Dear Margaret + Be

a little reminder of the
pleasant times we have had
together.
Love
Jan + Rob/x

MargaretPerry
Little Gwengenny,
Wormbridge
Herefordshire HR2 9DT
Tel. 01981 570 689

A Definitive History of Dore Abbey

Drawing of the interior of Dore Abbey when in use as the parish church in 1840.
Note the position of the pulpit in front of the screen

A Definitive History of Dore Abbey

Edited by

Ron Shoesmith & Ruth Richardson

with contributions by

John Eisel, Francis Evans, Stuart Harrison,
Joe Hillaby, Sue Hubbard, Dennis Monger,
Ruth Richardson, Ron Shoesmith, Richard Stone,
Malcolm Thurlby, Jim Tonkin, Alan Vince,
Esther de Waal & David Williams
and the Rt. Revd. John Oliver (Bishop of Hereford)

Logaston Press 1997

LOGASTON PRESS
Little Logaston Woonton Almeley
Herefordshire HR3 6QH

First published by Logaston Press 1997
Copyright © author of each chapter 1997

ISBN 1 873827 84 9

Set in Times 10 on 12 pt
by Logaston Press and printed in Great Britain
by Redwood Books

Contents

Acknowledgments

In a book such as this there are many people who should be acknowledged—those who have helped an individual contributor, those who have helped unearth photographs and illustrations, those who have advised the editors and publishers. It is almost without doubt that someone will have been missed from the ensuing list, for which apologies for our combined oversight are given.

As regards illustrations, the publishers would like to thank Brian Byron for producing the maps and plans which have been drawn for this volume, Ken Hoverd for many of the photographs and Mrs. Mildred Colman for that last essential check of the text before it was delivered to the printers. For the illustrations of Rievaulx and Fountains abbeys thanks are due to Dr Glyn Coppack; for the aerial photograph of Dore Abbey used in Chapter XII thanks are due to the Ministry of Defence; for the photographs of the manuscripts from Hereford Cathedral Library thanks are due to the Dean and Chapter and the Mappa Mundi Trust and to the former only for the use of the seal of Abbot Jordan; material in the British Library used in Chapter III and its related appendices has been reproduced by permission of the British Library; material from manuscripts held by Exeter College, Oxford, is reproduced by permission of the Rector and Fellows; and material in the Public Record Office has been reproduced by permission of the Controller of Her Majesty's Stationery Office.

Malcolm Thurlby and Stuart Harrison would like to express their thanks to Dr. David Robinson for discussing Dore with them and for sharing his vast knowledge of Welsh Cistercian architecture. Brian O'Callaghan kindly made available a copy of his paper on Dore prior to publication and Paul Williamson generously gave of his expertise on matters relating to the Gothic sculpture at Dore. Thurlby's research for Chapter V was funded in part by the Social Sciences and Humanities Research Council of Canada. Stuart Harrison also wishes to thank Dr Richard Morris for help with dating the moulding profiles; Bernard Nurse and the Society of Antiquaries for help with the Rowland Paul collection of drawings; Richard Stone for help with recording and Joe Hillaby for keeping him on the right path.

Richard Stone would like to thank Dr Glyn Coppack for advice, and Ruth Richardson expresses her appreciation of help from Elizabeth Taylor and David Whitehead.

The Rt. Revd. John Oliver acknowledges that the lines from 'Little Gidding' by T.S. Eliot are reproduced by permission of Faber and Faber Ltd. from *Four Quartets*.

Many people with an interest in Dore Abbey have been involved in this work and particular thanks are due to Gerald Powell of Tan House Farm and Rev. Dr. Arthur Moore, the Priest-in-Charge of Dore. This project could well have foundered but for the stirling efforts of The Friends of Dore Abbey who have stimulated interest in the Abbey, its history and architecture through their efforts to maintain it as a place of regular worship.

The known abbots of Dore

1186-c.1216	Adam I
c.1216-26	Adam II
1230	Godfrey
1236-57	Stephen of Worcester
1257	Reginald
1257-73	Henry *(? King)*
1274-81	William Wroth
1282-92	William of Hereford
1293-98	Hugh Cromus
1298-1304	John of Grosmont
1305-12	Richard of Madeley *(? Straddell)*
1312-46	Richard Straddell
1346-47	Roger
1347-62	Robert Wroth
1362-84	John Wysbech
1385	Richard
1396-98	John Holand
1398-1403	Jordan Bykeleswade
1405-13	Richard Grisby
1435	Richard Clifford
1441-72	Richard Rochester *(al. Rowchester)*
1448, 1453	*John*
1476-95	Philip Morgan *(al. Llywelyn)*
1495-1500	Richard Dorston
1500-16	John Longdon
1516-23	Thomas Cleubery *(al. Olebery)*
1524-28	John Glyn
1529-36	John Redborn(e)

CHAPTER I

Dore before the Abbey

by Ron Shoesmith

'The Dore (falling from the north) cuts its way through the middle of the valley, which the Britains from the river call Diffrin-Dore [Dyffryn-dwr - water valley] but the English, that they might seem to express the force of that word, have called it The Gilden Vale, which name it may well be thought to deserve, for its golden, rich and pleasant fertility; for the hills which encompass it on both sides are cloathed with woods, under the woods lye Corn-fields on each hand, and under those fields lovely and fruitful meadows. In the middle, between them, glides a clear and crystal river, upon which Robert Earl of Ewyas erected a beautiful monastery, wherein many of the nobility and gentry of these parts were buried.'[1]

It would be very surprising if such a fertile and pleasant valley did not have many traces of human occupation well before the abbey was founded in 1147. However, during the Neolithic Period it is on the surrounding hills that the main traces of occupation have been found, for at that time the valleys would probably have been well-wooded and relatively impenetrable. The ridge separating the Dore from the Wye includes several burial sites such as Arthur's Stone, Cross Lodge long barrow and Dunseal long barrow - the latter a bare 2.5km north of Abbey Dore. On the opposite side of the valley, some 4km north-west of Dore is the chambered tomb in Park Wood. On the same ridge there has been found several flint scatters, several axes and a settle-ment site on Dorstone Hill.[2] During the Bronze Age, finds indicating a possible settlement have been found to the south-west of Dore on the high ground around the Monnow and Olchon valleys, but with still no indication that the valley bottoms had any permanent use. By the time of the Iron Age, hill-forts had been built at Poston, above Vowchurch, and a short distance to the east in Timberline Wood. These were both quite small and would probably have only had control over small territories.[3] Once again the indications are that the area had a very limited occupation, mainly on the edges of the valley of the Dore.

It was probably with the coming of the Romans that man started to abandon the hills and penetrate the valley of the Dore. The members of the Woolhope Naturalists' Field Club, the Herefordshire Society devoted to 'the practical study, in all its branches, of the Natural History and Archaeology of Herefordshire ...' established the first piece of evidence. It was on Thursday 25 July that the Woolhope Club held their 1901 Ladies' Day meeting in the Golden Valley. They caught the 9.22 a.m. train to Hay where they changed to the then two-year-old section of the Golden Valley Railway that took them through Dorstone and Peterchurch to Abbey Dore.[4] One reason for their visit was the recent exposure of an ancient road in the grounds of the Railway Station. The road, first exposed in 1893[5], was further examined by Mr. G. H. Jack, the County

Surveyor in 1908.[6] He excavated the surface for a length of about 30ft. and for its full width. He recorded it as consisting of 'unworked nodular limestone hand pitched on the virgin soil (a hard red marl). There was no sign of a concrete bed or any cementing material between the stones, which were of all sizes, varying from 3 to 12 ins. in their longest diameter. The road was not kerbed ... the width 12 ft. 9 ins.' Jack noted two sets of wheel ruts, with a gauge of 4ft. 6ins., one apparently replacing the other, and both on the eastern side, leaving a 5ft. wide walkway to the west. Found on the road were 'two Roman nails ... and a fragment of a Roman horseshoe.'

Jack was certain that this was the road described in the Antoinine Itinerary as running northwards from Caerleon via Abergavenny and Kenchester to Wroxeter. Whilst Watling Street, the road joining these two Roman legionary fortresses, is well attested, the precise route between Abergavenny and Kenchester has been a problem for many years. The route that eventually goes through Abbey Dore follows the main road to Pandy where it picks up the Monnow valley to Pontrilas and then up the Golden Valley to Black Bush Farm, some 2km north of the abbey, where there was a temporary Roman fort provisionally dated to before 80AD. From there it follows the known course of Stone Street to the river Wye and Kenchester. The often-quoted alternative route follows the Monnow upstream to Longtown (where Roman coins were found when the school was built on the Castle Green in 1869)[7], and then north-eastwards over the hills to Black Bush Farm.[8] Indeed, there is even the possibility of yet another Roman road running from Longtown through Craswall and down to the Wye valley to Hay-on-Wye.[9]

Since Jack's work there have been various developments, but the uncertainties still remain—is the Abbey Dore section a Roman road, and if so is it part of the road leading from Abergavenny to Kenchester? However, the discovery of Roman forts at Clifford, Kentchurch and Monmouth bring forward the possibility[10] of a military link leading to Wales along the valleys of the rivers Monnow and Dore. The alignment has been traced up-river from Dore to Mantooth near Vowchurch, where a section was excavated. This road was evidently the same as the one at Dore—12ft. wide, of large stones and with wheel ruts on the east.

It can be seen, therefore, that the Abbey Dore road is most likely to be of Roman date, but a slim possibility still remains that it was built at some time during the medieval period. There is one other aspect to the problem—what was the alignment of the road to the south-east? Was it deliberately left outside the monastic precinct when the boundary wall was built, or was it ignored or the course even totally lost, so that it went directly through the precinct? It has apparently been found to the south of the precinct, but the course between the two exposures remains uncertain.[11]

The Roman presence in the Golden Valley would appear to have been associated more with the invasion rather than the peaceful occupation that followed and lasted for over 300 years. There is apparently no trace of villas or farmsteads and hardly any finds of Roman material. This out-of-the-way and unprotected border area between the Roman civil and military zones would not have appealed to cosmopolitan Romans, who would have settled in far less remote areas with all the adjuncts of civilisation available in a Roman town in the locality. When the Roman legions withdrew from Britain at the beginning of the fifth century war lords such as Vortigern, Ambrosius Aurelianus and the semi-legendary King Arthur, all of whom may well have been associated with Herefordshire, came to the fore.[12]

Virtually nothing is known about the Golden Valley area during the two or three hundred year period after the Roman troops abandoned the country. The few people who were left probably held on to small farms of which few traces can be expected to survive. Slowly, a measure of order came out of the chaos and small kingdoms began to emerge. The Saxon kingdom of Mercia was formed in the Midlands and under the rule of King Penda its boundaries extended westwards with the incorporation, probably by agreement, of south Shropshire and north Herefordshire at some time between 630 and 650. By the time

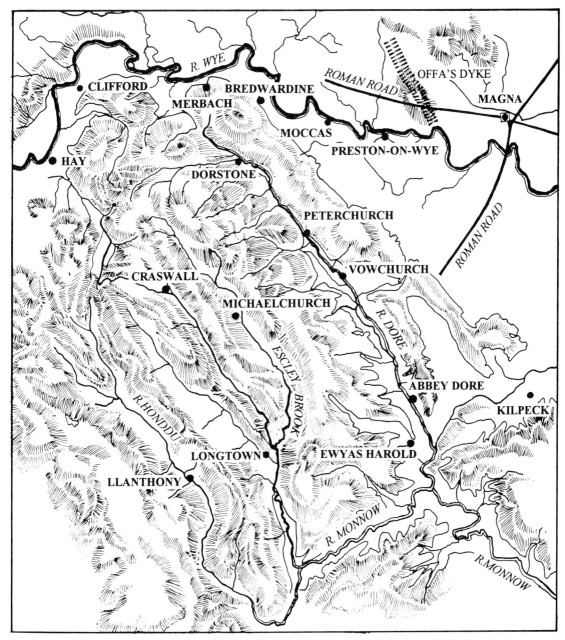

Fig. 1: The Golden Valley Area

that Penda died, in 655, the kingdom of Mercia extended from the Welsh border to the North Sea. This huge midland state was basically a federation of several peoples and, with Penda's death, it appears to have been split into several parts.

However, the southern part of Herefordshire was following a completely different path to its northern neighbour. By the middle of the sixth century it had become a small independent kingdom in its own right—the Welsh kingdom of Ergyng.[13] It included lands on both sides of the Wye and was named after the Roman settlement of Ariconium, in the south-east of the county near Ross. A glance at a map of the county shows a massive concentration of Celtic and British field-names and place-names in the southern part of Herefordshire as compared with the rest of the county and the neighbouring counties to the north and east.[14] It is now considered likely that Christianity continued in the Ergyng area right through from the Roman period.

Indeed, there seems to be every reason to suppose that there was an early religious site somewhere in the Golden Valley. It was around 606AD that 'King Cinuin gave Mafurn to bishop Aidan.[15] A few years later, about 625, King Athrwys gave *ecclesia Cynmarchi* with its *territorium* which included *podum Mafurn, Lann Calcuch* and *Lann Cerniu* to Bishop *Comereg* (Abbot of Mochros).[16]

About 745AD, there is a note recording that King Ithael returned eleven churches, which had previously belonged to Dyfrig, to Bishop Berthwyn, after Saxon devastation in the Hereford area. Included was *Cenubia Cornubium, id est Lann Cerniu super ripem Dour, podum Mafurn ...* . It was over a century later, about 860, in a composite record that *Britcon* son of *Deuon* is recorded as giving six churches with their *territoria* to Bishop *Gaecielis* which previously belonged to Dyfrig. The list includes *Mafurn*.

It would appear that *Podum Mafurn* (the estate of Mafurn) is a religious settlement, considered by Wendy Davies to be probably somewhere between Dore and Peterchurch. However, the identification of Lann Cerniu with Dorstone has been questioned[17] and the suggestion made that it was at Abbey Dore, in which case podum Mafurn is placed at Peterchurch.[18] Whichever is the case, it would appear that there are good arguments for a religious presence in the immediate neighbourhood of Dore from the beginning of the seventh century. Traces of such buildings would be extremely difficult to find as they would almost certainly have been built of wood, which would eventually disappear.

By the early seventh century it appears that Ergyng had come under the control of the kings of Gwent, though at least part of it continued to preserve its own identity. It gained a new name—Archenfield—and was still sufficiently independent to have its own bishop, Cyfeiliog, in 914. The older kingdom of Ergyng had extended some distance east of the Wye, perhaps as far as the Severn.[19] During the sixth and seventh centuries, according to the Book of Llandaff, the then kingdom of Ergyng had also incorporated an additional area to the north and west, including the Dore valley, with a northern frontier following the river Wye as far as Hay. To the west of Ergyng, and north of the kingdom of Gwent, was the Welsh commote of Ewyas, apparently centred on the area around Clodock and Longtown in the Olchon valley.

It was in 757 that Offa took the throne of Mercia and attempted to define the boundary between Wales and his kingdom of Mercia by the construction of the great earthwork that still bears his name. Offa's Dyke runs from the estuary of the Dee near Prestatyn to a point close to the confluence of the Wye and Severn near Chepstow, a distance as the crow flies of almost 200kms. It was described in detail some 40 years ago.[20]

The Dyke is not continuous throughout Herefordshire—apart from a 7.5km. long gap south of Lyonshall, there is a total lack of any trace from Bridge Sollars, 8km. west of Hereford, to Redbrook in Gloucestershire. The northern gap could possibly have been defended by a strong timber palisade—the area was well wooded—but the long southern gap requires a more pragmatic solution. Rather than accepting suggestions that this massive embankment and its associated ditch had mysteriously been totally flattened throughout much of Herefordshire, it would seem far more likely that the reason for the lack of a marked out frontier was associated with the presence of the semi-independent and privileged buffer state that had earlier been called Ergyng and was by then known as Archenfield. By Offa's time there were two parts of this miniature state, separated by the Wye from a point near Monmouth in the south to Holme Lacy in the north.

During Offa's reign, and indeed for some considerable time afterwards, this eastern area was still apparently considered to be part of Archenfield, although it would appear that the two halves had been gradually growing apart.

If it is accepted that the Wye was the eastern and northern boundary of the western part of Archenfield at the time of Offa, then the lack of any demarcation in this area would suggest that the Welsh of this semi-independent buffer state had come to a successful arrangement with the king that the Wye would act as a frontier. This would have accelerated the break-up of Archenfield into its two component parts, for it can be assumed that from that time onwards Welsh law and customs were accepted on one side of the river, whilst on the other side Mercian law began. The river would provide a line of separation and, although it has been suggested that it would be a poor barrier because of low summer levels and frequent crossing places[21], it would surely have been as good a barrier as the embankment and dry ditch of the main part of the Dyke. If it was indeed a patrolled boundary, the main problem would be the length—the Wye from Ross to Fownhope follows a tortuous course some 29km long whilst the direct line is a mere 11km. As a boundary it is acceptable, but as a line that was regularly patrolled, it would have had obvious difficulties. Even as a boundary, it could still have been used by boats travelling from one part of the river to another as happens with many international rivers today.

Although Offa had fixed the border between England and Wales in Shropshire and the northern part of Herefordshire, and Archenfield filled the gap in the southern part of the county, this did not mean that there was peace throughout the 300 or so years between the Dyke being built and the Norman Conquest. It does appear that there were some lengthy intervals when peace prevailed, but they were interspersed with periods of border raiding and open warfare.

The independent state of Archenfield seems to have continued to exist well into the tenth century, but only to the west of the Wye, and probably with the loss of its northern territories. For several generations the people of Archenfield on the east of the Wye had gone their own way taking up the English laws and customs. The situation was apparently regularised when the 'Ordinance concerning the Dunsæte' was drawn up, probably by King Athelstan in consultation with the Welsh around 926. It is suggested that the Dunsæte included the people of both parts of Archenfield and possibly those of other surrounding areas. The Ordinance was a set of laws providing regulations and penalties to be observed between the Welsh section of the Dunsæte on the one side of an unnamed river and the English section on the other. It is assumed that the Wye was the unnamed river. The presence of such a document infers that the separation of the Dunsæte into two distinct parts was of long standing. The rules may have lasted for a short while, but the elaborate procedures concerning the tracking of cattle thieves outlined in the Ordinance may well have fallen into disuse once the Wye ceased to be considered as a boundary and the division of the area into 'Hundreds' became of more importance. To a certain extent the medieval Deanery of Archenfield reflects the Welsh Dunsæte, whilst the Deanery of Ross may provide a similar indication of the extent of the English Dunsæte.

Changes came with the Norman Conquest. The invaders not only brought their own laws and regulations, they also encouraged colonisation, with French knights, monks and tradesmen dominating and exploiting the local populace. At that time Abbey Dore was not a parish in its own right; indeed, it would seem that the abbey was built in part of the parish of Bacton (Bacca's

Estate), described in Domesday as being held by Roger de Lacy. 'In *Valle Stradelie* Roger also holds Bacton at 5 hides and Wadetune at 1 hide. Gilbert holds these two manors from Roger. Edwy and Alfward held these 6 hides; they were waste. In lordship 1 plough; 1 slave. 3 Welshmen pay 3 sesters of honey. Value 9s.'[22]

However, it would appear that there was a parish church serving Dore although its origin is quite a mystery—was it the church mentioned in the early charters either at *Podum Mafurn* or *Lann Cerniu*? The church is mentioned in the Schedule presented to be read at the Consecration in 1634. 'That the said Parish Church being so long ago demolished, as that the very Place of it is not now certainly known. Nay there remains not the least Mark or Token of the place. The very ground is converted to a Corn Field, about a mile higher up, in the Gilden Valley; the same Field near *Dreuth-Lan-dee, i.e.,* Black Bush, still retaining the name of the Church-Yard: Which makes it credible enough, that (according to tradition) the Church formerly stood there.'[23] The 1839 Abbey Dore tithe apportionment names field 191 on Black Bush Farm as 'Churchyard Field'.[24]

Abbeys such as Dore were usually founded on virgin ground and there is no reason to suppose that this was not the case here. The original village (probably little more than a few build-ings) was probably at Black Bush Farm in close proximity to the church. There may have been a gradual movement to the area outside the abbey precinct, but this not need be so, for abbeys were very self-contained institutions and had little need of hangers-on. The remainder of the Golden Valley was becoming settled well before the Norman Conquest with settlements at Dorstone, Wilmastone, Poston, Monnington and Bacton mentioned in the Domesday Survey as well as the pre-Conquest English settlements such as *Almundestune, Alcamestune, Beltrou, Elnodestune, Edwardestune, Wadetune and Wluetone*,[25] that appear to have been re-named in the post-Conquest era.

The early name or names for the Dore area are shrouded in mystery. At the foundation of the abbey, it has been implied that Robert I de Ewyas gave *Blancharbesal as* the site of the new church and it has been suggested that this could possibly refer to the parts of the parish on the west of the river Dore.[26] Recent research makes this suggestion unlikely.[27] Leland notes 'There was ay Dour afore, the edification of the maner called *Blak Berats Haulle* and that the abbey was 'in the diocese but not in Herefordshire.'[28] Abbey Dore was apparently first used as a name for the parish at some time between 1727 and 1831.[29]

CHAPTER II

The Cistercians

by Esther de Waal

In 1147, the year in which Robert of Ewyas brought a group of European monks to found his new community at Dore he was, in current estimation, bringing the best men then available. By this time the monks of Citeaux in Burgundy with their many offshoots and new foundations, were at the height of their power.

They were very much a reflection of the century which saw their birth. The twelfth century was a vibrant and energetic period pushing out its boundaries in new directions. Underlying the dynamism lay economic growth and a population explosion which saw the population of Europe double between 1050 and 1200, encouraging the search for new lands to colonise, whilst cities and urban wealth expanded, and transport and communication improved. These were the years of the new learning, when translations of hitherto unknown works of Plato and Aristotle reached Europe bringing new tools for questioning, for analysis and synthesis, exciting the minds of wandering scholars and encouraging the establishment of universities. It was essentially a time of self-questioning, a search for identity, and one which did not leave the monastic orders untouched. It was into this world that the Cistercian order was born, shaped and influenced by the needs and demands of contemporary society.

Although the Cistercians based their lives on the Rule of St. Benedict they did not wear the black habit of the Benedictine monks. Their distinctive white habit says much for who they were and what they stood for. White is a symbol of purity, of newness and they saw their lives as a return to the original vision of their founder and to the simplicity of life which they felt had been lost. Instead of buying cloth already woven and dyed they preferred to spin and weave it from flocks reared in their own pastures and wear it in its natural undyed state. But white is also the colour associated with Our Lady to whom all Cistercian churches are dedicated. Love for her was a strong element in their personal lives, and in their shared liturgical life. At Dore she is represented in two of the remaining bosses (see Chapter VIII) and there is also the *Tract on the Blessed Virgin Mary* (see Appendix 2) by Cadwgan of Bangor. Each day ended, as it still does, with the singing of the *Salve Regina*.

Highly intelligent men, influenced by the intellectual revival of their day, they studied ancient texts as fresh and living books composed for their benefit, as Christopher Brooke points out[1]. By following the Rule of St. Benedict they did not have to bind themselves to the letter of the law but to return to the well-springs, as they believed, of the original monastic ideal. In these earlier years this was to be a great liberating force which showed itself in a surge of creativity in every sphere of life, not only the spiritual, but also the organisational, architectural and agricultural fields.

Origins

Any study of Cistercian origins must start with the story of the exodus of Robert, abbot of Molesmes, to Citeaux in the year 1098—even though present day scholarship warns that these earliest texts are 'riddled with as many problems as a colander has holes.'[2] Finding the Benedictine community which he had himself founded twenty years before, falling short of his vision, Robert set out to establish a life of greater austerity and discipline. He and twenty brothers settled in a 'desert' amongst the woods and marshes south west of Dijon in a place bearing the name of Citeaux. In their own (alleged) words they describe how 'they set out eagerly for a wilderness known as Citeaux, a locality in the diocese of Chalon where men rarely penetrated and none but wild things lived, so densely covered was it then with woodland and thorn bush. When the men of God arrived there and realised that the less attractive and accessible the site was to laymen, the better it would suit themselves, they began after felling and clearing the close-growing thickets and bushes, to build a monastery...'[3]

These years in 'the howling waste of the wilderness' gave an experience which proved too demanding for some of the exiles and Robert returned with half the brethren. This seeming betrayal welded those who remained into a unity of mind and will that was to shape the future and become a hallmark of the Order.[4] They endured years of extreme hardship, austerity, poverty and illness which at first discouraged anyone from joining them, although ultimately they began to attract others. They gained because that they had among them two wise leaders, first the Frenchman, Abbot Alberic, and subsequently the Englishman, Stephen Harding, from Sherborne. But it was the arrival of Bernard in 1112, making his dramatic entry with a large company of nephews, brothers, uncles and cousins, that proved the turning point in the fortunes of this hitherto little-regarded monastery. Within three years Bernard had risen to be the abbot of a new foundation, Clairvaux, and for the remaining forty years of his life he proved himself one of the most vigorous and powerful men in the Church. The man was a polymath who exercised a tremendous influence on the political, literary and religious life of the Europe of his day, a reformer, a preacher of Crusades, an intransigent accuser of heresy, an ascetic in his personal life, an ardent preacher and writer, his teaching inspired as much by his study of scripture and the Fathers as by his own experience of mystical union with Christ. 'In his day Bernard determined who was accepted as pope and king ... So dynamic was his appeal that when he spoke at the University of Paris half of the students are reported to have withdrawn to flock to the monasteries ...'[5]

Who could have guessed what was to follow from this small beginning? Those pioneers had chosen the isolation of Citeaux believing it would be easier there to restore the monastic rhythm of body, mind and spirit, in a life of prayer, study and manual work. This original balance had become lost, partly because the liturgy had acquired unwieldy accretions, especially in the monastic life of Cluny founded in 910 in Burgundy, while manual work had virtually disappeared. In addition, increasing numbers of schools, guests and lay patrons inevitably meant more involvement in secular society. Whether the concern of this small group of men in their Burgundian desert was protest, escape, or reform is difficult to establish. The later controversies which were to embroil the Order brought the temptation to read into the earlier sources what the protagonists hoped to find. Perhaps it is best simply to recognise that these were men impelled by their desire to live the life of the Gospel, to which their monastic vows committed them, 'The Rule of St. Benedict is an exposition of the whole Gospel, not allegorically but in terms of simple experience and visible works'.[6]

Their first task therefore was to free the *Opus Dei*, the work of God, the saying of the daily offices which lay at the heart of their life, from all the accretions of litanies and prayers, elaborations of chant and ceremony. Their concern was to restore the ability to listen to God through the reading of the scriptures and the singing of the psalms. The day began in the dark with the monks getting up for Vigils during the night and coming down the night stairs into the choir, a symbolic living out of the movement from dark to light, from death to life. Then followed the saying of the other offices, seven times during the day, starting with Matins, followed at once by Lauds, which was sung some time between midnight and 4a.m.—times would vary between winter and summer. The morning offices were Prime, Terce and Sext. The afternoon hours were None at 2p.m. and Vespers, and the day would close with Compline around 6.30p.m. Mass was celebrated before Terce in summer, after in winter. This was their daily commitment, year in, year out. In addition they also lived out the drama of the liturgy as it unfolded annually from Advent through to Pentecost, together with the successive feasts of Our Lady, the Annunciation, the Visitation and the Assumption. In this lay the heart beat of their life.

By restoring two periods of manual labour, one in the morning and the other in the after-noon, they not only recovered that balance of body, mind and spirit which they felt had become lost, they also reasserted their close ties with the earth itself. Perhaps it is not without significance that they should have included the figure of a green man in one of the bosses of the nave roof which they would see daily. Taking into account time spent in prayer, in study and in devotional reading (*lectio divina*) with time for eating and sleeping, as well as Sundays and festi-vals, the working week amounted to at most thirty hours. Not able to afford hired labour and having renounced serfs, they desperately needed practical help if they were to subjugate and make fruitful the wildernesses in which they had chosen to plant their new houses. The solution was to use the system of lay-brothers, or *conversi*, already in use with the Tironese and Grandmontine orders. The result was to bring into their communities great numbers of unlet-tered local peasants who were clothed with brown robes and cloaks. These simple illiterate men found their vocation in working the land, handling tools, and caring for livestock and bees. They were not expected to say the offices; their prayers were the Pater, the Ave, and the Gloria. They lived apart from the choir-monks, whether in separate buildings in the mother-house herself, or increasingly in small numbers of granges scat-tered throughout the surrounding countryside which David Williams describes as model farms. Originally no more than a barn or byre they often became a complex of farm buildings, a small oratory and living quarters, possibly surrounded by a wall, where squads of lay-brothers took it in turn to spend weeks at home and weeks out on the granges. During the twelfth century the numbers of *conversi* were very considerable and without them the monks would never have been able to acquire and cultivate areas hitherto deemed waste. This was agriculture at the margins and the Cistercian monks were in a very real sense frontiers-men. In Britain they were engaged in large scale pastoral farming, raising sheep in their thousands and making sheep-walks in places that had before been largely unused. Their ownership of great tracts of land laid the foundations of later wealth and also of consider-able unpopularity. But they did much to improve the methods of cultivation. They did not hesitate to make use of any new technology, sometimes as pioneers, sometimes adapting existing advances to their own purposes.[7] They also grew cereals, which meant establishing mills and constructing waterways to work them. Where the climate was favourable they had vineyards. Fishing was particularly important in providing a diet which excluded the flesh of four-footed beasts. Their careful estate management and expertise was reflected in Wales in the initiative and impetus they brought to wool production, to trade and to the early Welsh mining industry.[8] Their emphasis on manual labour was, and still is, an essential part of the Cistercian ideal.

The expansion of the order
The vigorous intellectual and economic climate of the twelfth century, coupled with the energy that came from a return to the original vision, in the hands of a group of men with brilliant leader-ship skills, led to a phenomenal growth of the order. During the first twenty years the number of foundations had risen from one to seven, but in little more than fifty years the total grew to more than three hundred. 'In 1152 the Cistercian

Fig. 2. Rievaulx Abbey

General Chapter forbade the foundation of new abbeys, but after a short interval growth began again with one foundation in 1155 and 1156, five in 1158, one in 1159, fourteen in 1160, and so on with an average of about 4.5 a year till the end of the century.' In 1200 the total stood at 694 abbeys.[9]

The first arrival in Britain of the white monks was to the comparative obscurity of Waverley in Surrey in 1128. But the really significant moment came in 1132 with the foundation of Rievaulx (Fig. 2), as a daughter abbey of Citeaux, by St. Bernard, followed a few months later by the exodus of a band of reformers consisting of the usual 12 monks and future abbot from the Benedictine abbey of St. Mary's in York to form the nucleus of Fountains Abbey (Fig. 3). For the next twenty years the foundation of new abbeys and the growing numbers of men joining them continued without any slackening. In 1152 there were forty Cistercian houses, the daughter houses (with four exceptions) of the three original foundations of Waverley, Rievaulx and Fountains. Their presence was particularly felt in the north, in areas that had had until then had few religious houses. At the height of its

success, Rievaulx had 150 choir monks and some 500 *conversi*. Nunneries were also founded in great numbers, for women had been important in the Order right from the outset, with St. Bernard's own sister, according to tradition, entering it at the same time as her brother. The early nunneries had been almost exclusively peopled by the daughters of the wealthy, but now, as with the men, the Cistercians gave the opportunity for uneducated women to become lay sisters.

The decree of 1152 forbidding new foundations slowed down growth and from that date until 1216 there were only half a dozen new foundations made in England. But in Wales the decree held less force. Already in about 1140 St. Bernard had sent a colony to west Wales which ultimately settled at Whitland where they drew many Welsh recruits. Both Whitland and its daughter, Strata Florida, were wealthy and attracted novices from the ruling families of Wales. From them sprang a family of half a dozen new foundations in north and central Wales while colonies were also sent to Ireland. This pattern of expansion was frequently interrupted by what Dom David Knowles has called

Organisation

This amazing success story owed much to the genius of Cistercian organisation, one of the masterpieces of medieval planning. Their biggest innovation lay in the decision to be determinedly separate from feudal society. They created a structure that was at once centralised and flexible; which helped to prevent anarchy and disintegration during years of meteoric growth. The clarity of mind of Stephen Harding, third abbot of Citeaux, is revealed in the first edition of his *Carta Caritatis*, or Charter of Charity, which was to guarantee the unity and uniformity of the order. Although they might declare themselves faithful to the Rule of St. Benedict they were in fact creating something new. A Benedictine house was essentially a self-contained and separate entity, whilst the Cistercians presented a simple chain of authority running from top to bottom with a single supreme legislative body, the General Chapter, consisting of all Cistercian abbots, which met once every three years. Each daughter house was to be visited every year by the abbot of the founding mother house, who was to examine the community with full powers of correction and punishment. This created a closely knit religious order, the first of its kind in the church. Professor Southern has called it the first effective international organisation in

Fig. 3. Fountains Abbey, from the south. Wood block of about 1850.

'the disturbed state of the country and the semi-barbarism of its upland population'[10] which meant that the General Chapter was constantly forced to send out arbitrators and visitors to settle disputes and enforce discipline. The high water mark of the Cistercian presence was reached in the mid-thirteenth century and after this came a continuous, though slow, decline.

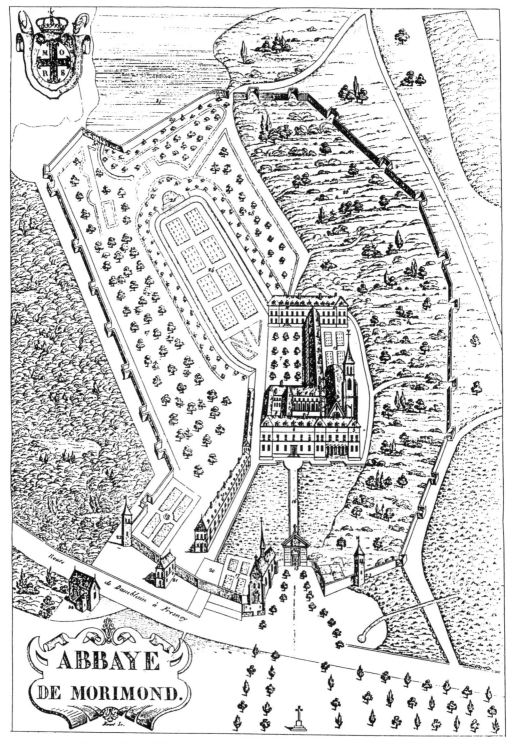

Fig. 4. Plan of Morimond Abbey, the founding house of Dore Abbey

Europe, even more effective than the papal organisation of its day since it had narrower aims and a smaller field of operation.[11] There are undoubtedly overtones of aristocratic control, also true of the intensely regulated life in each house which we glimpse in what Walter Daniel, the biographer of Aelred, shows us of the hot-house atmosphere of Rievaulx under Aelred.

Spirituality

The primacy of charity had been apparent right from the start in the very name of their founding charter. It was charity by which the monks in their abbeys, though separated in body in different countries of the world, would be indissolubly united in spirit. They had a good reason to name this decree the *Charter of Charity* 'because ... it had for its object charity alone ... We wish ... that we may live united by one charity, one Rule...'[12] Love is the key to the Rule of St. Benedict, lived out love in a family of brothers, a love that is *fervens*, ardent, burning. St. Bernard, when he spoke of the fullness of the love of God, said it was as though a great flame of love was enkindled in the soul.[13]

It is almost impossible to write of the early Cistercian life and not to place the person of St. Bernard at its centre as the incarnation of its spirit, the keystone which held everything together. His influence on the order was incalculable, and undoubtedly without him the order would have remained relatively small, perhaps half its actual size. His personal magnetism and his spiritual power were far-reaching and irresistible. The first Cistercian fathers had been hidden and silent, Bernard was neither. He became influential in word and deed far beyond the walls of the monastery. He was at the centre of more than one controversy, he fought many battles in his life on behalf of the church. His zeal for the church was simply an extension of the love of God which informed and directed his whole life. He was a deeply passionate man, for whom the *Song of Songs* was the book which throws most light on the Gospel.

A modern edition of St. Bernard's writings fills nine volumes. But in this he was typical, for scholarship and writing held a high place in Cistercian life. Lives of asceticism and renunciation did not include renouncing the gift of writing theological treatises. Well versed in the tradition of meditative theology, a theology defined as 'prayerful reflection upon God's revealed word and all the depths of meaning which it contains'[14], we owe to the Cistercians works that must rank amongst the classics of the spiritual life. They have been called the last of the Fathers[15]. They did not write in definitions and rational analysis but in symbols and analogies which lead the reader into a mystery that has no limits[16]. Whether they were preaching or writing, their one concern was a desire to make God known more closely to men and women, and to make them aware of that abounding love which would draw them closer to Him. This is the vision common to all the great twelfth century writers—Aelred of Rievaulx, William of St. Thierry, Guerric of Igny and many more—whose works are increasingly becoming known and valued today.[17]

Later years

The early fervour instilled by these twelfth century monks was inevitably to fade. Instead the ruthless and aggressive side of the Order's life came increasingly to the fore in battles and law-suits, whether in internal tensions between lay-brothers and choir monks, or in fights over property rights and interests. By the thirteenth century the Cistercians were themselves showing those very qualities which they had vowed to correct. No longer were they the frontiers-men of the church, literally and metaphorically: that role now went to the new order of friars. They became both a reactionary force and great land-owners; rich, and thus open to all the burdens and temptations that prosperity brings.

Today

Present day scholarship can be seen in the editing of Cistercian texts, the publications of numerous learned articles in *Cistercian Studies Quarterly* and elsewhere, and in a yearly academic conference. This is testimony not only to the power of the past but to the strength and energy of present day members of the Cistercian order. There are houses throughout the world and not least in the third world, indeed the present Abbot General comes from Argentina. Women play a significant role and abbesses votes with abbots when they meet in Rome. What underlies such strength and such continuity?

In the Middle Ages their writing was a reflection of their personal experience of the contemplative life nourished in their communities. That remains true today. Cistercian houses do not justify their existence by the doing of good works, by hospitality and by the undertaking of pastoral activity, but by prayer. But that is the paradox of the monastic life: the closer men and women come to God the closer they come to the world.

It is a paradox seen in the life of the twentieth century American Cistercian Thomas Merton in which his apparently enclosed years of withdrawal brought him to the very heart of the pain and hurt of the contemporary world. Since he first started writing in the 1940s he has demonstrated to thousands of people that the Cistercian expression of the monastic tradition remains a living force today, just as it has been in the past, speaking to men and women of the priority of prayer beyond all barriers or divides of time or place.

CHAPTER III

The Abbey of Dore

by David H. Williams

The Cistercian Order in the Middle Ages was divided into five great families, of which one consisted of those monasteries in lineal descent from the abbey of Morimond, the fifth senior house of the Order situated on the dividing line between France and Lorraine.[1] Most of Morimond's daughter houses lay in central and eastern Europe, but it also had oversight of the military order of the Knights of Calatrava in Spain.[2] It had only one daughter-house in England—that of Dore Abbey, and seemingly one, Macosquin, in Northern Ireland.[3] Abbey Dore was founded (probably on 25 April) in 1147, a year known in the Order as a 'wonderful year' because of the boost the Cistercians received by the incorporation of the Norman congregation of Savigny, and the affiliation of the dependencies of the French abbey of Obazine, as well as the foundation of several new monasteries—twelve of them in Britain alone. Why should the founder of our monastery, Robert, the grandson of lord Ralph of Ewyas, have sought to bring, exceptionally for England, monks of Morimond to settle at Dore? The answer may lie in the fact that 1147 was the year of the Second Crusade, strongly promoted by St. Bernard of Clairvaux and in which Abbot Rainald of Morimond took what has been described as 'a lively interest'.[4] It is at least possible, if not probable, that the foundation of Dore resulted from contacts made in the early stages of that Crusade by Robert of Ewyas, or

others of his family, with the monks of Morimond. At any rate Dore became the nineteenth daughter-house of Morimond in chronological order; one authority sees a close similarity in plan between its church and that at Morimond itself[5], and contacts with the mother-house can be traced throughout at least the thirteenth century.[6]

As for the monks of Dore, they themselves settled three daughter-houses. The first, Trawscoed Abbey in Cantref-selyf, Breconshire, was probably founded about 1173 by Walter de Clifford who had sought to build an abbey 'for the increase of the Cistercian Order'; he granted 'all materials in his forest which were necessary for its construction', a clear pointer that many of its early buildings would have been raised in timber. He also gave rents and tithes of fisheries 'provided that the abbey shall remain in Cantref-selyf for ever'. It didn't.[7] The General Chapter of the Order in 1189, and again in 1204, ruled that if a monastery didn't get off the ground, and in particular if it failed to continue to attract a community of at least thirteen monks, then 'it should be reduced to a grange, or dissolved altogether'.[8] We have it on the critical authority of Gerald of Wales that Trawscoed was degraded to the status of a grange (a Cistercian model farm) during his life-time, somewhere perhaps in the very early years of the thirteenth century.[9] The second daughter-house of Abbey Dore was at Grace Dieu, a few miles west of Monmouth, on

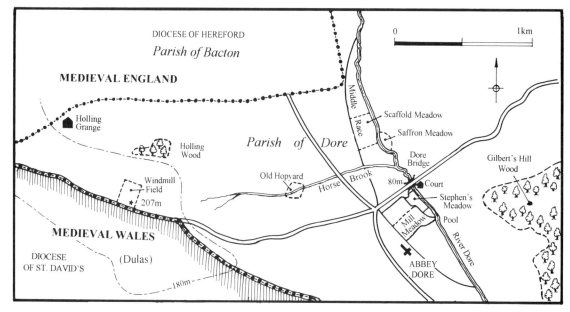

Fig. 5. Parish of Dore, west of the river (1840)
(based on the diocesan copy of the tithe map)

the present Hendre Estate. Founded in 1226, it was completely burnt by Welsh forces in 1233, and refounded on the opposite, eastern bank of the Troddi stream. Nothing can be seen in the field there today, but foundations have been revealed by a limited excavation.[10] Thirdly, came the abbey sited first at Darnhall in 1273, moving to Vale Royal in 1285, both sites being in the county of Chester. It had a royal founder, Prince Edward, later Edward I, grateful to the monks of Dore who had ministered to him whilst held a captive in Hereford during the Barons Revolt of 1265.[11]

A Border Site

It is fashionable by some students of monastic history today to play down the idea of the Cistercians as being essentially monks who went deliberately to remote areas to build their monasteries, to be in effect 'frontiers-men'. Of some monasteries it was undoubtedly true, if only because much of the better land in a kingdom, or a county or a diocese, or a parish, was already settled, that the Cistercians found themselves at the borders of temporal or ecclesiastical administrative units. It was certainly true of the mother-abbey at Morimond, where the frontier between France and Lorraine passed through its dining-hall, so that one writer could say: 'the monks prayed and sang in France, but ate in Germany'.[12] Abbey Dore, too, was such a border-house, on the very edge of England and on the very verge of the diocese of Hereford. Situated in the lordship of Ewyas Harold, perhaps on land carved out of the parish of Bacton, Dore was practically in a 'no-man's land', and indeed on more than one occasion was administratively grouped with the Welsh houses of the Order.[13] Its borderline position meant that, even after the Edwardian conquest of Wales in 1277-82, it 'suffered by the wars between the English and the Welsh' (1345)[14]; its monks were particularly fearful at the time of the Glyn Dŵr Revolt (1405) gaining royal leave 'to treat with the rebels for the safety of the abbey, which is in great peril of destruction and burning'.[15] Clearly, Dore walked a tight-rope in such years, not wishing to give aid and comfort to the king's enemies, but not wanting either to suffer in the process (Fig. 5).

In about 1540 the travelling antiquary, John Leland, described Dore as having been 'in the diocese, but not in the shire of Hereford'.[16] This

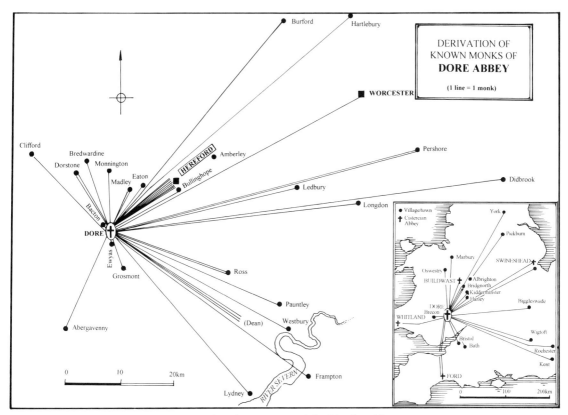

Fig. 6. Catchment area of the Monks of Dore

fact had been a bone of contention nearly three centuries before. About 1283 the bishop of St. David's, possibly for political reasons in the aftermath of the Edwardian Conquest of Wales, claimed jurisdiction over the monastery 'saving', he said, 'the rights of the monks'—for Cistercian houses were to all intents and purposes exempt from interference by their diocesan bishop. The bishop asserted that Dore lay in the parish of Ewyas Harold, itself in the diocese of St. David's, until as late as 1847. Bishop Swinfield of Hereford resisted this claim; in August 1284 he wrote to the General Chapter of the Cistercian Order, about to meet that September at Cîteaux, protesting at the seemingly one-sided appointment of the Welsh abbots of Neath and Strata Marcella to investigate the matter. Bishop Swinfield argued that the abbey had always been in the parish of Bacton, in his diocese of Hereford, and pointed out that it was his immediate predecessor, St. Thomas Cantilupe, who had consecrated the abbey church a few years

previously—a ceremony, tradition has it, which Cantilupe undertook at some personal risk for the Welshry assembled a show of military force to try to deter him. (Another source has the bishop of St. David's as having dedicated the abbey church).[17] In replying to Bishop Swinfield, the General Chapter sat on the fence, stating that Dore should obey the *de facto* diocesan bishop.[18] Clearly, this was the bishop of Hereford, and certainly there is no doubt that from at least 1284, almost all the abbots of Dore were blessed on assuming office by the occupant of that see.[19] (A strange twist in the tale came on Palm Sunday, 1634, when the bishop of St. David's, deputising for the bishop of Hereford, re-dedicated what remained of the abbey church).

The Monks

Where did the monks come from? The names of quite a number of those who were professed at Abbey Dore are known[20]; in 54 cases they bear a

17

surname or ascription, like Robert of Dorstone or Henry of Bullinghope, which enables a map to be drawn of Dore's catchment area (Fig. 6). Its principal source of vocations was the city of Hereford which generated eight of the fifty-four. Others came from local villages like Clifford and Grosmont, a number from wider afield but within easy reach—from localities in Shropshire, Worcestershire, Oxfordshire and Gloucestershire. One may have come from York, another from Ireland. Very few showed any real Welsh connection. A few came from other Cistercian houses or their environs, like Thomas of Buildwas, Matthew of Whitland, and Richard of Swineshead. They may have been vocations gained from the neighbourhood of those monasteries attracted by some contact with Dore, or they may have been monks of those houses transferred to Dore because of particular skills, or because their own communities had been temporarily dispersed due to an economic crisis, or, and this was sometimes the case, they may have been monks sent permanently away from their own abbeys because they had been troublemakers there. It was a two-way traffic, for monks hailing from Dore or its locality could on occasion be found as monks of other abbeys—at Hailes, at Stanley, and at Tintern.

As regarding the spiritual lives of the monks there is but patchy evidence, the details of relatively minor infringements of the *Rule* contained in one or two extant visitation charters—as that of 1318 when the abbot of Hailes, Gloucestershire, as commissary of the abbot of Morimond, inspected Dore[21]—are far from being sufficient to give a general picture. The house knew some great abbots and in their days at least a high standard was probably maintained. It is true of any monastery's history, (as indeed in today's newspapers), that often only the bad news hits the headlines; the scores of monks living at any given time at Dore, humbly observing the usages of the Order and seeking holiness thereby, hardly ever get a mention. There is one pointer—such evidence as there is suggests that Dore had a reasonably fine library and that its monks read their books.

The Library of the Monastery

A Cistercian library was never as ambitious as those of some large Benedictine abbeys, but a gift of books could help supplement it or form a nucleus for further development. This probably happened at Dore in 1236 when Bishop Cadwgan of Bangor retired there and brought with him 'his store of books', these becoming the property of the monastery.[22] As for the interest of the monks in their books, the words of the abbot of Hailes in the 1318 visitation charter are worth noting: 'All books belonging to the community are to be entered on a common list [in other words they were to be catalogued], and if anyone was found to have a book which he had not handed in for listing, he was to be treated as a thief'. Moreover, the abbot continued, 'all the books were to be kept in a common bookcase, and not kept out overnight without leave of the precentor or succentor, on pain of bread and water penance the next day'.[23] One of Dore's books was, of course, its 'register' or 'cartulary'—that was for

Fig. 7. Liber monachorum sancte Marie Vallis Dore per manum Johannis Bathoniensis—The book of the monks of Saint Mary of Valley Dore, by the hand of John of Bath. Contemporary inscription in an early thirteenth century manuscript of Osbern of Gloucester's Panormia.
(Hereford Cathedral Library, MS P.V.5, f.i^v)

Fig. 8. Extract from the Annals of Dore (BL Egerton MS 3088)

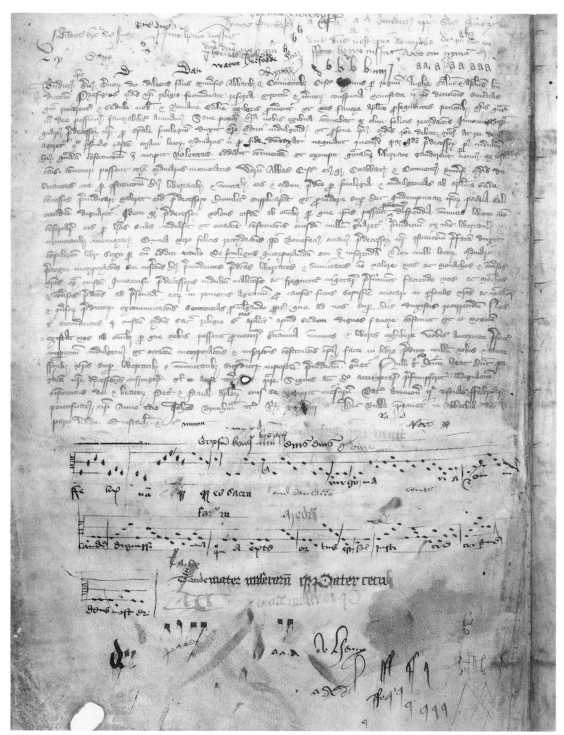

Fig. 9. Extract from Exeter Coll. (Oxford) MS 1 (f. 75ᵛ)
(by permission of the Rector & Fellows of Exeter College, Oxford)

20

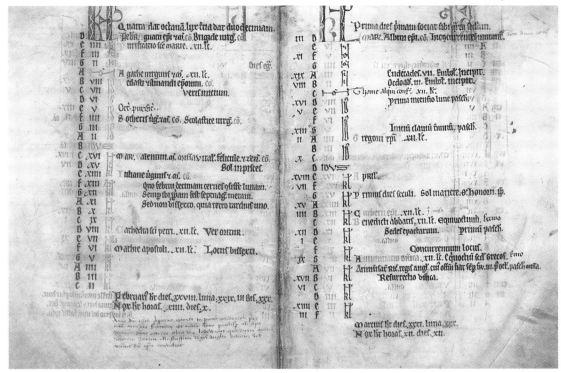

Fig. 10. Extract from Exeter Coll. (Oxford) MS 1 (ff 3ᵛ⁻⁴r)
(by permission of the Rector & Fellows of Exeter College, Oxford)

sometime after the Suppression at Holme Lacy (close to Hereford) but has long since disappeared.[24]

Some ten books known to have belonged to Abbey Dore have survived, all of them twelfth or thirteenth century copies of standard works.[25] Four of these now repose in the British Library, including a work by Bede; three are in Oxford libraries, including a work by Augustine (an author much favoured by the Cistercians); one is in the ancient cathedral library of Hereford, and one, *The Rule of St. Basil*, is at Trinity College, Cambridge. The Hereford manuscript is a thirteenth-century transcription by a monk of Dore, John of Bath, of the *Panormia* or 'Latin Dictionary' of Osbert, a monk of Gloucester (Fig. 7, Plate 7).[26] Books lent out were not always returned, and perhaps sometimes stolen; so to the usual monastic *ex-libris* inscription: 'The book of the monks of St. Mary of Valley Dore.' The Trinity manuscript adds: 'let him who deceitfully takes it be anathema'.[27]

Two of Dore's books are of considerable interest. First, the work by Bede in the British Library—for bound in the volume almost as an after-thought is a chronicle which can only have been compiled at Dore itself[28] (Appendix 1). Written mostly in a late-thirteenth century hand, it has additions down to 1362 when, unfortunately, it stops short. It is this chronicle which tells of the foundation of Grace Dieu Abbey near Monmouth by monks from Dore, of the miracle wrought by Matilda Burnel, and of the doctorate of Abbot Straddell. Arranged in two columns, the left hand deals mostly with secular history and the right hand with ecclesiastical affairs. It tells, for example, that in 1208 William, prior of Goldcliff, was elected bishop of Llandaff, and that William de Braose, 'father and son', fled to Ireland (Fig. 8).

Second, at Exeter College, Oxford, and fittingly its *MS No. 1*, is what has been described as a *Regula monachorum*, perhaps a copy of the Cistercian *Ecclesiastica Officia*. It is a very detailed customary, with kalendar, which awaits and would be worthy of full transcription. The style of handwriting apart, its thirteenth century compilation is attested by later additions made to the kalendar; such include the feasts of St. Louis (a great ally of the Cistercians), canonised in 1297, and of St. Thomas Aquinas—raised to the altars of the Church in 1323. Clearly the work precedes both those dates. Like many other monastic volumes, additional interest is to be found in the rough notes added by monks in the margins and on the fly-leaves. As to the kalendar for February in this same work, we read at the foot of the page of a comet appearing 'towards the east' in 1515. Other pages of the Exeter manuscript have jottings of plain chant, and notes telling of some of the disputes and problems the monastery endured in the fourteenth century (Figs. 9 & 10).

An interest in books was maintained at Dore in the early sixteenth century by the last abbot but two of the house, Thomas Cleubery. Not only does his signature appear on one of the back pages of the Exeter manuscript, but also on an Harleian manuscript in the British Library.[29] The Latin script is debatable, but one interpretation of this line runs: 'this little new work is compiled and put together by Cleubery, this long time of Dore, 1526'. The book is a composite volume of several short works, two of the sections being Lichtenberger's *Prognosticatio* printed at Strasbourg about 1500. On folio 47 of these prophecies foretelling the extinction of the monasteries has 'A.D. 1539' added in manuscript in the margin, and a forecast of two years of tribulation has '1522' similarly appended, probably by Cleubery himself, those being the very years of his own misfortunes and persecution.

Miracles, and Pilgrims

To Abbey Dore, despite its remote position, came also pilgrims. They may have been attracted by a miracle noted as happening in 1318, 'by virtue of the venerable matron, Matilda Burnel, who lies before the high altar'.[30] The chronicle gives no further detail. Sometime, too, miraculous happenings both at Dore and at its

Trawscoed Grange (Breconshire) were alleged in a fourteenth century manuscript. They concerned *conversi* (lay-brothers) whose mouths the Blessed Sacrament would not enter on account of their unresolved sins. The 'Miracles which took place in the house of dore' were related in a composite volume, now in Hereford Cathedral Library[31], but possibly emanating from St. Peter's Abbey, Gloucester (Fig. 11).

The year 1318 was also the year of the visitation of Dore by the abbot of Hailes of which a detailed record survives.[32] Drawing up his visitation charter, the abbot noted that 'large numbers came to venerate the cross in the conventual church'. Which cross was that? The annals of Dore tell (under the year 1321) that 'on October 6th, and then a Tuesday, came to Dore the lord W(illiam) de Grandison, bringing with him a portion of the wood of the Holy Cross, very beautifully adorned with gold and precious stones, he handed it over to the monastery'.[33] Some of the dates in the annals of Dore are suspect, but not this one, as 6 October was a Tuesday in 1321. Otherwise, it would be tempting to assume that this was the cross referred to in the visitation of 1318. Dore had another precious cross, described by its last abbot, John Redborne, as 'a cross of gold called a little relic cross'.[34] So as to which cross the pilgrims came to venerate, we are little the wiser.

Early History

Little is known of life at Dore from its inception in 1147 through to the abbacy of Adam I (from about 1186 to 1216). It was in his time that the monastery became the subject of critical attacks by the archdeacon of Brecon, Gerald of Wales (*Giraldus Cambrensis*) and the archdeacon of Oxford, Walter Map. Amongst the accusations levelled at the monastery were allegations that the monks frequently ate meat breaking their custom of total abstinence, and that drink was a problem in the abbey; that they extended their lands—obtaining property by fair means or foul, that for financial reward they induced men and women to take the monastic habit on their deathbed, and that they had reduced Trawscoed Abbey in Cantref-selyf to the status of a grange.[35] There

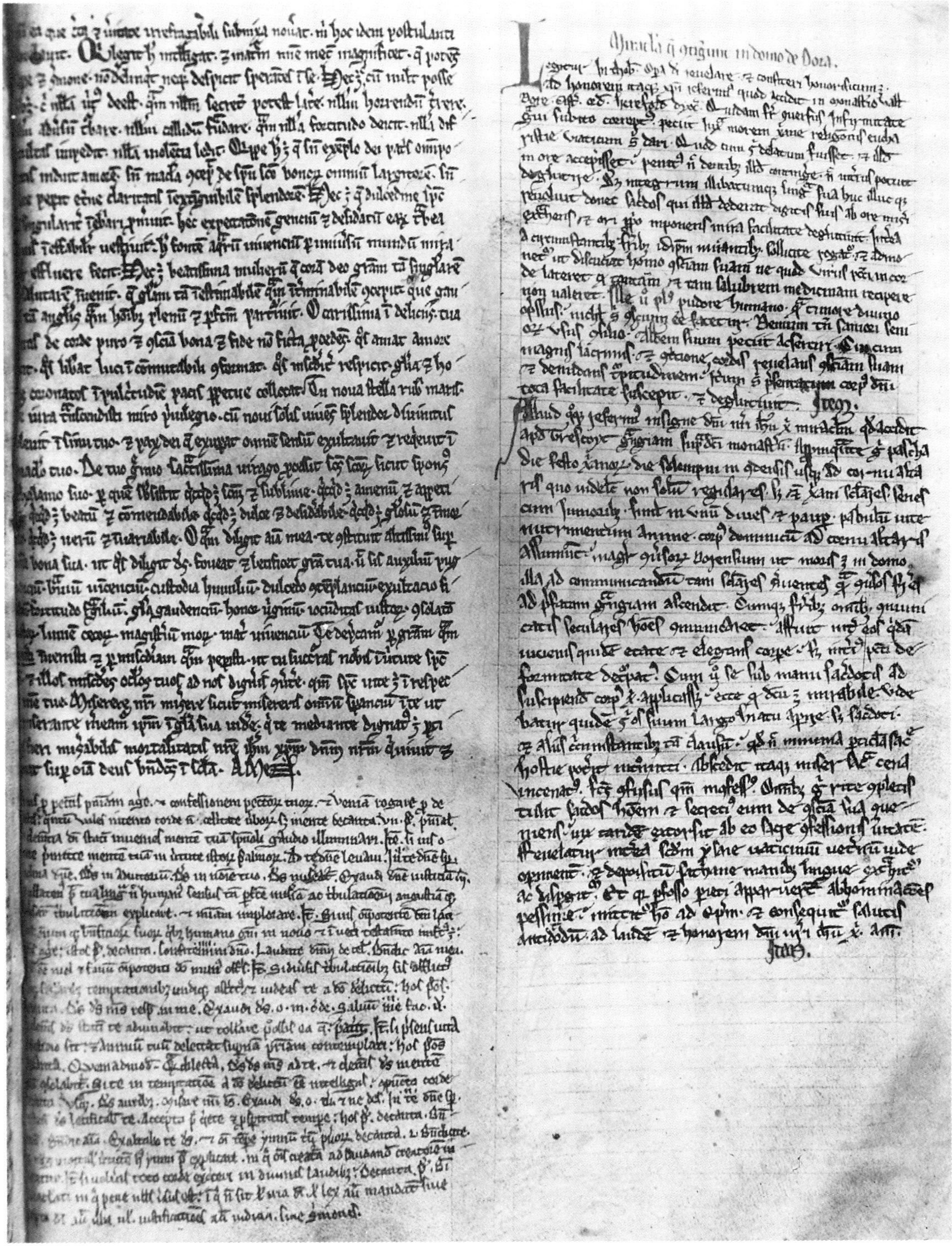

Fig. 11. Miracula que contingunt in domo de Dora—miracles which took place in the house of Dore. From an early thirteenth century manuscript of the works of Hugh of Fleury and others, possibly from St. Peter's Abbey, Gloucester. (Hereford Cathedral Library, MS P.I.13, f.142)

may have been some truth in these criticisms, though perhaps not in the particular ways that Gerald painted them. He was in his later life embittered by having been passed over for promotion to the bishopric of St. David's, and for this he blamed in large measure the Cistercians, and especially abbot Peter of Whitland.[36]

It is a pity that the reply penned by abbot Adam II (who ruled from about 1216 to 1226) to these attacks on the monastery is no longer extant, for a very different picture might then emerge. (It was a custom of the time—not just at Dore—for dying people to seek a sort of spiritual life insurance by taking the habit of a monk in their last illness. Further, the General Chapter had not long since ordered that abbeys which failed to maintain a community of thirteen monks were to become granges, or be closed down altogether).[37] Formerly a Cluniac monk, Adam II was given credit by Gerald of Wales for entering the more austere Cistercian Order. It was but limited credit; Adam was, Gerald said. 'modest in a mediocre way'.[38] Adam II was given to literary work; he is reputed to have written a bible in verse, and a treatise entitled *The Rudiments of Music*, a term which can refer either to music or the music of poetry.[39] Certainly, the monks of Dore took an interest in music at that time; along with the community of Tintern they were rebuked by the General Chapter (in 1217) for using three- and four-part tones instead of the plain Cistercian chant.[40]

A long-serving abbot was Stephen of Worcester (1236-57). In his time there is evidence for the expansion of the estates and economic privileges of Dore[41], and for the abbey following a common monastic practice of acting as bankers, both taking deposits (for safeguarding) and lending out money.[42] Of the character of Stephen himself nothing is recorded. He must have been a good abbot to have held the office for twenty-one years without apparently any serious complaint, and to have encouraged the literary activity of John of Bath and perhaps others. He was deposed in 1257, but no reason is known; perhaps with age he had lost his grip on things. It was a time when little in the way of

especial privileges were formally accorded to retired or deposed abbots. He was literally 'placed in the cloister', and one can imagine how he might then be treated by monks whom he had to discipline (perhaps have soundly flogged) whilst he was superior. It was for this reason that the precentor of Hereford Cathedral wrote to his successor, abbot Henry, offering the new abbot a palfrey if he would ensure that the deposed Stephen, 'my great friend', was not ill-treated.[43]

In the history of Dore abbot Stephen will perhaps be best remembered for having received the renewed profession of Cadwgan, formerly abbot of Whitland in Carmarthenshire (1203-15) and then bishop of Bangor in Gwynedd (1215-36). Retiring after twenty-one years in the episcopate he returned to finish his days (he died in 1241) as he had begun adult life, in a Cistercian cloister. He chose to come to Dore, transferring to the monastery all his goods, books and horses.[44] Cadwgan was a noted theologian and spiritual writer whose known works, written more probably during his time at Bangor than at Dore, included a penitential, several commentaries (as on Genesis 1, the Eucharist, and St. Bernard), and tracts (on the Blessed Virgin Mary [Appendix 2], and on the 4th verse of the 79th Psalm). His work has been described as 'thoroughly Celtic in spirit and expression'.[45] Alas, his days drew to a close on an unhappy note. The General Chapter (of 1239) heard that Cadwgan neglected to keep the observances of the Order (both by breaking silence and his mode of living) and that he fostered dissension and scandal.[46] The extent of the truth of these allegations, if any, is unknown. As a bishop he perhaps had a certain freedom, and there may have been those jealous of this and indeed of his reputation. For many years, and certainly as late as 1727, an effigy carved in oak was to be seen in the south walk of the ambulatory at Dore; rightly or wrongly it has been conjectured as representing Cadwgan (Fig. 12).[47]

Troubled Years
The mid-thirteenth century saw the abbacy of Henry (1257-73), previously cellarer of the monastery. The position of cellarer was

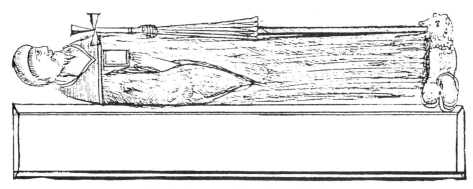

Fig 12. A drawing of the effigy of Cadwgan

extremely important in the economic well-being of an early medieval Cistercian house, and numerous cellarers are on record as being translated from that position, with the experience and business acumen it gave, to the post of superior with overall command. His abbacy was not to be an easy time. Money had to be raised to complete the 'sumptuous church'—aided by an indulgence issued by the bishop of Hereford (1260).[48] The monastery suffered 'more than most' in the Baronial Rebellion against Henry III (1263-65).[49] There were several long-running disputes—not least over the possession of the manor of Holme Lacy (which it leased from the chapter of Hereford Cathedral) (1259-64), and with the Knights Hospitaller (probably regarding property and rights in Herefordshire) (1266). As for the trouble concerning Holme Lacy, which was raided more than once, the abbot said that 'a single membrane of parchment could not contain the full tale of injury'.[50] In the litigation with the Hospitallers the abbot used one of his monks, brother A. de Madel, as his emissary, urging him by letter to 'carry through and hasten our business, all our hope rests on you'. He added: 'Love knows not loathing, and feels no toil'.[51] The close of Abbot Henry's rule saw Dore said to be 'deficient in temporalities' (1273).[52]

These difficult years resulted in Dore having a succession of 'conservators' of its privileges appointed by the Holy See.[53] A typical mandate was that addressed to the Precentor of Llandaff Cathedral in 1262 commanding him to 'assist the abbot and convent of Dore, by ecclesiastical censure [excommunication] to prevent them from being disquieted or molested in their persons and goods'.[54] Despite his many preoccupations, in 1265 the abbot was successful in obtaining pardon for an alleged murderer in Cheltenham[55], and in January 1273 he was commissioned by the king to travel with the Abbot of Haughmond, Shropshire, to the Ford of Montgomery, Powys, to receive the fealty of Prince Llywelyn the Last (of Wales).[56] The prince failed to turn up. That same year, on 20 November, Abbot Henry died.[57] The last decades of the thirteenth century saw the foundation of a daughter-house at Darnhall, Cheshire, (in January 1274—just after Abbot Henry's death), a brief stay in December 1282 by Archbishop Peckham of Canterbury at Dore on his return from Wales[58], and the consecration of the abbey church.

A Great Abbot

For thirty-five years, much of the first half of the fourteenth century, Dore had for abbot a monk widely respected and of considerable scholarship, who stood head and shoulders in general esteem above those who preceded and followed him. More than that, he was long remembered. Richard Straddell, abbot by 1312, took an Oxford doctorate early in his abbacy, and found time to write several theological works.[59] He composed, in Latin of course, commentaries on the Bible, a paraphrase of the Lord's Prayer, various homilies and sermons, some of them upon the angelic salutation, 'Hail Mary, full of grace', and some of them still extant, while seventeen of his sermons which have survived are based upon texts from the Book of Daniel. Another of his sermons, *Of St. Benedict*, and based upon the text, 'Blessed are you in the firmament of heaven', from the *Song of the Three Holy Children*, told us 'to scorn earthly things, to love virtuous things, and to hope for things eternal'[60] (Appendix 3). When on 15 August 1330, the Feast of the Assumption, he preached at the consecration of the abbey church at Vale Royal, it was naturally a sermon 'touching the Blessed Virgin' which 'refreshed the people in his accustomed way with food of special nourishment'.[61]

By this time Straddell had a growing reputation as an arbiter and diplomat, and was frequently engaged as a member of missions on behalf of the Crown, especially in the problems arising from Anglo-French conflict. In 1321 he carried a message from Humphrey de Bohun, earl of Hereford and Essex, to Edward II.[62] The following year he went with the abbot of Margam to Ireland on a visitation of Cistercian houses, arranged by the General Chapter of the Order at the king's request[63], and, in the company of the archbishop of York, he journeyed to Scotland in 1327 to treat for peace between the English and the Scots.[64] The rector of Wickwar, Worcestershire, attended upon Straddell in the year of 1332 to 1333.[65]

Abbot Richard went three times on royal business to France; in 1330 to Aquitaine, in 1334 to Paris, and in 1335 to Poitou. On the latter journey he was allowed to carry abroad 'the silver vessels used in his household'—a reflection of the restrictions currently placed on the transference of money and silver abroad so that ready cash didn't fall into enemy hands[66]; it was a contemporaneous note, too, of the style in which abbots had become accustomed to live. On his return from Poitou, Straddell journeyed to Berwick to wait upon Edward III. The travels of 1334 and 1335 necessitated the total absence of Dore's abbot for at least seven months—not always good for a monastery as St. Bernard's community had found much earlier. On the other hand he became a

personage with influential and perhaps helpful contacts. His itemised accounts for his last two French journeys are still extant, and show that as well as his passage, he was allowed daily expenses of 30 shillings in England but £2 in France.[67]

Edward III appreciated Straddell's 'great labours', and by way of recompense gave especial privileges to his monastery.[68] His death came on 29 July, 1346, and the monastery was not to see his like again. But his fame lived on, and when two centuries later, after the suppression of the abbey, the travelling antiquary, John Leland, visited Hereford, he met an elderly bibliophile, a man in his late sixties and now resident in the city. This was Thomas Cleubery (abbot of Dore from 1516 to 1523), and Leland recorded that Cleubery 'told me much about Straddell'.[69] This little incident shows how highly Straddell must have been regarded not only in his own day but also in the traditions of the abbey handed down through later generations of monks. It also tells us something of the respect shewn locally for Cleubery in his retirement; he was obviously pointed out in Hereford as a man Leland ought to consult.

Power Struggles at Dore

Little is known of the abbacies which immediately followed that of Straddell (Appendix 5). Robert Wroth ruled the monastery from 1347 to 1362; he came of an old local family. The phrase *Robert Wroth me fecit* occurs on a detached stone which may formerly have formed part of a pillar in the north transept.[70] His successor, John Wysbech (1362-84) went on to be abbot of Tintern in the Wye Valley for another twenty or more years.

The concluding five years of the fourteenth century were perhaps some of the worst in the history of the monastery. Not only did two monks contend as to whom was the rightful abbot of the house (there is unfortunately no official record of the episcopal blessing of either), but also the community and its properties were subject to armed raids and depredations from without—possibly as a result of the power struggle within.

The ruling abbot about 1395 was John Holand, previously a monk of Dore. Around this time he was dispossessed of the abbacy by a monk of St. Mary Graces (near the Tower of London), Jordan Bykeleswade (*al.* Biggleswade) with the help of armed force. In (probably the late summer of) 1396 a provincial chapter of the English Cistercians held at St. Mary Graces confirmed Bykeleswade in the abbacy, but the king gave protection to Holand as the true abbot.[71] The matter dragged on, with both men trying to administer the properties of the abbey. Both, for example, presented different priests to the living of Wigtoft, Lincolnshire, (of the abbey's patronage) when a vacancy occurred there. The resulting dispute between the two nominees led to riot and even bloodshed during Mass in Wigtoft church.[72] In 1398 Bykeleswade seems to have received backing from both the pope and the bishop of Hereford, and from then on until he was indicted of a felony in 1403 was *de facto* abbot.[73]

Both abbots had many problems with the local populace. Members of the Scudamore family, probably towards the close of Holand's abbacy, came to the abbey armed, assaulted the abbot (presumably Holand), chased him away, and rustled horses, oxen and cows. They then went to the daughter-house at Grace Dieu, where the abbot had tried to take refuge, and at both monasteries stole money, goods, charters and muniments, as well as the common seal of Dore. Worse still, they imprisoned one of the monks (Thomas Baker, *al.* Thomas of Abergavenny) in Ewyas Harold Castle.[74] Jordan Bykeleswade too was troubled. In the late summer of 1398 he sent a petition to the king seeking redress after depredations done by John and Gruffydd ap Henry, Thomas de la Hay, and John Oldcastle, to the buildings and lands of Dore, both in the Golden Valley and in Breconshire. At Trivel Wood, for example, they felled and removed ninety-four 'great oaks of the best'; they raided Morehampton Grange with 'a great multitude of archers' and killed thirty beef cattle there. Not content with the damage they had inflicted, the Henry brothers came again to Dore and took three of the monks (Richard Clifford, a young man and later abbot of Dore, was one) from

the abbey, imprisoning them first at Snodhill Castle and then at Urishay Castle. Clifford paid a fine for ransom and was released, but David Oswestry and Richard Madley were to suffer further. They were taken to Gwenddwr, one of the abbey's Welsh granges, and there, off-and-on for three days, were hung from trees upside down.[75]

These troubles may have reflected the power struggle for the abbacy, or increasing Welsh-English tensions, or the growth of Lollardy. John Oldcastle, who took the least part in them, was a notable Lollard. Certainly they were times of lawlessness, and in Wales abbeys such as Cymer and Strata Florida were to know similar troubles.[76] Hardly had Richard Grisby become abbot of Dore (1405-13) than the monks feared for the safety of their monastery as Glyn Dŵr's Revolt swept across the Welsh Border country.[77] (Four years later Grisby felt able to journey to the General Chapter at Citeaux[78] and was appointed to participate in a visitation of the Cistercian house of studies at Oxford).[79]

In 1435 Abbot Richard Clifford obtained the bishop of Hereford's inspection, 'all interested being assembled', of papal bulls in the defence of Cistercian privileges. The monks, having obviously experienced some difficulties, said that no new rights were sought but only that 'which is ancient should be preserved'. The papal bulls presented had been addressed to the monks of Llantarnam in Gwent.[80] It is possible that Dore's bulls had been lost in the raids on the monastery. It is of interest that no less than three leaden papal *bullae* formerly attached to some of Llantarnam's deeds have been unearthed within the last few years very close to that abbey.[81]

The long abbacy of Richard Rochester (*al.* Rowchester; 1441-72) was punctuated by further troubles. Little is known of the abbot himself, save that he had been a monk of Dore since at least 1414, and as he did not die until 1472 he more than achieved the golden jubilee of his profession.[82] The few indications are that the spiritual life of the house was healthy under his rule; the abbot went on a pilgrimage to St. David's sometime before 1460[83], and one of his monks (Edmund Thornebar) had become abbot of Basingwerk in North Wales by 1466.[84] The monastery had to receive Crown protection and be placed for a time under secular guardianship in 1453 because it was 'oppressed by sons of iniquity, taking and distraining of goods and chattels, abductions and carryings away'.[85] This ended a five or six year period when Rochester seems to have lost control of the abbey to an abbot John.[86] In 1471 when Rochester was an old man of about seventy-five years he was temporarily ousted unlawfully as abbot by a monk, Robert Ford. The General Chapter, 'being sufficiently informed of the assaults and divers torments on the lord Richard Rochester, abbot of Dore', deprived Ford of his pretended dignity.[87]

Tudor Times

Two abbots ruled at Dore in the last quarter of the fifteenth century. Philip Morgan (*alias* de Llywelyn), a monk of Dore by 1455, was blessed as abbot in 1478 and held that position until deposed when of 'great age' about 1495.[88] He was then technically professed as a monk of Whitland in Carmarthenshire, but in practice was allowed 'for his comfort in his age' to live at the house of Friars Preacher in Hereford, and there some ten years later he died and was buried. He was alleged to have taken with him to Hereford in retirement books and charters of the monastery as well as quite a sum of money and jewels.[89] Morgan was succeeded by Richard Dorston, formerly abbot of the daughter-house of Grace Dieu (1485-95), which he continued to try to rule.[90] He appears to have been deposed in 1500 for mismanagement of the monastery's affairs[91], yet managed to become abbot of Strata Florida in Ceredigion (by 1509-13).

His successor, John Longdon (*alias* Langdon; 1500-16) had to try to bring the monastery back to greater prosperity. At least one monk, John Ledbury (*alias* Mardio) preferred to live apart from the community.[92] As for Longdon, he seems to have been keen on hunting and the possession of saffron (used for flavouring).[93] In his time the monastery appears to have offered medical assistance to local folk; one Thomas Cokeshutt was indebted to Dore for 'a bleeding in his pins [legs] with cloves, spices, and other things.'[94] All three abbots had external worries:

Morgan drew up in his own hand a list of debts owing to the abbey by Harry Griffith[95]; Dorston (and later Cleubery) had problems with their own steward, Henry Miles[96]; and Longdon found it necessary to evict a widow from the tenancy of one of Dore's houses in Hereford.[97] By late August 1516, Thomas Cleubery, the scholar and bibliophile had succeeded as abbot of Dore. His entire abbacy was marked by problems. In 1518 he had occasion to complain of grave defamation by one Richard Jerneyn of the diocese of Worcester[98]; and of Henry Webb who for some years had wrongfully taken the tithes of the parish of Dore.[99] In 1519 the abbey was still in dispute with its steward and Cleubery drew up a list of his debts to the house going back over twenty years.[100] The abbot himself was menaced at a manorial court held at Dore by Miles' son-in-law.[101] Miles' son (Miles ap Harry) about this time (or a little later) removed from the custody of the abbey papers relating to his lands and those of Philip Scudamore of Kentchurch. (It was commonplace in those days for monasteries to act as safe-deposits for not only money and jewels but also for private deeds). Miles ap Harry's stated reasons for removing the coffer containing 'divers charters, writings and muniments' perhaps gives the background to troubles yet to come. Miles said that he 'perceived that the monastery of Dore standeth in a wild quarter where resided divers and many persons of light demeanour, and some of the monks being of that condition' he feared 'lest the said coffer and evidence should be embezzled or misordered by such persons.'[102] Not a very respectful reference to the community, and clearly not true of its abbot.

Cleubery's abbacy ended with harassment at Dore in the late summer and autumn of 1523 by Thomas ap Richard and an armed band. On 12 August they assaulted his sister and beat his brother, and on 7 October they lay in a wood near the abbey intent on killing the abbot himself. The worst attack was on Sunday, 20 September, when led by Thomas ap Richard some fifteen men, some of whom were said to be 'open thieves and indicted of felony' invaded the church during high mass, armed with 'bows and arrows, swords, bucklers, bills and spears', so that Cleubery fled the church for fear of his life.[103] The background to the attacks is unknown; it might have been a deliberate attempt to force him to give way to his unworthy successor. It was nearly two-and-a-half years before the community gave him a reasonable pension and his own accommodation (a complex of three rooms called 'the new chamber') with a chapel adjacent, on the north side of the monastery.[104] After the suppression Cleubery went to live in Hereford and was still alive in 1557. Said to be 'not married and of religious conversation', he was then 71 years old.[105]

His successor at Dore, John Glyn (1524-28), had already been expelled for misrule at Cymer in Meirionydd, and now proceeded to squander the financial resources of Dore. More than that, it was said that he lacked any stability.[106] The Reformator of the Order in England and Wales (abbot Henry of St. Mary Graces) deposed Glyn, and formally released the monks from their profession of obedience to him. Despite all this, Glyn managed to become the last abbot of Cwmhir about 1535[107]—it was a time when abbacies were much sought after in the not unrealistic hope of a pension on the expected Dissolution.

Property and Income
The basic unit of exploitation of Cistercian lands was the grange, a model farm in those days. Ideally it had an oratory, accommodation for the resident *conversi* (lay-brethren), and the necessary barn, stable, and animal sheds. Its inner enclosure was often surrounded by a wall or hedge or ditch, and there might be a protective gate-house. Dore had some seventeen such granges, nine of which lay in the Golden Valley, four were in north Gwent, and three in Breconshire (Fig. 13). Apart from these there were many other scattered possessions. Most is known of the grange of Llanfair Cilgoed sited well to the south of Grosmont. Originally a hermitage, it was granted to Dore in the early-thirteenth century by Hubert de Burgh, lord of the Three Castles of Grosmont, Skenfrith and White Castle (1201-43). As well as being a grange for the

abbey, it housed at first a cell of monks and later of secular chaplains to say Mass for the souls of de Burgh and other benefactors. This duty was still being performed at the Dissolution, when the chapel served the local populace who were far from a parish church.[108] In those days 'mattyns, masse, and evensong' were said on Sundays and holydays, Wednesdays and Fridays.[109] The chapel came to be a centre of recusancy with burials taking place in its ruins until towards the close of the eighteenth century.[110] Extensive foundations yet visible, and a field-survey by the late Richard Kay of Hereford (to whom the author owes a great deal), show that the grange was built on a courtyard pattern, and had a connected series of three or more fish-ponds, with terraced slopes for vine or fruit-growing.[111] Documentary evidence of the latter monastic days tells of a heronry at Llanfair.[112]

Other granges in north Gwent included Llyncoed (Campston) with 443 acres (180 ha.) of tithe-free land enduring into modern times; Cold Grange—associated with the manor of Blackbrook, where for a time (1360-69) Dore held St. Noye's Chapel[113]; and Morlais—now the 'mynachty' in the parish of Llanddewi Rhydderch. The granges in the Golden Valley included Kingstone—granted by Baldwin fitz Miles in the reign of Henry II (1154-89), and extended later (as most Cistercian granges were) through to the end of the thirteenth century by grants of contiguous land from at least four benefactors. It was primarily an arable grange, but with the mixed economy essential in the Middle Ages.[114] There were moated sites at Dore's Morehampton and Blackmoor Granges—perhaps for protection from wandering animals.[115] The latter had a 'Sheepcot Field'. The other granges in the Golden Valley were Bacton, Godway, Hollings, New, Newborough, and Whitewall; there was a somewhat detached grange at Benfield near the river Wye. There were more scattered lands—especially in the Gwent parishes of Grosmont and Skenfrith[116]; the abbey held the township of Dore itself, and for a time leased the manors of Albrighton (Salop; 1327 to about 1360)[117] and Holme Lacy, near Hereford (1259-65).

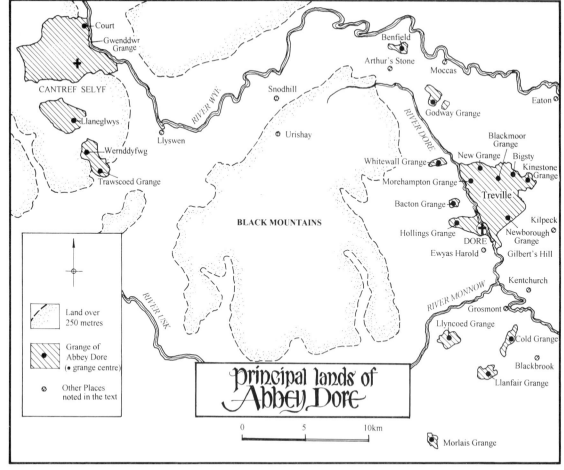

Fig. 13. The lands of Dore

A survey of 1540 showed the demense lands in the township of Dore to comprise over 400 acres (160 ha.) of arable, as well as 160 acres (65 ha.) of pasture and meadow. There was at least one water-mill, barns, 'Sheephouse', 'Ox-house', and dovecots.[118] The parish tithe-map (300 years later) shows field names which may have survived from monastic days, including: Scaffold Meadow, Saffron Meadow, and Stephen's Meadow.[119] At the eastern border of its territorial complex Dore owned (by 1213) some thousand acres (400 ha.) of the former Forest of Trivel. 300 acres (120 ha.) had come by purchase (for 300 marks) from King Richard I in 1198—for Trivel was then a royal chase.[120] Gerald of Wales criticised Dore for its wholesale clearance of woodland in Trivel, telling how the monks had

changed 'an oak wood into a wheat field', but, acknowledging their foresight, commented that the timber 'when sold in Hereford for building purposes brought back the three hundred marks more than three times over'.[121] Trivel included the property now called Jury (Jewry formerly), and in the remainder of the former forest, Grace Dieu Abbey owned a chapel.[122]

There is much evidence of the monks buying up land within, or contiguous to, their properties, or achieving it by exchange or outright grant. This is recorded, *inter alia*, at Benfield from 1225 to 1295[123] and Morlais from 1318 to 1342.[124] It was this deliberate policy which allowed Dore to unite six granges into one unbroken landholding stretching across the Golden Valley from Hollings Grange in the west to Kingstone Grange and Trivel in the east. Such an achievement allowed of careful land management and economic efficiency, giving freedom of movement and avoiding certain duplication of expenses. Some of the benefactors who gave these additional lands to Dore, (as Roger de Clifford[125], Roger de Evereus[126], and Walter of Kingstone[127]) did so partly in return for the privilege of being buried at the abbey. One benefactor, Walter of Homenesse, surrendered land (by 1263) in return for a corrody.[128] The *minutiae* of the relevant deeds reveals much local history of interest, with references (in Benfield alone) to 'the Summer Way'[129], 'the Ferryman of Bredwardine' (*ca.* 1235)[130], and to 'Arthur's Stone' (*ca.* 1235-70; now an Ancient Monument).[131]

Walter Clifford (the first) in about 1170 gave Dore considerable lands in the Breconshire lordship of Cantref-selyf. Here the abbey's properties, worked later on manorial lines, consisted of three units—the granges of Gwenddwr, Llaneglwys, and Trawscoed. There is also mention in 1241 of Wernddyfwg Grange of which little more is heard.[132] Trawscoed Grange (so called in 1263) was the former abbey of that name. In Cantref-selyf there was a bridge called *Pontum Monachorum*, where in 1268 an agreement was reached between Prince Llewelyn the Last of Wales and Earl Gilbert de Clare of Gloucester[133]; its choice as a meeting-place shows the borderland nature of Cantref-selyf. The lands there were essentially pastoral ones, and at Trawscoed in later monastic years was 'a great house called the Sheepcote.'[134] Dore's enjoyment of its pasture rights and other liberties in Cantref-selyf were challenged or usurped several times in the first half of the thirteenth century. Consequently there were disputes with Strata Florida Abbey (1209)[135], Walter Clifford (the third; 1240-52)[136], and William and John of Ford (1263)[137], among others. In all the major disputes Dore won its case and in 1264 felt able to say that 'it had established its rights in the land of Cantref-selyf.'[138] The extent of Dore's interests, both in England and Wales, is reflected in the two great confirmatory charters of its lands issued by Henry III[139] and Edward III.[140]

Most Cistercian monasteries owned houses in neighbouring towns, especially in the local see city. These provided a place to stay for monks on business, a place to store goods for sale and to do trade, and, when leased out, a source of income. In the early thirteenth century Adam Seys gave the monks of Dore 'a piece of land in Hereford that they may have a hostel there when they come to Hereford.'[141] In 1263 his son, Adam, granted Dore money for this purpose 'in place of certain tenements and rents now ruinous and decayed'[142]—possibly a reflection of the current Marchland disturbances. Dore also came to own houses in Barton Street, King Street (seven), and Wyebridge Street—the latter 'in the parish of St. Nicholas.'[143] One of the houses in Wyebridge Street was given to Dore in 1334 by the vicar of Bacton[144], and, whilst temporarily shared with a previous tenant's widow; it had for the monks' immediate use, a stone chamber and cellar, kitchen and stable.[145] When abbot Longdon evicted John Williams from the house in Hereford he rented from the abbey, it was on the grounds that the holding was worth more than the 5s. annual rent originally charged. His widow, Katherine, managed much later to get an enquiry held into the circumstances of her late husband's eviction. In the depositions then given mention was made of how half the garden was planted with saffron, and that abbot Longdon, having evicted Williams, 'gathered the flowers of the saffron there growing.'[146] Dore also owned a burgage in Castle Street, Ewyas Harold.[147]

Revenues

The sources of income accruing to a Cistercian monastery were threefold. Firstly, came income from demised granges and other properties. Especially towards the Suppression much monastic land was rented out, and by 1536 Dore had very little land left under its direct management. Exactly how long major properties had been demised is uncertain. For Cantref-selyf there is extant an inventory of forty-four monastic indentures and leases going back to at least 1457, but of these eighteen date from the last abbacy, that of John Redborne (1529-36), showing the acceleration of the process in those years.[148] Of other properties, Bacton Grange had been demised by 1458, and Kingstone by 1468, but there is no extant note of any lease of Morehampton Grange until 1527, Llanfair until 1529, Blackmoor until 1530, and Morlais until 1534.[149] Some smaller individual properties had been farmed out very much earlier.[150] Apart from paying a cash annual rent (£15 6s. 8d. for Morehampton[151] but only £6 13s. 4d. for Kingstone[152]) monastic tenants had other conditions to fulfil, not least the duty of maintaining and, indeed, improving the property. Thomas Baskerville (Dore's last Steward) who received Morehampton was within five years (and largely at his own expense) to build or cause to be builded anew, 'a barn, an ox house, a kitchen, a day house, and all other houses necessary'. Baskerville, clearly a man of influence and perhaps with a certain hold over the monastery, was also the tenant of Kingstone Grange. There he was not only to build 'a dwelling house, a barn, and other cottages, meet and convenient', but also 'to repair, maintain and sustain all manner of hedges and dykes within the precincts of the grange'. He could have sufficient housebote (wood for the repair of buildings) and heybote (wood for the repair of fences) out of the abbey wood at Dore, but he was not to cut down 'the grete oak, elm, or polle [pollard] wood'. How far he carried out the improvements is unknown.

Secondly, there were tithes and income from appropriated parishes, or, in other words, 'spiritualities', which formed nearly a quarter of the abbey's gross value in 1535. The major parishes so impropriated to Dore were Avenbury and Bacton in Herefordshire, Duntisbourne in Gloucestershire, Albrighton in Shropshire, Wigtoft in Lincolnshire, and Gwenddwr in Breconshire.[153] Dore also laid claim at some stage to at least the advowson (right to present a parson to the living), if not the tithes also, of Iddeshale (Shifnal) in Staffordshire[154] and Lugwardine in Herefordshire.[155] It had too the tithes of what came to be known as the 'parish of Dore' which (in 1518) consisted of 'wheat, barley, rye, oats, straw, fish, hay, wool and lamb's wool'[156] - i.e. the 'greater' and 'lesser' tithes.

The churches of Avenbury and Duntisbourne were granted to Dore by their lay patron, John le Rous, in 1318 and by 1328 respectively. Mass for his soul was still being offered at St. Edmund's altar in the abbey church in 1446.[157] The process of appropriation could be lengthy and costly, because of the fees payable to various personages, including the diocesan bishop and the pope. The monastery had to justify its need for the income a parish would yield; in the case of Avenbury it was to help in providing charity for the poor;[158] in the instance of Duntisbourne it was because of the privations the abbey had suffered, including 'sterility of lands ... murrain of animals ... wars, and other external disturbances'.[159] Once episcopal permission had been gained, the next stage was the resignation of the incumbent rector, who was compensated. This act took place in the case of Avenbury (1 July 1321) in the bishop of Hereford's chapel at Whitbourne;[160] in the instance of Duntisbourne (7 Sept. 1330) at Dore 'in the porch of a chamber next to the great infirmary.'[161]

Only on the resignation of the rector could a vicar be appointed, almost always a secular priest, to perform divine service and pastoral care. In the prior negotiations terms were agreed as to the stipend and rights of the new incumbent. At Avenbury the monastery retained for the use of the monks two chambers in the manse and the greater tithes, the vicar receiving the rest of the house, the lesser tithes, and a small stipend.[162] The tithe barn there was called 'the Abbot's Barn'. Papal confirmation of the grant and arrangements was often sought and (at Avenbury) granted in 1330.[163] At Duntisbourne the relevant deed makes it clear that the abbey was responsible for the upkeep and repair of the chancel of the church. Two copies were made of the agreement in the case of Duntisbourne; one for the abbey and one for the vicar, whilst the terms were also transcribed into the bishop of Worcester's register.[164]

Albrighton church was appropriated in 1327 on the condition of requiems being chanted in the monastery for the grantor, John la Warre, lord of Ewyas.[165] The same donor gave Wigtoft church in 1330, an act confirmed in 1345 because the abbey had 'suffered by the wars between the English and the Welsh.'[166] Wigtoft was Dore's most valuable church, worth some £30 in the fourteenth century but declining in value thereafter.[167] Out of its income an annual payment had to be made of £3 6s. 8d. to the bishop of Lincoln.[168] The greater tithes of Gwenddwr were demised by Dore in 1529 to its local bailiff, Robert ap Glyn Llywelyn[169], and the advowson of the church there in 1530 to Jenkin ap Rhys and his father.[170] When the then 'curate incumbent' should die or resign they could nominate his successor, but first they were to 'present any such priest unto the abbot and convent, as to his ordinary, who shall admit him to ye cure'. Gwenddwr church perhaps arose from the grange chapel, hence the abbot rather than the bishop was the ordinary—the ecclesiastical authority with the final say. The vicar received the lesser tithes, as well as 'all altar dues, offerings, and mortuaries'. It was provided that 'if the abbot be willing to have the tithing lambs of the parish of Gwenddwr, then the vicar shall see them to him for his money before any other man'.

Thirdly, income came from sales. Save in the case of wool and timber (of which mention later), we have little knowledge of sales in the case of Dore. There is, however, a late and odd reference, when Thomas Havard sent to the abbot 'five sacks, beseeching your lordship to send me in every sack four bushels, and I trust my lord when your lordship and I meet that we shall not vary over a reckoning.'[171] Abbey Dore also received income from occasional gifts and bequests and pilgrim offerings. Very important, in the earlier centuries, was the 'hidden income'—income received in kind, the produce sent from the granges for the sustenance of the community. Another valuable asset was the freedom from paying tithes on lands it had brought under cultivation.

Despite its varied revenue Dore was never very rich. Early on, and indeed in 1321 (to William de Grandison), it had made loans to those in need[172], but for two-thirds of its recorded history there are periodic references to its financial difficulties, a reflection in part of the hazards of economic life in the Border country. In 1255 it borrowed nearly four hundred marks from a merchant-cum-money lender of Siena.[173] In 1273 it was said to be 'deficient in temporalities.'[174]

In 1281 it was classified by the General Chapter amongst the Welsh Cistercian houses for taxation purposes, after pleading poverty.[175] In 1295 it owed over £100 to Earl Edmund of Cornwall[176], and in 1340 £150 to Edward Frankys of Bristol.[177] When subsidies for pope or king were levied, Dore (often a sub-collector) was frequently in arrears of payment, a situation which continued down to 1517.[178] Part of its later stringency came from the failure of some tenants to pay their rents for years on end.[179] In the last centuries, too, as paid lay-officials and hired servants became increasingly common, the greater the wages bill must have been. Among the more interesting outgoings, as recorded in 1535, were 6s. 8d. to the choristers of Hereford Cathedral (a pension due from the appropriated church of Avenbury), and £1 16s. for the distribution of money and bread to the poor on that great day of Christian charity, Maundy Thursday.[180]

Economic Activity
A jealously guarded commodity in the Middle Ages was timber, relatively abundant but in considerable demand. While in their earlier days the monks of Dore received several rights of cutting timber, there is evidence that they became careful conservators of their own woods. Hand in hand with grants of land went lumbering rights in order to construct buildings thereon, and for fencing newly cleared land. Gerald of Wales asserted that they sold much timber in Hereford. In Cantref-selyf (1241) the monks could 'take in the wood which they require for the granges of Trawscoed and Wernddyfwg, for building, for fuel, and for making hedges.'[181] In northern Gwent (1233) for 'making their buildings in the grange of Llyncoed they may take in Grosmont Forest all that is necessary in the view of the foresters, and dead wood for fuel.'[182] King John confirming

part of Trivel Forest to the abbey also 'deforested' it—a legal term which meant that it was no longer Crown land, and thus the monks could have freedom of action therein though they had to pay heavily for the right.[183] In 1254, Henry III 'allowed' Dore to make clearings in its woods 'with all haste'; probably more of a command to ensure that Welsh and other rebels could not hide away near thoroughfares during the then current Border warfare.[184]

Apart from restrictions on felling trees placed on its tenants, evidence suggesting planned tree growth and conservation on the lands of Dore comes in surveys made in 1540, just four years after its suppression. These show that at Gilbert's Hill (a wood owned by the monks east of the abbey, a remnant perhaps of Trivel Forest, and possibly the wood in which abbot Cleubery's would-be assassins laid wait), the trees were 'closed with a hedge containing 120 acres, whereof 13 acres be of fifty years growing, and the residue of an hundred years growing and above.'[185] Morehampton Wood was 'set with oaks of eighty and one hundred years growth', and occupied fifty acres[186], but woods growing on lands belonging to nearby Bigstye (*alias* Pigsty, Boggestye) would 'hardly suffice to repair the houses and maintain the hedges there.'[187] There was still much woodland in Gwenddwr, and on some of the granges—including ten acres at Llanfair Cilgoed.[188]

Woodland clearance (assarting) was generally accompanied by some form of enclosure, so far as monastic lands were concerned, both for purposes of delineation and to discourage wandering animals. In early-thirteenth century grants there is phraseology such as 'to build a dyke around it and plough it' (at Oxmead)[189], 'to dyke, enclose, and treat at their pleasure' (at Bacton)[190], and to 'till, assart, and enclose' (at Gwenddwr).[191] Of the actual type of cultivation on Dore's granges we know little, but arable was certainly important—420 acres (170 ha.) at the dissolution on the immediate demesne of the monastery.[192] Kingston Grange was an important arable farm, and the several mills and barns Dore owned is another pointer. One insight into farming at Dore came in the visitation charter of

1318 when it was enjoined that young monks were not to work at carting unsupervised, and the sowing of flax was forbidden—as this meant women had to come in 'to pick, wash, and prepare it.'[193] A second glimpse comes in the detailed agreement between the abbey and Philip Tew and Robert Balcott (Bulcote) in 1533 when, for nine years, Tew and Balcott entered into partnership with the monks in cultivating the three fields called 'the odde marks.'[194] The abbey was to find four teams of oxen (twenty-four oxen all told) and was to provide 'corn waynes, dong waynes [dung carts], ploughs, and harrows with harrowing horses'. The lessees were to provide all necessary seed, and they were to have 'four ridges in every field without division'. 126 acres (51 ha.) of arable were involved and 47 (19 ha.) of pasture; of the arable wheat occupied nearly 50 acres (20 ha.), oats 40 (16 ha.), and rye, barley, and pulse were also grown.

Dore's extensive lands and rights of pasture supported some 3,000 sheep in the late-thirteenth century, according to the *Taxatio Ecclesiastica* survey of 1291[195], but this is not an entirely reliable source. 1,760 of these sheep were enumerated on its English lands, 980 on its Welsh lands—but no figures were given for those Welsh lands lying in the diocese of St. David's. The survey also underestimates the number of cows, ascribing a total of only 54 to Dore, surprisingly small considering the grant to the abbey of forty by one donor alone, not long before in 1280.[196] Broad pictures can be gained from this great survey of church lands, but it is not an infallible witness. Apart from its own pastures (mountainous in Cantref-selyf, valley floor and hillside in the Golden Valley)[197], pastoralism was assisted by rights of common pasture—as granted to Dore in a number of localities[198], especially Grosmont Hill in northern Gwent. There, Hubert de Burgh, early in the thirteenth century, allowed the monks 'pasture in forest and field' for its 'oxen, cows, sheep and pigs'[199], and Prince Edmund (in 1268) gave pannage for fifty pigs.[200] Rights of way assisted stock movement. Dore had, *inter alia*, 'free entry, exit and passage' in Cantref-selyf (1241)[201], and two

Fig. 14. A wool receipt of 1303 (PRO E326/B. 5527)

rights of passage there were more specific: 'by the way above the Wye going from Llyswen to Builth'[202], and 'on that footpath which leads from Nanteglwys to Gwenddwr.'[203] Nearer home the monks could approach their grange at Benfield on a twenty-foot wide cart road given them by Hugh of Radnor[204], whilst William de Furches gave them an approach road to Kingstone Grange, allowing the monks to enclose and ditch it.[205]

The upshot of pastoralism was much wool production. Dore's wool in the late-thirteenth century was (in company with that of Tintern) the highest priced monastic wool in England and Wales in Pegolotti's valuation. The same source recorded Dore's output for export each year as being 16 sacks, its best wool being valued at 28 marks per sack—whether this was its total output, or that sold to a single merchant, is uncertain.[206] Wool was the basis of Dore's early trade. It had contacts (probably based on wool) with Flanders as early as 1211.[207] In 1216 the monastery sent seven cartloads of wool to Windsor.[208] Later in the century the monks concluded an agreement (drawn up in London in 1270) whereby for the five years of 1272 to 1276

two merchants of Douai could buy all the medium quality wool and better locks of Dore. ('Locks' were the poorest type of English wool). The merchants were to prepare the wrapping for the wool; the monks were to weigh it and take it to Hereford for collection.[209] At this time (in 1275) comes an interesting note, for when Dore's newly-founded house at Darnhall was selling wool to a merchant of Cambrai, it was ordered to be 'as good as the better crop of Dore, to be weighed by the weight of Dore.'[210]

By this time Dore had its first contacts with Italian merchants when borrowing 392 marks from Matthew Rayner of Siena, 'computing a mark at 13s. 4d.'[211] In the early-fourteenth century comes clear evidence of the Italian wool trade. Dore sold in 1303 to members of the Company of the Portinari of Florence, 17 sacks and 2 weights of good wool, 3 sacks of medium wool, and $4^{1}/_{2}$ sacks of locks for £266 8s. 0d. (Fig. 14).[212] In 1333 it sold to merchants of the Society of Peruzzi of Florence all its wool for that year: 11 sacks and 9 weights of good wool, 10 sacks of medium wool and chosen locks, and 2 sacks of lamb's wool. The merchants' quittance—they seem to have paid in advance, as was often the case to help a monastery in financial need—is dated 8 September.[213] The final extant record of Dore's wool trade comes the following year when again it sold to a merchant of the Society of Peruzzi 'all its own store of wool', 23 sacks in all, with 4 weights of says.[214]

The only other direct mention of trade by the abbey is the bringing of four cart-loads of salt to the monastery from Worcester in 1233[215], but it may be seen too in the holding of a small property in the port of Bristol[216], and may be implied in Richard I's quittance for its monks 'of toll, passage, and pontage, throughout the realm of England'[217]—unless that relates to crossing over from its Welsh lands. Little is known of the abbey's other economic activities. It possessed at least four watermills and possibly a windmill, as well as two fulling-mills in Cantref-selyf. There was a tannery at or near the abbey.[218] There were fishing rights in the river Wye at Benfield[219] and Eaton[220], and of free warren in Trivel and Kingstone Grange.[221] Grants of taking clay in Kilpeck (1248[222] and later[223]), and of marl, gravel, slate and stone (probably referring to the local 'tufa'), near Moccas (1272)[224] were made to the house. Dore thus practised many forms of economy typical of the medieval Cistercians, but the complete lack of extant cellarer's rolls and grange records, let alone the careful accounts each department of the monastery would have kept, leave us so far as Dore is concerned, with a wholly incomplete picture of its economy.

CHAPTER IV

The Buried Evidence : the Opus Dei

by Joe Hillaby

Four men bestride the history, the story as we now know it, of the church of Dore. The character and personality of Abbot Adam I is firmly stamped on the late-twelfth and early-thirteenth century rebuilding of the transepts, crossing and east end, that is the church as it stands today. More importantly he was responsible for Dore's polygonal chapter house, the first of that outstanding series that grace so many of England's greater churches. Abbot Richard Straddell dominates the later history of the abbey in a manner not dissimilar to that of Adam I in the earlier period. In the same way the religious convictions of John, first viscount Scudamore, are impressed ineradicably on Dore's 1634 reconstruction as a parochial church. Last was Roland Paul who, when that church had reached its lowest ebb at the end of the nineteenth century, restored it with great sensitivity. In the process he retrieved and replaced many of Dore's artistic treasures from its monastic days.

Roland Wilmot Paul

Born at Weston-super-Mare, Roland was the son of Henry Thomas Paul, manager of the local branch of Stuckey's Bank. In 1887 he exhibited a drawing of the shrine of St. Alban at the Royal Academy. The next year he was awarded the Pugin Travelling Studentship to study medieval buildings in Hampshire, Dorset and West Somerset, a studentship held by W.R.

Lethaby six years before.[1] Paul's pen and ink drawings and meticulous plans began to appear in *The Builder* in the early 1890s. Most notable were contributions to the journal's long-running series on 'The Abbeys of Great Britain'. Between 1893 and 1900 these included Ripon, Winchcombe, Glastonbury, Malmesbury, Llanthony, Tewkesbury, Tintern, Abbey Dore, Selby, Sherborne, Great Malvern, Pershore, Bayham, Valle Crucis, Cartmel, Dorchester (Oxon) and Buildwas.

At Abbey Dore he found ample opportunity to exercise his skills as a draughtsman. In all, between 1895 and 1931, he produced six different plans of the monastic buildings, some with only minor amendments.[2] Paul was elected a Fellow of the Society of Antiquaries in 1900. His collection of plans and drawings of Dore Abbey, including the originals of some of the plans referred to above, together with plans, drawings and details of many other Herefordshire churches, were left to the Society with a legacy of £50 on his death in 1935. Paul kept a *Diary* over the years 1895-1907 in which he recorded day-by-day his finds at Dore. This is not amongst his papers at Burlington House, but it is known from brief extracts quoted in correspondence with George Marshall.

Paul continued to exhibit at the Royal Academy until 1904 when drawings of his reredos for Dore and screen for Dymock were displayed. Given this range of experience and his

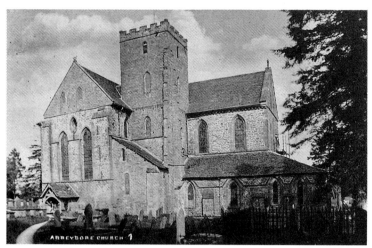

Fig. 15. Abbey Dore church from the south in the 1920's

deep affection for his subject, it is no surprise that he provided such a sensitive and informed restoration at Dore. Eventually Paul returned to the West Country as architect to the Dean and Chapter of Bristol Cathedral. There his work on the Lady Chapel has been described as 'amongst his most successful accomplishments' but, according to the obituary in *The Builder*, 'within his profession' it was his 'careful and sympathetic restoration work at Abbey Dore' for which he would be remembered.[3]

Oratorium: the monastic church

Paul's interest in Dore had been aroused initially by Thomas Blashill's discoveries on the chapter house site, but he soon turned his attention to the nave of the monastic church of which, as now, only the eastern pair of piers were visible. The presence of graves restricted his 1895 excavations to the area of the north arcade. In this undisturbed area he was able to obtain a fairly clear idea of the layout of the nave. This was reported, with a detailed reconstruction plan in *The Builder*.[4] Exploration began at the west end. A westward extension of the foundations of the north wall of the nave, with those of a southwest angle buttress, proved to be a vestige of the west range of cloister buildings, the cellarium, (A on Fig. 16). The dormitory of the lay brothers would have been on the first floor above the cellarium. Twenty-eight feet to the east Paul

found traces of stonework which he took to be the west wall of the nave (B on Fig. 16). The position of the west end of the nave apparently established, the foundations of the north arcade were brought to light: the plinths of piers 2 to 7 counting from the east and the bases of the shafts of piers 2 to 5 (see Fig. 16). These were similar to the pier still standing at the eastern end of the arcade, that is cylindrical piers on square bases. Had Paul had indeed found the west wall, this would have given a nine-bay nave. Between 1897 and 1907 minor excavations were carried out in the nave and, to a lesser extent, in the conventual buildings, as opportunity offered.

The restoration of Scudamore's parish church in 1901-9 provided Paul with further opportunities. A much more thorough examination of the presbytery, transepts and crossing was now possible. As part of the programme the paving and tombstones were taken up and 'in nearly every part ancient levels were found'. Finds were reported, somewhat randomly, in a series of contributions to journals between 1893 and 1931.[5] The only other evidence available is in the papers which he bequeathed to the Society of Antiquaries and a few letters to George Marshall.

The details of the internal layout which Paul recovered throw considerable light on the nature of and changes in the spiritual life of the Dore community over four and a half centuries. In the zest for unravelling building sequences and tracing possible architectural affiliations and allied matters, the *raison d'etre* of the abbey church—the *opus dei*, the work of God—must not be neglected. Even Père M-Anselme Dimier, in his monumental study of Cistercian churches throughout Europe, is content, in all but a very few cases, to provide plans which give the architectural design but no clue as to the liturgical divisions within the churches.[6]

Restoration has transformed our perceptions of the great medieval churches—the dominant aesthetic introduced was the long view, an aesthetic taken over from landscape architects. In the Middle Ages Cistercian churches did not present the great vistas at which we gaze in wonder today, such as at Kirkstall and Fountains. The basilican ideal inherited from the ancient world had finally been abandoned. In its internal layout the church of the white monks differed little from that of the Benedictines. It was divided by screens and walls into a series of compartments related to the major liturgical foci. Four were imperative: the presbytery with its high altar, the choir of the prayer monks, the retrochoir, and the choir of the lay brothers—the *conversi*.

Fundamentally the church was but a shelter for the altar. The altar dominated the church. Here took place the central act of worship, 'thanks-

giving', eucharist. It thus had its own space at the east end, in the presbytery or sanctuary. In early Cistercian churches this had taken up all the area east of the crossing. By the end of the twelfth century ambulatories with chapels beyond were being built behind the high altar to provide space for processions and further altars for the celebration of private masses incumbent on monks in priests' orders. Byland, which presents one of the earliest examples of this development, inspired Dore. In such cases the high altar was in the second bay from the east on a raised platform whilst the presbytery was divided from the aisles by an arcaded screen. This extended to and sometimes beyond the eastern piers of the crossing, thus enclosing the presbytery on three sides but leaving it in clear view from the west, from the choir of the prayer monks.

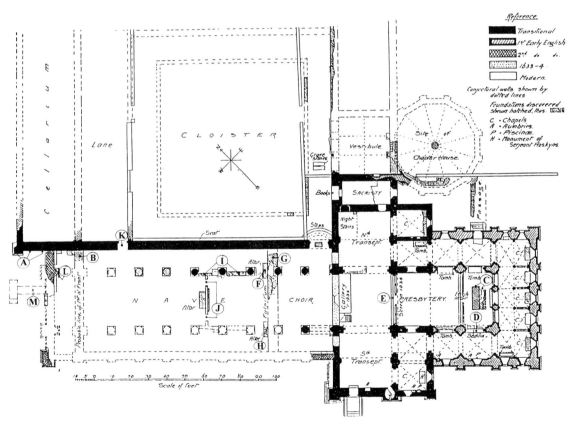

Fig. 16. Part of Paul's 1931 plan annotated with the letters used for reference in the text

The presbytery with the altar remained the dominant space within the church to which all others were subordinate. This was achieved by simple but highly effective architectural devices. A number of steps, the *gradus presbyterium*, led up to the sanctuary. A further step gave access to the altar itself behind which stood a reredos, a decorated screen or wall. The fact that the presbytery was devoid of other elements further heightened the commanding position of the altar. The only exceptions were those essential for the service of the altar: the sedilia, three seats to the south for the celebrant and his two assistants, a deacon and sub-deacon; the credence or *ministerium*, for the preparation of the sacrifice, whence the bread and wine were taken to be offered at the high altar; and finally the piscina, for ablutions during the ceremony. The foundations of the monastic high altar, reredos and sedilia were uncovered by Paul during his work of restoration in the chancel (C & D on Fig. 16). On either side of the presbytery would have been holes for the pulley for the Lenten veil, the *velum quadragesimale*. At Dore hooks to hold the veil are still visible.

By the later Middle Ages the stone altars of the greater churches had become awesome in their size. Great stress was laid on their integrity, held to symbolise the unity of the church, broken neither by error nor schism. After a century of profane use as a farm salting table, Dore's medieval stone altar was rescued by Scudamore in 1634. The timber altar mentioned in his accounts must have become surplus to requirements. Matthew Gibson in his *View of the Ancient and Present State of the Church of Door* (1727) explains that 'the Lord Scudamore, when he rebuilt this Church, with great Awfulness ordered it (the stone Altar) to be restored, and set upon three Pilasters of stone.' (Chapter X)Today the stone altar impresses us by its size, 12 feet by 4 feet, but it was only typical of its period: the Lady Chapel altar at Ely is 16 feet 4½ inches in length, that at Tewkesbury, cut in two for seats in the eigteenth century, was 13 feet 8 inches; whilst at Christchurch it is similar in length to Dore. Smaller medieval parochial stone altars can be seen not far away in the churches at

Peterchurch and Patricio, together with the chapel at Urishay.

The second compartment was the ritual choir, the choir of the prayer monks. In Cistercian churches it usually occupied the western part of the crossing, the first bay and often, as Paul showed to be the case at Dore, the second bay of the nave. The monks' timber stalls flanked the choir to the north and south, backing onto stone walls built flush with the fronts of the nave piers and extending half-way into the crossing. The stalls would then return against the great stone screen called the pulpitum to the west, which divided the choir from the retrochoir. The open area left in the eastern half of the crossing, between choir and presbytery, provided spaces for the prayer monks to enter their choir. These were known as the upper entrances, *superiores introitus*. Paul revealed the foundations of a wall dividing the western end of the north transept from the crossing to the south, thus confirming that the standard arrangement was observed at Dore.

The primary duty of the choir monk was prayer, the Divine Office, the *Opus Dei* in the terminology of St. Benedict. This was the recitation of prayers at fixed hours during the day and night. 'Nothing', said Benedict, 'was to be set before the work of God.' All other monastic occupations depended upon it. The liturgy fixed the *horarium* or timetable; it claimed almost all the hours of the monks' day, and those the best. There were two monastic seasons; each divided night and day into twelve equal hours. At the eighth hour of the night the monks rose for Vigils, the night office, followed immediately by the office of the dead. At dawn was sung the first of the day offices, Lauds, followed by Prime; then, at three-hourly intervals, Terce, Sext and None with Vespers. Soon after, Compline ended the day. In winter, Vigils could be shortly after 2a.m. when the monks, in their night shoes, would enter the choir directly from their dormitory on the first floor of the eastern range of the buildings around the cloister. At Dore this lay to the north rather than, as usual, on the sunnier south side. The doorway which gave access by way of the night stairs to the upper entrances can be seen at the western end of the north transept, 8 feet 6 inches above ground level. Vestiges of the foundations of these stairs were found by Paul.

When Scudamore restored Dore as a parish church in 1634, he also restored the internal organisation to a pattern similar to that of its monastic forebear. Once more the presbytery was an open area, dominated by the stone medieval altar. The *gradus presbyterium* was now marked out even more firmly by the presence of Abel's great oak screen (E on Fig. 16) and the platform of the altar by the Laudian communion rails. Pews for the congregation were installed to the west of the screen, in the crossing, not far from the site of the monks' choir stalls. The only intrusions were the pulpit, in front of the communion rails at their northern end, and what appears to have been a patron's pew just inside the screen on the north, as shown on Paul's plans. The invasion of the presbytery by 'chairs and rough forms' came in the nineteenth century. During the 1901-9 restoration, the seventeenth century pews were moved from the crossing to their present position east of the screen, within the sanctuary of the former monastic church.

The third compartment, the retrochoir, was for monks excused choir duties by reason of age, ill-health or the annual blood-letting. At Roche the stone benches on which they sat are still visible. The retrochoir was separated from the monastic choir to the east by the pulpitum, the western face of which, even in Cistercian houses, came to be elaborately decorated. By the second pier of the north nave arcade Paul made one of his most important discoveries in 1896, the foundations of the pulpitum. About 5 feet thick, its eastern face aligned with the centre of the pier. Where it passed in front of the pier there was a projection, the foundation of a side altar (F on Fig. 16). Retrochoir altars were found at Fountains, where they were dedicated to St. Mary and St. Bernard, Kirkstall and elsewhere. Their lateral position was dictated by the presence of a central doorway in the pulpitum. This was the lower entrance or *introitus inferior* which gave the weekly *Asperges* procession access from the retrochoir to the ritual choir. As the pulpitum was ruined to its foundations Paul found no evidence for this door but did establish that the pulpitum crossed the north aisle at its full 5 foot width (G on Fig. 16).

Foundations of the south altar on the other side of the pulpitum were discovered during the digging of a grave (H on Fig. 16). A similar arrangement was uncovered at Furness in 1896-8 by W. St. John Hope. There a permanent pulpitum had been built in the early-thirteenth century. At some Cistercian houses the organ (in medieval parlance, a 'pair' of organs) was, like the 'Cryers' at Durham, carried on such extensions, usually over the aisle opposite the cloister. Abbot Adam I (1186-c.1216) had a strong interest in music; he wrote a study of *The Rudiments of Music*. Further the General Chapter had reports that Dore was indulging in three- and four-part chanting to the detriment of Cistercian plainsong. There is thus a distinct possibility that the pulpitum extended over the aisle to provide firm support for an organ. Certainly one was there in the late middle ages, for John Scudamore bought 'the organs in the quire' at the dissolution.[7]

The rood screen closed the retrochoir on the west. This second screen is found in all Cistercian churches. At Dore it lay 33 feet west of the pulpitum. The retrochoir thus occupied two bays, more precisely one whole and two half bays, rather than the usual one bay; but other two-bay retrochoirs are known. At Byland, which provided Dore with the inspiration for an eastern extension to form ambulatory and chapels, it measured some 35 feet. As one would anticipate, the fourth and fifth bays of the north arcade were linked by screen walls, dividing the retrochoir from the aisle (I on Fig. 16). These were 2 feet thick, plastered on both faces, the north side painted white, that facing the retrochoir red, blue, yellow and green. It was here that Paul found traces of the coloured and gilded architectural fragment which he believed to be part of a shrine. (Chapter VI).

The fourth compartment, the western part of the nave beyond the rood screen, formed the lay brothers' choir. In this respect it differed from churches of the black monks and the canons where the nave to the west of the rood screen was open to the laity and in many places, as at Leominster Priory, it was used as the parish church. At the east end was the nave altar, behind which would be a decorated reredos or retable. This was situated against the rood screen which would have had a passage along the top, lined with panelling, forming a loft. Above and dominating all, was the great rood, Christ Crucified with Mary and John on each side, carried on a large wooden beam.[8] On either side of the rood altar doors gave access to the retro-choir. Their position at Dore is clearly indicated on Paul's plan (J on Fig. 16).

A number of English monastic rood screens survive. At Tynemouth, c.1195, where the east face is more elaborate than the west. At St. Albans, late fourteenth century, and Crowland, c.1400, both sides are decorated. At the latter the east face now appears more ornate but originally the west face was enriched with moveable panel-work, probably of alabaster.[9] Similarly the painting and gilding found by Paul in the retro-choir probably represents a continuation of even richer work around the altar on the western side of the rood screen.

The nave altar was the site of one of the most solemn occasions in the weekly calendar of the monks, and one of great antiquity. It is found in a copy of the *Gelasian Sacramentary* of c.790— and, locally, in the early-eleventh century Leominster prayer book. On Sunday, immediately before high mass, the ceremony of the *Asperges* took place. The name came from a chant based on David's prayer in Psalm 51:

'Purge me with hyssop and I shall be clean
Wash me and I shall be whiter than snow.'[10]

In full procession the whole community passed through the church, blessing the altars with holy water, and then entered the cloister, by the door to the eastern alley. There the monks visited chapter house, parlour, dormitory, rere-dorter, warming house, refectory, kitchen and finally the lay brothers' quarters in the western range. The procession then re-entered the church by the west door. At Dore it had first to pass through the west porch, known as the Galilee. The name was also derived from the *Asperges*

procession, symbolising Christ leading his disciples into Galilee. 'Then said Jesus unto them, Be not afraid: go tell my brethren that they go into Galilee, and there they shall see Me' (Matthew 28: 10).

Moving down the nave the procession then took up position in front of the rood and nave high altar. The holy water bearer, followed by the monk carrying the processional cross, the thurifer with his thurible, the incense burner, between two candle bearers and the celebrant with his deacon and sub-deacon would lead the members of the convent. At Fountains, in the floor of the nave, there are 23 slabs of white limestone, each 27 inches square and incised with a circle, with intervals of 11 inches between them. Further east are two other squares and in front, in the middle, a single square.[11] These marks the stations of members of the procession 'in front of the Great Cross'. The abbot, who had taken up the rear, then advanced between his monks. After the bidding prayer the procession passed through the doors on either side of the altar into the retrochoir and thence by the door in the centre of the pulpitum into the choir, the abbot taking up his place at the rear. Sunday high mass could then commence.

At Tintern, Strata Florida and elsewhere there are considerable remains of stone side screens which closed the lay brothers' church from the aisles. Although Paul found no foundations of such an arrangement at Dore it is likely that the wooden stalls of the *conversi* would have backed onto a screen wall, similar to, if less grand than, those of the prayer monks. In the westernmost bay alone would the arcade have been left open, to provide access from the lay brothers' entrance. At Dore this doorway is still intact, visible from the stockyard to the north (K on Fig. 16).

From his initial excavations Paul believed he had found the west end of the nave. However, excavations in 1905 revealed the northern end and southwest angle buttress of a 'later west front', together with 'the respond of the north arcade (L on Fig. 16) ... and some interesting fragments of the west doorway'. Paul thus assumed the addition of a western bay to the nave, possibly with 'older material re-used'. In

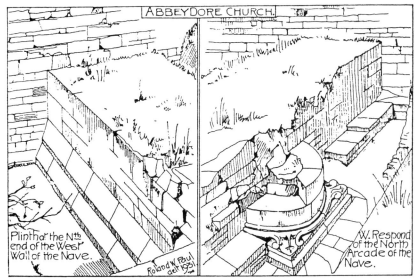

Plinth at the N<u>th</u>
end of the West
Wall of the Nave.

Roland W. Paul
del. 1931

W. Respond
of the North
Arcade of the
Nave.

Fig. 17. Paul's drawing in The Builder *(25 September 1931), showing (left)
the plinth at the north end of the west wall of the nave, and (right)
the west respond of the north arcade of the nave*

1927 he referred to this as part of a west front, 'largely remodelled', and believed that the 'carved details' found in 1905 'pointed to a fine west doorway with possibly a triplet of lancets over it.'[12]

Paul's 1893 identification of a nine-bay nave was mistaken. In his 1931 article he sketched the west respond of the north arcade of the nave, showing a semi-circular pier on a base with spurs at the angles (Fig 17). Similar spurs can still be seen on the easternmost respond of the same arcade, indicating a similar construction date. What Paul had found in 1905 was not a one-bay addition to a nine-bay nave but the west end of a ten-bay nave.

In addition the 1931 plan outlines the foundations of a small structure attached to the west end (M on Fig. 16). This would have been a Galilee porch. It did not span the whole of the west end, merely the area in front of the west portal and in this respect was similar to the western porches of Dore's rivals, the Welsh houses at Tintern and Neath.[13]

The claustral buildings of a Cistercian house differed from those of the black monks and canons in that here again provision had to be made for the lay brethren. The western range was set apart for their use. In addition, the refectory or frater was situated not along, but at right angles to, the range opposite the church, thus giving space for the kitchen at the western end of the same range, where it could serve the refectories of both the choir monks and the lay brethren, to the east and west respectively.

The cloister was a study area for the choir monks. During a hard winter the Cistercians at Dore and Buildwas, and the Benedictine Black Monks at Leominster, must have lamented their northern cloister. Today the cloister area is represented, approximately, by the walls of the former rectory kitchen garden.

In 1904 the Bristol and Gloucester Archaeological Society visited Dore. A new, third, plan accompanied Paul's description in the Society's *Transactions*. It threw light on the size and position of a number of the claustral buildings—the west wall of the eastern range; parts of the rere-dorter, warming house, refectory and kitchen on the north; and the cellar and 'lane' on the west. It also added a few more details relating to the chapter house—some masonry, presumably the floor, within the southern part of the chapter house itself and two grave slabs outside the vestibule. These latter Paul was to place inside the church.

The eastern range was on two levels. The choir monks' dormitory extended the full length of the first floor with the rere-dorter or necessarium extending at right angles above the watercourse, an arrangement well illustrated at Whalley. Because of its high conical roof Adam I's new polygonal chapter house had to be sited beyond the building line of the eastern range and the former chapter house with its low vault was converted into a vestibule (Chapter X). Documentary evidence shows that, in 1330, next to what is described as 'the great infirmary' was 'a certain chamber with porch' in which the abbot conducted formal transactions.

Towards the end of his life, after a silence of 26 years, Paul was stung into taking up his pen to write once more for *The Builder*. In 1931 the first of the Royal Commission on Historical Monuments' *Herefordshire* volumes was published. This included a ground plan of Dore in which the position of nave and the claustral buildings was 'said to be taken' from one of Paul's drawings. This, he pointed out, was published without any reference to him and more important was 'incorrect in important details'. The frater, for example, was shown on the plan 'at the *south* end near the church, an obviously impossible position!' So that purchasers of this first volume 'should be put in possession of an accurate plan' he now published his sixth and final plan of Dore. This was accompanied by an article, with hitherto unpublished sketches, summarising his finds and conclusions.

The challenge which Paul had so publicly thrown down in the columns of *The Builder* could not be ignored by the Commission. An amended plan was published as an appendix to the third *Herefordshire* volume in 1934 with an explanation as the first item in the *Addenda et Corrigenda*. How far Paul was mollified by the amended plan and corrigenda published, without apology, is not known but the Royal Commission's blunder certainly elicited further valuable detail on church and cloister.

CHAPTER V

An Architectural History

by Stuart Harrison & Malcolm Thurlby

Of the fifty former Cistercian abbey churches in England only two now serve as parish churches, Holmcultram, in Cumbria, and Dore. At Holmcultram just the former nave is in use, minus its aisles and three eastern bays.[1] At Dore just a fragment of the nave remains but remarkably the entire chevet (eastern arm) and transepts survive as the parish church. There remains the three-bay presbytery with its north and south aisles and five-bay ambulatory and eastern chapels returning across the square east end, the crossing, and the transepts with their chapels. What story do the remains tell us? Is the medieval church the product of a single build which was conceived as a single entity by a patron and master mason? Or are there two or more phases of building activity? To what extent is the church typically Cistercian? Does it represent something new in the region? The Cistercians have been called the 'missionaries of Gothic'[2] and specifically in connection with Dore strong French Gothic influence has been suggested.[3] On the other hand, several authors have commented on the relationship of details at Dore with the so-called West Country School of masons, even though Dore was not included in Brakspear's survey of that school.[4] The documents are silent on these matters and therefore we are left to read the evidence in the fabric itself, to play the role of architectural sleuth, in order to determine the roles of patron(s) and master mason(s) and the training of the master

mason(s). The exercise is analogous to a detective story. Just as Sherlock Holmes or Miss Marple might piece together seemingly insignificant scraps of evidence to solve a case, so to understand the fabric of Dore we must meticulously observe even the smallest details in the quest to visualize the original form and subsequent evolution of the church.

The requirements of a Cistercian monastic church

Before examining the fabric itself we must determine what were the requirements of a Cistercian monastic church. Nothing was to be excessive or luxurious. Figurative sculpture was outlawed, although as we shall see that did not preclude its appearance at Dore in the thirteenth century. There is a remarkable uniformity amongst early Cistercian churches of the so-called Bernardine plan, even though there is no documentary association of the plan with St. Bernard.[5] In these churches the high altar is set in a square-ended sanctuary which usually projects one bay beyond the transept chapels which are also square-ended. The monastic choir extends through an undifferentiated crossing. Stairs for access from the dormitory to the church for night services are located in the transept. A separate choir for the lay brothers is provided in the nave beyond the pulpitum and rood screens. Lay brothers generally outnumbered choir monks and therefore their choir usually occupied a proportionally larger space. They were also provided with stairs for night services, commonly situated at the west end of the nave. The Statutes of the Order demanded simplicity and none of the excessive decoration associated with Benedictine and Cluniac houses, reflections of which may seen locally at Kilpeck Church which was given to the Benedictine Abbey of St. Peter at Gloucester, now the cathedral, in 1134. To what extent does Dore conform to this Cistercian ideal of simplicity?

In order to start a Cistercian community it was required that there should be an abbot and twelve monks and that wooden buildings appropriate for their requirements should be provided by the patron.[6] Dore Abbey, dependent upon grants of lands from patrons, would have taken several years to have achieved the *Stabilitas* required before substantial buildings in stone replaced those initially of timber. That this state was achieved by the 1170s is shown by Walter de Clifford's grants of around 1173. It may seem unlikely that wooden buildings would have sufficed for a quarter of a century. However, at Jervaulx, Yorkshire, the monks moved to the present site in 1156, and while work was soon commenced on the lay brothers and other ranges, the church seems not to have been begun before 1180.[7] Similarly at Revesby, Lincolnshire, founded in 1142, and at Vaudey, also in Lincolnshire, founded 1147, work on the stone churches may not have commenced until about 1170.[8] Thus it is possible that the building which has come down to us represents the first stone building on the site as commenced around 1173. Alternatively, we must consider the possibility that there are elements of a pre-1173 stone church incorporated into the present fabric. A third possibility for Dore is that there was an earlier stone church, or even churches, on the site and that these were not large enough and were therefore completely replaced after 1173 with the present structure. The parallel for this is at Fountains Abbey in North Yorkshire, where around 1135 work commenced on a stone replacement for the wooden church. This church was damaged by fire in 1147, and was quickly rebuilt only to be replaced around 1150 when a start was made on the present much larger church.[9]

The third possibility could only be determined through excavation, though the whole floor of the church was dug up and replaced by Paul who

Fig. 18. The corner of the north transept and the presbytery. The semi-circular-headed doorway originally led to the sacristry

reported no evidence for an earlier building. So we are therefore left to discover whether or not there is any evidence for a pre-1170s church immured in the present fabric.

The fabric of the abbey

It is generally agreed that the two eastern bays of the presbytery and the ambulatory with its chapels belong to a later phase of construction than the transepts, crossing and nave of the church. Analysis of the details supports this contention. There is also much evidence to support the proposition that the earliest extant parts of the church are in the north transept, crossing and part of the western bay of the presbytery. This makes good sense given the location of the monastic buildings on the north side of the church. These are now largely lost but the semicircular head of the doorway (Fig. 18) leading from the north transept to the slype (sacristy) with its continuous quadrant moulding belongs to a tradition in the west of England going back to the late-eleventh century as in the wall arches of the presbytery aisles at St. Peter's Abbey at Gloucester.[10] The east window of the chapel of the north transept is round-headed and attenuated, although this is no longer obvious because of a partial blocking above the original sill level. It stands in contrast to all the other windows in the church which are of lancet design. The solid wall between this chapel and what is now the north aisle of the presbytery (formerly the inner chapel of the north transept), conforms to earlier twelfth century Cistercian practice, as is still well-preserved at Fountains and Buildwas, Shropshire.

The phasing of the north transept chapels is not easily determined. There are three possible interpretations. First, that we are dealing with earlier barrel-vaulted chapels which have been refaced to the west and revaulted. The unevenness of the wall faces of the lateral walls of the chapels may suggest that barrel vaults have been removed, although the later plaster precludes certainty on this point. The unusual placement of the entrance arch mouldings under the outer plane rather than towards the middle of the wall accords with this view. It is also suggested by the

absence of ashlar in the north-east angle of the north transept below the spandrel of the arch. In other words it is possible that the lower wall is pre-1173 and where the ashlar starts is post-1173. This interpretation suggests a plain building, probably of aisleless plan, with simple barrel-vaulted spaces, which was extensively remodelled when the present church was commenced (Fig. 19). The transept chapels at Fountains provide a parallel for the proposed barrel vaults and are of further interest because originally each chapel there was provided with a separate gable and roof which intersected with the main sloping aisle roof like a dormer.[11] Something similar seems to have existed at Dore though with the distinction that each chapel roof was carried back to the main transept wall where it was provided with a stone hood moulding which still survives beneath the present chapel roof.[12] The hood mould of the former roof line of the inner chapel of the north transept against the presbytery wall can be traced as far east as the line of the east wall of the transept chapel, that is to the junction with the later extension of the presbytery.

Secondly, that the chapels had the roof arrangement just described but that they were rib-vaulted from the first, like the transept chapels at Buildwas, and that they followed an *en echelon* plan. The chamfered arch at the east end of the north transept inner chapel—now the first bay of the north aisle—is similar to the one from this chapel to the presbytery but quite different to the richly moulded arches of the extended presbytery. This indicates that the two chamfered arches are contemporary and that the chapel continued further east to give an *en echelon* plan to the transept chapels before the construction of the presbytery extension.[13] This was the arrangement used by the Cistercians at Fountains, Melrose and Rievaulx. Arches leading from the transept inner chapels to the presbytery, as at Dore, combined with *en echelon* plans, were used by other monastic orders. At Benedictine Ewenny, Glamorganshire, a doorway communicated between the west end of the presbytery and the adjacent chapel, a smaller version of the Dore arch.[14] Closer to Dore, at

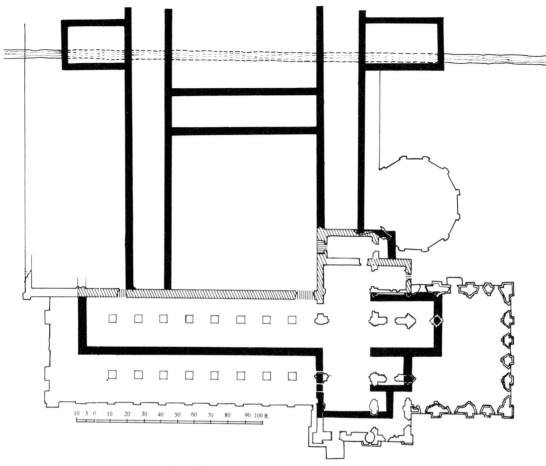

Fig. 19. Tentative plan of aisleless church

Llanthony Priory, a similar arrangement existed in a house of Augustinian canons.[15] Ultimately this plan derived from the classic Romanesque *en echelon* arrangement of parallel apses in the transepts, in which the arch had the purpose of providing a means of access to the presbytery from the nave through the transepts when the crossing was occupied by the choir stalls. The arch in the first bay of the presbytery at Dore should therefore be seen as the upper choir entrance.

Thirdly, Roland Paul's excavation plan, preserved at the Society of Antiquaries in London, does not indicate any footings for an extended inner chapel but does show continuous footings beneath the eastern chamfered arch. This may suggest that the arch was inserted into the former eastern wall of a one-bay chapel. Support for this reading is found in the east wall of the south transept inner chapel where a string-course set at windowsill level is truncated to the south (right) of the jamb of the chamfered arch into the presbytery south aisle. However, Paul also exposed continuous footings beneath the entrance arches to the north transept chapels which demonstrates that the presence of footings does not necessarily mean that a wall was constructed.

Paul claimed that prior to the remodelling that resulted in the present extended eastern arm, the presbytery comprised three bays.[16] That the first (western) bay of this earlier presbytery is still standing and formerly continued further east is confirmed by the high vault shafts and capitals between the western and middle bays on both the north and south walls of the presbytery. Here the shaft groups do not course with the jamb of the arch of the middle bay, and the crocket capitals and angled abaci are quite different from the high vault capitals further east with their sparse stiff-leaf foliage and round abaci. This shows that the former presbytery had at least two bays, but Paul's excavation plan does not provide conclusive evidence that it was three bays in length. Certain variations in the footings suggest that those to the east of the western bay date from the construction of the present extended presbytery and therefore it is uncertain whether the former presbytery comprised two or three bays.

First phase of construction of the enlarged church

The first phase of construction in the north transept is characterized by a sparing use of ashlar for arched openings and jambs; the rest of the wall is of rubble construction and there are no buttresses. Externally the walls are devoid of even a simple chamfered plinth and have only a continuous stringcourse set above floor level. The single moulded order of the north transept chapel entrance arches has triple rolls towards the outer plane of the arch surmounted by a hood with stylized foliate pyramids (Fig. 18). These soffit rolls have a somewhat doughy appearance and are typologically earlier than the crisper mouldings elsewhere in the church. They are most closely paralleled in the West Country in the nave arcades and aisle ribs at Malmesbury Abbey, Wiltshire, probably under construction in the 1160s. The rib profile of the outer chapel has paired rolls while the inner chapel has triple rolls, an indication not of any chronological difference but rather the love of subtle variety which was much favoured at Dore. The trajectory of the diagonals is semi-circular and the junction of the web with the wall is pointed without wall arches. This is the normal arrange-

ment in French early Gothic, albeit usually with wall arches, while the same geometry is found in the nave aisle vaults at Malmesbury Abbey. The ribs of the Dore chapels are carried on angle-set corbel capitals carved with a range of foliage types which suggest a date around 1175.

The waterleaf capital in the north-west angle of the outer chapel and the south-west angle of the inner chapel, characterized by broad plain leaves topped with inward turning volutes on the angles of the capital, makes its earliest appearances at York Minster (1154-81), the nave of the Temple Church in London before 1161, and at St. Andrews Cathedral-Priory, Fife, (1162), and continues in use to the turn of the century.[17] The stylized acanthus at the south-east angle of the inner chapel relates to the Temple Church nave aisle dado arcade and the presbytery of St. Cross at Winchester (c.1158-71). The plantain leaves on the south-east capital of the outer chapel derive from French Gothic and interestingly find a remarkably close parallel for the basic form and upright central leaf with a capital from Morimond.[18] The crocket capital at the south-west angle of the outer chapel is French inspired, but in this case there is a lower range of trefoil leaves with upright main veins or mid-ribs which are characteristic of the stiff-leaf convention and make their earliest appearance in England at Wells Cathedral commenced by Bishop Reginald soon after he took office in 1174.[19] A similar fusion of stiff-leaf foliage on a French inspired crocket capital is evident in the entrance arches of the north transept chapels.

Other capitals in the north transept and crossing such as the trumpet scallop support the c.1175 date. They may be compared with the western bays at Worcester Cathedral which are traditionally dated after the fall of the 'new' tower in 1175.[20] The south capitals of the eastern crossing arch have a ring beneath the abacus (pl. 8), a common feature in French early Gothic capitals but one confined to works of the 1170s and early 1180s in England as in the choir of Canterbury Cathedral (1175-84) and the eastern-most early Gothic capitals of the choir arcade at Wells cathedral. The quinquepartite high-vault shafts in the north transept (Fig. 18) have been related to French sources and in particular the nave of Le Bourg-Dun, Seine-Maritime[21], though this has been questioned by O'Callaghan.[22] Certainly there are significant differences between Dore and Le Bourg-Dun; at Le Bourg-Dun the capitals and bases are treated as five distinctly separate elements while at Dore the semi-octagonal base plinth and capital abaci frame the works. This has a good English Cistercian pedigree as in the chapter house at Fountains Abbey before 1170 and also in the chapter house at Buildwas. Furthermore, five-shaft groups already appear in the West Country in the early-twelfth century north nave aisle responds of St. Peter's Abbey, in Gloucester, and fragments of five-shaft groups survive from the Augustinian abbey of Keynsham, founded in 1166.

Fig. 20. *The south-western corner of the presbytery with the crossing ceiling visible through the arch*

The chamfered responds of the entrance arches to the transept chapels at Fountains and the transepts at Sawley Abbey, Yorkshire, also provide a possible source for the semi-octagonal responds at Dore.[23] Furthermore, octagonal piers are used in the chapter house at Buildwas in which the diagonal ribs have triple rolls, as in the Dore north transept inner chapel, and a combination of simple leaf and multi-scalloped designs as in the north transept at Dore. Closer to the French work are the western high vault capitals of the Dore presbytery which also belong to the first phase of construction of the enlarged church Crocket capitals are ubiquitous in French Gothic churches of the 1160s and 70s[24], while analogues in England appear in the presbytery aisles and triforia of St Fridewide's, Oxford[25], the west bays at Worcester Cathedral[26] and the Lady Chapel of Glastonbury Abbey (1184-1189).[27] These high vault capitals in the presbytery at Dore demonstrate that the aisleless presbytery was intended to be vaulted and was as tall as the present building (Fig. 20). At a lower level these triple shafts are banded by a stringcourse which is now terminated next to the later masonry to the east, but which formerly continued eastwards presumably in line with the presbytery window sills.

In the transepts the five-part responds were planned to carry the transverse and diagonal ribs of a high vault and wall arches. The latter are still extant and rest in the corners of the transepts on cone-like terminations which flank the angle-set capitals planned for the diagonal rib. Corbels are common in Cistercian contexts and are doubtless used here to economise on ashlar. Whether or not a high vault was actually constructed has been doubted because of the relative thinness of the walls—just 4 feet—and the popularity of wooden vaults in early Gothic architecture in Britain, not least in the West Country. The plastered surfaces do nothing to aid a decision on this matter although the uneven-ness of the masonry above the northern crossing arch must surely be read as the remains of the webbing of a stone vault. This would probably have been of tufa, a very light porous rock of sponge-like appearance, found round mineral springs. Tufa was used in the Romanesque chapter house vault at Worcester Cathedral[28] and in the two early Gothic western bays of the south nave aisle there, and in the south transept chapel of the great Church at Glastonbury after 1185. Gervase mentions its use in the vaults of the eastern arm of Canterbury Cathedral after the 1174 fire[29]. There is also a large quantity of tufa blocks at Llanthony Priory where the walls are just one inch thicker than at Dore.

The crossing

At the junction of the north transept arcade and the north-east crossing pier the masonry courses through without interruption indicating that they were built together. Therefore, if there are remains of an earlier church in the north transept chapels one must assume that they belong to a church with an undifferentiated crossing and probably with a much lower elevation as in the Cistercian abbey church at Fontenay, Cote d'Or. The eastern crossing piers differ from their western counterparts in that they are fully articulated from the ground whereas on the western piers the responds of the western crossing arch are supported upon a broad shallow pilaster which is stopped short of the floor with a wall like projection some 12 feet in height. This indicates that the choir stalls continued into the nave. The elongation of the western crossing piers on the east-west axis is a traditional West Country Romanesque feature as at Tewkesbury Abbey. At first sight it may appear that the crossing was planned for a four part ribbed vault. The evidence is in the upper angled corbels in the corners of the arch spandrels of the crossing. However, there is no corbel in the north-east angle and, most importantly, no trace that vault springers were ever let into the masonry above the corbels, nor marks for trajectory of a vault web. On balance it seems likely that these corbels were provided to support wall posts for a timber floor in the crossing.

This interpretation is borne out by a second, later series of corbels set at a lower level. These are clearly inserted into the existing fabric to carry a vault in the crossing. The curvature of this vault—the traces of which are clear in the north spandrel of the western crossing arch, the east spandrel of the northern crossing arch and the north spandrel of the eastern crossing arch—shows that it would have risen above the present flanking wall tops and indicates that either the crossing walls were raised high enough to accommodate the vault or that there was a central tower. In either case masonry has been removed from above the crossing arches to accommodate the present flat ceiling. It is a general misconception that the Cistercians were forbidden to build towers on their churches. Towers were allowed provided they were moderate in height and did not contain more than the prescribed number of bells. Indeed, towers were common on Cistercian churches in England as surviving details show at Fountains, Buildwas, Furness and Kirkstall. The oft-quoted legislation

Fig. 21. The south transept showing the stair lights in the corner buttress and the Scudamore porch. (c. 1910 postcard)

of 1157 and 1182 served only to prohibit the building of elaborate towers and cannot be interpreted as a complete prohibition.

The south transept

The south transept contains many differences from the northern arm. There are broad angle buttresses but none on the north (Fig. 21). The west clerestory window is taller in the south transept and on the east side the clerestory windows are larger in the south transept and have double external chamfers, rather than a single chamfer as in the north transept. Instead of a solid wall separating the two chapels an arch communicates between them. The vaults in the chapels are carried not on corbels but on capitals atop detached shafts and bases. The entrance arches to the chapels in the south have two orders rather than the one in the north, and the inner order of both south transept arches is flat with angle roll mouldings in contrast to the doughy triple rolls of the north transept. The outer order of the inner chapel arch has a continuous chamfer as in the nave arcade at nearby Llanthony Priory, and the outer order of the outer chapel arch has an angle roll flanked by hollow rolls. The pier between the chapels is wider in the south transept than the north. The profile of the inner order of both south transept arches is typically French and was used in England only for a limited time as typified in the transepts and nave of Roche Abbey, Yorkshire (c.1170), the eastern arm at Canterbury Cathedral (1174-84) and the rebuilding of Chichester cathedral after the fire of 1187.

As in the north transept a high vault was planned for the south transept and again the evidence above the south crossing arch speaks in favour of its construction in stone; the projection in the plaster in the west spandrel suggests the trajectory of the vault web. The differences between the north and south transepts suggest that the south transept is later. The opening up of the chapels, the larger clerestory windows, and the huge lancets in the south and west walls, all indicate a move towards Gothic which is characterized by the reduction of the wall to maximize openness and light. Ashlar is used more liberally

in the entrance arches of the south transept chapels than in the north. The western arch of the presbytery south arcade matches its northern counterpart but with a minor change to a moulded outer order in the arch head exactly as on the south transept outer chapel entrance arch.

Of the exterior faces of the transept windows only the two lancets on the south transept facade are decorated (Fig. 21). In both cases there is just a plain chamfered continuous inner order but the outer order has a nibbed angle roll moulding against a hollow chamfer carried on plantain, waterleaf and beaded foliage capitals atop detached shafts.

The south transept doorway, now covered by Scudamore's timber porch dating from the 1630s, is similarly treated, though with coursed rather than detached shafts, and with the additional enrichment of a dog-tooth hood mould. It was used by the monks to carry their dead to the monastic cemetery east of the church. The enrichment of the south transept front seems to have no great chronological significance and can be paralleled in the north transept at Strata Florida, which also had an elaborate doorway, surmounted by huge lancet windows. The extra decoration may well have been introduced for the facade of the church in public view, as opposed to the plain monastic side, like the rich north transept doorway at Furness Abbey.

The stair turret

Access to the upper parts of the church was via a stair turret located behind the south respond of the south transept arcade (Fig. 21). This is an unusual position but one that seems to derive from a West Country Romanesque tradition as at Tewkesbury Abbey and finds a near-contemporary parallel at St. David's Cathedral and in the north transept at Strata Florida. The stair ascends to give access to the roof space above the eastern chapels and then to the main transept roof. At the top of the stair there is a short passage which has a stepped lintel ceiling and just above the top of the stair newel is a vertical square hole and sockets for a horizontal cross beam to support a vertical post in the hole. This marks the position and size of one of the original twelfth-century vertical posts which braced the ends of the roof rafters. Similarly a setback in the internal wall face of the east gable may mark the position of a tie beam in the presbytery roof frames. The main roofs of the church appear to have been stone tiled since Paul reported finding fragments of these in his nave excavations.

The nave

Only a small fragment remains of the nave (Fig. 22) and what we know of its plan comes from Paul's excavations[30] (Fig. 25). He originally thought that there was an eleven bay nave[31], then, after excavation, he revised this to nine bays[32], and subsequently discovered substantial evidence which showed that it was ten bays. The details of the west respond of the north arcade

are late-twelfth century and suggest that ten bays were always intended.[33] The surviving piers at the east end were retained to buttress the crossing and though less remains on the north the pier is still complete (Figs. 22-24). The capitals of the piers differ substantially in design as do the eastern responds and it seems likely that this variety was carried throughout the arcades.

Two loose capitals survive from the nave, one with side-turned stems and leaves, the other, which Paul discovered,[34] with regularly spaced crockets and small flat trilobed leaves beneath them. The first bay on the south has a large drum pier supporting a pointed arch and the springer of the second bay, but only the reset springers of the first bay remain on top of the pier of the north arcade. The inner order has the same profile as in the south transept chapel

Fig. 22. The western end of the present church showing the outline of the nave and transepts

*Fig. 23. The surviving pier and arcade arch of
the nave viewed from the south-west*

*Fig. 24. The same fragment from the north-west
with part of the north pier on the left*

arches but interestingly the springer of the second bay of the south arcade has a different profile.

There was a variety in the colour of the piers, grey on the north versus red on the south, and in the capital form, scalloped on the north but leaf on the south.[35] Related decorative forms and various arcade profiles appeared in the nave of Strata Florida.[36] The columnar piers belong to a well-established tradition in the West Country as at Great Malvern Priory and Cistercian Buildwas. What is unusual about the Dore piers, however, is the use of corbels at the back for the ribs of the aisle vault (Fig. 23). This has been compared with the nave piers at Lausanne Cathedral[37], but the exact nature of this connection is elusive. It is possible that the arrangement at Dore evolved from examples of corbelling on columnar piers in England. In West Country Romanesque architecture corbels appear on the columnar piers in the Bishop's Chapel at Hereford and the presbytery arcades at Tewkesbury Abbey.[38] In a Cistercian context

corbels are used at Fountains at the back of the nave arcade piers to carry the transverse arches of the aisles[39], while in the east guest house also at Fountains the two northern piers have all eight sections of the capital for the vault ribs supported on moulded corbels.[40] The corbels of the surviving piers at Dore have different designs and yet a third corbel from amongst the loose stonework collection is different again. Clear evidence for the vault remains in both the north and south aisles with the pointed scar of the former web above the arches to the transepts arms (Figs. 23 & 24). In the north-east corner of the north aisle the vault rib is carried on a diagonally set stylized acanthus corbel-capital but its counterpart at the south-east angle of the south aisle is supported on a round moulded corbel-capital. Paul reported finding two bosses from the north nave aisle[41] and though only one can now be traced its angle of intersection matches the geometry of the aisle bay and its mouldings agree with the surviving springer in the south aisle.

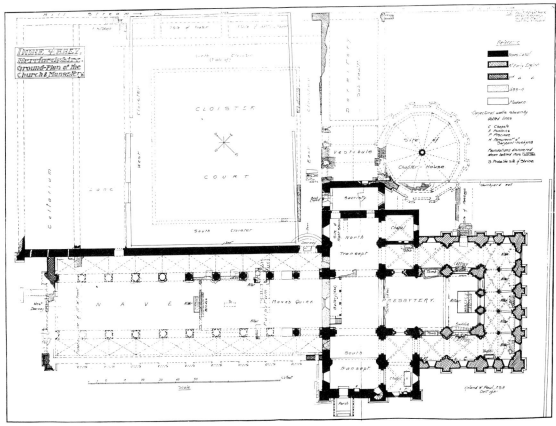

Fig. 25. Paul's plan of Dore dated 1931.

Above the south nave arcade are the jambs of an upper storey. Whether this was an integrated triforium and clerestory as in the nave of Llanthony Priory and St. David's Cathedral or just the extension down of the clerestory window jambs has been a matter of debate. The jamb is worked with an angle roll against a broad hollow chamfer, otherwise the stonework is plain and set at right angles to the main arcade, although this may be reconstituted.[42] Fortunately one of the nave clerestory windows survives complete, carefully rebuilt in the wall which blocks the western crossing arch (Fig. 22). It has identical mouldings to its inner jambs and, most importantly, an unusual segmental form to the arch head with a moulded rerearch. This arrangement means that though there was a substantial splay on the window jambs, the internal and external heads are at the same level. Furthermore, this segmental type of arch head is usually employed

beneath the vault web and set concentric with it. The window shows no sign of alteration and is the right width to fit in the nave elevation (Fig. 26).

The nave had a high vault as shown by the springer which survives corbelled off the wall adjoining the south-west crossing pier. The corbelled triplet above the first pier of the south arcade would have carried triple detached shafts for the high vault. Preserved in the eastern chapels are some figurated vault bosses in which the profile and angle of intersection of the ribs confirm Paul's opinion that they came from the nave high vault. The figure style with broad-fold draperies and the stylized oak-leaf foliage are obviously later than the classicizing trough-fold draperies and stiff-leaf foliage of the mid-thirteenth century 'Samson and the Lion' boss from the Cistercian abbey at Hailes, Gloucestershire.[43] Athough these bosses have generally been attributed to the early-fourteenth century[44], the consecration of Dore by Thomas Cantilupe, Bishop of Hereford (1275-82) surely marks the completion of the church. The broad-fold draperies of the figures on the bosses belong to a tradition established in English seals in the 1260s and 70s[45] and are used on the seal of Thomas Cantilupe.[46] Naturalistic foliage, including oak, appears in the vault bosses of the Angel Choir at Lincoln Cathedral (1256-80) and, in a West Country context, in those of the Lady Chapel and retrochoir of Exeter Cathedral where work on the new east end was in hand before 1279.

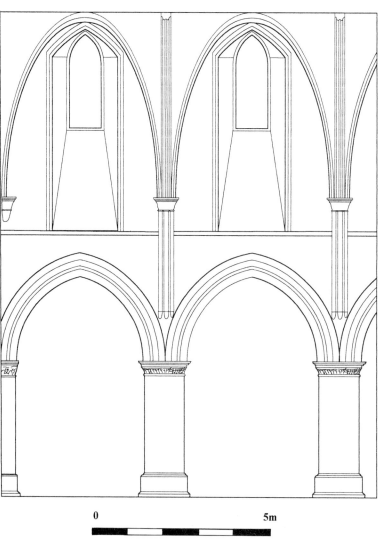

0   5m

Fig. 26. Reconstruction of two bays of the nave arcades, showing the single lancet clerestory windows, one of which survives re-used in the wall which blocks the western crossing arch. The internal arch head was segmental and set concentric to the curvature of the high vault.

The presbytery (Plate 1)

The remodelling and extension of the presbytery was probably commenced soon after the ambitious Abbot Adam took office in 1186.[47] It represents a radical departure from the aesthetics of the earlier twelfth century as the contrast between the western bay and the two eastern bays demonstrates (Fig. 27). In the western bay the arch is triple chamfered, although with a moulded outer order on the south side. In the eastern bays the main arcade arches are also of three orders, but in contrast to the western bay they are richly moulded with two continuous outer orders and an inner order carried on a shaft and a foliate capital with round abacus. The eastern arcade of the presbytery rises to the same height as the north and south arcades but it springs from a higher level because the bays are narrower than those of the lateral arcades.

As if to further enrich the design, the eastern arcade is different; the continuous orders with single roll mouldings of the north and south arcades are not used and instead there are triple roll mouldings in the arch carried on capitals and shafts which are conceived as triplets for the inner and outer orders on the two free-standing piers and on the inner order of both responds. The clerestory windows have the same design details throughout the presbytery with a continuous inner order and an outer order carried on a foliate capital atop a detached shaft. However, while the lateral windows have two orders, the east clerestory windows have three. Also, the sill is higher in the western bay which suggest either that the windows here were inserted or that the upper walls were completely rebuilt with the extension of the presbytery. The various forms of the capitals in the presbytery arcades and their aisle responds support a start early in Adam I's abbacy. The continued use of waterleaf and trumpet scallops after 1180 is paralleled at St. David's Cathedral, but the stylized upright acanthus is virtually unknown elsewhere after 1190 by which time it had been replaced by the stiff-leaf convention. The unusual stiff-leaf with floppy intertwined stems on the capitals of the north presbytery aisle and the north respond of the east arcade is closely paralleled in the presbytery arcades at Lichfield Cathedral (c.1180-1200) where the capitals share round abaci with Dore, a relatively unusual feature in the West Country.[48]

The change to a richer aesthetic is not peculiar to the Dore presbytery but rather conforms to a general trend that took place in Cistercian and other monastic and cathedral churches in the late-twelfth century. The enlarged eastern arm with square ambulatory and eastern chapels was used at Citeaux in the remodelling completed in 1193 and at Morimond.[49] The Morimond east end is undated and is different in many details from Dore. Formally closer in plan and detailing but not in terms of structure to Dore is Byland Abbey with a range of five chapels across the flat east end.[50] At Byland the detailing is much richer than in the earlier Cistercian work in Yorkshire as at Rievaulx, Fountains and Kirkstall, although the chapter houses of the three monasteries

Fig. 27. The eastern end of the presbytery

presage a more elaborate approach.[51] The elaboration at Byland responded to Archbishop Roger of Pont l'Eveque's work at York Minster and Ripon Minster, both of which may also have had square ambulatory plans. The tradition of Cistercian richness continues into the thirteenth century with the lavish eastern arms at Fountains and Rievaulx. In the West Country the nave of Cwmhir, Powys, provides the most direct analogy for the new Cistercian richness.

Whatever the connection between the earlier fabric at Dore with French Gothic there can be no doubt that the links for the eastern extension are firmly rooted in the West Country tradition. Variously multi-shafted compound piers and deeply cut complex arch mouldings are present in the western bays of Worcester Cathedral, at Wells Cathedral and in the Lady Chapel of Hereford Cathedral. Specifically, the three-order arch with two continuous outer orders and a non-continuous inner order is paralleled in the western bays of the nave of Llanthony Priory. At Llanthony the orders are chamfered rather than moulded, although towards the aisles at Dore a single continuous chamfered order is use. For the moulded continuous order there are analogies at the entrance to the Becket Chapel off the north transept of St. David's Cathedral[52] and in the Great Church of Glastonbury Abbey commenced in 1185.

The triple shaft to carry a single order of an arch has a good pedigree in the West Country as in the external apse arcade at Dymock, Gloucestershire, (c.1120) and the gatehouse dado arcade of Evesham Abbey (1130-49). Moreover it is one of the most popular motifs of West Country Early Gothic architects[53] and an identical arrangement to the Dore eastern arcade— with alternating triple and single shafts on the free-standing piers, and triple shafts for the inner order and single shafts for the middle and outer orders in the responds—is found in the former nave arcade of Cwmhir Abbey since re-erected as the north nave arcade at Llanidloes church, Powys.[54] This variety in pier form extends to other aspects of the eastern arm of Dore.[55]

Aside from the wide range of capital types there is the rather more unusual play between round and square abaci. In the north aisle the respond capitals have round abaci, except at the west end of the middle bay where they are square. In the south aisle the abaci are square and set parallel to the wall for the transverse arches but on the diagonal for the diagonal ribs. In the ambulatory and radiating chapels the abaci are all round except in the north-east and south-east angles where they are set on the diagonal. The ribs in the south presbytery aisle have a single filleted roll but in the east bay of the north presbytery aisle they have triple rolls with the central one filleted.

There is even more extreme variety in the middle bay of the north presbytery aisle where the rib towards the north-west corner has angle rolls to either side of a central hollow, while the other ribs have a triple roll as in the adjacent bay to the east. This profile is also used throughout the ambulatory and eastern chapels, except for the transverse ribs of the ambulatory which have plain angle rolls flanking a hollow roll and hollow side chamfers. Wall arches are used throughout the presbytery aisles and eastern chapels, but with variations in design. In the presbytery aisles and eastern chapel walls the wall arch is a continuous roll moulding as in the eastern aisles of the transepts at Wells Cathedral, the presbytery aisles of Lichfield Cathedral and the aisles of Glastonbury Abbey Great Church, but on the north and south walls of the chapels and ambulatory the wall arches are only articulated at the heads of the windows where they double as hoodmoulds. The piers of the ambulatory are unusual in a West Country context in combining four coursed and four detached shafts, with the latter on the cardinal axis, although the lowest section of the pier is coursed throughout all eight shafts (Fig. 28). The pier capitals are highly finished and may be cut from a grey marble which could have taken a dark polish. At the east side of each pier is the stub of a wall which divided the eastern chapels.

The roof of the presbytery

The presbytery has triple shafts for a high vault for which wall ribs remain (Fig 27). Most recently this has been reconstructed as a wooden vault.[56] Unfortunately, when the present roof

Fig. 28. The eastern ambulatory from the north

acting as Regent in his absence. De Grey was instructed 'to cause work to go on both in winter and in summer until the king's chapel of Windsor is finished, and to have a high wooden roof made after the manner of the new work of Lichfield, so that it may appear to be stonework, with good panelling and painting ...'[58] Perhaps the clearest archaeological evidence of a wooden vault is in the nave of Llanthony Priory where the high vault responds survive in the form of trumpet-scallop capitals atop triple shafts. A short distance above the vault capitals at Llanthony start the stone pointed wall arches. At no point, either immediately above the vault capitals or immediately outside the wall arches, are there any signs of disturbance in the masonry which would have been brought about by the removal of the stone webbing of a vault. On the contrary, the flat rubble stonework or the ashlar at the junctions with the west front, courses quite regularly throughout the vault spandrel area. This technique contrasts with that in the parts of the church which were stone vaulted. In the north and south aisles of the nave, voussoirs remain from the stone vault webs, and the penultimate western bay of the north aisle preserves half of the vault web. Above the south crossing arch and on the south wall of the south transept, there are chases in the wall in which the rubble voussoirs of the vault were set, and fragments of this rubble remain above the south-west vault capital. An analogous chase is also visible above the four ashlar voussoirs of the diagonal rib springer of the high stone vault at the south-west angle of the presbytery. This difference in technique, plus the lack of abutment for a high stone vault in the nave of Llanthony strongly indicates that the nave was covered with a high wooden ribbed vault.

was constructed the former vault springers were removed from the walls, to leave deep sockets behind the upright wall posts of the seventeenth century roof (Fig. 20). The aisle walls feature prominent, though shallow, pilaster buttresses and their absence from the clerestory suggests that a wooden high vault is a likely solution. Such wooden vaults seem to have enjoyed popularity in early Gothic churches in the West Country and even though no examples survive from the region their former existence may be reconstructed from archaeological and documentary evidence.[57] Thus in the autumn of 1243 Henry III wrote from Bordeaux to the Archbishop of York, Walter de Gray, who was

Original paintwork

The traces of the original painted decoration in the east end of Dore are a very precious survival and probably constitute the most extensive remains of twelfth-century Cistercian church painting in England.[59] The evidence is clearest on, and immediately to the west of, the north respond of the arch from the south presbytery aisle to the ambulatory, and on the ambulatory side of the southern free-standing pier of the east arcade.

To start with the former: the basic wall decoration to the west of the respond has a cream ground with narrow parallel paired red lines which suggest the outline of imitation mortar joints. The same scheme is used on the central shaft and dosseret (pilaster) of the respond, but the flanking shafts are plain cream. There are traces of red and yellow ochre on the impost of the central capital, and red on the abacus. The inner order of the transverse arch which springs from this respond is cream with three rows of triple red 'mortar' lines after which there are paired black 'mortar' lines. The outer order has traces of yellow ochre and there is a very faded red line between the two orders to the level of the black 'mortar' lines on the inner order. The effect is one of syncopation, in which richer decoration is found on the central section of the respond and outer orders of the arch, while the simpler scheme is on the outer section of the respond and inner section of the arch.

On the opposite southern respond there are chevrons on the eastern reveal of the pilaster (Plate. 4). Many other traces of cream, red and yellow ochre are preserved on this respond, while immediately to the east, on the west jamb of the ambulatory south window, the shaft is yellow ochre with broad cream mortar joints and the hollow moulding to the left of the shaft is red. On the ambulatory side of the southern free-standing pier of the eastern arcade the triple shaft is painted with a cream ground whilst the middle shaft is picked out with a chevron pattern outlined with red and black lines and broad cream and pink bands.[60]

The painted decoration at Dore follows the simpler, earlier schemes of the Fountains slype

and that which can be reconstructed at Byland, although in both these cases the 'mortar' joint lines are relatively thick.[61] Closer to Dore was the decoration of the Rievaulx frater which had similar thin red lines and stippled flower motifs on a pink ground, with red mouldings to the wall arcades. Some of the piers have deep red bandings and this resembles in part some surviving paint in the transepts at Strata Florida.

The general internal appearance of the church now gives a false image of its medieval condition because during the restoration the areas of ashlar were cleaned of the plaster and limewash coatings and this has left several areas with ugly tooling marks. An impression of the previous appearance can be gained from the north-east crossing pier where subsequent removal of the pulpit sounding board has revealed an untouched area of limewash. The nave was also brightly painted and Paul excavated a capital which had its foliage highlighted by a bright red ground, slight traces of which still exist.[62]

Externally the church still has large areas of decaying white mortar covering both its rubble and dressed ashlar surfaces. A close inspection shows that it formerly covered the whole building and, against the south wall of the south transept where it is most completely preserved, shows a floated polished finish with false masonry joints incised into the plaster which were probably picked out in red. Thus the external appearance of the church today is also radically altered from its original state. We must imagine it brightly limewashed and glowing in the sunshine—an evocation of Heavenly Jerusalem on earth.

Other medieval stonework

The tower, in the angle of the south transept and presbytery, was inserted by Scudamore's masons and uses windows, arches and doorways that were re-used from the nave and monastic buildings. It may prove possible to identify their origin within the complex more closely in the future.

The north transept was connected to the dormitory and still retains two distinct rooflines on its northern face which show that the dormi-

Fig. 29. The north face of the north transept showing the two distinct roof lines associated with the dormitory range

aisle roof, but the stonework between them retains medieval plaster and beneath the present roof there is no provision for such gables which would have fronted the aisle vaults. The roofs above the transept chapels are set higher than the presbytery aisles which reflects the greater height of the chapel vaults. The aisle roofs have a prominent chamfered weather moulding which angles upwards where the two roofs join. This can be seen clearly on the north side but is obscured by the tower on the south, although it can be examined closely inside the ringing chamber.

tory was raised in height (Fig. 29). The weathering strips of the dormitory lower roof line are formed from the same stones as the quoins of the transept and are therefore integral with them, while the upper roof line is cut into the quoins and is therefore later. Hard to detect externally, but plainly visible inside the roof-space, are the remains of a pair of lancet windows which used to light the gable flanking the apex of the dormitory roof. Their outer edges are now cut by the gable of the transept which suggests that the main roofs of the church were lowered in pitch during Scudamore's restoration. Clearly visible is a blocked doorway which gave access to the upper section of the raised dormitory roof.

On the north side of the presbytery is an inserted doorway, which retains its medieval door and ironwork[63], to provide access for the old and infirm monks to attend services. The windows throughout the presbytery and eastern chapels are lancets with a horizontal billet stringcourse carried over the windows as decorative gablets. It has been suggested that these originally formed dormers in the main sloping

Conclusion

This review of the architecture of the abbey church of Dore has highlighted the complexity of various phases of the construction of the building. What may at first glance appear to be a building of one period has been shown to be the work of several successive campaigns. The visible evidence for an earlier church of much smaller scale is slight, but at the present stage of research the matter should be left open, not least because at other Cistercian sites, such as Fountains and Waverley, modest aisleless churches were replaced by much larger aisled buildings and the original claustral complex were substantially enlarged. The latter certainly happened at Dore, suggesting that the monks undertook a massive replacement of the entire monastic complex and that this began with the rebuilding of the church.

This rebuilding, which commenced in the north transept, was itself quite drastically revised from the original Bernardine plan. The church was designed in the new Gothic style which presumably reflected the patron's desire to emulate the up-to-date French elements seen in

York Minster and Canterbury Cathedral and, in the West Country, at Keynsham Abbey and Worcester Cathedral. The exact nature of the French link is difficult to determine, but the handling of details suggests that this was a local and not very sophisticated interpretation of the style.

High vaults were intended from the first and it appears that these were built over the transepts and probably over the original presbytery. Numerous detail differences show that the south transept was built after the north transept, and work on the nave would have been commenced at this time. Similarities between certain capitals from the nave and the presbytery suggest that before the completion of the nave, work had started on the lavish enlargement of the presby-tery under the patronage of the ambitious Abbot Adam.

Dore is the best surviving example of the change in Cistercian aesthetic attitudes that took place in the late-twelfth century. In contrast to the earlier austerity, the Dore presbytery displays the new Cistercian desire to rival the most richly decorated contemporary buildings including Wells Cathedral, Glastonbury Abbey, and the Lady Chapel of Hereford Cathedral. The love of variety, at first expressed cautiously in the north transept, is now boldly asserted. In addition the taste for lavish adornment of the fabric continued at Dore well into the thirteenth century with the figurated bosses from the nave and the refurbishment of the screens.

CHAPTER VI

The loose architectural detail

by Stuart Harrison

Lying in the eastern chapels of the ambulatory of the church at Abbey Dore are a remarkable collection of architectural fragments. To my knowledge they have never been studied before with a view to finding out what they can tell about the buildings of the abbey nor have the majority of the pieces been published. Pieces of loose stonework at the abbey are first mentioned by Thomas Blashill in a very astute article in which he recognised that the abbey possessed a chapter house which had a polygonal plan and then identified the base from its central column which was lying in the rockery of the rectory garden.[1] Alas this promising start was not continued by other investigators and though the main commentator and excavator of the abbey, Roland Paul, mentions finding some stonework, in the main he did not identify fragments in any detail, nor did he publish what he found.

During this study of the material it has become apparent that although Paul had the evidence before him he did not avail himself of all the information it could impart, nor did he actually understand how some of it must have appeared when complete. In the late nineteenth and early twentieth centuries usually very little attention was paid to architectural fragments, interest being more focused on the recovery of building plans. However, Paul was sufficiently interested to draw a few pieces of arcading in detail and attempt a reconstruction of some of the micro-tracery he discovered together with

parts of what was described as a shrine.

In 1976 the stones were marked with a series of coded numbers by G. Gilchrist, then head of the Sculpture Department of Dyfed College of Art and the hand list made at that time gives a guide to the coding. This list quantifies the stones, but its descriptions are very brief and do not relate in detail to where the stones were formerly located in the buildings and there is no reference at all to their provenance. Thus the knowledge of exactly where the majority of pieces were discovered is limited to the blanket areas of Paul's excavations and is largely reliant on comments made by Blashill and Paul. Fortunately Paul annotated one of his plans of the church with the location of some finds and these can still be identified.[2]

Despite this lack of information it is possible to tentatively ascribe an origin to a considerable quantity of the material with some confidence. However, it should be stressed that the present study should be regarded simply as a beginning of the analysis of the material. It does not pretend to be a definitive account. In fact it is only the more obvious and easily reconstructable features which have been picked out and there are many intriguing and unexplained elements which remain to be explored. Only a systematic and detailed analysis of all the pieces will explain more about the abbey buildings. During recent years increasing notice has been paid to the large numbers of carved stone fragments which have been excavated at medieval sites over the last hundred years. Usually consigned to a dump at the fringes of the site they form a rich treasure trove of material for someone skilled enough to understand how to relocate them back into the original fabric of the buildings. It is this aspect that has been studied at Abbey Dore for the collection, though small by the standards of collections at sites such as Rievaulx or Fountains which number over a thousand pieces, is nevertheless very important and unusually rich.

The Rood Screen and the 'Shrine'

It was Thomas Blashill and possibly the Rev. Phillips who first instigated investigations into the nave at Dore with an excavation apparently to establish its length. In this they appear to have failed but they did recover an object of very great interest. This was part of the superstructure of what was described as an elaborate 'shrine' of mid- to late thirteenth century date, apparently retaining considerable traces of painting and gilding.[3] Apart from noting its discovery nothing was done to illustrate the find nor to discuss why such an elaborate object should be found in the nave of a Cistercian church.

Following on from Blashill and Phillips, Paul excavated a further section of the nave and noted that more fragments of the 'shrine' had been discovered. His plan shows the position as being virtually on the centre line of the nave between the first pair of piers west of the pulpitum screen and records that the fragments were found in August 1895.[4] In the same year Paul prepared a coloured drawing of the parts of the 'shrine' discovered by Blashill which shows that it had by then largely lost the bright polychromy described at the time of its discovery.

The surviving pieces comprise parts of the upper section of the structure forming one and a half pointed arches in length by one narrower arch in width (Fig. 30). Each arch is heavily moulded and set below a gablet, with the section between originally painted red. The corners have a decorated pilaster buttress. On the end face these have incised sunk quatrefoils, which were painted red and on the return face a blind lancet arch. The triangular sections above the gablets are pierced with trefoils and have a moulded string course along the top edge which is returned around the corners and end of the shrine. In the soffits of the side arches are rebates to take tracery inserts. These also appear to be the pieces found later by Paul.

Paul's second undated coloured drawing of the structure is a partial reconstruction incorporating these tracery fragments and elements of the foiled openings along the top edge between the gablets.[5] Now kept in display cupboards in the vestry, they comprise a considerable number of fragments of micro-tracery designs (Figs. 31 & 32). They have all the appearance of full size

Fig. 30. The object long known as the 'shrine,' but now thought to be part of the rood screen

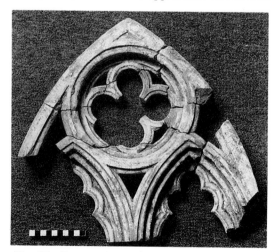

Fig. 31. Tracery insert for the 'shrine,' cut from a single stone, painted and gilded

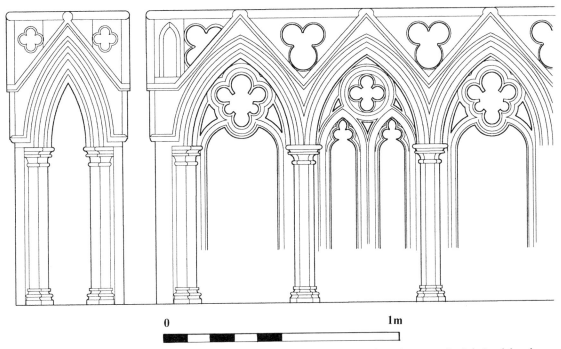

0   1m

Fig. 32. Reconstruction of one end of the structure previously thought to be part of a 'shrine,' but has now been identified as forming the top of the rood screen. This diagram shows the section of masonry shown in fig 30 and tracery inserts from figs. 31 and 33

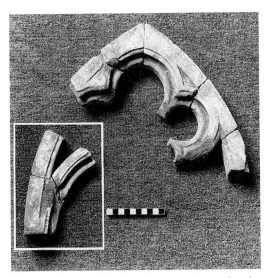

Fig. 33. Second design of tracery insert for the 'shrine,' also painted and gilded

window tracery including fully detailed mould-ings, but are worked to a very small scale. Cut from a single piece of stone the tracery sections form two distinct designs. The most complete has a quatrefoil contained in a circle in the arch head with blunt cusps and cinquefoil cusping to the paired lower openings (Fig. 31). The second design has a different pattern in the arch head with a foiled opening and, at the top, a central large lobe flanked by two smaller lobes and the start of a third smaller lobe (Fig. 33). The lower section of the tracery is incomplete, but has the springing from the side with an arch which projects suffi-ciently to show that it cannot have been paired with a central arch division. This arrangement shows that the foils in the arch head must have been completed in the lower section by a sixth foil which was linked to the tracery springing from each side. It follows that Paul's reconstruction, which shows this section with an ogee lower section to the tracery head, instead of a sixth foil, supported by a central mullion, must be wrong.

These pieces of tracery are highly unusual and form superb examples of the mason's craft. The structure must have been supported on piers and capitals which have not yet been identified though three quatrefoil bases seem to be part of the assemblage and Paul intimates that they may have formed part of the structure.[6] One aspect of these bases that needs to be explored in more detail is the absence of any indication that they supported the inset tracery within the arches. It seems that the side responds and central mullions cannot have extended down to the level of the bases. This suggests that there was some form of horizontal sill set at a higher level to accommodate the uprights of the tracery.

The foiled openings between the gablets are now largely broken but sufficient pieces were recovered to indicate the whole design (Fig. 32). These smaller sections appear to have never been properly cleaned since they were excavated and retain considerable traces of white paint and also gilding on the tracery. The foiled openings have a white ground with motifs such as chevrons painted in black along the top edge. The whole structure must have been very bright, though probably not appealing to modern tastes. The top has a lead insert in one corner which indicates that it had an upper section now lost and the ridge of the surviving gablet has been crudely pierced with a circular hole, for a fitting of some description. Paul discovered the sections of tracery in the retrochoir between the rood and pulpitum screens[7] and no doubt influenced by the finds location, indicated on his 1931 plan that the 'shrine' stood in the centre of this area.[8] However, there is strong evidence to indicate that this was not the case.

The Screen Walls and Arcading

The evidence for early screen divisions in Cistercian churches seems to indicate that the aisles of the nave were screened by solid walls, which in early churches such as Rievaulx, Fountains and Kirkstall were simply butted up to the piers. In later designs such as Byland and Jervaulx the piers were adapted at the front to accommodate the walls and at Strata Florida and Tintern the walls were bonded to the piers or the arcade was built on top. At Dore the excavated evidence seems to indicate that the walls were simply butted up to the piers.

The debris from the excavations indicates that the layout of screens at Dore was modified in the late thirteenth century. Paul's excavations showed that though the rood screen stood on a narrow base wall, the pulpitum was a screen of considerable thickness which contrary to earlier practice, closed off the aisles as well as the nave of the church. The pulpitum, at 5ft 6in thick, must have been a substantial structure. It undoubtedly had a single central doorway, though Paul failed to trace its width. With such thick screens it was common for there to be a longitudinal staircase in the wall thickness, starting from within the central entrance lobby up to the top of the screen. Such was the case with the pulpitum at Tintern. This screen, which has recently been reconstructed in detail, was of early fourteenth century date and shows that Cistercian pulpitum screens at that time could rival those in the great cathedrals such as that at Exeter.[9] Unfortunately it has not yet proved possible to identify any material from the example at Dore and it seems that Paul was correct when he thought that it had been removed at the Dissolution.

Few rood or pulpitum screens have survived in a Cistercian context but the rood screen at Roche Abbey, which stands to a considerable height, has a plain wall pierced by a thirteenth-century central doorway, with benches on the east face for the infirm monks. The rood screen at Furness, of fourteenth-century date, also has a central opening with mouldings for blind tracery on the west side, though a large detached fragment shows tracery panelling on each side, it also seems to have had benches on the east face. Paul's plan of the Dore screen shows that this too had a bench on the east side. At Rievaulx the fifteenth century rood screen also had a central doorway but was constructed of timber which stood on a stone base and this must have looked very similar to the surviving rood screen in

Aysgarth Church which was removed from Jervaulx at the Dissolution.

At Dore many other details from this area of the church have been recovered and these include considerable sections from the top of a screen wall. These consist of flat copings 47cm wide with a filleted roll moulding along each edge which was supported by a structure 39cm wide. These copings show that it must have been at least around 5m long. An identically moulded piece shows the junction of an arch hood mould with the horizontal coping and a radial angled joint, its extent shows that it covered a round-headed or slightly pointed arch. Fortunately one voussoir from this has survived and shows mouldings to both faces with a prominent rebate on the soffit. Like the hood mould it is elaborately painted in white and red with the rebate completely outlined in red. This shows that there was never a door casing, with the door being hung from hinges set directly into the rebates of the jambs.

Paul found there was a central nave altar base, set against the west face of the rood screen, with a pair of flanking doorways, though only the northern one was seen. This still retained its moulded south jamb and though not shown in great detail on his plan it is around the right size and shape for the reconstructed doorway.[10] Some of the copings have sockets for fittings and these form three distinctly different types. Firstly on top of the doorway section is the outline for a support extending across the width of the coping with a tulip-shaped base at each side joined by a web. Secondly there is a large coping which has a pair of trefoiled outlines which exactly match the three small bases found by Paul and which seem to have supported the corners of the shrine previously described. Thirdly there are two pieces with a 10cm square socket which pierces the coping and also a shallower 5cm square socket, one of which has the circular outline for a base. The spacings are regular in each case and suggest an alternation of major and minor sockets.

The location recesses for the bases which supported the 'shrine' show that it must have stood on top of the screen walling but give no indication of exactly where this might have been. However the size and location of the other recess, above the doorway, seems most likely to have formed the position for one of its intermediate base supports and if this was the case it is most unlikely that we are dealing with the simple three bay structure which was reconstructed by Paul. It is far more likely that what survives is just one end of a structure which extended across the whole of the top of the rood screen, or possibly three separate structures which were spaced towards the sides and centre of the screen. If this interpretation is correct then we should discount the interpretation of the structure as a shrine and see it as a very elaborate cresting arcade which supported the rood and its fittings.

Also amongst this material are sections of arcading which are mentioned by Paul within the remains of the pulpitum screen, 'and some

Fig. 34. Paul's 'Early English Arcading' from the top of the nave side screen walls. The soffits are rebated for tracery inserts.

Fig. 35. Reconstruction of the arcading (fig 34) which stood on top of the walls which screened the aisles from the central part of the nave. Like the arcading on top of the rood screen (fig 37) it was heavily poly-chromed and painted with white floral motifs

very beautiful pieces of Early English arcading were found in its core, showing that either the present wall was the second on the same site, with earlier work re-used in its construction, or that the "pulpitum" had been thrown down at the Dissolution, and the carved work of neigh-bouring shrines had been broken up and thrown into it.'[11] This statement is hard to reconcile, for the arcading still retains considerable traces of paint which suggests that it has never been reused as core work within a later screen and also Paul's statement that the pulpitum had been largely reduced to its footings.[12] This very fine arcading was drawn in detail by Paul largely to record the painting which was then well

preserved.[13] The arcading consists of pointed arches with fine moulding which merge with a horizontal string course which links the arches at the apex (Fig. 34). The integral capitals have a combined leaf and moulded design worked with the arch springers. The separate voussoirs are finely jointed to the springers and the span-drels on each side have sunk circles and trefoils. They retain considerable evidence of red paint and white-painted flowers in the spandrels. The arch mouldings are finely moulded with rolls and fillets and the soffits are rebated for separate tracery or cusps. Some separate cusps have also survived and show similar remains of paint, but though they are the right width to fit

Fig. 36. Reconstruction of the upper part of a five-light tracery insert

0   15cm

the soffit rebates of the arches they are from a larger arch. The delicacy of the arches and capitals together with the high quality of the decorative scheme suggest that it formed some sort of screen work. Paul tried to reconstruct a tracery infilling set within the rebates which suggests that the fragments of tracery on which his reconstruction was based were found associated or close to the arcading. This is perhaps confirmed by a note on his plan which mentions 'portions of cusped arch gilt and colour.'[14] However, this description could equally apply to the separate cusps mentioned above. Certainly the tracery pattern he drew within the arches can be recognised and reconstructed amongst the other micro-tracery fragments found in the vestry cupboards.

However, whilst most of these fragments show a tracery pattern with a single mullion supporting paired cusped arches and a cusped circle in the arch head there are similar pieces which show at least one other tracery design. This can be reconstructed as a five light opening with a trefoiled cusped centre light flanked by paired lancet openings with a cusped circle above (Fig. 36). The central pair of mullions are larger and support two arches which frame a larger circle in the main arch head. This was undoubtedly cusped though the tracery is too incomplete to determine the details.

Both these tracery patterns are of a similar scale to the surviving containing arches, but they are much narrower than the rebates in their soffits. Though this indicates that they may originate in another series of arches, it might simply be a mistake on the part of the masons in making the rebates too wide. However, it seems likely that the arcading must be associated with the screen wall copings mentioned above because the bay spacings of the larger sockets correspond exactly with that of the arcade and if they were subdivided by tracery the smaller holes would have held the central mullions.

The coping shows that the 'shrine' stood in isolation so that the arcade cannot have stood on the same length of wall as that structure and its seems most likely that the side walls of the retrochoir, which were the same thickness as the rood screen, supported this arcading (Fig. 35). Paul reported that the north wall was still standing 2 feet high and brightly painted in red, green, blue and yellow towards the nave, but plain white towards the aisle.[15]

These various elements allow a tentative reconstruction of the rood screen to be attempted. Basically a blank ashlar wall across the nave, it was pierced by a pair of doorways and capped by a moulded coping. Standing on this was the structure known as the 'shrine,' extending for fifteen bays almost across the

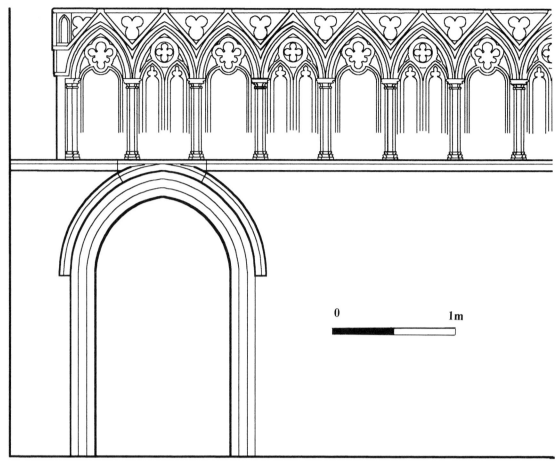

*Fig. 37 . Reconstruction of the rood screen (northern half) based on Paul's excavation plan and the frag-
ments shown in figs 30, 31 & 33 and incorporating the reconstruction in fig 32*

whole width of the screen, with some form of
lost superstructure or cresting, possibly of timber
(Fig. 37). In the centre was the nave altar and
high above the rood, depicting the crucifixion
with possibly flanking statues of the Virgin and
St. John. On the east side was a bench for the
infirm monks. The overall impression must have
been extremely rich, both in terms of architectural design and the associated polychromy.

Paul also reported that part of the space
beneath the arcade in front of the pulpitum was
occupied by altar bases and from the late thirteenth century it seems to have been common
practice to divide the nave aisles in Cistercian
churches into separate chapel and family chantry
spaces. Amongst the loose stonework are several

sections which derive from trefoiled arched
piscina recesses similar to those which survive in
the transepts and presbytery. These have a trait
particular to Dore in that they are commonly cut
to take a shelf, in particular at the springing of
the foil. This peculiarity is present on the loose
pieces and whilst the fragments show two, probably early, simply chamfered examples, one
elaborate section shares the same moulding
profile as the cloister arcading and must be from
the same rebuilding. These surviving pieces can
only derive from the church and whilst Paul
reported finding some fragments of piscinae and
aumbries in one of four holes discovered in the
floor of the east end of the church, which may
account for some of the material[16], some of these

pieces must come from the nave; presumably they come from Paul's excavations on the north side, though some may have been unearthed by Blashill. They show that besides the single altar definitely discovered by Paul under the north arch, against the pulpitum screen, there must have been a whole series of others and that the nave aisles must have been subdivided into several chapel spaces. This common feature of Cistercian naves can be best seen at Rievaulx where the screen divisions and altars are relatively intact, though less perfect examples survive at Roche, Byland and Jervaulx and are known to have existed at Fountains and Kirkstall.

The architectural details of the rood screen indicate a date for its construction in the years following the middle of the thirteenth century. It was at this time in 1260 that the bishop of Hereford had had to issue the twenty days indulgence to those who contributed to the building of 'the sumptuous church of Dore.'[17] Could the screen have been a product of this building campaign? It may have been completed when the later bishop of Hereford, Thomas Cantilupe (1275-82), consecrated the church. Certainly the reconstruction shows that the rood screen and its associated screen walls was a sumptuous design and that by the middle of the thirteenth century any Cistercian pretensions towards simplicity in architecture had long been forgotten.

The Tomb or Shrine Base

Paul commented on the discovery of parts of a possible tomb chest during the renewal of the flooring in the church. 'In the north aisle a very delicately carved stone, probably the angle of a canopy of a tomb, was found and some shafts and bases belonging to the same'[18] and the actual location of the discovery in the second bay is marked on one of his unpublished plans.[19] Though this is an imprecise description it is possible to identify some loose pieces of stone which may be the ones referred to. In the vestry cupboards is a stone of thirteenth century date, evidently from the corner angle of a structure

Fig.38. Fragment of possible tomb or shrine base

such as a tomb chest. It has a trefoil shaft with a stiff leaf capital and moulded round abaci. Above this is the springing for a moulded arch on the left and on the right an unusually-shaped leaf decoration. Also amongst the material are seven fragmentary moulded bases which have trefoiled shafts. These can be matched to those on the larger piece. Enough of the surrounds survive to show that the arch was part of a blind arcade.

Amongst the larger collection of stone in the ambulatory is a similar but more complete stone which has a trefoiled blind arch with the remains of a capital on the left side which had trefoiled shafts (Fig. 38). Unfortunately the lower sections are incomplete and though it seems most likely that these two pieces formed the ends of the structure the trefoil shafts are not worked on the corner angles but are set in and worked only on the end face. The spandrels are decorated with sunk moulded trefoils with foliate decoration. There is also a section of arcading which consists of a trefoiled springer which formed two halves of a pair of open

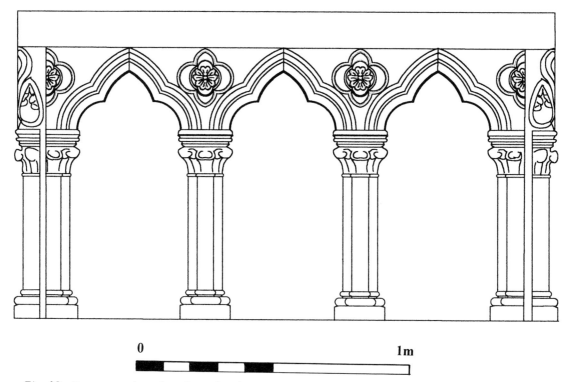

Fig. 39. Reconstruction of tomb or altar base, of thirteenth century date, perhaps with trefoiled open arches along each side and a single blind trefoiled arch at each end

arches. It has an attached trefoiled capital of foliate design and foliate decoration in the spandrel. The return sides are plain and would have appeared noticeably so if they were ever visible. The rear face is also plain and it seems most likely that it was not visible. All three pieces of arcading show evidence for metal cramps set into the top face to hold it together. If it was some form of tomb chest it would seem most likely that the blind arches formed the end sections with the open arcading along the sides. This was probably overlapped by the ends of the chest and concealed the section of plain return masonry along the angle.

The open arcaded sides are hard to explain in terms of a tomb chest of this date which would normally have solid sides, but if it was possibly a shrine, there would be no objection to the open arches along the sides (Fig. 39). The effect would have looked very similar to the upper part of the Cantilupe shrine base in Hereford Cathedral. Early shrines in their simplest form were composed of a table design with a large stone slab standing on columns to support the feretory or movable container which actually enclosed the bones. Such a slab has recently been recognised amongst the material dismantled during the recent work on the shrine of St. Alban.[20] Slightly more elaborate versions have solid sides pierced with holes or foils such as that in Ilam Church, Staffordshire.[21] These apertures allowed pilgrims close access to the relics and were provided so that they might insert an affected limb or even crawl into the shrine base. As time went by shrines became more elaborate with the feretory supported at a higher level upon a row of arches, often with some form of gabled design and usually with some form of elaborate cover which could be raised by a rope and pulley. Unfortunately there is insufficient remaining to be sure but it may be that the extremely elaborate decoration of the nave rood screen and retrochoir was part of a shrine scheme and that these pieces formed the base of the structure which supported the feretory.

The High Vault

The nave at Dore was vaulted in stone in the late-thirteenth or early-fourteenth century and the surviving bosses form an interesting collection. The three bosses from the transverse ribs, two in the church and one built in the churchyard wall, feature large human heads including a green man. The five diagonal rib bosses show figurative scenes including some with a Marian theme, only to be expected in a Cistercian context. There is the Virgin and Child, the Coronation of the Virgin, Christ in Majesty, and St. Catherine with her wheel. The bosses are described in detail in chapter VIII.

Though the series of bosses is far from complete it is clear that those remaining show a typical group of scenes which could be expected in any medieval church context and the Marian theme would suggest that others such as the Annunciation, the Nativity and Assumption of the Virgin are likely to have featured in the series. They are remarkably well preserved and show little damage. Their good condition has led to the suggestion by Ruth Richardson that they were intentionally saved and removed from the vault following the Dissolution, though this would have been a difficult procedure. One explanation may be that the vault had become dangerous with age and had already been dismantled and that the bosses were kept somewhere on site, like those from the dismantled Presbytery and Nine Altars Chapel vaults at Fountains, though there is no specific evidence to confirm this theory.

One aspect of the design of these bosses has significance in regard to the understanding of the development of the nave. Richard Morris has examined the rib profiles and concluded that stylistically they date to the early thirteenth century, though the foliage and decoration show that they must date to the late thirteenth or the early fourteenth century. This suggests that either the masons continued using a profile which had gone out of fashion or, more likely, that the ribs were cut to this pattern to match existing vault springers from an earlier vaulting scheme that was either never built or supported a timber vault.

The West Front

Paul also excavated the west end of the nave and reported finding parts of the west windows; he expressed the opinion that they were most probably a triplet of lancets.[22] He also mentions elaborate mouldings which he thought came from the west doorway. Now Paul can only have deduced a triplet of lancet windows if he saw evidence for such a group of windows amongst the loose stonework. This would normally be a jamb shared by two splays. Such a double splay with a base for a shaft set between the jambs survives amongst the loose stonework (Fig. 40). There is also a single jamb base with the same profile and a pair of foliate capitals which would fit such a single jamb. In addition there are a number of elaborate voussoirs that match with the window jamb mouldings and appear to have derived from the window heads. With a radius of nearly 2 metres, they confirm Paul's idea of a group of lancets and enable a reconstruction of the window plan to be drawn. Though different in profile the

Fig. 40. Base from between two of the angled splays of the lancet windows in the west front. The base supported a detached shaft

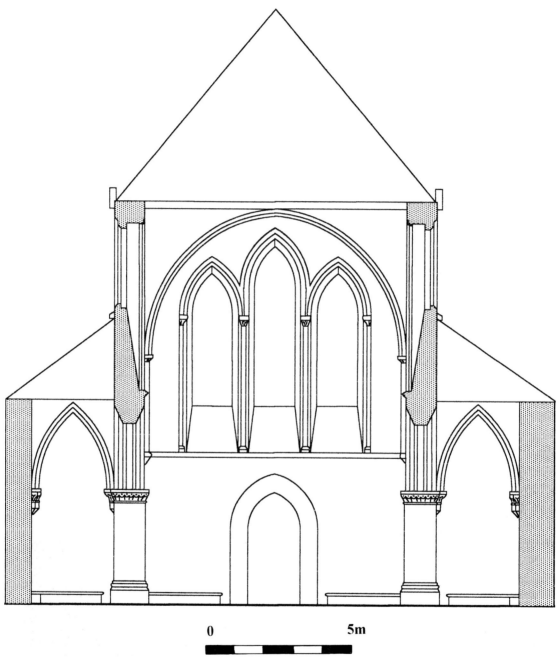

Fig. 41. Reconstruction of the interior of the west front, based on the surviving lower parts excavated by Paul and the loose masonry which he recovered. The outline of the west doorway survived in plan together with the north-west arcade respond base. Detached fragments of the lancet windows include sections of the bases, the capitals and the arch heads. The outline of the vault survives at the east end of the nave.

mouldings show a close similarity in arrangement to the clerestory windows of the presbytery indicating that the west windows would have been very similar in appearance.

Though the west doorway had been largely robbed away, part of the step remained and from this and the robbing line shown on Paul's plan it is possible to estimate with some accuracy the size of the doorway. It was flanked on the north (and presumably the south) by a wall bench with a moulded capping. A similar bench filled the end of the north aisle and was returned along the north wall. From these isolated pieces of evidence it is possible to draw a tentative reconstruction of the inside of the west front with a modest west doorway and a triplet of lancet windows graduated to fill the area beneath the high vault (Fig, 41). Externally, there were traces of substantial walls flanking the west doorway which may represent a later porch or galilee such as are known to have existed at Tintern, Margam and Holmcultram, possibly as at the latter replacing an earlier galilee which extended across the full width of the west front.

Paul excavated a considerable section of the west front and exposed the north arcade respond and the south-west corner angle buttress plinth, part of which was removed during grave digging a few years ago and is now lying in the churchyard. The respond was a half cylinder pier with a moulded base and large foliate spurs on each angle[23], Paul's pencil scale drawing of the northern half of the west front[24], shows it standing about 5 feet high, with a double-chamfered external plinth. It also shows the angled outline of the central doorway splay with two large slabs forming the external doorstep. As mentioned above, at each side of the respond, was a stone wall bench with a moulded capping. Part of a pier base with an identical spur survives amongst the loose stone and shows that other piers in the nave also had this type of decoration. This loose base appears to be of late twelfth to early thirteenth century date and Paul obviously recognised that the respond was similar to the nave pier bases and suggested that it may have been reused material.[25]

However, this might not be the case and raises the question of what he did see in his earlier excavation—was it really an earlier west front, or could it have been the base for the lay brothers night stair, which would probably have been in the last bay of the nave? Unfortunately the actual extent of the excavation is not shown on his plan though the section of walling is clearly shown as being about 4 feet in thickness and extending southwards for just over half the width of the aisle. No indication of depth is given in relation to the floor so it is not possible to establish the relationship of the wall to the rest of the nave.

From the excavations indicated on his plan it is clear that many were small in scale and were essentially keyhole archaeology. Unfortunately it is hard to be sure exactly what he saw, but extending an existing nave by only one bay would seem an unusual thing to do, especially when it is considered that it would involve the demolition of the existing western bay. Certainly, the design of the respond seems to indicate an earlier rather than later thirteenth century date, at least for the lower parts of the work.

One solution might be that in his first excavation, Paul found the west front of an earlier, probably aisle less, church which was demolished when the present nave was built. Richard Morris considers the mouldings of the west windows and the vaulting of the south aisle to be of the middle years of the thirteenth-century which, at first sight, would seem to confirm Paul's idea of a substantial rebuilding of the west end. However, it is also quite likely that work on the nave may have been suspended for a considerable time whilst the monastic buildings were extensively rebuilt and only when these were finished would work have resumed on the nave and west front. Delays in building work in the early-thirteenth century may have been related to the financial difficulties with King John .

The Cloister Arcade
Amongst the loose fragments are several trefoil bases and matching foliate capitals supported by three detached shafts. There are also sections of an arcade which it seems to have supported (Fig. 42). Three springers survive and two voussoirs and apex stones. Enough remains to reconstruct a

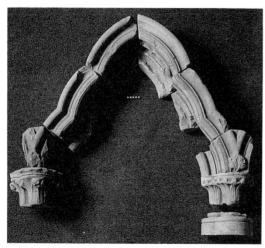

Fig. 42. Sections of the arches, capitals and bases from the thirteenth century cloister arcade

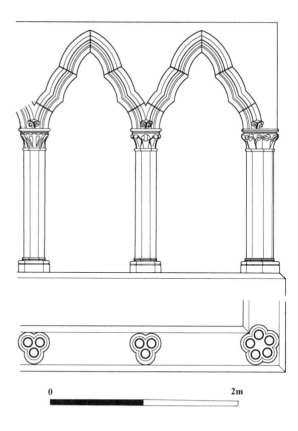

Fig. 43. Reconstruction of two bays of the cloister arcade, based on surviving fragments. A cluster of five shafts supported the corner.

single arch of cinquefoil design elaborately moulded towards the front but plainer to the rear with a prominent step rebate (Fig. 43). This was provided to accommodate a second inset layer of arcading also moulded towards the front but chamfered to the rear. This is an unusual arrangement but one which presages later developments where tracery or cusping was set into rebates in the soffits of arches such as on the rood screen arcading. Possibly the arches were subdivided by tracery, though no evidence has survived to show that this was the case. When reconstructed on paper the arcading resembles that commonly found in cloisters to support the alley roofs, though the traditional form from the eleventh century was usually of paired shafts, supporting round-headed or pointed arches.

Although Paul carried out some excavations in the cloister and found the footings of the arcade base wall, he never reported finding evidence for its arcades. It may be that these pieces are the unreported product of his excavation. Although cinquefoils arches are uncommon in such arcades its thirteenth century date makes it a relatively late design. The one of similar date at Norton Priory, reconstructed from fragments also has trefoiled supporting shafts. At Dore, in addition to the trefoil capitals there is also a fragmentary capital which was supported by a cluster of five detached shafts which must have been used to turn the arcade at the corner of the cloister alley. When seen in plan its layout fits exactly into a corner position, matching up with the trefoil bases of the normal arcade on each side yet turning the arcade perfectly around the corner.

CHAPTER VII

The Medieval Floor Tiles

by Alan Vince

The surviving tiles

The first recorded discovery of medieval floor tiles at Abbey Dore took place at the beginning of the twentieth century when tiles were found as part of the architectural work carried out by Roland Paul. It seems from notes deposited at the Society of Antiquaries Library at Burlington House, London, that Roland Paul made notes on his discoveries but, if so, these have not survived (or at least their present whereabouts is not known). There is a plan of the church prepared by Roland Paul which is annotated with notes to say that floor tiles were found at particular places. There is nothing on this plan to suggest that the tiles were still *in situ* when found and, since some were recorded outside the church to the south, it is quite likely that they were already in a secondary context when discovered. Notes by Roland Paul and circumstantial evidence (some of the loose tiles were still wrapped in the remains of a 1901 newspaper when studied in 1996) confirm that all the floor tiles now in the church were found by Paul.

A few floor tile fragments have been observed in patches of loose soil outside the church and there is therefore a strong possibility that the collection we have now could be augmented in the future by excavation of the abbey remains or as a result of unavoidable disturbance to the archaeological levels, such as the provision of services or grave digging.

The surviving tiles from the 1901 excavations are now either relaid to either side of the altar or are loose in cabinets in the vestry. The collections are rather different in character, evidence of the prevailing taste at the time of the renovation (and a warning against assuming that any surviving collection of tiles is going to be a random selection of the original assemblage). The relaid tiles are predominantly heraldic two-colour tiles and lozenge-shaped relief tiles whereas the loose collection is mainly composed of non-heraldic two-colour tiles (Plate. 5).

History of the study

In the 95 years since their discovery the Abbey Dore tiles have received attention from several scholars. However, they have all assumed that the relaid tiles were representative of the whole collection and have therefore overlooked an extremely interesting body of evidence for the internal fittings of the abbey. The relief tiles are described briefly in Ward-Perkins' 1937 study of medieval relief tiles, where the section on Abbey Dore appears to be based on the tracings in the collection of Lord Alwyn Compton (held in the Society of Antiquaries library). Ward-Perkins quotes Mr. R. McN. Rushforth's suggestion that they date to the early-thirteenth century and are part of the original fabric of the abbey. The heraldic tiles, described in the RCHM inventory, are included in Wilmott and Vince's 1991 study of a lost tile pavement from Tewkesbury Abbey (which was based on research carried out between 1974 and 1977, plus a site visit in the early 1980s in order to trace the designs of the heraldic tiles). The loose collection, however, appears to have been examined for the first time in 1996, as a direct consequence of the need to prepare this book. All the loose tiles were laid out and divided into design types. They were then drawn by Lyn Harper, of Monmouth Archaeological Society. A sample of six relief tiles and six two-colour tiles was then thin-sectioned and subjected to Inductively Coupled Plasma Spectroscopy (ICPS) in order to study the clay from which the tiles had been made.

The relief tiles

At the time when Ward Perkins undertook his study of British relief tiles there were very few tiles earlier than the late medieval period known. The intervening sixty years has not really changed this pattern although several of the tiles included by Ward-Perkins have since been recognised as being of late Saxon date. In the author's research on medieval ceramics in the Severn Valley no further examples of relief tiles have been found in the counties of Gwent, Hereford and Worcester, Gloucestershire or Avon[1]. In addition to the lozenge-shaped tiles which form a patch of relaid tiles to the east of the altar and stamped with two dies, a single example of a third design, probably from a square or rectangular shaped tile, was

found amongst the loose material (Fig. 44). The fabric of all these tiles is distinctive, containing abundant rounded fragments of calcium carbonate (Fig. 45), together with abundant silt-sized quartz and white mica. This carbonate occurs as nodules in the Devonian marl which outcrops along the southern part of the Marches and medieval tiles and pottery of similar fabric are found in a small area of southwestern Herefordshire and northeastern Gwent. Some of this pottery appears to have been tempered with a coarse sand or gravel containing calcareous grains and rounded sandstone fragments. At

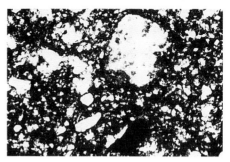

Fig. 45. Photomicrograph of relief tile

Hereford, this fabric was classified as Hereford Fabric A2 and it was suggested that it might have been produced in or on the outskirts of Hereford, since the gravel underlying Hereford itself is very similar in composition to the inclusions in the pottery fabric. The Abbey Dore tiles, however, do not include rounded sandstone fragments and it is more likely that in this case the clay itself was calcareous.

Perhaps the closest parallel to the fabric of the Abbey Dore tiles comes from Kilpeck, where excavations by the City of Hereford Archaeology Unit on a site immediately north of the church produced fragments of Roman-style (ie. tegula and imbrex) glazed roof tiles in a calcareous, silty, micaceous fabric. Apart from a single fragment of a tegula tile from Bewell House, Hereford, these tiles are only known from this one excavation. Whilst it is likely that future archaeological work will show that such tiles are not as uncommon as they now appear (there are still less than a dozen sites in the country which have produced them), it is clear that the Kilpeck

0   10cm

Fig. 44. Relief tile

roof tiles, like the Abbey Dore floor tiles, represent an introduction into the Marches of a non-local technology. Whether the two sites are connected more closely may become clear should any excavations take place at Abbey Dore, for then it could be established whether or not the abbey church ever had a glazed tile roof.

The two-colour tiles

The two-colour tiles from Abbey Dore were made from a much finer clay than the relief tiles. In

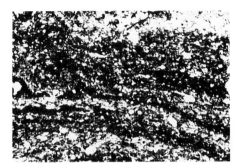

Fig. 46. Photomicrograph of two-colour tile

broken sections it can be seen that the fabric is variegated. This is shown clearly in thin-section (Fig. 46). This variegated texture is not present in the fabric of other two-colour tiles in the southern Marches, which actually contain sparse rounded calcareous nodules and sandstone grains, similar to those found in Hereford Fabric A2 (and classed at Hereford as Hereford Fabric A9). No other examples of this tile fabric have been identified. The main characteristics of the fabric, however, are silt-sized quartz grains and white mica. These confirm that the tiles were made from a locally-available clay, though the precise location of the clay source (and thus the tilery) cannot be determined using scientific evidence alone.

The ICPS analysis confirms that the fabric of the two-colour tiles is clearly distinguishable from that of the relief tiles. This is unlikely to be simply a result of the two-colour tiles being made from a better-prepared clay since this difference is present in the frequency of most of the elements measured (See Appendix 6 & Fig. 47). In comparison with the relief tiles the design cutting on the two-colour tiles is poor—

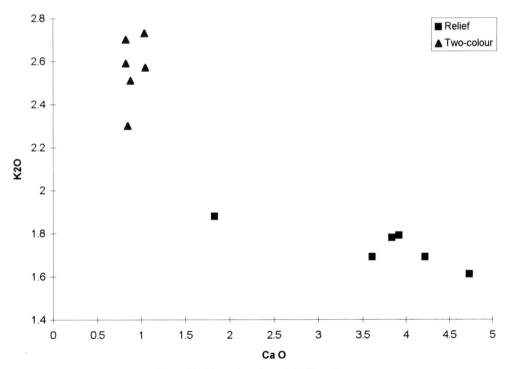

Fig. 47. Plot taken from ICPS analyses

curves appear to have been cut without the use of compasses and there is no consistency in the appearance of letters in the inscriptions.

Heraldic tiles

The heraldic tiles from Abbey Dore were made using at least seventeen separate dies. As with other coats of arms used on tiles there is always a difficulty in identifying the arms with any certainty since the tilers could not use the correct colours, being limited to 'white' clay (ie appearing yellow or light brown under the lead glaze) and 'red' clay (varying from deep reds through browns to greys, depending on firing conditions. The Dore Abbey tiles seem to be consistently oxidized and well fired, having a brick red colour. Bearing these difficulties in mind, Tony Wilmott has taken the Dore Abbey heraldic tiles and compared the arms present with those found in a number of dated rolls of arms. He concludes that the Dore Abbey tiles are likely to form a mid-thirteenth century collection, since they include the arms of Leon and Castile, which must date later than 1254, and the arms of a Walter de Clifford II, who died in 1261[2]. Furthermore, a number of arms found in later-thirteenth century and early-fourteenth century rolls of arms are absent. These missing arms are present in other southern Marches collections, such as Ludlow, Hereford, Bredon, Tewkesbury and Gloucester.

However, with the exception of Bredon all of these collections have had the fabric of their tiles examined and all belong to the Hereford A9 fabric group described above. Bredon, considering its similarity in the range of designs to the others, is likely to be the same. Thus, Dore Abbey again appears to stand alone.

Other single patterns

No non-heraldic two-colour tiles are present in the relaid patches of floor tiles but the majority of the loose tiles are of this type, being roughly equally divided between tiles which have designs which can be used singly (although they would in the main probably have been used in groups of four) and those which only make sense in groups of four, mainly employing a quarter circle as a major element of their design.

The single designs include one with a circular band containing the inscription *Martin me fecit* in Lombardic script and an angel with trumpet in the centre (Fig. 48). One of the tilers involved in the manufacture of these tiles was therefore presumably called 'Martin.' This design is specifically mentioned by Roland Paul as being amongst the tiles he found. The other single designs of note consist of a quatrefoil containing a winged, horned beast with cloven hoofs (Fig. 49) and a lion's head (Fig. 50).

Fig. 48. Tile including Martin me fecit

Fig. 49. Tile with winged and horned beast

80

Four-tile patterns

The four-tile designs appear in the main to have a circular band of Lombardic script with a floral motif in the outside corner and another motif in the centre. Only one central motif is identifiable, a lion's head (Fig 51). Some of the inscription bands have narrower bands to either side whilst others are plain. The bands on some of the tiles with narrow additional bands have a very large diameter, suggesting that they either occurred on tiles with a large quarry size or were designed to fit together as groups of nine or sixteen tiles (Figs. 52-60). The script on these tiles is cut in reverse, which may be an indication that the die cutters were illiterate. Fragments of similar tiles were found at Berrington Street, Hereford[3].

Dating

Since Ward-Perkins wrote his survey of relief-decorated floor tiles it has been shown that there is a long history of the use of this type of tile from the late-tenth or eleventh century (at Winchester Old Minster), through the later-eleventh/early-twelfth century and into the twelfth century (at St. Alban's Abbey Chapter House, for example). There is therefore no need to be cautious, as Ward-Perkins clearly felt he had to be, when dating the earliest medieval relief-decorated floor tiles. One might see in the Abbey Dore lozenge design a development from the Romanesque patterns found on the St. Alban's tiles. There seems little doubt that the Abbey Dore tiles belong to a late-twelfth to early-thirteenth century milieu and it is interesting to note that the Kilpeck roof tiles, described above, have similarly been dated to this period.

The two-colour tiles are clearly later. Wilmott's dating of the arms used on the heraldic tiles clearly gives a date range of 1254 to c.1261 for the cutting of the dies. The non-heraldic tiles have close parallels with the

Fig 50. Tile with traces of a lion's head

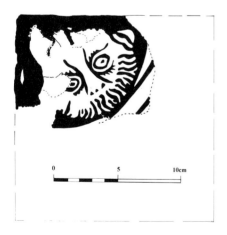

Fig. 51. Part of four-tile design with a lion's head

Fig. 52. Four-tile design in reverse script

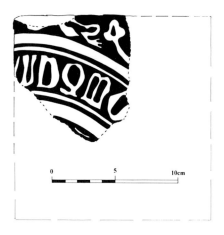

Fig. 53. Part of a four-tile pattern

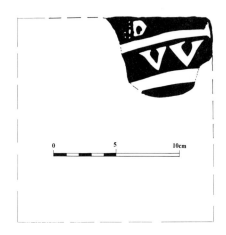

Fig. 55. Fragment of a four-centre pattern

Fig. 54. Part of a four-tile pattern

Fig. 56. Fragment of a four-centre pattern

Chertsey-Halesowen tile series. For example, the four-tile patterns with Lombardic inscriptions are paralleled at Halesowen (see the Halesowen tile from Coventry, published by Chatwin[4]). The lion's head on the Abbey Dore tiles is set within an arc which when repeated on four tiles produces a quatrefoil. The same feature is found on Chertsey-Halesowen tiles[5]. The grotesque beast found at Abbey Dore inside a quatrefoil is paralleled in the Chertsey-Halesowen school by the grotesque figures found at Kenilworth Abbey[6]. The Halesowen pavements can be dated

to the late-thirteenth century on the basis of one of the inscribed tiles, which includes a dedication by abbot Nicholas, who died in 1298. The Abbey Dore tiles are clearly not the work of a craftsman from the Chertsey-Halesowen school. Their design cutting is poor and the characteristics of the tiles themselves are quite different. For example, the Chertsey-Halesowen tiles are much thicker, sometimes reaching 30mm, whilst the Abbey Dore examples are between 20 and 25mm thick. The Abbey Dore tiles are also more heavily bevelled than the Chertsey-Halesowen

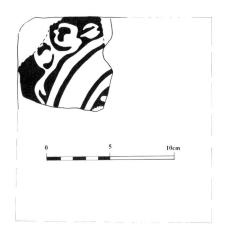

Fig. 57. Fragment of a four-centre pattern

Fig. 59. Fragment of four-centre pattern

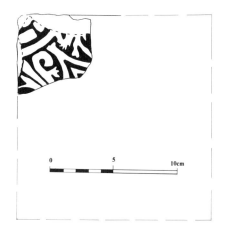

Fig. 58. Fragment of a four-centre pattern

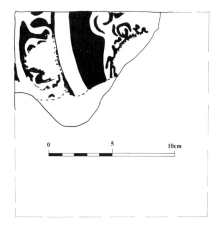

Fig. 60. Fragment of a four-centre pattern

tiles. We must therefore imagine that the Abbey Dore die cutter, possibly the Martin mentioned earlier, had seen a pavement of the Chertsey-Halesowen school, probably somewhere in the west Midlands rather than at Chertsey itself. There is no reason why this should not have taken place in the later years of the thirteenth century, exactly how late depends on the earliest dating possible for the start of the west Midlands activities of the school. The school was evidently still active in the 1330s, since Chertsey-Halesowen tiles were found at Maxstoke Priory,

founded in 1336[7]. Given the much poorer quality of the execution of the Abbey Dore designs it is highly unlikely that the relationship can be reversed. As for the heraldic tiles, it seems that those at Abbey Dore are earlier, and quite possibly ancestral to, the other heraldic tile pavements of the southern Marches.

Source

There is no reason to doubt that both groups of tiles were made somewhere in the southern Marches, using the widely-available Devonian marl. Both the petrological analysis and ICPS results show that the two groups of tiles were made using different sources of clay but in the absence of comparable studies of other locally-made ceramics of known provenance there is no means of localising the source more closely.

Importance

The relief decorated tiles are highly unusual and are perhaps to be seen as the latest of a tradition of Romanesque relief-decorated floor tiles in which the overall pattern of the pavement was paramount. Later tiles seem to use their designs in a more self-contained manner. The carpet nature of the Abbey Dore tiles can be illustrated by looking at the corners of the tiles, where the border is clearly meant to be seen as a lattice covering the entire floor. Ward-Perkins notes the similarity of the lozenge pattern to some from Switzerland, and it is entirely possible that the Abbey Dore pavement (and perhaps the Kilpeck church roof?) were products of craftsmen from the continent.

The later, two-colour tiles are more common, although Abbey Dore would still rank amongst the first of the religious houses in the Marches to have such tiles. As noted above, the heraldic tiles seem to have been created for Abbey Dore without benefit of a local prototype. In terms of its early use of floor tiles, the abbey can be compared with those at Halesowen, Evesham, Kenilworth, and Hailes, and St. Bartholomew's Hospital at Gloucester, all sites to the east of the Severn. In the Marches and Wales itself there are fewer sites with floor tiles of such an early date—Tintern Abbey and Goodrich Castle are the closest. In both the latter cases the thirteenth century tiles were imported to the site from tileries to the east of the Severn.

Clearly, then, the floor tiles from Abbey Dore suggest that in its early years the abbey could afford to employ innovative craftsmen at the forefront of their craft and was one of the earliest houses in the Marches to use such materials. To set alongside this distinction, however, there is the poor quality of the die-cutting as compared with the Chertsey-Halesowen prototypes and the use of the reversed script.

Conclusions

The Abbey Dore floor tiles are at present unique. The relief decorated tiles appear to be of early-thirteenth century date and perhaps the product of an immigrant craftsman from Switzerland. The two-colour tiles are perhaps a generation or two later and appear to be the earliest two-colour tiles to have been made in the southern Marches. It is likely that we have the name, Martin, of the die-cutter for these tiles and it is also likely that this die-cutter used a Chertsey-Halesowen school pavement as the prototype for the non-heraldic tiles whilst devising the heraldic tile series himself. The Abbey Dore two-colour tiles are the prototype for a widely-distributed series of heraldic and sub-Chertsey-Halesowen tiles, perhaps produced in Hereford, in the early-fourteenth century. The style and quality of these Hereford-made tiles is very similar to those at Abbey Dore and it is not outside the bounds of possibility that the die-cutter moved on to Hereford, having completed his commission for Abbey Dore. Certainly, there are some dies used at Abbey Dore which in the early-fourteenth century were in use at the later tilery.

CHAPTER VIII

People in the Abbey

by Ruth Richardson

Dore Abbey was designed, built, paid for and used, by people for the glory of God. Many involved may indeed have acted from deep religious motives. However, it is also true that to the workmen, whether clerical or lay, regular work meant regularly assured meals, while the patrons may have viewed such a use of their wealth as a form of religious insurance policy. Locally, feelings about the abbey may have always been mixed—a haven in time of trouble or an oppressor causing more trouble, depending on the period and the personnel involved. The monks had a tradition of hospitality and the poor could expect help, but the abbey was also a feudal landlord.

Medieval churches were colourful and the present building would appear unfinished to its original users. Church walls were covered by lime wash[1] at the Reformation and the fact that any traces of mediaeval decoration survive at all in the abbey does suggest a degree of weatherproofing between the 1537 Dissolution and the 1630s Restoration. A roofless shell would not have needed lime wash to cover its walls. More colour would have survived but for the nineteenth century fashion of scraping away the lime wash and plaster to reveal the stone—the marks of this work can be clearly seen in the ambulatory:

'The walls, columns, and vaulting ribs of the aisles and chapels, and the greater part of both transepts are entirely covered with whitewash. In the case of the ambulatory and transept walls the whitewash conceals paintings and fresco, some of medieval, others of Scudamore's date. The whitewash should be carefully removed so as to expose any colour decoration, and to show the ashlar work of the walls and columns and vault ribs which were never intended to be so covered.'[2]

Unfortunately, little coloured decoration survived this work. Only the seventeenth and early eighteenth century texts, and the skeleton, appear to be in their original form, while 'restoration' was carried out on the other paintings.[3]

Medieval decoration was not static and paintings were frequently changed in parish churches. However, the Cistercians were an austere order, initially favouring painted lines to resemble masonry, though with time, and not always approved by the General Chapter, becoming more ornate. Roland Paul found that: '... many of the caps and shafts at the east end retain considerable traces of colour ... Much colour remains on the caps and columns of this eastern ambulatory, the shafts appear to have been treated with a scheme of zigzag in red, yellow, and white, and several of the caps have had somewhat flat carving brought into greater relief by coloured backgrounds of red and green ... A portion of a shrine[4] ... with considerable traces of gold and colour came to light ...'[5]

Therefore, the ordinary monk and worshipper would have found the abbey a riot of colour and

Fig. 61. Traces of lettering on the pillar in the south aisle

used or noted down instructions for their workmen. Before the keeping of parish registers the local priest sometimes used this method of recording genealogical information or the arrival of disasters, be they floods, tempests or plague, to his village.

The examples of graffiti so far discovered at Dore are all on the plaster of the pillars in the south aisle. They are faint and difficult to see unless the light strikes them at the right angle, so it is possible that there are others still awaiting discovery. It is likely that there would have been more, but most of the pillars in the abbey have been stripped of their plaster in the course of cleaning and restoration and it is only by chance that anything has survived.

On the pillar to the east of the effigy are traces of lettering, including an ornate T (Fig. 61), and part of three roughly drawn coats of arms. Too little remains of the arms for them to be definitely identified, but one shows a chevron, borne by many notable families, including Fitzwalter and de Clare. Another has three wheels or stars above a band of lozenges which, again, bears a partial resemblance to the arms of both Clifford and Ewyas. Some idea of the date of the writing, at least, may be gained from the fact that it is incised on top of the horizontal red lines of painted decoration.

It is tempting to think that the arms were drawn there as a guide for larger paintings or carvings, perhaps to commemorate noble benefactors to the abbey, but they may equally well have been scratched there by some early visitor, a reminder of a time when a man's coat of arms and pedigree were as well known as his signature.

More graffiti appear on the pillar to the west of the effigy, but here again the restorers have been busy and only a few fragments survive. These are all in different hands, possibly fifteenth century and are incised in a small area at varying heights between 1.5 and 2.5 metres

not the tranquil grey it is today. Of the three doors into the present church—that to the sacristy is the oldest, while the oak door in the north aisle with thirteenth century ironwork of scrolls, foliage and wolf's head led to the abbot's lodging—Sledmere suggested that the south door was added to allow lay people access to the chapels.[6] It is more likely, as Malcolm Thurlby has shown, that an existing door was utilised for this purpose and this could also explain the graffiti, which are on the nearby pillars.

Graffiti (by Sue Hubbard)

The existence of graffiti, the scratching of words or pictures onto the stone or plasterwork of a church, is a widespread phenomenon but one which frequently goes unrecorded, as has been the case at Dore Abbey until now.

Often written in Latin, and dating from the twelfth to the sixteenth centuries, graffiti may appear on walls, windowsills, doorways or any other convenient flat surface, but the most favoured place seems to have been the pillars of the nave. Their content is equally varied: the pious inscribed biblical verses, the love-sick wrote admiring comments about their girl friends, and builders kept accounts of materials

Plate 1. The south-eastern corner of the Presbytery with the altar, communion rails and pulpit.

Plate 2. The East Window

Plate 3. The Royal Arms of Queen Anne on the north wall of the north transept

above the ground. They include another ornate capital T, something which looks like 'voster' or 'wister' and a possible word ending in 'mynach'. These remains are too slight to be reconstructed, but their position one below the other and the variety of handwriting could point to a list of names or messages such as might be inscribed by visitors near a shrine or image in the abbey.

Sue Hubbard's examination of the graffiti has led to a further examination of the site. The area opposite the southern effigy has what was probably a piscina, though any drainage hole has gone. In the centre, under the window, is the only surviving socket base in the abbey. It is a small square stone with a shallow depression in its centre. A chantry chapel often had a processional cross fixed in a socket behind the altar. These several pieces of evidence do suggest such a chapel opposite the present position of the southern effigy.

Inscribed Stones
Although many hundreds of people were involved with the Abbey when it was in use, only four names survive carved on stone. One is a small burial while the other three are semi-octagonal stones. The inscriptions are in early Norman Latin, the writing being lombardic capitals, and would originally have been painted. The T is very similar to that shown on the graffiti:

ROBERT ∶ VICA / RI ∶ DE WRMBRE / GGE

'ME' FEC·IT

(Robert Vicar of Wormbridge made me)

This inscription is beautifully cut, having the smallest lettering of 4 cm. depth. The letters are evenly positioned on three sides of the stone, and it is enclosed by two lines with a suggestion of a further line top and bottom. The diameter is c.77cm., depth 12cm., and each written face 32 cm. with c.8cm. remaining of two other sides. The long side is bevelled as if to fit in another stone. It is eroded and some of the letters are now flaking. It was obviously part of a larger

structure and it is suggested that it was probably a pillar base marking rebuilding or repair work.

It is ironic that the many monks who led blameless lives in peaceful times are rarely recorded. It is only when there were disputes that names appear, usually in legal documents. Robert of Wormbridge was sub-prior of the abbey in 1266. He was summoned to appear in London with Abbot Henry, in a legal dispute with the Knights Hospitallers of Saint John of Jerusalem. Cistercian monks were exempt from being made to travel more than two days from their monasteries and Robert was given protection against a similar summons by the Abbot of Llantarnam.[7] As Cistercian monks were often skilled craftsmen it is very possible that Robert carved this himself and was not just the donor.

'+ H / UGO OLIM D / ECCAN DE / WEBBELE' M / E
FE

(Hugo formerly dean of Weobley made me)

This inscription is cut in half horizontally and follows three sides of the two stones with the additional overlap of the +H and the final E. The diameter is 78 cm., the depth of bottom stone 12cm. and the top stone 8cm. In the centre of the long side which forms the rear of the stone is a shaft measuring 9cm. across and cut about 5 cm. into the stone. It may be original or could be connected with the stone's re-use. The FE had to be carved separately below the W, leading Roland Paul to suggest that the inscription was unfinished. It does not have the enclosing lines that the other inscriptions show but the lettering, of 5cm. depth, is as fine. These inscribed stones are the best preserved of the examples, with clean lines, but there is considerable flaking of the corner with M D, and the W does not seem to be as deeply incised as the other letters.

Paul found the stones 'upside down' being used as the font step, 'a simple octagon ... perhaps made up from other worked stones', which he suggested 'was either introduced by Scudamore, or brought by him from the old parish church of Dore, which had fallen into decay'.[8]

Paul further suggested that the stone, which he moved, 'may perhaps have been a portion of a churchyard cross, of which there is more than one in the neighbourhood.' The abbey had at least one churchyard cross. Robert, elder son of the Robert of Ewyas who founded the abbey, was said to have been 'slayne at the stony crosse beside the Abbey of Door. And many others with him and lieth in the Abbey of Door in the middle of the Quyre,'[9] an event dated to 1196[10]. This cross appears to have been outside the abbey. However, the clarity of the lettering does indicate that the stone was protected from weathering by being inside the abbey so it is unlikely to have been a feature of this cross.

In 1267 the abbey is recorded as sending $2\frac{1}{2}$ marks of silver to the dean of Weobley who was collector of a clerical tenth for the king, two monks delivering the money.[11] In addition, in Weobley Church, there is a thirteenth century coffin-lid carved with a very beautiful foliated cross that commemorates Hugo Bissop of Norton Canon.[12] It cannot be demonstrated that these are connected to the same person, but each shows a man of influence. It is certainly possible that Hugo, dean of Weobley, is the Hugo Bissop buried in Weobley church. Hugo may have been the carver or the donor of the stone at Dore.

ROBERT / WROETH / ME : FEC

(Robert Wroth made me)

This is cut on three sides and is the only stone where the words are proportional to the sides. It has the largest letters with a depth of 6cm. and there are lines above and below the words. It has a diameter of 71cm., depth of 11cm. with each written face c.31cm., though the right side appears broken with the possibility of another letter(s), perhaps IT for FECIT. The two further sides now measure c.12cm. and c.17cm. on the broken side. The long side is uneven and bevelled as if to fit another stone and it is obvious this was part of a larger structure. Flaking is occurring on one corner. It has been suggested this stone was a pillar base in the north transept.[13]

Robert Wroth was abbot from 1347 to 1362, following Richard Straddell. There was also a Robert Wroth at Ewyas Lacy (Longtown) in 1286, so he was from an old local family. Indeed, Sledmere quotes 'Llyfr Baglan' as stating that a Sir Robert Wroth, knight, actually built much of the abbey[14], although whether this refers to the initial building, repairs or extensions is not known. The inscriptions on the stones cannot be precisely dated so, again, it is not possible to identify the abbot with this stone with any degree of certainty. It is quite possible that Robert Wroth was the carver, while a donor of that name could have been another member of his family.

One problem with all these stones is what they represent. The stones are small for pillar bases and it is not likely that anyone would commemorate just the making of a pillar. They could record carrying out repairs, in which case the person named would have been the organiser on behalf of the abbey. However, to go to the trouble of carving a name would seem to indicate that one, or all, of the stones could be those for statue bases. It may also be important that each inscription is on one half of the stone, indicating a 'front' and 'back' for viewing purposes. Certainly the quality of the lettering suggests something special and, while other non-funerary inscriptions are known, they are not common. It is also apparent that those named must have been pleased with the results as the stones continued to be seen in the abbey, showing no signs of alteration or mutilation.

Fig. 62. The heart burial stone

The diminutive effigy of a bishop in eucharistic vestments lying with his head on a cushion probably commemorates a heart burial. It is *c*.39cm. long, by 25cm. at the head but tapering to 23.5cm. at the bottom. There is a slight possibility that the slab, which would have been painted, was originally longer; the figure is complete but there are no upper or lower borders (Fig. 62). The inscription is along the two sides and again is in Latin, the lettering, of 2cm. depth, being in lombardic capitals:

> (SER) VA ⁞ PONTIFICIS ⁞ COR . . .
> on the right side
> (S)A(NCTUM) ⁞ XPISTE ⁞ IOH (ANNIS) . . .
> on the left side
> (O Christ, preserve the holy heart of
> Pontiff John)[15]

The thirteenth century marked a period of change in ecclesiastical vestments, which were established but generally not embellished. The figure is shown wearing an alb, or under tunic, which can be seen just above his shoes. Albs usually had apparels, that is embroidery at the wrists and as panels at the front and back hems, but this cannot be determined here due to the deterioration of the stone. It is possible that his left hand is concealed by his long sleeve, considered an act of humility.[16] The stand-up collar at the neck is an embroidered amice, or scarf, to absorb sweat and to prevent chafing of the neck by other garments. The elevation of the host was formally recognised in 1210[17] and this posed the problem of how the celebrant could raise his arms. One solution was the very full, circular, chasuble shown here. Originally of fine wool, silk became popular but chasubles were not ornamented until the fourteenth century; there is no suggestion of even a vertical front seam here. He also wears a mitre which by the thirteenth century had three forms, though a tall form was also beginning to develop, and had changed to a sideways dent from the front-to-back dent that was common in the twelfth century. This one seems to be the simple, short, form suggesting, a date in the thirteenth century.[18] His head is on a cushion and he has a very defaced crosier, apparently held by his left hand. He is defaced. The effigy was formerly in the large recess, or aumbry, in the north aisle of the ambulatory.

Two heart burials are recorded in the abbey, Bishop John's and Margaret, possibly a member of the Clifford family. Margaret's was the earlier, in 1260, and she also gave 15 marks for expenses.[19] Roland Paul found an uninscribed leaden heart case in the centre of the presbytery. In a period when relics of saints were highly prized, heart burials would not have seemed strange.[20] Though there is no documentary evidence for Bishop John's, the figure suggests the thirteenth century. The only candidate in that date range is John de Breton, Bishop of Hereford 1269 to 1275.

Bishop John de Breton may have come from Dore as he granted permission in 1270 for his parents, John le Bretun and Margaret, to be buried in the abbey. The bishop had been a canon of Hereford Cathedral. He was a Doctor of Laws and Keeper of the King's Wardrobe.

The previous bishop of Hereford had been Peter de Aquablanca whose body was buried in a splendid shrine in Hereford while his heart was sent to his native Savoy. He had been extremely unpopular, placing clerics from Savoy in all the best posts and, despite being an astute financier and a builder of the cathedral, was at one time taken prisoner in the cathedral itself by Sir Roger de Clifford, whose effigy is probably one of the knights in Dore.

John de Breton had thoroughly resented clerical posts being given by the previous bishop to his relatives and friends. When he was elevated to bishop in 1269 he deprived several of them of these preferments giving them to others including Thomas Cantilupe, who became the next bishop (later canonised as Saint Thomas Cantilupe) in 1275. Peter de Aquablanca's numerous relatives took Bishop John de Breton to the papal courts and are recorded as physically fighting to retain their official seats in the choir stalls.[21] Perhaps it is not surprising that Bishop John, while his body was buried in his cathedral, chose to have his heart buried near his parents at Dore!

People on the Bosses

The bosses are beautifully sculpted, would have been vividly painted and probably date from the late thirteenth to early fourteenth century rebuild.[22] Traces of plaster remain on some stones. They were projections of stone placed to cover the intersections of the vault ribs—here probably from the nave or presbytery. Eight bosses are known. It appears, on stylistic grounds, that they were designed by one sculptor and close examination shows that the same figures are repeated on the different bosses. There are two groups, the first including:

Christ in Majesty with surrounding foliage

With right hand raised to bless, Christ's left hand rests on an orb, a symbol of majesty and kingship originating in the Byzantine Empire. He wears a semi-circular cloak suspended from the shoulders, which is brought round over his knees, and is barefooted. He is bearded, with wavy hair which shows the place for a crown to be painted. He is surrounded by naturalistic foliage of oak leaves and acorns, though only one side is intact (Fig. 63).

Known as a 'Majesty' such depictions of the ascended Christ—another is at Rowlestone church—are frequent in the thirteenth and early fourteenth centuries.[23] The treatment of the foliage, which is the same on all the bosses, is also typical of about 1300.[24] This boss was treated with particular reverence. As with all the bosses it must have been deliberately saved after the Dissolution, otherwise it would have broken on crashing to the floor. It was then kept safe, or buried, until in about 1633 it was placed in a prominent position in the new west wall.

Roland Paul noticed 'traces of carved work ... at the back of the gallery.' It was found when the plaster was removed. 'From its having been hidden by the gallery and from its position having been exactly central with the lancet window above it, it was evidently placed there to form a central ornament.'[25] It must have been a focal point, viewed from the chancel through the screen, for the new Laudian design.[26] However, Archbishop Laud was executed in 1645 and puritan views then dominated. A 'Majesty' would have been defaced. It must be that someone saved it a second time by plastering it over; possibly it was even forgotten about when, in the early eighteenth century, the gallery was built in front of it.

The Coronation of the Virgin with Christ and surrounding foliage

The Virgin wears a gown—by the thirteenth century called a cote—full skirted, with tight sleeves and a wide girdle at the waist that hangs down centre front (Fig. 64). Over it she wears a

Fig. 63. Christ in Majesty

Fig. 64. Coronation of the Virgin

semi-circular mantle, which should be fastened across the shoulders, and which is brought round to cover her knees; traces of blue paint can be seen. Her hands are in an attitude of prayer. Usually, a veil was worn, kept in place by a linen band, only young girls wearing their hair loose. This figure is already stylised; her virginity shown by wearing a band, or a diadem, on loose, wavy, hair and clothes that, with a waist girdle and no surcote, date from about 1200.[27] Christ, in a loose, belted, long-sleeved tunic and cloak, is bearded, has a diadem, or crown, on wavy hair and holds an orb. The four ribs can be seen on this boss. Also carefully saved at the Dissolution, this was preserved by being built into the face of the reputed tomb of Robert of Ewyas in the eastern chapel. It is not clear if it was hidden or visible. It was removed by Paul when he re-sited the effigy.[28]

An abbot, almost certainly the benefactor responsible for the vaulting, kneeling before the Virgin and Child with surrounding foliage

Two of the bosses show an abbot. Here he wears the white Cistercian habit of undyed wool with a black scapula, or shoulder apron; the hood of the scapula can be clearly seen. There is no belt. He holds his crosier and is tonsured. The Virgin is dressed as above, while the Child, standing on her knee, is wearing a long loose tunic, still with traces of red paint, and with tight sleeves. She holds him with her left hand while her right hand holds the Child's right hand. The Child's left hand appears to hold a small orb. This is so beautifully carved that it is a pity the Child is defaced (Plate. 6).

All Cistercian churches were dedicated to the Virgin, which is why a lady chapel was not required. It is very probable that the abbot is the famous Richard Straddell, abbot possibly from 1305, certainly from 1312, to 1346. He was a noted theologian, poet, and diplomat for Edward II and Edward III, his fame lasting for more than two hundred years.[29] He was probably abbot when the refurbishment took place, paid for by the wealth from wool. This was the other boss that was preserved by being built into a tomb then in the eastern chapel, reputedly that of Roger de Clifford. Again it is unclear if it was

visible or not but it was removed by Paul when he re-sited the tomb.[30]

A monk, on the left, kneeling before a standing abbot who raises his right hand in blessing

This is the second boss to depict an abbot. He wears similar eucharistic robes to Bishop John de Breton, of alb, amice, full chasuble and here the sleeves are more clearly seen. Some abbots were mitred but mitres were not worn on the back of the head, and this figure has his hair showing— he is bareheaded with tonsure. The monk, who clasps his hands in prayer, is clearly wearing a Cistercian habit. The foliage has been cut away and with it the abbot's hands. The folds of the robes are beautifully sculpted.

The abbot is once again very probably Richard Straddell. The suggestion has been made, for instance in Sledmere, that the figure is a bishop; it appears that both bosses show the same figure. Bishop, later Saint, Thomas Cantilupe, who probably consecrated the abbey in c.1282, would be the best episcopal candidate for such commemoration. No certainty can be achieved and probability determined only by architectural date and style of vestments, which are eucharistic. The depiction of either Straddell or Cantilupe would have been a sufficient reason for preservation.

In the nineteenth century it was found in the Dulas Brook at Ewyas Harold[31] and kept in Ewyas Harold church before being restored to the abbey.

A monk praying to Saint Katherine with her emblems of a sword and wheel with surrounding foliage

The medieval church depicted saints with recognisable emblems, based on their lives or manner of their deaths, to allow easy identification.[32] The monk with hands clasped is dressed in Cistercian habit. Saint Katherine of Alexandria is standing, holding her emblems and carved in a very similar manner to the Virgin, though when painted her clothes would have looked different. The boss shows the four ribs. This boss was buried in the rubble of the nave and was only found recently when a grave was dug (Fig. 65).

Fig. 65. Monk praying to St Katherine

Fig. 66. The young head

Fig. 67. The old head—the 'green man'

Each member of the second group of bosses joined two ribs. They form a set of three and each show a single head and have the same dimensions.

In the first one the face is young, rounded with a pointed chin and wavy hair (Fig. 66). In the second it is older and bearded, lines furrow his forehead and his cheeks are slightly sunken. It is presently set in the boundary wall south-east of the church. In the third the face is sunk in foliage of large oak leaves that replace his hair and beard—perhaps he had died. It is the image of a 'green man', and retains a covering of what appears to be yellow ochre and is a recent discovery in the churchyard (Fig. 67).

These three bosses are very striking and, although it could never be demonstrated, do seem to show the same person. If this is true then perhaps we are looking at one of the workmen, or even the master sculptor himself.

The Knights' Effigies
Two stone effigies remain, though not in their original positions, having been re-sited in the ambulatory by Roland Paul. He found the tombs already changed by having two bosses built into them. 'During the excavations a fragment of considerable size was found, still retaining considerable traces of bright blue colouring on the surcoat, which may possibly have been treated heraldically.'[33] Paul found them in the eastern chapels. If these had been their original sites, then the chapels may have been their chantries as well.

They depict medieval knights, which tradition has assigned to Robert of Ewyas (the northern effigy) and Roger de Clifford (the southern effigy). Both are on raised slabs and positioned with crossed legs. Originally they would have been brightly painted, even gilded, and their identities easily recognised by heraldic coats-of-arms on both the surcoats and the shields. Medieval sculptors were paid less than the painters[34] and as neither shield has a device etched on to it the painting would have been crucial.

A.C. Fryer considers them effigies made under the influence of the Bristol craftsmen. While executed locally, using local stone, the

Fig. 68. Effigy in north ambulatory

sculptors and painters probably travelled to the site from Bristol. One characteristic of these workshops was to carve the mail on the arms of the hauberk, from shoulder to wrist, in parallel lines[35], and this occurs on the northern effigy. The later deeper outline of drapery[36] is particularly marked on the very fine, realistically posed, southern effigy.

Now sited in the northern ambulatory: 'Unknown knight; ... Effigy (6ft. 5ins. present length). In suit of mail ($^1/_2$in.), flat-topped coif, hauberk with mail in parallel rows from shoulders to wrists, mail gloves, hose, sleeveless surcoat to calves, sword-belt ($1^3/_4$in.) with 16in. of strap beyond buckle, sword (scabbard, present length, 2ft. 3in., hilt with straight quillons, 7in.), kite-shaped shield on left arm (2ft. 10in. by 1ft.

4in.), right hand on hilt of sword and left on scabbard, head on one cushion set diagonally (1 ft. 2in. by 1 ft. 2in. by $2^3/_4$in.). Effigy much worn and mutilated, but was originally a fine figure and made from block of light-coloured calcareous sandstone. Date 1240-1250.' (Fig. 68)[37]

The date has been thought too early and 1250-1270 has been suggested.[38] The mail running in lines down the arms is very clear on shoulders and wrists, and quite different from the other effigy. Traces of blue colouring noticed by Paul are still visible. The legs are broken below the knee though the fragments are adjacent.

Now sited in the southern ambulatory: 'Unknown knight; attributed to Roger de Clifford. Effigy (6ft. 2in. present length). In suit of mail ($^5/_8$in.), round-topped coif with fillet,

Fig. 69. Effigy in south ambulatory

hauberk with lace at wrists and mail gloves, having divided fingers, hose, sleeveless surcoat to calves, cingulum ($1/2$in.) hanging 9in. beyond buckle, sword-belt (2in.) loose and wrapped round scabbard with 11 in. beyond buckle, sword (1ft. of scabbard remains, hilt, 9 in., circular pommel and quillons lost), kite-shaped shield (2ft. 4in. present length by 2ft.), guige ($2^{1}/4$in.), right hand on hilt of sword and left under shield on breast. A fine figure, sadly mutilated, head severed from body, made from block of old red sandstone. Date c. 1280.'[39] (Fig. 69) He is drawing his sword. In 1985 the head was stolen and a replica is in its position.[40] The effigy may have been inspired by the earlier tomb of John of Monmouth formerly in the priory church at Monmouth but which was destroyed during a restoration of the church carried out in 1737.[41]

The question of portraiture is difficult to determine. It certainly appears that some of the Bristol craftsmen produced effigies that are so individual that portraits would seem very plausible.[42] However, others appear stylised, although defacement adds to the problem. Again, painting would have been important in giving any personal appearance especially to a fully mailed knight. There are instances of effigies being made long after death but these are usually of someone regarded as a saint.[43] Most effigies were produced wearing the clothes prevalent at the time of the person's death. Indeed, a stone effigy may perhaps copy the wood figure sometimes carried at a funeral. As a result, effigies can be dated, albeit approximately. At Dore the northern effigy is likely to be the older, dating about 1250, while the southern effigy is dated to about 1280. They are superb works of art from sculptors well-known in their day and, therefore, were commissioned by wealthy patrons, whose surviving relatives would have expected to approve the work. The absence of inscriptions means that the identities are unknown but, given the dates and the quality, suggestions can be made.

The two names associated with the effigies may help provide the actual identication as they have been preserved by tradition. Unfortunately, medieval families had the habit of using very few given names and the same Christian name can appear in each generation. Indeed, in these cases there are at least five Roberts, Lords of Ewyas, and three Rogers de Clifford, as the family tree illustrates (Fig. 70).

The first Robert of Ewyas, son of Harold, was the founder of the abbey in 1147[44] and although he was buried in his new abbey the effigy dates from at least 100 years after his death. In 1195 Robert's grandaughter Sybil was married to Robert de Tregoz [Troisgots in the department of Manche] in Normandy. He was King Richard I's Bailiff in the Contentin Forest and he had a castle on the River Vire.[45] Her father, the second Robert of Ewyas is said to have been killed the following year, with others, by the stone cross beside the abbey and to be buried in the middle of the quire.[46] Again he is too early for the effigy.

Robert de Tregoz, married to an heiress, became lord of Ewyas and had the use of the great barony, though he may not even have visited it. He is known to have been still alive in 1212.[47] The date of his death is not known but he is possibly too early for the effigy and anyway is more likely to be buried in Normandy.

When Robert died, Sybil was once more an eligible marriage prospect. Any new husband would become lord of Ewyas—but only for his lifetime as she already had a small son, Robert, who would in due course have a claim on the barony. She may have married William of Newmarch, another Norman marcher lord, but this is uncertain.[48]

Sybil was perhaps more interested in the area than her first husband and is recorded as giving the abbey pasture for 200 sheep by the Dulas brook.[49] Indeed, most of her family were buried in the abbey and, unless she died in Normandy, it is likely she was too.

Then in 1214 Roger de Clifford of Tenbury, a younger son of Walter de Clifford, paid the enormous fine of £1,000 (more than £500,000 at today's value) to King John to marry her.[50] It shows the importance placed on the castle and barony of Ewyas Harold by the Cliffords, especially as this was only for Roger's lifetime. Roger became lord of Ewyas, becoming also

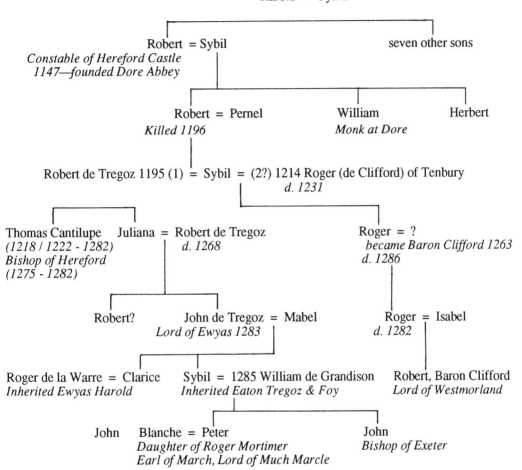

Ralph, Lord of Ewyas
possibly the same as Ralph (the Timid) Earl of Hereford, nephew of King Edward the Confessor

Harold = Gytha

Robert = Sybil
Constable of Hereford Castle 1147—founded Dore Abbey

seven other sons

Robert = Pernel
Killed 1196

William
Monk at Dore

Herbert

Robert de Tregoz 1195 (1) = Sybil = (2?) 1214 Roger (de Clifford) of Tenbury
d. 1231

Thomas Cantilupe
(1218 / 1222 - 1282)
Bishop of Hereford
(1275 - 1282)

Juliana = Robert de Tregoz
d. 1268

Roger = ?
became Baron Clifford 1263
d. 1286

Robert?

John de Tregoz = Mabel
Lord of Ewyas 1283

Roger = Isabel
d. 1282

Roger de la Warre = Clarice
Inherited Ewyas Harold

Sybil = 1285 William de Grandison
Inherited Eaton Tregoz & Foy

Robert, Baron Clifford
Lord of Westmorland

John

Blanche = Peter
Daughter of Roger Mortimer
Earl of March, Lord of Much Marcle

John
Bishop of Exeter

Fig. 70. Simplified family tree of the Lords of Ewyas[52]

Constable of St. Briavels' Castle and Warden of the Forest of Dean.[51] He died in 1231 and was buried in Dore Abbey, which is too early for the southern effigy attributed to a Clifford, and a little early for the northern effigy.

In 1236 Sybil's son by her first marriage, Robert de Tregoz, became lord of Ewyas presumably on his mother's death.[53] She was in her late 40s or early 50s. Robert married Juliana the sister of bishop, later Saint, Thomas Cantilupe of Hereford.[54] The Bishopric of

Hereford was a powerful position in the marches and Juliana was not only the bishop's favourite sister but she was also related to the de Montfort family.[55] This marriage was another alliance of marcher lords.

When witnesses were examined at the canonisation enquiry, there is a glimpse of Robert de Tregoz himself. On one occasion Robert, sitting at table with Thomas, was rebuked by the bishop 'for insulting a young woman by implying she was trying to attract the attention of men.'[56] Relationships with women were always a problem for medieval clerics. Thomas did not even allow his sisters to stay overnight and, although he had kissed Juliana before, when she visited him at his palace at Bosbury to congratulate him on becoming bishop, 'he held out his hand for her to kiss, thereby emphasising his episcopal authority rather than their kinship.'[57]

Robert died in 1268 as a grant made by 'Sir John de Tregoz, son and heir of Sir Robert de Tregoz deceased of Ewyas to Lady Juliana, late the wife of Robert' concerning two manors, Alington and Etone, in Wiltshire, confirms.'[58] He is a possibility for the northern effigy, which is dated to about this period. There is no way of telling the exact age of the person depicted by the effigy, especially as he wears chain mail.

There is a suggestion that Juliana and Robert also had a son called Robert[59] but it was their son John who was the last of the Tregoz name to hold Foy[60] and Ewyas Harold. He had two daughters, Clarice inheriting Ewyas Harold. His other daughter Sybil married William de Grandison and both were buried in the abbey.[61] So the younger Robert is yet another possible candidate for the effigy, though it is most likley to be his father.

Sybil's son Roger by her second husband, Roger de Clifford, may well have felt aggrieved that he could not inherit Ewyas from his mother, and his father seems to have left him more debts than land. He seems to have tried very hard to repair his fortunes and he was active in the politics and intrigues of the time. This was a very troubled time as King and barons manoeuvred for power. Roger's position only became more secure in 1263 when he succeeded to the barony of Clifford on the death of his uncle.

Roger de Clifford led a group of fully armed barons to Hereford cathedral where they seized Bishop Peter de Aquablanca, who was out of favour with King Henry III, and imprisoned him in Eardisley Castle for three months, making him watch the division of his goods.[62] Clifford had to do penance and pay 300 marks for this but when, in later years, he continued cattle-raiding and ill-

treating his tenants Bishop Thomas de Cantilupe forced him to walk bare-foot to the high altar of the cathedral, the bishop beating him with a rod.[63]

Roger had a number of financial dealings with Dore, as in 1263 when he bought oxen from the abbey. It was an eventful year as he also sent his men to seize corn from Holme Lacy manor, leased by the abbey, causing the furious abbot to have to travel to London to resolve the matter.[64] He later acknowledged the difficulties he caused the abbey in his will where he confirmed 'all the land which they have by gift of William of Ewyas, about which I have sometimes vexed them.'[65]

His enthusiastic support for the King in 1264-65, which included fighting for him at the battle of Evesham, certainly helped his fortunes.[66] It brought him land, the cancellation of his debt and a marriage for his son Roger to Isabel, co-heiress of the barony of Appleby, though in 1308 the Cliffords acquired the rest.[67] Roger's and Isabel's son, named Robert, was not only baron Clifford but also lord of Westmorland.[68]

Roger, Isabel's husband, died in 1282, before his father, and in his will of 1284 Roger de Clifford asked to be buried at Dore next to his son. The abbot was his executor and he was presumably buried, as requested, and 'with his body his war-horse trappings or thirty marks.'[69]

The southern effigy is dated c.1280 so it could be either Roger, the son who died in 1282, or Roger de Clifford himself who died in 1286. A grieving father could easily have commissioned a figure for the son's tomb. However, thirty marks was more than enough to pay for a priest to say regular prayers and to pay for an effigy and this effigy is more probably the father. Perhaps burial at Dore was his religious insurance policy, considering his earlier deeds which had angered both bishop and abbot.

These traces of the people who knew the abbey are few. Of the many who lived at Dore over the centuries, only a handful are represented in the abbey. They serve to remind us of the monks, the landowners, the workmen and the local people with no memorials.

CHAPTER IX

Cults, Patrons and Sepulture

by Joe Hillaby

More precious than the corporal remains of the saints were relics closely associated with the Holy Family. These emanated from the discovery of 'the saving wood of the Cross' during Constantine's reign. As the symbol of redemption the Cross was supreme but there were others: Prato claimed the Virgin's girdle; Perugia stole the Virgin's wedding ring from Chiusi; and Loretto received the Holy House, that is the house in which the Virgin Mary was believed to have lived at the time of the Annunciation, brought to the west not by travellers or Crusaders but by angels.

Two Cistercian houses in the British Isles could boast such relics. In Gloucestershire, Hailes Abbey was founded by Henry III's brother, Richard, Earl of Cornwall, for family burial. In 1270 Edmund, his second son, presented the abbot and convent with a phial containing a drop of the Holy Blood bought from the Count of Holland, with guarantees of authenticity from the Patriarch of Jerusalem and Pope Urban IV. This 'Blood of Hailes' was preserved within a beryl, similar to an emerald, adorned with chased silver and was displayed in a shrine in the elaborate polygonal apse behind the high altar.[1]

In Ireland the Cistercians of Holy Cross near Cashel had a fragment of the True Cross. The date of acquisition of this famous relic is in dispute. Some suggest it was the gift of Donald (Mor) O'Brien, King of Thomond, whose father had received it from Pascal III in 1110. Others insist it

was the gift of a Plantagenet queen. Whatever the case, the abbey was lavishly rebuilt in the fifteenth century from pilgrims' offerings. Hidden in the seventeenth century, two fragments are now on display: one with the Trappists of Mount Melleray; the other, returned by the Ursuline nuns of Blackrock, in the restored church.[2]

Dore was in the same category as Hailes and Holy Cross. Under the year 1321, during the long abbacy of Richard Straddell, the annals record that on '6 October, a Tuesday, the lord W (illiam) de Grauntsoun (Grandison) came to Dore bringing with him a fragment (*portionem*) of the wood of the Holy Cross adorned, very beautifully, with gold and precious stones. And in honour of the Holy Trinity, and in return for the grace and favour of the lord Straddel, abbot of the said house, he handed it over to the monastery on the morrow—his obligation ... being totally cancelled by the said abbot lord Richard.'[3] The relic, acquired more than 30 years after the completion of the rood screen, can explain the subsequent alteration of the west end of the nave, and the suggested enhancement of the screen itself by the addition of a feretory and gilding.

How could this precious relic have come into the hands of a Herefordshire knight? William was a Savoyard who came to England with his elder brother, Otto, the family claiming descent from the Holy Roman Emperors. The brothers were key figures in the conquest of Wales.[4] Otto, who has been described as Edward I's 'friend and counsellor' and 'greatest of all the Savoyards who served Edward', became Constable of Caernarfon and first justiciar of Wales. William was appointed constable of the newly-completed castle at Harlech and a deputy justiciar in 1287. Two years later William took his brother's place at Caernarfon when the latter was called abroad on the royal service.

Both were content with royal office rather than the acquisition of wide estates. Nevertheless the king's service did bring rewards. William was given the manor of Ashperton and Stretton where in 1292 he had licence to crenellate his dwelling. In 1285 he was granted the hand of Sybil, grandniece of St. Thomas Cantilupe and younger daughter and co-heiress of John de Tregoz of Lydiard Tregoz in Wiltshire, and Ewyas Harold, the last male heir of the family of Dore's founder. His eldest son, Peter, married Blanche, daughter of Roger Mortimer future Earl of March, and became lord of Much Marcle in addition to the lands inherited from his father. Another son, John, Bishop of Exeter (1327-69), author of the cathedral's remarkable west front, was one of the major artistic patrons of the age. Straddell thus linked the fortunes of his house to one of the rising families of the county.[5]

How could this treasure have been acquired by William Grandison? The answer is, apparently, in the same way as so many other relics, as a consequence of the Crusades. His brother, Otto, had accompanied Edward to the Holy Land in 1270. When a Muslim attacked Edward with a poisoned dagger Otto, not the queen, sucked the wound clean, according to the St. Bertin chronicler. Some 20 years later Otto served a second time in the Holy Land, leading the advance guard of Edward I's proposed second crusade. In May 1291 the Mamluks launched their final assault on Acre, the most important Crusader stronghold remaining. With the Templars, and the King of Cyprus who fled betimes, Otto commanded the defence. When Acre was overwhelmed he escaped in a Venetian vessel.[6]

By the thirteenth century Acre had become the largest city of the kingdom of Jerusalem. As lands were lost to Islam it became the home for a concentration of religious houses both monastic and regular. In 1187 the patriarch had to move here from Jerusalem and in 1262 took over the see of Acre. A number of the military orders were based here and by the late thirteenth century there were more than 60 churches. Contraction of Christian territory led to an accumulation of relics. As soon as the city's fate became evident all relics would have been removed, above all those of the cathedral church—itself dedicated to the Holy Cross. As Otto never married he left his English estates, with the lordship of the Channel Islands, to William's sons, Peter and Otto. His relic, or a fragment from it, apparently passed into the hands of his brother, William.[7]

The timing of Grandison's gift seemed opportune, for the diocese was in a fever over the translation of its own newly canonised saint, Thomas of Hereford, the bishop who had dedicated the completed church at Dore. Ever since his installation as bishop in 1282 Richard Swinfield, who had been Thomas Cantilupe's chaplain and secretary, had worked unremittingly for his predecessor's canonisation. Pilgrims flocked to his monument, the scene of many miracles, their offerings providing resources for an extensive building campaign. Large sums were spent in Rome to no avail. When Swinfield died in 1317 his life's ambition was unfulfilled. After almost forty years of negotiation it was the combination of Edward II's determination and money and the adept diplomacy of Swinfield's successor as bishop of Hereford, Adam de Orleton, which persuaded Pope John XXII to admit Cantilupe, the bishop who had apparently died excommunicate, to the roll of Holy Confessors in 1320. Once again, it was hoped, pilgrims would flock to Hereford with their offerings. Elaborate preparations were made for the saint's translation from the north transept to a splendid new shrine behind the high altar. The cathedral records for 1321 detail payments for marble and craftsmanship in electrum and silver. This was the year in which William de Grandison made his gift to the abbot and convent of Dore.[8]

The acquisition of the fragment of the Holy Cross provided the occasion for a major reconstruction of the nave at Dore but more general forces were at work altering the life of the abbey in other ways. Firstly there was a sharp decline in numbers of the lay brethren due to a combination of economic factors and acute problems with discipline, particularly drunkenness and violence. As a consequence in a number of Cistercian houses the choirs of the lay brethren were already silent and deserted. With their disappearance many Cistercian communities used the area to the west of the rood screen merely for processional purposes. In several Irish houses this space was left to decay or was even demolished.[9]

On the other hand there was an increasing willingness on the part of Cistercian abbots to promote lay sepulture within their churches. At Furness monumental effigies of two knights in flat-topped helmets of c.1250-60 were found in the presbytery and an early fourteenth century knight and his lady in the north aisle. At Roche, about 1300, the stalls of the conversi were removed to provide space for lay burial. A rhyming inscription on the tomb of Peryn and Ysabel of Doncaster shows that the laity was admitted to the confraternity of the abbey with 'a share in the prayers of the abbot and convent and in the merits accruing from their works of charity and piety'—in return for a suitable grant. One tomb was even enclosed by stone screens, thus forming its own considerable chantry chapel.[10]

The process can be traced in edicts of the Chapter General. In 1152 and 1180 it had ruled that only kings and queens, archbishops and bishops could be buried within the church. Even for the dukes of Burgundy, founders of Clairvaux, infringement of the edict was not permitted. On the other hand, after canonisation in 1178, Saint Bernard was placed in a marble sarcophagus behind the high altar. By the mid-thirteenth century burial in the cloister came to be accepted for important benefactors. According to Leland 'the Botears' had been buried in the chapter house. A Robert Boter was a benefactor of Canon Pyon church in the thirteenth century and the Boters held half a knight's fee in Wormsley in 1316 and 1332.[11] Paul's 1931 plan shows two coffin lids in the east

cloister walk, just outside the entrance to the chapter house vestibule. One of these, decorated with a foliated cross in relief and plain shield, is now with other fragments at the east end of the church. The privilege was eventually extended to burial within the church.

In England the lead was taken by the royal family. Richard I's first queen, Isabella, was buried at John's foundation, Beaulieu. Richard of Cornwall's second wife, Sancha of Provence, was buried at Hailes in 1262, as was his son, Henry, murdered by the de Montforts at Viterbo in 1272. A year later Richard himself was buried close to them in front of the high altar.[12] At Bordesley this process began in the late thirteenth century. On the basis of surviving effigies Coppack has suggested that patronal burial commenced at the same time at Dore, Furness, Jervaulx, Margam, Neath, Rievaulx and Strata Florida.[13]

The original site of the two remaining effigies at Dore is not known. They were moved to their present position by Paul during the 1901-9 restoration. The use of effigies indicates that they were originally within the church. Their worn condition suggests a site in the nave whence they may have been rescued during Scudamore's 1634 restoration. On early plans Paul showed them in two of the eastern chapels.

For Abbot Straddell, burial within the church was the prime means of attracting regular income through the appropriation of parish churches. In this he was following the Benedictines, Augustinians and even the nuns of Aconbury but was contravening the dictates of the *Exordium*— that the possession of spiritualities, income from churches, advowsons, tithes and church dues, should be utterly renounced. In Straddell's defence it has to be said that compromise on these matters had begun a century and a half earlier, during St. Bernard's own lifetime, with the absorption of the Savignac houses into the Cistercian order in 1147.

Sometime between 1219 and 1234 Dore itself had received a grant of tithes from 40 acres in Treville from John de Kilpeck and Adam I had had no qualms about the appropriation of the parish church of Bacton.[14]

Straddell had considerable success. A dissolution document of 1536/7 lists Dore's income from rectories and churches as: Wigtoft (Lincolnshire), £13 6s. 8d.; Albrighton (Salop), £6 13s. 4d.; Avenbury with the chapel of Bredenbury (Herefordshire), £5 6s. 8d.; Gwenddwr (Brecon), £5 6s. 8d.; and Duntisbourne Rouse (Gloucestershire), 13s. 4d., totalling £31 6s. 8d. All, except possibly Gwenddwr, were acquired by Straddell between 1320 and 1330. Assertions of deep impoverishment were necessarily made to press claims with the diocesan authorities. At Duntisbourne, the fourth appropriation in ten years, an even stronger case was made. Straddell claimed that the 'sterility of their lands and possessions, murrain of animals, wars and other disturbances' were such that he could not sustain 'even the hospitality due to Christ's poor; a situation which deteriorates daily.'[15]

Analysis of burials in this period shows Straddell using sepulture within the by then probably deserted lay brothers' choir as an inducement to local landed families to make grants of the spiritualities they held as patrons. Put the other way round, the grant of the advowson of parish churches was the price such families were prepared to pay for the right to 'share in the prayers' of the monks of Dore and 'in the merit accruing from their works of charity and piety.' Leland provides a 'list of burials' at Dore to which additions can be made from other sources.[16] From these a picture can be drawn of the interrelationship between sepulture and patronage.

The first major appropriation was short-lived. The important church of Lugwardine, together with its chapels of St. Deinst, Llangarron, St. Dubricius, Hentland and St. Weonards, was granted in 1318/19 by Alan II de Plugenet, lord of Lugwardine, Kilpeck and the Forest of Haywood. In 1325 Alan II died, without heirs, and was buried at Dore as was his father '1st Alanes lord of Alanes More', who had died in 1298. If ever formalised, the grant was not held long. Joanna, his sister and heiress, and widow of Henry de Bohun, grandson of Henry, third earl of Hereford and Essex, succeeded to the Plugenet lands. She had other ideas.[17]

Sir John le Rous (d. 1346) was of higher social standing than the de Plugenets. He was sheriff of Herefordshire in 1332-34, represented the county in six parliaments 1330-43 and was lord of Harescombe and Duntisbourne Rouse in Gloucestershire. In 1319 licence was made 'at the instance of Humphrey de Bohun, earl of Hereford and Essex' for the 'alienation in mortmain by John le Rous to the abbot and convent of Dore of a garden in Avenbury and the advowson of the church.' According to a 1327 charter confirming Dore's privileges le Rous gave the advowson not only of Avenbury but of Harescombe with the chapel of Pitchcombe and Duntisbourne Rouse with the chapel of Pinbury. Later sources refer to an 'abbot's barn', for tithes, at Avenbury. At Duntisbourne, whilst Bishop Orleton reserved the former rectorial manse with its croft to the vicar, the monks were to have adequate space for 'granges, barns or other buildings.'[18]

John de la Warre's wish to be buried at Dore is readily explained. His father, Roger, had married Clarissa, eldest daughter and co-heiress of John, last of the Tregoz lords of Ewyas Harold. John shared the inheritance with Sybil, the other daughter and co-heiress who had married William Grandison. De la Warre received the castle and manor of Ewyas 'with all things pertaining to it in the parts of Wales' together with Albrighton (Salop), Chelwood (Somerset) and Allington and East Kennet (Wilts); to Sybil de Grandison went Eton Tregoz, Lydiard Tregoz (Wilts) and Burnham (Somerset).[19]

Soon after his arrival, the abbey began to foster its relationship with the new lord of Ewyas Harold. Thus, in 1305, the Dore annalist recorded the birth of his son, John, at Ewyas. Apart from the death and election of abbots this is the only local entry in the chronicle. As lord of Ewyas John de la Warre was anxious for burial at Dore, but a price had to be paid. In 1327 he obtained licence to alienate in mortmain to Dore land in Albrighton and the advowson of the church there. In return the convent was to find three monks to act as chaplains to celebrate divine service daily in their abbey for the souls

Fig. 71. Tomb of Joanna de Bohun in the Lady Chapel of Hereford Cathedral

monument still in the Lady Chapel at Hereford (Fig. 71). In return she gave the dean and chapter the advowson of Lugwardine with its chapelries, thus revoking her brother's grant to Dore. The account rolls of the warden of the lady chapel show the income for 1356 as £45 6s. 8d.—almost double the revenue received by Dore from all its appropriated churches in 1536-7. From this gift Bishop Charlton provided eight priests, one deacon and one sub-deacon to 'say the canonical hours night and day in the choir, and mass for the donor daily.' Such was Straddell's loss.

Straddell had hoped that a combination of lavish decoration, architectural remodelling and the presence of the relic would provide a sufficient sense of grandeur to of John and his ancestors. In 1330 Straddell received from John the even more valuable gift of the advowson of the church of Wigtoft, Lincolnshire. For the de Grandisons, however, no such grants of advowson were required. William's gift of the fragment of the True Cross was more than compensation.

However, the shrine proved but a partial inducement for sepulture. The new lady of Kilpeck, Joanna de Bohun, had higher aspirations. She was buried in 1327 in the remarkable induce local families, now expending large sums on funerary monuments, to select Dore's nave as their preferred place of burial. The list of appropriated churches indicates some measure of success but the cases of Lady Joanna de Bohun and Peter Grandison were to show that Dore could not compete with the Lady Chapel of Hereford Cathedral with its shrine of St. Thomas. In 1321 the shrine was almost completed when Edward II announced his intention of attending the translation. Political events, however, led to a

Fig. 72. Tomb of Peter de Grandison next to that of Joanna in the Lady Chapel of Hereford Cathedral

28-year postponement. Joanna can be forgiven for believing the delay would not be long, but translation only took place, in the presence of Edward III, in October 1349. This was incentive enough for Peter de Grandison whose elaborate tomb was, in 1352 placed between that of Joanna and the shrine (Fig, 72).[20] His father's fragment of the True Cross was no challenge to the shrine of St. Thomas. Amongst the possessions of Dore sold at the Dissolution on 1 March 1537 was 'a cross of beryl.'[21]

CHAPTER X

Superfluity and Singularity

by Joe Hillaby

The polygonal chapter house was one of the most remarkable achievements of English medieval architecture. It found august expression at such cathedrals as Lincoln c.1220/30, Lichfield c.1240, Westminster c.1250, Wells c.1250/1300, Salisbury c.1260, York pre-1300, Old St Paul's c.1332 and finally Hereford c.1340. The form spread to Scotland but was never adopted on the continent.

These buildings were not merely objects of great beauty; they were the greatest technical achievements of the age, for the great stone vaults had each to be carried on a single, slender shaft. Naturally they were the source of pride and rivalry. The most famous, at Westminster, was described by Matthew Paris, the chronicler, as 'a chapter house beyond compare'. More important it was built by Henry III as a meeting place for his Great Council from which Parliament evolved. 'The very shape may have moulded that institution. It was "in the round": theatrical.' In the tiled floor a damaged inscription commences: *ut rosa phlos phlorum sic est domus ista domorum ....*; 'as the rose is the flower of flowers, so this house is the house of houses, which king Henry, a lover of the Holy Trinity, dedicated to Christ ...'. The same claim is found at York. Ironically, for here the builders lost their nerve and fearing the weight of stone, they roofed it with wood.[1]

Thomas Blashill, 1830-1905

The first truly polygonal chapter house was at Dore.[2] Credit for its discovery goes to the London-based architect, Thomas Blashill. Between 1863-9 he had assisted William Heywood, Surveyor to the City, with the detailing of Holborn Viaduct. He became Architect to the Metropolitan Board of Works and then Superintendent Architect for the London County Council. One of his achievements was Westminster Technical College (1893), between Victoria Street and Vauxhall Bridge Road.[3]

Although Blashill was born in Sutton-in-Holderness, Yorkshire, his parents lived for many years at Downshill, Bishopstone in Herefordshire where his father was land steward for Sir Henry Cotterell's Garnons estate. As a 22-year-old Blashill was already an enthusiastic antiquarian and natural historian for he had joined the Woolhope Club in 1851-52, the year of its foundation. Although based in London, he retained a strong interest in Herefordshire. In 1863 he restored the church at Yarkhill where three years later he designed the National School. The restoration of the churches at Westhide (1866-7), Stottesdon, Salop (1868), Putley (1875-6) and Dormington (1877) and the tower of Westhide (1880) followed. Blashill spent some time in Herefordshire indulging his interest in archaeology. When the British Archaeological Association's annual congress

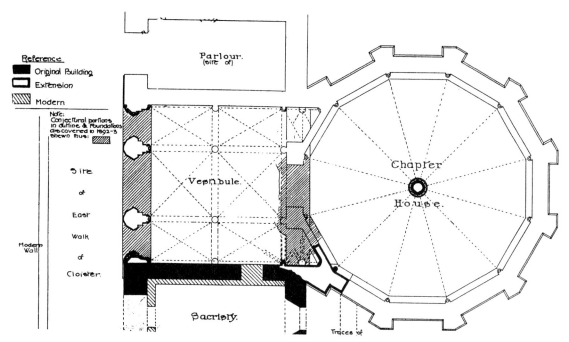

Fig. 73. Plan of Dore Abbey chapter house, vestibule etc. R.W. Paul, The Builder *(8 April 1893)*

was held at Hereford in 1870 he led the visits to Kilpeck, Rowlestone and Dore Abbey.

Seven years later the Royal Archaeological Institute held its Annual Meeting at Hereford. Sir George Gilbert Scott, doyen of the architects of the Gothic Revival, was the guide for the visit to Dore. He knew Hereford well through his work on the cathedral between 1856 and 1863. Nevertheless his note books show that he had taken care to visit the abbey the previous month, for a sketch which he made at the time is in the British Architectural Library. Significantly one member, Mr. Fairless Barber, drew attention to 'a small excavation recently made at the entrance of the vestibule to the chapter house which has disclosed the base of the shafts by which the portal was decorated'. He had 'little doubt that a careful and not very expensive exploration of the other remains would yield mouldings and details of very considerable interest'.[4]

Blashill was elected President of the Woolhope Club in 1882. For the first Field Meeting he took members to the churches of the Golden Valley which 'by its new railway has but

recently been made easy of access'. Connecting Pontrilas and Hay, this line was built 1876-89 and the final section closed in 1957. Some members preferred to eschew the new-fangled train, making their way instead on horseback. At Dore the party was received by the rector, the Rev. Alfred Phillipps who 'had caused some search to be made for the remains of the destroyed buildings before the arrival of the visitors' and who, presumably, was responsible for 'the small excavation' made in 1877.[5]

Blashill 'formed the opinion that the chapter house was a polygonal building'—and realised the full significance of his conclusion. 'This was very surprising as all English Cistercian chapter-houses then known were quadrangular, except that of Margam in South Wales, which was of about the same date and 50 feet in diameter.' He continued: 'I have since ascertained that the chapter-house of Dore was a twelve-sided building of beautiful thirteenth-century design, having a clustered column in the centre, the base of which, prepared for six large shafts and six smaller intermediate shafts, I identified in a

104

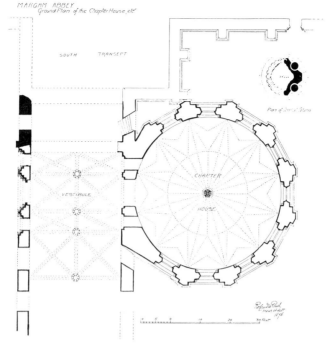

Fig. 74. Plan of Margam Abbey chapter house, R.W. Paul, (1895)
in W. de G. Birch, A History of Margam Abbey (1897)

rockery in the Rectory Garden [now in the south transept]. I found also in the belfry a base from one of the angles of the interior, prepared for a large vaulting shaft, and two smaller shafts that carried the wall-ribs thus fully establishing the shape of the building. I think also there are remains of the small arcade that ran round the lower parts of the walls, forming stalls for the abbot and monks in their chapter. Those who knew the splendid chapter-houses of Westminster, Salisbury and Wells will easily picture this at Dore which seems to have been a most worthy example of that class of buildings.'

Blashill's findings, published 1882-85[6], were instrumental in introducing Roland Paul to Dore. Having drawn a detailed plan of the structure remaining Paul decided to excavate to 'discover, if possible, the exact extent and position of some of the destroyed buildings'. With the rector's consent work began in 1892 and continued into the next year. His findings, presented to the Leeds and Yorkshire Architectural Society in March 1893, were published in *The Builder* the following month (Fig. 73).[7]

Paul established 'the exact dimensions' of the chapter house, explaining that 'the only remains above ground are an angle with a vaulting shaft, and a small portion of one side, with a stone bench projecting 15 in. from the wall still remaining. The foundation of this side was followed as far as its junction with a cross-wall, running north from the vaulting shaft which still remains at the east end of the vestibule wall.' The angle shaft can still be seen but there is now no trace of the bench. The length of one side and an angle having been obtained, the twelve-sided figure was restored. 'To complete the picture the [central shaft] base, circular below and showing the bases of twelve shafts above, which was in the rectory garden (and had been discovered by Blashill) was placed with the springing of its vaulting over it'. This stone had long been lying in the field. 'It would fill the cap a great deal better than that at Margam.' The internal diameter at the angle was 45 feet, 4 feet less than at Margam.

The Margam Chapter House

At Margam most of the chapter house still stands. After the dissolution only the nave of the monastic church was retained for parochial worship. Vestibule and chapter house were kept, as outbuildings for the mansion built by Rice Merrick. In 1736 the former was a brewhouse whilst the latter was a coalhouse. The chapter house vault collapsed in 1799 but not before a drawing had been made of the interior in its complete state (Fig 75).[8]

Paul, like Blashill, recognised the importance of the relationship between the chapter houses of Dore and Margam. In 1893 he visited the latter and published plans of the chapter house (Fig. 74) and of the bases of the central shafts of Margam and Dore. Margam was not a pure polygon. Circular internally, externally it was an irregular eleven-sided figure, lit by nine lancets. Eight sides were regular but the three about the entrance differed considerably in length. The vaulting system, however, was based on a regular dodecagon, for the ribs divide the roof into twelve equal bays.

Margam was also a Cistercian house. It was founded, as a daughter of Clairvaux, by Robert earl of Gloucester in 1147, the year of his death, and colonised by monks from Waverley. By the late-twelfth century it had acquired widespread estates in and around the fertile valleys of the Afan and Kenfig. In the thirteenth century it was the richest ecclesiastical institution in Wales, its only rivals being Meath and Tintern. In the late-twelfth and early-thirteenth century abbot and convent were thus able to embark upon an ambitious programme, ultimately rebuilding their church as far west as the pulpitum. Chapter house and vestibule belong to the first part of this rebuilding programme. By the end of the twelfth century the chapter house was becoming the expression of the authority and personality of the abbot. It is a stark indication of Abbot Gilbert's priorities that his chapter house impinged uncomfortably on the eastern arm of the church.

The relationship of the two chapter houses

This relationship has yet to be fully explored. The Early English work at Margam stands in marked contrast to that of Dore. It lacks sophistication in detail. Within the church the proportions of many capitals are unfortunate, plate tracery is left raw and unadorned on the inner faces of the choir and transept windows. The chapter house vaulting ribs fit ungainly on their capitals. Thus, for Paul, Margam was the hybrid and Dore the perfected form.

Not everyone is convinced that Margam came first. Neil Stratford is 'inclined to award priority to Dore on the evidence of the surviving details' but does not develop this argument.[9]

In fact there is an important difference between the two buildings. Rings are found on almost all the Margam shafts. Originally a functional element, they were first used decoratively at Glastonbury lady chapel in 1184-6. At Hereford they are not found in de Vere's retrochoir, c.1190, but are a marked feature of the multiple shafts of the lady chapel, c.1220-30. Rings were used to great effect at Brecon Priory, 1201-08, the latter date established by the flight of its patron, William de Braose, to Ireland. From 1203 to 1208 de Braose was entrusted by King John with the government of Glamorgan. He is the outstanding figure in the annals and records of Margam for that period. Four bands of rings were adopted for the east end of St. David's Cathedral. Under Marcher influence this design was used at Christ Church Cathedral, Dublin[10]. Would the Dore masons have rejected such fashionable ring shafts if they were indeed copying and refining the detail from Margam?

Other evidence suggests that building continued later at Margam than at Dore. In 1208 the pope placed England under an Interdict. The churches were closed, the dead could not be buried in consecrated ground, marriages were not solemnised, and the laity was denied the sacraments of the altar. Soon all but two bishops had quitted the kingdom. John replied by seizing all ecclesiastical property which he then farmed back to the clergy—at a heavy price. It might be thought that the Interdict brought all construction work to a halt at Margam for six and a half years as it did at Dore and most other churches, but this may not have been the case.

The two houses fared very differently during John's reign. The time-serving abbot Gilbert (1203-13) was, according to the Margam annalists, first the close associate of Braose, author of the Abergavenny massacre, described by Sir John Lloyd as 'perfidy and barbarity of a deep dye'; then the intimate of King John. In 1210 the latter, balked in his attempt to capture Braose, exacted vengeance on his wife and child whom he had starved to death in one of his dungeons, a crime which shocked even the most hardened chroniclers of the age—and haunted the king on his deathbed. In that year John stayed, with his army, at Margam on his way to and from his Irish expedition against Braose. He placed Margam under his special protection and favoured it almost as much as his own foundation, Beaulieu. About the Interdict the Margam chronicler even suggested that 'all the laity, most of the clergy and many monks were on the king's side'. Unlike his Dore colleague, who counted each day to its end, the chronicler ignored its lifting.[11]

More significant, in August 1213, immediately after the restoration of relations between king and pope, but a year before the lifting of the Interdict, the Margam annals record the arrival of messengers from Citeaux. They brought letters peremptorily deposing Gilbert, who was banished to end his days at the distant Cistercian house of Kirkstead. Neither annals nor statutes offer an explanation. For this one should probably turn to the abbey of Vaucelles where in 1192 the official visitor was formally reprimanded for not correcting extravagances, particularly 'the building of a church that is too costly and superfluous, shocking many' and delegates were ordered to suppress all that failed to conform to 'the simplicity of the order.'[12]

Pride, Superfluity and Singularity

As Pevsner says, 'the very splendour of Dore's double ambulatory was a denial of Bernardian ideals.'[13] What then of the two chapter houses? They were not merely 'superfluity' but each the very essence of 'singularity'. How could such an outstanding architectural development, so much at variance with the ideals of the rule, have been pioneered in two Cistercian houses? This is the fundamental question.

The order had originated in a rejection of the riches and luxury that had characterised the life of many monasteries, especially the Cluniacs, in the early twelfth century. The founders sought to return to the early forms of western monasticism and the apostolic life on which they were based, in all their simplicity and severity. These ideals found formal expression in such documents as the *Exordium Cistercii, Carta Caritatis* and *Exordium Parvum.*[14]

For the Cistercians the three fundamental characteristics of the human soul were simplicity, immortality and free will. The removal of superfluity was part of the striving for simplicity. 'There is no virtue more indispensible at the beginning of our conversion than simplicity.' Furthermore, 'He Who is subsisting Truth has no love of singularities; divisions do not please Him. He "standeth in the midst", that is to say, He is found in the common life and discipline; uniformity of observance is His delight'. Singularity was a seeking of one's own interest, an indulgence of one's 'own will' at the expense of the common will. Thus for the Cistercians unity of plan and construction was the architectural expression of the monastic ideal of community; of the common will and its desire for simplicity.[15]

The *Exordium Cistercii* stated categorically that 'in the house of God wherein they desired to serve God devoutly by day and night they would have nothing that savoured of pride or superfluity, or which might ever corrupt the poverty, which they had chosen of their free will, as the custodians of the virtues'. Such things were an impediment to the life of contemplation and prayer. 'Every ornament, vessel and utensil must be without gold, silver or precious stones except the chalice and communion reed. We are allowed these two things of silver or gold plate but never of pure gold. The altar linen and vestments of the ministers, except the stole and maniple, must be without silk. The chasuble must be of one colour. We may not have sculptures anywhere; we may have paintings but only on crosses; and we may have crosses made only of wood.' Statutes of the

General Chapter insisted that windows should be only of white, that is grisaille, glass without pictures or crosses, bells should not exceed 500 pounds so that they might be rung by a single person and two bells should never be rung together. Bell towers of stone were forbidden.[16] To the outsider, however, the Cistercian ideal found its clearest expression in the undyed white habit.

This inevitably led to conflict with the Cluniacs. In his *Apologia* St. Bernard denounced 'the immense height of (their) churches, their immoderate length, their superfluous breadth ... and strange designs which, while they attract the eyes of the worshipper, hinder the soul's devotion'. He continued: 'but a monk myself, I do ask other monks "Tell me, O ye professors of poverty, what does gold do in a holy place?" To speak plainly, is it not avarice—the worship of idols—from which we do not expect spiritual fruit but worldly benefit? Money is laid out that it returns multiplied many times. By the sight of costly vanities men are prompted to give rather than to pray ... O vanity of vanities what has all this to do with monks, with professors of poverty, with men of spiritual minds?'[17] This is the context in which the building of the first of the great series of English polygonal chapter houses, at Dore, has to be explained.

The order also provided a well-defined machinery to maintain these austere ideals. Overall legislative and judicial power lay with a General Chapter held annually each year at Citeaux, which every abbot was obliged to attend. As a further control mechanism 'the abbot of the mother house shall visit all the monasteries he himself has founded once a year'. Such annual visitations to the Welsh march would have been 'long, arduous, expensive and occasionally fraught with danger'. The journey from Tintern to Citeaux took some three weeks and the return journey cost £10. As the abbot of Morimond had twenty-six other houses to visit, a

Fig. 75. Engraving of Margam Abbey chapter house before the vault collapsed. From: W. de G. Birch, A History of Margam Abbey *(1897)*

certain laxity had developed by the end of the twelfth century.[18]

Given these controls, how can we explain such indulgence as the Dore and Margam chapter houses? Interest in the neglected subject of Cistercian chapter houses has recently revived. In a 1982 review of archaeological work on the English and Welsh Cistercians Butler concluded 'there is far less opportunity in England (than on the continent) for pioneer architectural studies ... Probably the way forward lies in the study of specific structures such as multi-sided chapter houses ...', a comment which provoked the article *The House of Houses* published in 1989 from which this chapter has evolved. Two years earlier Gilyard-Beer had examined *The Graves of the Abbots of Fountains*, a subject returned to by Butler in 1993, and in 1976 W.S. Gardner had considered *The Role of Central Planning in English Romanesque Chapter House Design*. In 1994 Fergusson and Harrison sought to account for the 'conceptual qualities' of the second Rievaulx chapter house, described by Gilyard-Beer as a 'remarkable lapse' from St. Bernard's aesthetic and by Gardner as 'bizarre'. Built by Ailred c.1150-60, this two-storey structure had cylindrical piers carrying a clerestory divided into four bays. To the east this was carried round an apse where four piers provided an ambulatory. At the centre Ailred placed the shrine of Rievaulx's first abbot, William, now popularly held to be a saint.[19]

For Fergusson the unique character of the Rievaulx chapter house arose firstly from its quasi-liturgical function under Ailred. Is this to underestimate Ailred's ambitions as the 'spokesman of articulate power'? Recently we have been warned against the sentimental portrait conveyed by Walter Daniel's propagandist *Life*, with its 'gentle abbot, meek and mild, the sensitive soul with a genius for friendship, otherworldly because clearly too good for this world.' That view, it has been suggested, 'has too long obscured the man who shows himself in his own *Works* to be bold, 'brilliant, ambitious and powerful.' Do we see in this 'remarkable lapse,' as in Daniel's *Life*, the growth of the cult of the abbot?[20]

There is no evidence that liturgical factors played any significant part in the origins of the polygonal chapter house at Margam and Dore. The key factor here was the role and personality of the abbot. Geography also contributed. The remoteness of these houses, together with political conflict, weakened the central authority of the General Chapter. In consequence the abbots had greater freedom to exercise their ambitions.

Adam I (Abbot 1186x7-c.1216)

As Fergusson pointed out in *Architecture of Solitude*, 'the attitude of the abbot was ... critical. As the formulator of the programme, as the presiding on-site authority watching all develop-ments and as the most widely travelled and thus the most knowledgeable person about developments elsewhere, the abbot exercised decisive control over the work.'

It was Abbot Adam I who was responsible for reconstructing the presbytery and building the polygonal chapter house. When the new hand began work, 'soberness and restraint were firmly set aside in favour of robust decorative interest[21]' inspired by neighbouring West Country workshops.

The end of the twelfth century witnessed the emergence of a group of highly ambitious and not altogether scrupulous Cistercian abbots. An aggressive and highly acquisitive landlordism led to widespread social distress. The Cistercians became 'harrowers, herdsmen, merchants and in each calling most active.'[22] In an economy based on the system of granges and sheep runs worked by lay brothers the local peasantry often found themselves disinherited of their small holdings. This is reflected in the quantity and quality of wool production of such houses as Margam, Tintern and Dore.

The order began to lose its formerly high reputation for piety and charity. This was seized upon as a handle for reproach by a number of not entirely disinterested writers from whom we learn much about Adam and Gilbert, his contemporary at Margam.

In the words of Walter Map the Cistercians 'recognised their prey as the hawk spies the frightened lark'. In the *Speculum Ecclesiae* (c.1217) Gerald of Wales describes how the dying Sybil, Lady of Ewyas, was 'made a monk with tonsure and cowl complete'. In return Dore received common of pasture on the side of Dulas for 200 sheep. The dying, 'especially the Welsh who are more simple minded and easy to deceive with promises of salvation in return for appropriate gifts', were carried off to Dore. Yet Adam was only engaged in what, for other orders, was standard procedure—rights of monastic sepulture in return for favours received or to be granted. Not infrequently this led to unseemly conflict. At Gloucester in 1143 the Benedictine monks of St. Mary's, now the cathedral, and the Augustinian canons of Lanthony Secunda, just outside the town wall, fought bitterly over the body of Miles, Castellan of Gloucester and Earl of Hereford. Only in 1197 was a full composition achieved between the two houses.[23]

Adam's detractors provide further instructive anecdotes. Gilbert, a local knight, was filled with wine and then his seal affixed to a forged grant of lands 'large, spacious, fertile and fruitful'. The grant is confirmed by the Dore survey of 1213. Rents and lands of Bacton Church were taken, despite the order's prohibition of the holding of parish churches or cure of souls.

Such a sketch of the new style, managerial, market-oriented abbot who provided the resources for the ambitious building programme in presbytery and chapter house is but part of the picture. Adam was more than an ambitious builder; he was a true son of the twelfth-century Renaissance. In intellectual interests he was very much a man of his times. Not for him, as for many English Cistercians of his day, talk merely of litigation, 'the progeny of bulls, ploughs ... and the yield of fields.'[24] His literary clashes with Gerald of Wales and Simon de Fresne, and other evidence, show that Adam was closely associated with the Hereford cathedral school which, under Bishop de Vere (1186-99), was one of the major cultural and intellectual centres of the kingdom. Gerald and Simon did not have it all their own way. Adam's counterblast, in the form of satyric verse, obviously hit its mark, for it drew replies from both.[25]

There is further evidence of Adam's intellectual talents. A series of sermons with verse endings, now in the British Library, and biblical passages rendered into a mixture of prose and verse, in the Bodleian, have been attributed to Adam. This is of particular interest because the General Chapter ordained in 1199 that any monk indulging a taste for poetry should be sent to another house.[26] Adam has also been credited with the authorship of the treatise *Pictor in Carmine*, a collection of 510 types and 138 antitypes, that is Old and New Testament subjects, intended for use in the decoration of cathedrals and parish churches. All thirteen extant manuscripts of the *Pictor* are English. The fly leaf of one is ascribed to 'Adam, abbot of Dore'.[27]

Adam's interest in music is well documented from his authorship of *The Rudiments of Music* and introduction of three- and four-part chanting at Dore.[28]

As early as 1169 Pope Alexander III had written to the English Cistercians, warning them that their entire way of life had undergone injury and change, leaving behind the original manner of life. Little changed. At Waverley, the premier English house, the abbot had to be replaced in 1187. Next year the General Chapter dismissed the abbots of Tintern, Bordesley and Flaxley. At Garendon the abbot was replaced in 1195 by the abbot of Merevale who, within a year, was stabbed and grievously wounded by one of his own lay brothers, at night in his infirmary. At Bordesley in 1199 Richard, who had replaced an earlier abbot, was himself removed.[29] At Dore there is no evidence throughout Adam's abbacy of some 30 years of breaches of discipline serious enough to merit the attention of the General Chapter.

The most serious trouble was, however, amongst the *conversi*. In the 1190s almost every abbot in the province had difficulty controlling them. At Margam beer drinking at the granges was a serious problem and in 1191 the abbot was sentenced by the General Chapter to remain out of his stall for 40 days on account of unspecified 'enormities' committed in his house. In 1206 the *conversi* rose in revolt and, armed, chased abbot Gilbert for fifteen miles. Gilbert had to have them carried off to dungeons in a nearby castle. Adam's wide cultural interest did not prevent him from ruling with a firm hand. Drunkenness and rioting were not found at Dore.[30]

In a recent analysis of the architecture of Dore, O'Callaghan comments that 'the date for the start of the eastern extension is usually given as *c*.1190 and I see no reason to quarrel with this'. He suggests that 'the upper parts of the choir must have been nearing completion by 1220 at the latest.'[31] The political history of John's reign is highly relevant to building history but often eludes the architectural historian. The six-year Interdict, 1208-14, and the financial exigencies subsequently experienced by Dore strongly suggest completion of the eastern extension and chapter house by 1208. Even at

Plate 4. Chevrons on a pillar in the ambulatory

Plate 5. Re-set floor tiles adjoining the altar

Plate 6. Boss with abbot kneeling before the Virgin and Child

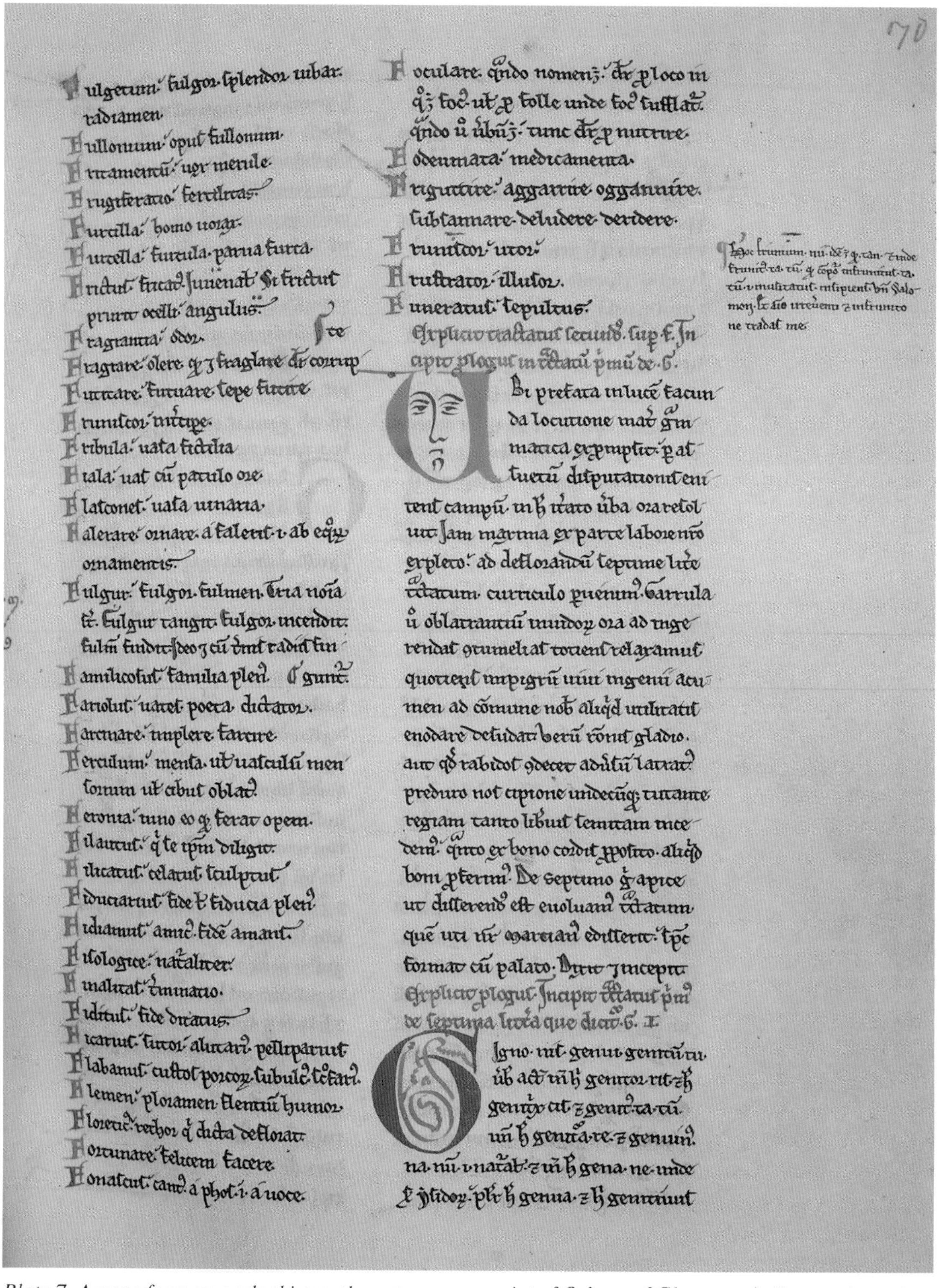

Plate 7. A page from an early thirteenth century manuscript of Osbern of Gloucester's Panormia, written and probably decorated by the scribe John of Bath, which belonged to the monks of Dore Abbey (Hereford Cathedral Library MS P.V.5, f.70)

Waverley, the new church laid out in 1203 was only completed after 1231.[32]

Relations between John and the Cistercians had been strained since 1200 when they had opposed his imposition of a carucage as contrary to their immunities. The king uttered dire threats but the conflict was temporarily resolved. Indeed, in 1204 John founded one of the largest English Cistercian abbeys, Beaulieu. During the Interdict, however, they suffered more harshly than any other order from John's exactions. According to Roger Wendover they were fined £40,000 in 1210 and Ralph of Coggeshall records a further levy of £22,000 in 1212. These may be exaggerations but many Cistercians sought refuge in other monasteries.[33] Apart from Beaulieu, Margam was one of the few houses to prosper, for reasons already noted. The imposition of the Interdict, and with it John's resumption of monastic lands in 1208, provides the critical date when Adam I's resources came under acute strain.

On 2 July 1214 the Dore annalist recorded the lifting of the Interdict which, in a poignantly precise note, he explained had 'lasted six years, three months and seventeen days', but its lifting did not solve Dore's financial problems.[34] Renowned for 'haunting woods and streams and greatly delighting in the pleasures of them', John stayed regularly at Kilpeck to hunt in the forest of Treville. He knew the forest well and was keenly aware of how his brother Richard's need for money in 1198 and 1199 had been exploited by Adam wishing to promote his own candidacy for St. David's. A 1213 survey shows how large a holding Adam had purchased and established—some 1,200 of the 2,000 acres. John had used 'the discord between us and the clergy of England' as an excuse to resume this land. However, on reaching an accommodation with the pope in August 1213, John was obliged to return Dore's part of Treville. But the monks had to pay, and pay heavily—they received no indemnification for John's financial depredations during those years, and in 1215 he levied a fine of £400 for a charter confirming the possession of the lands Adam had acquired between Dore and Treville brooks. Next year there were further demands.[35]

Even after the opening of the new reign Dore's finances did not improve. Hostilities with Llewelyn, ally of the rebellious barons, were only terminated in 1218 and conditions on the march remained precarious for a number of years due to his feuds with various marcher lords, especially William Marshal the Younger. In addition Henry III continued the heavy fines imposed by his father. In 1223 yet another survey was ordered of 'the assarts made by Dore in Treville wood'. In 1226 Dore had to pay £433 for a further charter of confirmation of their Treville lands.[36] Gerald of Wales' description of Adam's successor, Adam II (c.1216-c.1226), as 'modest in a mediocre way' is not altogether surprising. Given such a financial drain anyone would have found it hard to emulate Adam I's architectural achievements. The overall building programme was completed only with difficulty. The evidence from the architectural fragments indicates that completion of the nave was long delayed.[37]

The Chapter House as the domain of the abbot

By the end of the twelfth century the monastic chapter house had a status second only to that of the church. It was the administrative and disciplinary centre of the house. The reading of the rule, the management of monastic affairs, the chapter of faults, the making of confession and the commemoration of benefactors all took place here. From his stall at the centre of the east wall, the abbot presided over these functions with his principal officers, the obedientiaries, to his left and right and the brethren to north and south. The abbot exercised both spiritual and civil authority. He was both judge and lord of his house and its dependants. The chapter thus came to be an expression of the authority and personality of the abbot for here, from his abbatical stall, he ruled. This received further emphasis at the annual visitation when the Cistercian abbot had to give up his stall to the abbot of the mother house or his deputy. Further, serious transgressions on the part of a Cistercian abbot were punished by exclusion from the abbatial stall, a far more public humiliation than fasting on bread and water.

As during his life the abbot ruled from his chapter house, so there he was buried. At

Fountains the grave stones of thirteen abbots extend down the middle of the chapter house in front of the abbot's stall. The increasingly elaborate decoration illustrates vividly the growth of the cult of personality amongst Cistercian abbots.[38]

The Dore and Margam chapter houses reflect desire for status and freedom from control but they could not have been built without technical help. This was developed by masons of the West Country school. There in the 1170s the vaulting of naves, 'almost rejected in the north, sporadic elsewhere, was provided for consistently'. By the end of the century the structurally most adventurous group of buildings was to be found in the west, one of the earliest signs being the vaulted nave aisles of Malmesbury in the 1160s.[39]

For his retrochoir Adam had followed the model of Byland.[40] For his chapter house he apparently turned to local sources. There is a strong family likeness between Hereford Cathedral and Dore in terms of capitals, trumpet-shaped scalloped and upright stiff leaf, and the triple shafts carrying the vault, but it was in the use of space that Adam was really inspired by bishop de Vere's new retrochoir at Hereford. Only the central compartment now remains but originally it was composed of three tall and spacious two-bay compartments spanning the east end. The plan was derived from Wells and Glastonbury where choir aisles were taken around the eastern end as an ambulatory and four chapels constructed to the east. The Hereford retrochoir differed from its predecessors in the outstanding sense of space achieved from a more open plan. As Malone has said, 'one would have emerged from the lower aisles to the choir into the unusually large spatial units of the retrochoir ... an early and one of the more exciting examples of the English taste for treating space as an element of dramatisation'. One would have experienced precisely the same sensation on leaving the vestibule and entering the chapter house at Dore.[41]

In his ambulatory, beautiful as it is, Adam was unable to create this effect for, unlike Hereford, the Dore retrochoir does not reach the full height of the presbytery; it is a lean-to of less than half the height. It was in their chapter houses that Adam and his rival, Gilbert of Margam, achieved such a spectacular dramatisation of space.

What was the architectural model for Dore and Margam? One possibility is the polygonal fountain houses pioneered by the Cluniacs. They were to be found at Cluny and la Charité and at their English dependancies of Lewes and Much Wenlock. They became popular amongst the Cistercians—at le Thoronet, in France; Santa Creus near Tarrogona (c.1180); Poblet, Catalonia (c.1200); Alcobaca, Portugal; and the sumptuous octagonal house at Mellifont in Ireland. In central Europe there were at least five others that were hexagonal, six others octagonal and two with nine sides.[42] On the whole, however, the polygonal lavabo appears to have been a quite distinct development.

More plausible is the suggestion made by Paul and following him Bilson, that the design was inspired by the Worcester chapter house. Originally circular it was roofed with a rib vault springing from a central column; but in the late fourteenth century it was remodelled as a decagon in an attempt to relieve the pressure of the vault on the walls. Internally it retains much of the original circular design.[43] Indeed Stalley has pointed out that the vaulting system used at Mellifont is a miniature version of that used at Worcester.[44]

So much for design but what were the motives that lay behind the construction of the Dore and Margam chapter houses? Fergusson has asserted, without providing any evidence, that 'meaning' was adopted from Worcester where the central plan has been explained 'by reference to iconographical prototypes like baptisteries, funerary mausolea, buildings associated with the Virgin ...' Twenty years ago Gardner concluded that the popularity of the centrally planned chapter house in the thirteenth century was due to architectural fashion, especially a strong interest in stone vaulting, rather than 'the symbolic significance which had surely been intended in the *early* twelfth century.'[45]

If the precise architectural origins are not altogether clear, one thing is certain: the brilliant realisation at Dore of the polygonal chapter house should be viewed, not as a response to liturgical needs, but as an expression of status and ambition, personal as well as institutional.

CHAPTER XI

The Cloistral Ranges and a fresh look at the Chapter House

by Stuart Harrison

Cistercian monasteries were nearly always built to a standardised layout usually with the monastic buildings standing to the south of the church, but in some cases, the buildings were situated on the north side of the church. This was usual on a northward sloping site and meant that the more common southern claustral layout was reversed in its entirety. This was the case at Dore as the Paul excavations have helped demonstrate.

The standard Cistercian plan had a square cloister court around which were raised the monastic buildings. Abutting the north transept of the church was the eastern range, a long building subdivided into several ground floor rooms. In order, these were a single long narrow room forming the vestry and library adjacent to the transept. Next was the chapter house where the monks met daily to hear a reading from the Rule of St. Benedict, confess faults and conduct business. To the north was the parlour where monks might meet for conversation, silence normally being observed throughout the cloister. Then there was the day stairs to the monks dormitory which usually covered the whole of the first floor of this range. The rest of the range consisted of a passage at the north-east corner of the cloister leading through to the infirmary and an undercroft which seems to have served the monks originally as a warming house and day

room. Later twelfth-century developments in the plan indicate that at some houses this room was used for the storage of tools and a place to practice manual trades.[1]

On the west side of the cloister was a similar range but with a parlour passage at its south end and a very large ground floor room, divided into a cellarer's storage area at the southern end, and a cross passage parlour in the middle of the range, giving access to the cloister and forming a room in which monks might meet with relatives. The northern half of the range formed the lay brothers frater whilst over the whole of the first floor was their dormitory. This range was often longer than the east range, reflecting the greater dormitory space required by the lay brothers.

Joining the east and west ranges and forming the northern side of the cloister was, from the east, the warming house, monks frater and kitchen. Early Cistercian plans had followed the traditional Benedictine layout with the frater parallel to the cloister walk but in the later twelfth century the Cistercians developed a new plan in which the frater projected outwards at right angles from the range and this gave greater space for the kitchen and warming house.[2] The warming house was usually a moderate-sized room with at least one and commonly two large fireplaces. A fire was kept burning here throughout the winter months from All Saints Day to Good Friday, so that the monks could keep warm.

The frater was generally a large hall with tables arranged around three sides of the room and benches against the walls to accommodate the monks. Surviving examples of table layouts such as that at Fountains[3], show that benches were not provided in the central space and this meant that the superior could always closely observe his monks who all faced into the centre of the hall. Tables were also generally supported by fixed stone legs and examples of these survive at Fountains, Rievaulx, Jervaulx and Roche. At Dore, the senior monks would have sat at the northern end where the table was usually raised on a dais. In the west wall would be a pulpit which was normally corbelled out with an arcaded balustrade supporting a book rest. It was set high up and commonly approached via a stair in the thickness of the wall as at Tintern[4] or more elaborately with an open arcaded front, pierced by windows in the rear wall as at Fountains, Rievaulx and Beaulieu. From this a monk read from scripture or a suitable book whilst the monks ate in silence. In the twelfth and thirteenth-centuries the monastery would have operated a rota system for those having weekly duties and these included cooking and serving meals in the frater.

The monks communicated by a system of hand signs; a practice continued today in abbeys like Ampleforth. The Rule of St. Benedict forbids the eating of flesh meats except for those monks who were sick or infirm or those who had been periodically bled and were temporarily living in the infirmary. In the fourteenth and fifteenth centuries such rules were relaxed and the monks began to eat meat on a regular basis though this had to be cooked in a separate meat kitchen and served in a separate frater hall known as the misericord. These buildings were additions to the standardised plan and there was no firm rule about their location and they were usually built in a convenient place or converted from other buildings. The cloister kitchen could vary considerably in layout but commonly would have a series of large fireplaces, either in one wall or more commonly in a centrally arranged chimney stack carried through a vaulted ceiling. In the east and west walls would have been hatches, sometimes fitted with timber turntables or dumbwaiters, as at Fountains[5] and Rievaulx for passing the food to the monks' and lay brothers' fraters.

The cloister had four covered alleys which served as passageways and that adjoining the church was usually divided by partitions into carrels or desks for use by the monks in study or writing. The northern alley at Dore would have been provided with a laver or washing place which usually took the form of a blind arcade flanking the frater doorway with a trough for washing[6], though sometimes as at Mellifont[7] and Durham[8] there was a fountain house projecting into the cloister garth. Piped water was usually provided and the monks washed before entering the frater for meals. On Saturdays and Maundy Thursday they performed the Mandatum ritual when the abbot or prior washed the feet of the monks in emulation of Christ washing the feet of the Disciples.[9] The square central garth, framed by the arcaded alleyways, was often laid out as a formal garden, with defined pathways and raised beds, such as those which have recently been excavated at Haverfordwest Priory and may have been used for growing herbs and flowers. Although the high roofs of the surrounding buildings afforded some protection the cloister must have been a drafty cold place in bad winter weather, for its roofs were usually supported on rows of open arches carried on slender columns.

The reconstructed cloister arcade from Dore is very elegant but no evidence for glazing has been found. The monks met in the southern alley before the last service of the day to hear the Collation, a reading from the works of John Cassian. At some houses, such as Cleeve and Melrose there was a seat provided with an arched recess for the abbot or prior to sit in and at Byland and Strata Florida a porch projecting into the cloister for the reader to stand in.[10]

Each dormitory was usually a large room which though initially open, with the monks sleeping in common on mattresses, was often later subdivided by partitions into individual cubicles or cells. The dormitories were provided with a reredorter or latrine which normally had two doorways providing a one way traffic system of access and egress, sometimes with a lamp niche set between them. The reredorter would have had a row of first-floor open latrine seats set over a drain which provided a means of flushing away the waste.

Reredorters were normally set at right angles to the main range following the alignment of the drainage channel and the ground floor walls often had a series of open arches. In the early years of the order the abbot had to sleep in common in the monks' dormitory and it seems likely that in the revised plan of the south range the room over the warming house, which was connected to the dormitory, was used as the abbot's lodging. Gradually, as the rule relaxed, abbots moved into separate lodgings sometimes built onto the end of the reredorter, as at Fountains, and eventually by the fifteenth century into often quite palatial quarters sometimes converted from other buildings, such as the infirmary at Rievaulx.

To the east of the main buildings there was usually the separate infirmary complex with a large, normally aisled, hall and associated chapel and kitchen. The aisles of the hall were sometimes divided by timber partitions like that at Rievaulx and it was here that those monks too old, sick or infirm to continue in the normal life of the monastery resided. Often there was a second cloister, smaller than the main court but with similar open arcaded walls carrying the roof. These arcades are commonly less substantial and sometimes carried on single rows of columns as at Rievaulx. Possibly the badly damaged moulded double capital of dumbbell design, now lying in the church, could have originated in such an infirmary cloister. In the fourteenth and fifteenth-centuries many infirmary halls were subdivided by stone partitions into separate rooms provided with fireplaces and these seem to have been used by the monks during the winter months. This was just another symptom, like the changes in diet, of the change to a less rigorous regime with an emphasis on creature comforts and followed the decline in the numbers of monks.

On the west side of the cloister buildings, there was sometimes a similar infirmary complex provided for the lay brothers like that at Fountains and Jervaulx[11], together with guest houses for visitors; hospitality being a feature of the Rule of St. Benedict. Guest houses could form a considerable range of buildings as those surviving at Fountains show. There could also be a large guest hall with fixed tables standing on stone legs such as that recently discovered at Fountains.

The decline in numbers of monks during the fourteenth and fifteenth-centuries saw a fundamental change in the use of many buildings. This decline and change of use was often also reflected in the demolition and dereliction of parts of the buildings. At Rievaulx besides converting the infirmary into the abbot's lodging the convent saw the demolition of half of the west range and its conversion to a suite of ground-floor rooms and a first-floor granary, with substantial reductions in the size of the kitchen, chapter house, reredorter and warming house. The huge dormitory was in a dangerous condition and its southern half was dismantled and turned into a tannery whilst the remainder was remodelled to provide more modern accommodation. At Strata Florida, by the Dissolution, the infirmary and frater were ruinous and one wonders how the relatively modest number of monks at Dore modified their buildings to cope with their reduced numbers. Certainly the contraction and change of use of monastic buildings can be shown to be a general trend by the late fifteenth century. Certainly had the Dissolution of the monasteries not taken place many more buildings would have been swept away as the evidence from French Cistercian monasteries such as Clairvaux clearly shows.

The Visible Evidence
Little of this extensive monastic complex now survives at Dore but it is possible to determine the outline of the main layout. The main evidence for the claustral ranges visible to the visitor are the remains of the vestry and library attached to the north transept and the marks of two high roofs against its walls, where the east

range joined the transept (Fig. 29). These roofs had steep pitches and the highest shows that the roof was raised in height and pitch. This obvious change to the dorter roof was not apparently the first change made to the roofs in this area. Against the walls of the transept the upper parts of the east and west wall of the dormitory were not bonded into the transept wall. This could be expected in the area where the roof and its supporting walls had been raised in height but it is clear that the lack of bonding extends much further, below the line of the lower roof. On the west side the bonding of the wall stops some six feet below the lower roof line and indicates that the dormitory roof may have already been raised in height when the upper part of the present transept was built. On its first floor was the dormitory and the transept retains the doorway giving access to the church for the night services, though the staircase has been removed.

The details of the chapter house show that it was constructed after the church had been extended and the eastern parts of the nave campaign completed and it was presumably this rebuilding which caused the second alterations to the level of the dormitory roof. Without further excavations and geophysical surveys it is not possible to be certain how far this rebuilding extended. It certainly affected the eastern range but the fact that the north range follows the later Cistercian plan and the frater was a very large building, makes it likely that it was a comprehensive rebuilding of all the main claustral ranges to a larger size. Certainly the loose fragments of the cloister arcade show that the original arcading had been replaced by the mid-thirteenth century. Such a rebuilding of the claustral ranges would not be unusual, especially if the first layout was relatively modest in scale. At Fountains the ranges were comprehensively rebuilt almost immediately after they had been originally completed[12] and at Tintern the claustral layout was extensively remodelled and substantially enlarged, with a splendid new cloister arcade of syncopated design, in the first half of the thirteenth century, prior to the rebuilding of the church.[13]

The vestry is a long narrow room which was apparently barrel vaulted with a thirteenth century doorway on the west which was subdivided into two. North of the vestry is the site of the chapter house vestibule and a fragment of one corner of the polygonal chapter house which projected east of the range. Nothing more is standing to the north though the outline of the range can be discerned as a distinct platform extending for a considerable distance, almost to the remains of the dismantled railway line, which bounds the site on the north. To the east of the range there is another large platform which may be part of the infirmary complex or abbot's lodging.

At first sight nothing remains of the north range and frater but in fact two substantial pieces of the frater west wall survive. These have two very large trees growing over them which have encased the walling within their impressive root system, preserving the low walls when all the rest has been destroyed. Little of the west range survives apart from the marks of where its east side abutted the nave aisle wall and a short stub of the west wall. This retains a couple of courses of the doorjamb for the cross passage or southern parlour at the south end of the range, a detail apparently overlooked or not seen by Paul. East and west ranges normally had vaulted ground floors, often with simple groin vaulting in early layouts and simple ribbed vaults in thirteenth century buildings. These were usually planned in square bays, with a central row of piers, to form the most easily vaulted space. The high altar of the church is now supported by reused sections of piers and responds which show a large central drum with smaller attached shafts at the cardinal points and it is quite likely that they were robbed from one of these service buildings.

Without excavation we cannot be certain exactly how far to the north the west and east ranges extended but they may have been of similar length and have reached as far north as the frater. If this was the case we could expect the west range to have been vaulted with around eighteen double bays and be around 260 feet in length.

Roland Paul shows on his plans that there was formerly a mill leat or main drain running across the site from west to east parallel with the north cloister alley. Paul outlined on his plans where he thought the main lines of the ranges lay and interpreted a wall on the western side of the cloister as a division for a lane. This was a feature which can also be seen on some other Cistercian sites most notably at Byland Abbey[14] but which also occurred at Neath[15], Beaulieu[16] and Kirkstall[17]; though relatively rare. In houses with a lane between the west range and cloister, the lay brothers day stair was placed on the cloister side of the range as at Byland and Kirkstall, but in those without a lane it was usually on the west side which also had a covered pentice between the church nave aisle doorway and reredorter as at Rievaulx, Fountains and Jervaulx. Paul appears to have based his evidence for the presence of a lane on the junction of this wall with the south aisle of the church and the presence of a doorway immediately to the west. The doorway is relatively early in date, and the decorative base stops on the jambs are identical to those on the northern upper choir entry arch in the presbytery of the church. This shows that it dates from the same period as the construction of the aisleless presbytery, before the addition of the eastern extension to the church. It is unusual to have a doorway in this position without a lane so it is easy to understand Paul's interpretation. However, as Paul indicated on his plans, the masonry of the present wall appears to be largely post-medieval and the extreme width of the lane seems unusual. The position of the doorway, which now seems out of place, may in fact indicate the presence of an earlier claustral layout or plan for the nave, in which its position would not be unusual.

Having thought he had established the presence of a lane, Paul drew a conjectural plan of the claustral layout. Most cloisters are square courts or nearly so and Paul took the distance between the transept and lane as the basis for his square court and projected his cloister on this premise. Therefore his whole plan of the buildings was basically conditioned by the assumed presence of the lane. One aspect of lane planning was overlooked by Paul. In nearly all the known plans the lane is continued through the west end of the south range, such as at Kirkstall and

Byland. At Dore the precise position of the frater has been established (see below) and it is noticeably slightly offset from the centre of the cloister, towards the west. This was presumably to allow for new day stairs as well as the warming house on the east side of the frater. On the west side it is impossible to carry the very wide lane through the range because this would have left virtually no room for the kitchen. If the lane had formed part of the plan it seems clear that the frater would have been positioned further east to allow room for the kitchen. As we shall see below, there is an alternative interpretation of the putative lane wall, derived from the excavated evidence; one which may fit better with the development of the site as a whole.

The Evidence From The Excavations
Between 1893 and 1907 Roland Paul excavated several areas of the church, cloister and monastic buildings in an attempt to ascertain the plan of the monastery. Unfortunately the only records of his discoveries are the short published articles with their various versions of the projected monastic plan, a framed coloured, plan formerly hanging in the vestry of the church (now in Hereford Record Office), and sketch plans in the Paul collection of drawings at the Society of Antiquaries. There are no detailed plan or section drawings of most of the excavations nor are there any photographs. However, study of all this material indicates conflicting features within the plans and the unpublished evidence adds considerably to the overall picture.

The largest excavated area was that of the chapter house and its vestibule with most of the east cloister alley. Paul traced the foundations, which was all that was left, of the west wall of the east range for a considerable distance, to the point where it crossed the mill leat. At this point, near the north wall of the kitchen garden, he found a return wall on its west side. Quite noticeably in the published plans he shows no other wall junction along the east face of the wall, but in the surviving plans there is further evidence noted by Paul but never discussed by him. This was the foundations of a wall three feet thick running east to west across the cloister garth, about 87 feet north of the church. It is not certain what structure this wall represents, but on one of Paul's surviving early plans[18] it is clear that he originally thought that this was the north wall of the cloister and projected a much smaller claustral layout than he later published based on this wall. In the later plans he changed his mind and discounted it entirely, however, it is quite likely that he was right in his initial assessment and that it may have been the south wall of an earlier north range. If a square cloister court is projected on the 87 feet dimension there is room for a substantial west range around 27 feet wide, a width commonly used in early Cistercian cloister layouts, to the wall junction against the north wall of the nave that Paul interpreted as a lane. Such an arrangemnt would place the western doorway in the nave wall on the west side of the adjoining range.

At the time he was working out his theoretical claustral plan, the discoveries of the earlier layouts at Tintern and Waverley had yet to be made and it is probable that had he been aware of these he might have tried, by excavation, to establish if a similar rebuilding had been undertaken at Dore. Though he never investigated along these lines, as we have seen, it is possible to draw some conclusions based on his discoveries. Such an early monastic plan would have probably included narrower ranges which were based around a smaller cloister and may have included a church of aisleless design. Paul's discoveries, though relatively meagre, allow a tentative plan to be drawn which will hopefully stimulate future discussion and possibly archaeological survey.

Paul continued his excavations in the cloister and he appears to have excavated a small hole further west to try and find the kitchen. This showed another section of the wall he had found at the north-east corner of the kitchen garden, and part of another wall returning to the south, though the two do not seem to have been bonded together. Whilst Paul seems to have thought that this return wall was the north end of the wall of the lane it is too far north to fit in with his projected cloister layout; but if it was the west wall of an earlier west range it could be discounted from the later rebuilt medieval plan. The two sections of the north wall that Paul definitely did find were aligned with the southern side of the mill leat and it seems most likely that they mark the north side of the rebuilt cloister court. The eastern end forming the junction with the east range would be the north-east corner of the cloister. If this is correct then with a lane it would have been a most irregular cloister distinctly longer north to south than east to west, a possibility admitted by Paul.[19] However, if the theory of a lane is discounted then the cloister would have been about 137 feet from east to west and 125 feet from north to south, nearer to the equal proportions that Paul was obviously trying to maintain on his projected monastic plan.

On clearing the area west of the east range he discovered the base of the dwarf wall which carried the cloister arcades in the east alley and traced this for a considerable distance, locating the south-east corner for the south alley return and establishing that there was a wall bench against the north aisle wall of the church. This showed that the alleys were around 12 feet wide. In the east alley in front of the southern entrance arch to the chapter house vestibule were two burials with stone tomb covers, one of which is now lying in the ambulatory of the church. Burials in this position seem to have been common and many remain at Rievaulx and have been seen in excavations at Fountains and Meaux. Paul also showed that adjoining the kitchen garden north wall, which is aligned with the north wall of the cloister and mill leat, trenches on the north side revealed traces of the frater walls. No trace can now be seen because the mill leat has been filled in, but the position of the west wall abutment on his plan coincides with the surviving remains of the frater west wall mentioned above and in this position he discovered remains of the kitchen hatch, or cupboard.[20]

Paul also excavated further north, for his 1907 coloured plan is unusual in that it shows more than his published plans, including the full projected layout of the frater walls. It also indicates that Paul excavated the corner junction of its east and north walls which retained indica-

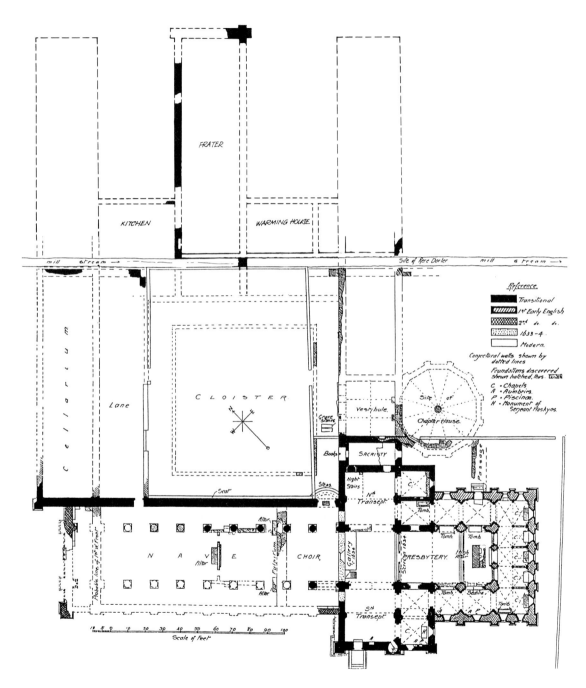

Fig. 76. Reconstruction of the plan of the church and main monastic buildings based on a re-interpretation of Paul's excavations.

tions for corner buttresses. An annotated sketch plan in the Society of Antiquaries collection gives more detail and shows that the frater was 33 feet 10 inches wide and 124 feet long, from its junction with the kitchen garden wall. Against its west and north walls he discovered traces of the wall benching provided for the monks to sit on during meals. This shows that the frater was a very large building, comparable in size to those at Fountains, Beaulieu and Rievaulx. Against the exterior of the west wall of the frater he noted traces of a cross wall 36 feet from the south wall of the range. This seems likely to be the north wall of the kitchen, which may have been aisled, like that at Rievaulx.

He also excavated part of the east wall of the east range where it crossed the mill leat and established that it extended further north beyond that point. He discovered a return wall on its east side just south of the mill leat and marked this as the probable site of the reredorter on his plan. It seems clear, from the position of this wall and the mill leat, that the reredorter would have been attached to the dormitory in this area and so this is probably one of its walls. Similarly, the reredorter attached to the west range serving the dormitory of the lay brothers would have projected along the line of the mill leat on its west side. From all these pieces of evidence it is possible to draw the claustral layout with some certainty and give a better idea of its probable extent.

The Chapter House

Blashill's promising start to the study of material from Dore and his identification of the polygonal chapter house was followed by Paul's more detailed investigation of its site. By excavating, around the area of remaining walling, he discovered that internally it had a wall bench, for the monks to sit on and determined the length of side to establish its full plan. Externally he discovered a substantial base plinth with three steeply chamfered courses, the top of which is 5 feet 6 inches below the surviving external string course.[21] Though mentioning the discovery of various pieces of its superstructure such as capitals he unfortunately never illustrated his discoveries.[22]

In fact the one illustration he published of the central pier plan is inaccurate for it shows all the shafts as being of identical size when it is clear that they alternated around the base from major to minor.[23] Similarly no previous commentator on the form of this pier seems to have noticed that another substantial piece of the base, which is possibly a grey false marble such as lias, also survives. This is shaped to fit on top of the piece found by Blashill and though the upper mouldings with the neckings are now lost, it clearly shows the same alternation of major and minor shafts. From these two pieces the full plan of the pier can be drawn and it becomes clear that it must have had a hexagonal core around which were arranged twelve shafts, probably of detached design (Fig. 77). These were most likely set into hollows worked into the pier core, a feature which also occurred on the central pier at Margam, though it may be that the minor shafts were coursed with the pier core and only the larger ones were detached. If this were the case then it is likely that the shafts were supported by annulet bandings midway up the pier or possibly at even more regular intervals. Paul's drawing of the pier also showed the form of the vault springer which sat on top of the capital. He indicated on the plan the direction in which he thought the ribs of the vault radiated. Unfortunately the moulding profiles indicated by this method cannot be matched to any of the surviving vault ribs.

However, if the mouldings are checked again on the springer it becomes clear that Paul took the wrong positions on the springer to draw his radiating ribs and that if the radiating pattern is adjusted then it is possible to match up the profiles of two of the types of surviving vault ribs. Fortunately one of the rib patterns matches with a foliate vault boss of tri-radial plan (Fig. 78) and the other profile with ribs and an apex joint for a pointed arch. When seen in plan it is clear that the latter formed the transverse ribs of the vault with a single pointed arch spanning from the central springer to the outer wall. The tri-radial spanned with a single rib from the central springer to the crown ridge of the vault and then split with two ribs spanning diagonally to the wall springers. The chapter house at Margam has long been compared with that at Dore and is more well known because of its almost complete survival. It has lost its vault but a drawing made before its collapse shows that its rib pattern was identical to that proposed here for Dore and a single plain tri-radial boss is now lying in the vestibule.

More details of the chapter house can be found amongst the loose pieces. Blashill reported finding a moulded base for a single detached shaft flanked by a pair of roll mouldings from one of its internal angles lying loose in the tower[24] and though this is now lost his description makes it clear that he was correct in his identification. Paul's unpublished drawings[25] show just such a base standing on the wall bench which ran along the base of the chapter house wall. The benching was capped by slabs which had a roll moulding worked along the front edge. The capitals, which Paul reported finding, have now been identified. The visible part of the surviving internal angle of the chapter house has

Fig. 78. Foliate vault boss of tri-radial form from the chapter house

paired roll mouldings separated by a hollow, confirming Paul's drawing. Several loose pieces of this corner shafting are amongst the loose stonework together with three of the capitals which they supported (Fig. 79). These are of stiff leaf design and confirm that the central hollow reflects the presence of a detached shaft which supported the main body of the capital. The outer roll mouldings rise at the sides of the capital and must have been continued as a wall rib to outline the abutment of the vaulting, a feature predicted by Blashill. An exactly similar rib can be seen in the small section of surviving vaulting in the eastern part of the vestibule.

The chapter house has now been reduced to a low level and the only masonry visible is its south-west side surviving around ten feet high (Fig. 81). This shows one of the internal angles with a triangular shaped vaulted compartment to the west. This has one remaining trumpet scallop capital with foliate decoration supporting a vault springer (unfortunately this section has recently suffered a collapse of masonry), with a second springer to the east. The vault webs are defined by a roll moulding wall rib. It seems clear from the height of the capital that its base, which Paul saw and illustrated[26], must be fairly deeply buried and from Paul's drawing it is possible to

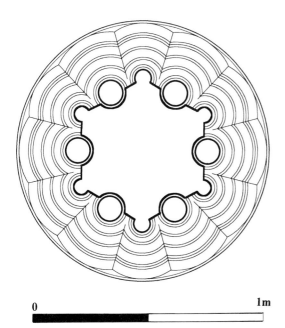

Fig. 77. Plan of the central pier of the chapter house with alternating major and minor shafts

Fig. 79. The chapter house—the internal angle junction with its associated capital

ascertain exactly by how much. Paul gives the height of this shaft from base to capital as 4 feet 7 inches. In addition the shaft base stands on a tall chamfered sub base, giving a total height with capital of nearly 7 feet. Only 4 feet is now visible showing that the floor of the vestibule and chapter house are buried 3 feet below the present ground level. Beyond the quadripartite section of vault springing there is a short section of plain barrel vaulting and along its eastern edge part of a rubble arch on a different alignment. This is the rubble backing arch for the window opening which flanked the entrance doorway.

To the west was the vestibule, probably a relatively low vaulted room to allow for the dormitory overhead. The arches, which fronted the windows, within the east wall of the vestibule were vaulted with quadripartite ribbed vaults and one of the diagonal vault rib keystones, identifiable by the angle of its intersecting ribs, has survived and has the same rib profile and similar foliate decoration to the tri-radial ribs from the chapter house. The surviving vault springers

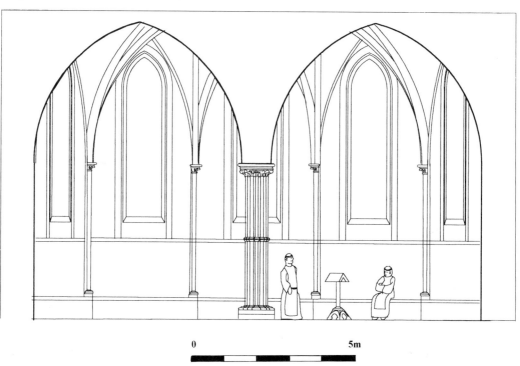

0   5m

Fig, 80. Reconstructed cross-section of the chapter house showing the central pier which supported the vaulting. The height is largely conjectural but cannot be far from that actually built.

though worn and not showing the full profile also clearly had this type of moulding higher up the springing. Paul's 1931 article shows a drawing of the northern jamb of the main entrance arches standing one course above its moulded bases and his unpublished plan shows the door jamb plan in detail with six shafts, on the reveal, of alternating coursed and detached design, an arrangement that was also employed at Tintern Abbey chapter house. His unpublished drawings also show that he located the central section of the chamfered plinth of the next door base to the north. Its position shows that like Tintern there was a group of three entrance arches, an architectural motif that was first employed at Fountains in the 1160s but which was relatively rare. Most houses of the Order employed the more usual design of a single entrance arch flanked by a pair of unglazed windows. The position of the plinth indicates that the doorways were of equal width and would have looked somewhat similar to the surviving doorways at

Fig. 81. The fragmentary remains of the chapter house

Margam. To the east there is a second group of shafts in the south-west angle of the vestibule with one attached and one detached shaft to carry the rerearch of the doorway and the corner vault springer respectively.

Paul shows a conjectural layout for the vaulting of the vestibule with three equally spaced aisles[27] and with two piers, although two unpublished drawings show possible arrangements of two and four piers. However, the angle of the surviving corner vault springer seems to confirm an arrangement of only two piers. Comparison with the surviving elements shows that it is most likely that the lost piers were a cluster of eight shafts and if there were only two with semicircular diagonal arches it is possible to show that the vaults must have been between 14 feet and 15 feet in height. The whole, with its slender pier supports, must have looked very similar to the vaults of the ambulatory of the church which are also supported on piers with eight shafts. Overall the details of the chapter house and vestibule seem to confirm that they form part of the same building campaign and it was not simply a case of adapting an existing chapter house as a vestibule to the new polygonal building. Paul may also have seen sections of the chapter house windows, but though several chamfered window sills, jambs and arch voussoirs survive amongst the stonework it is impossible to determine with certainty if any of them came from the chapter house. The close similarity of the chapter house to the more complete example at Margam makes it likely that Dore also featured single windows in each bay.

The question of which abbey first adopted the polygonal chapter house plan has been the subject of some discussion and is explored in detail in the chapter by Joe Hillaby. However, the details now recovered show quite clearly that Dore must have been built after the work on the abbey church and later than the chapter house at Margam and that besides the more advanced character of its decoration, the general form of the plan of the vestibule and its entrance arches, together with the complex arrangement of vaulted spaces in front of the windows flanking the entrance arch quite clearly show significant advances on the Margam design.

CHAPTER XII

The Monastic Precinct

by Richard Stone

If the church and the cloister were the focus of the spiritual life of a medieval monastery, it was the wide range of activities that took place in the precinct surrounding this central core that provided for the daily life of the community, controlling its income and welfare.

Unlike the formal disposition of the cloister, there was no predetermined layout for the components of the precinct. The form of an ideal monastery depicted in the tenth century plan of St. Gall never became accepted in practice, though it gives a good indication of what a precinct might be expected to include.[1] Whereas the central focus of the precinct was spiritual, the services provided in the wider precinct were mainly devoted to agriculture, industry and accommodation, and a large variety of land use was common. As the Cistercian ideal aimed to balance the spiritual life with manual labour it was normal for their precincts to be substantially larger than those of other orders, allowing for agricultural land to be cultivated by the monks without the need for them to leave the confines of the monastery.

The study of precincts has been much neglected. Typically the remains are not from substantial stone buildings with carved stonework and traceried windows, but from agricultural systems, timber structures and only a relatively small number of generally plain buildings. The status was not as high as the church and cloister, but it was by no means low. Many monastic churches survive, at least in part, as they were not easy to convert to other uses after the dissolution. However, most of the land and buildings of the precinct were claimed for other uses and it is rare to find complete structures surviving. Indeed, the vast majority of the layout of precincts is now lost to sight. Careful investigation of the evidence of the landscape, contemporary accounts and later maps and documents, can nevertheless reveal much evidence about its disposition beyond the cloister, which formed 90% of the enclosed monastery.

The precinct boundary was usually formed by a high wall, and access was strictly controlled through gatehouses.[2] The intention of the physical enclosure was primarily to act as a barrier reflecting the separation of the community from the outside world. The importance of security and defensibility was secondary, though this was not neglected. The fourteenth century Great Gate of the urban abbey of Bury St. Edmunds, for instance, was provided with portcullis and arrow slits. The gatehouse itself was a very important building, as the public face of the monastery. Often it was made impressive by its defences, its sheer size, as at St. Albans Abbey, or by decorative treatment, such as at Kirkham Priory.

The precinct was divided into a series of walled courts, each with a specific function and its own buildings. At the centre was the 'House', which consisted of the church and cloister with the surrounding ranges. The monastery's infir-

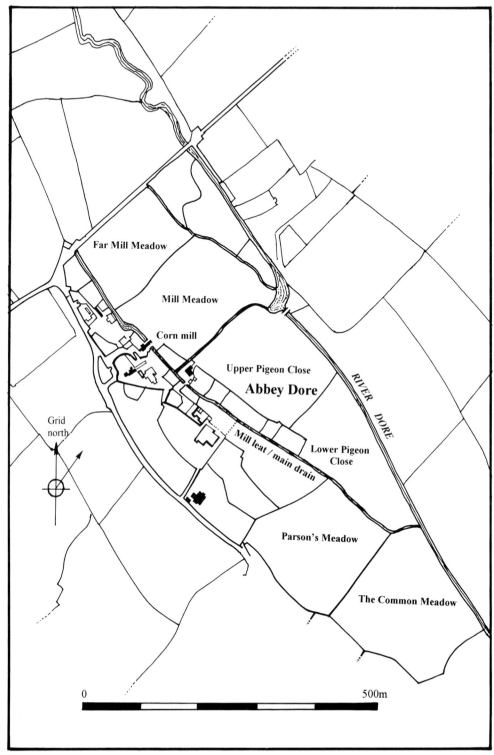

Fig. 82. A copy of the tithe map of 1839-40

mary and cemetery and the lodging for the head of the house, whether abbot or prior, were also included within this central core. Beyond this was what is now generally known as the Inner Court which included guest accommodation, stabling, granaries as well as bakehouse, brewhouse and storage for food and drink. The largest part of the monastery was the Outer Court where the lesser, ancillary buildings, such as barns, woolhouse, smithy and stabling would be found. In larger houses the precinct might include a range of other agricultural uses such as piggeries, dovecotes and orchards. The provision of water to all parts of the monastery was of critical importance for drinking, washing, drainage and for industry and agriculture.[3] Accordingly, much effort was put into its supply, including extensive piping, canalisation and the construction of mills, water meadows and fish ponds.

The sale of monastic lands after the dissolution and the subsequent changes in ownership and use of land have resulted in the loss of vast amounts of detailed information about the layout of individual precincts and it is only recently that serious study of this aspect of monasticism has been undertaken. At Dore Abbey there are, unfortunately, only very fragmentary standing remains of the precinct boundary and of the Inner and Outer Courts to show their extent and layout. Nor do descriptions of the abbey's layout exist in the form of dissolution inventories and the like. The *Valor Ecclesiasticus* of 1535 is too terse to be of value and the descriptions of the demesne lands granted to John Scudamore after the dissolution do not differentiate between the precinct and the lands beyond.[4] Instead, the information generated from the landscape must be used, together with early maps and documents to provide a better insight into the layout and functioning of the abbey precinct.

In the description of the precinct which follows liturgical orientation is used.

The Extent of the Precinct
The patronage of Robert of Ewyas was of central importance in determining the size and position of the abbey. The size of the precinct reflects the extent of land granted by him and the intended numbers of the community. Leland's description of the abbey, written shortly after it had been suppressed, noted that:

> The broke of Dour runneth by the abbay of Dour, and there it breketh a litle above the monasterie into 2. armes, whereof the lesse arme rennethe throwghe the monastery. The bygger arme levith the abbey a bowe shot of on the right hond or banke. The confluence is againe hard bynethe the abbey.[5]

The lesser arm mentioned is shown on the tithe map of 1839-40 (Fig. 82), and was marked on the 1904 Ordnance Survey 6 inch map as a mill race (Fig. 83). Its course continued through the abbey, as a drain for the claustral kitchen and lavatorium, before rejoining the Dore at the boundary of the precinct. The larger arm of the river formed the northern boundary of the precinct. Along the bank there are ephemeral traces of an embankment towards the east, which may not be related to the abbey but to dumping of material, whilst the few fragments of building stone in this area are not *in situ*. Although a wall along the bank of the river was not absolutely necessary one was nevertheless sometimes provided, as at Furness and Rievaulx.[6] At Abbey Dore there is no visible evidence for any direct exploitation of the river itself.

The western boundary of the precinct is represented by the road which runs past Abbey Dore Court. Directly west of the Court the road goes over a bridge, probably contemporary with the Court, which replaced an earlier one spanning the Dore. A hundred metres further south another bridge, probably of medieval date, spans a leat which flowed eastwards through the north-western part of the precinct, before joining the Dore 300 metres downstream. Along this boundary there is no trace of any masonry or of a platform to carry a wall. Instead it is marked by a ditch on the eastern side of the road, which was formerly part of the abbey's system of leats.

Further south is a junction of four roads, which clearly represents the south-western corner of the precinct. Just within the precinct at

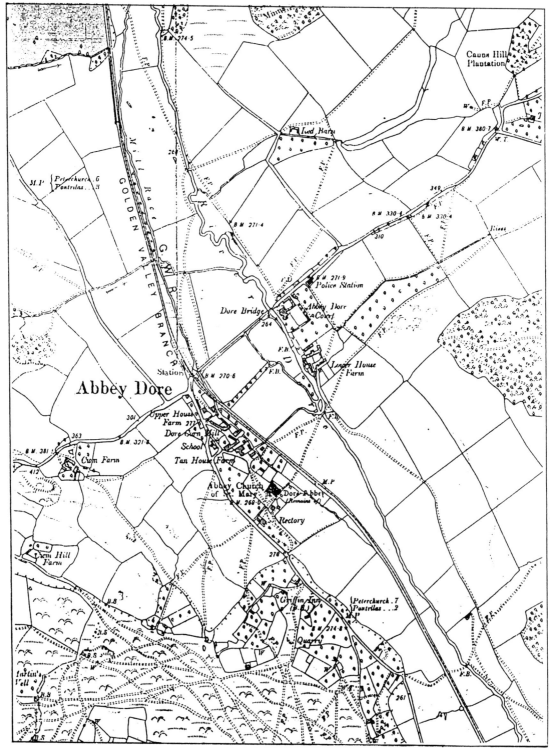

Fig. 83. The 1904 Ordnance Survey map of the Abbey Dore area (6 inch to 1 mile)

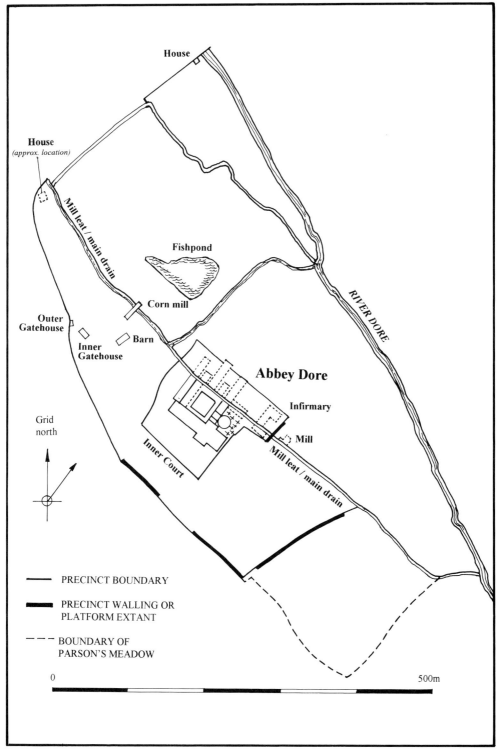

Fig. 84. The layout of the precinct

Within the figure, the following labels appear:

House

House *(approx. location)*

Mill leat / main drain

Fishpond

Corn mill

Outer Gatehouse

Inner Gatehouse

Barn

Abbey Dore

Infirmary

Mill

RIVER DORE

Inner Court

Mill leat / main drain

Grid north

PRECINCT BOUNDARY

PRECINCT WALLING OR PLATFORM EXTANT

BOUNDARY OF PARSON'S MEADOW

0   500m

Fig. 85. The precinct wall at the east, from the east

this point (Fig. 84) are traces of loose stone rubble in an otherwise wooded area. The traces are enough to suggest a demolished building just within the precinct, though this could be a post-medieval structure. A few metres north of this the main leat serving the community entered the precinct, having been canalised from the Dore some 1,300 metres upstream. It ran through the mill complex, then continued past the north cloister alley and, passing the site of the infirmary, continued eastwards to rejoin the Dore.

From the south-west corner of the precinct the road continues to the east, broadly parallel to the river. On its northern side the road is hedged, and many old trees, together with several large stumps, survive just within this line, indicating the antiquity of this boundary, though in the western stretch no traces of the precinct wall can be seen. Where the boundary reaches a point opposite the nave a flat platform, up to 3 metres wide, is visible. In some areas there is a slight ridge in the centre of the platform with a thick-

ness of about 1.3 metres, which is presumably the remains of the precinct wall. Beyond this, adjacent to the Rectory, masonry walling of a similar thickness survives to a height of up to 1 metre. Despite extensive rebuilding, this wall doubtless perpetuates the line of the precinct boundary. The precinct wall would have been about 3 metres high, comparable with the very imposing 3.4 metres of Fountains Abbey.[7]

Leland's statement that the leat rejoined the Dore 'hard bynethe the abbey' would suggest that the precinct included the 8 acre (3 ha.) field that was called The Parson's Meadow in 1839, and there is no doubt that the field to its east, called the Common Meadow in the tithe apportionment, was outside the precinct. The western end of the Parson's Meadow is defined by the remains of a stone wall along the line of which, after it had tumbled almost to ground level, trees grew, and it now appears as a tree-covered embankment. Some of the trees growing on top of the decayed wall are several centuries old, attesting to the antiquity of the wall. Where it marks the boundary of the Rectory garden, the wall is 0.6 metres thick, but further north it is up to 1.2 metres thick (Fig. 85). The wall continues only as far as the main leat or drain and no evidence survives in the landscape to suggest that it formerly continued to the river. The precise course of the precinct in this stretch is therefore unclear. It possibly followed the line of the wall northwards, but could equally have followed the bank of the leat eastwards.

The precinct was therefore a sub-rectangular enclosure covering about 48 acres (21 ha.), bounded by the the river to its north, and with roads to its west and south (Fig. 84). The church occupied a central position within the precinct. The boundary was marked by a wall at the east and along at least part of the southern edge, along the road. As at Tintern, it seems that the wall was not continuous around the whole precinct.[8] The size of the precinct reflected the needs and aspirations of the community at the time of its foundation, accepting the restrictions placed by land granted to the monastery. The initial community of an abbot and twelve monks was seen as only the starting point, from which further growth was expected. Once the size of the precinct was fixed, probably by the end of the twelfth century, it was to remain so until the Dissolution, when there were only nine monks, with sixteen or more servants.[9]

At Fountains Abbey, where the dorter of the 1160s could accommodate up to 120 monks, the precinct covered some 70 acres (28 ha.).[10] Furness was of similar size, while Rievaulx, intended by St. Bernard to be the base from which Cistercian influence was to spread throughout Scotland and the north of England, had an even larger precinct, of some 92 acres (37 ha.).[11] Byland Abbey, a great rival of nearby Rievaulx, had a precinct in excess of 100 acres. In the smaller communities there was still a substantial acreage, such as at Kirkstall with 40 acres (16 ha.) or Tintern, which is suggested to have had around 27 acres (11 ha.). This would have been an average size, serving a community which was envisaged as around twenty monks and fifty lay brothers.[12] If the extent of the precinct is a fair indication, Dore Abbey's acreage suggests that it had higher than average aspirations, particularly in comparison with other Cistercian houses in this part of Britain. These aspirations were doubtless connected to its role in establishing daughter houses and as a mission centre.

Outer Court

Access to the precinct was controlled at the gatehouse. In Cistercian monasteries there was an outer gatehouse, which formed the initial entrance, and then an inner, or 'Great' gatehouse, which was generally more substantial. At Furness Abbey the 'Great' gate was 170 feet (52 metres) south of the outer gate.[13] The sale of goods of Abbey Dore in 1537 following the dissolution included two cornwains 'within the great gate and the postern gate to the same.'[14]

No trace of either gatehouse remains and even their sites are uncertain. Roland Paul suggested that the entrance to the monastery was to the south or south-west of the church.[15] Even if he was referring to liturgical directions rather than to points of the compass this seems unlikely. It is more likely that the gatehouses were to the west, and it is in this area that the industrial Outer Court buildings described below would have been clustered. The tithe map shows a road or track, now lost, leading (liturgical) north from the triangle of land on which the school house was built and this is the probable location for the outer gatehouse. Such a position would have given access to the industrial and agricultural hub of the Outer Court, whilst also providing a direct route to the nave of the church.

Close to the gatehouse would have been a chapel, almonry, and possibly a lay infirmary and accommodation for the poorest guests. The sites of these are unknown, but their presence can be inferred from documentary evidence. A report of the visitation of 1318 noted specifically that provision was to be made for women pilgrims at the abbey gate rather than within the confines of the monastery, which suggests that they were—previously and most irregularly—being allowed into the Inner Court rather than being kept outside, at a chapel near the gate.[16]

131

As well as providing a chapel the Cistercians took their responsibility towards hospitality and almsgiving very seriously. For this, money was needed. In 1273 Dore was noted as being deficient in temporalities and the problem was cited half a century later, in 1329, as so acute that the requisite hospitality could not be given—'even that due to Christ's poor.'[17] Assuming that this was not an exaggeration it would have meant that many obligations, such as medical assistance, could not be fulfilled. Lay infirmaries had become a common feature of monasteries by the early thirteenth century, and Dore's probably dated from this period. It continued to be used, presumably until the dissolution, but at least into the sixteenth century when a Thomas Cokeshutt expressed his indebtedness to the monks for being bled.[18]

Besides helping the poor, the community would have provided accommodation for a range of guests of varying status, all of whom needed appropriate lodgings. These included the very poor who might be given a room with the animals, as was the case at Nunkeeling, where the 'house for poore folks' was with the hen-house.[19] The richer lay guests would need more spacious and well appointed lodging while visiting the monastery, and would be given accommodation in the Inner Court, as described below. Visiting monks were lodged in the dorter with the community's own monks.

In addition to receiving temporary guests, the abbey provided accommodation for permanent guests in the form of corrodies (annuities). The earliest reference to these at Dore was in the second half of the thirteenth century when Walter de Homeness was granted a corrody in return for the payment of two marks annually.[20] This small sum, if not augmented by an initial grant, was not large enough to warrant spacious lodgings and Walter was probably simply given a room within the normal guest accommodation in the Outer Court. Little is known of the locations of corrodians' houses, but they do generally seem to have been in the Outer Court, as has been shown at Rievaulx.

Besides these charitable duties the monastery sustained a varied economy within the precinct.

Most of the buildings are now lost but the south-western part is still extensively built up and although the buildings which survive in this area are of the post-medieval period they are likely to be replacements of earlier structures of similar function. It is in this area that the centre of the industrial activity of the monastery was to be found. At the west was a complex of uncertain function, identified simply as a homestead in the tithe map apportionment of 1839. To the east of this homestead was a corn mill. The course of the mill leat is clearly shown on the tithe map. Remains found during repairs and deepening of the mill stream in the late nineteenth century, when the corn mill was still in use were interpreted as being from its medieval predecessor. Unfortunately, the precise location of these remains was not recorded and soon after it was noted that 'there is nothing of interest to be seen there.'[21] The leat is now disused and largely infilled.

At the time of the tithe apportionment the two large fields to the north were called Mill Meadow and Far Mill Meadow. These were bounded on all sides by leats, as were the two fields between them and the river. In no other part of the precinct is such a developed network of water-courses found. This area, upstream of the main core of the monastery, would have been fed with clean water. An extensive depression in Mill Meadow, running diagonally across the field, may reflect the position of monastic fish-ponds, but no trace of leats serving them are visible (Fig. 86). Alternatively it has been suggested that the depression was associated with the construction of the railway in the nineteenth century and that the fishponds were to the east of the church.[22]

To the east of the corn mill was another complex, called a homestead in the tithe apportionment. This retains the name of Tan House Farm, indicating a possible use of this area in the monastic period. Adjoining the later farmhouse is a barn of four timber-framed bays with a threshing floor of stone flags. This barn was probably one of the important agricultural buildings associated with the corn mill. The details of the sale of goods after the dissolution refer separ-

Fig. 86. Depression in Mill Meadow, possibly fishponds

ately to wheat, barley and oats all as being in 'the barn.'[23] The range of crops would have derived from the various granges as well as from the immediate demesne and the precinct and other crops would also have needed storage within the precinct. There is no documentary evidence of what was grown within the precinct, but it is likely to have included several crops in rotation as well as areas of pasture and meadow land.

The barn which now forms part of Tan House Farm was a threshing barn and there may well have been a separate barn for crop storage at the time of the dissolution. There were probably also other barns, including a hay barn, as these were provided even in the smaller houses, for example Yedingham and Thicket, both in Yorkshire.[24] The tithe apportionment mentions a tithe barn in an entry called the 'piece below the churchyard including tithe barn and fold' is misleading. The Cistercians did not originally collect tithes and the map shows this 'piece' as being in the area of the cloister and to the east of the chapter house,

and so a post-medieval addition. Tradition states that the post-medieval tithe barn in fact lay to the north of the mill leat, under the present cowsheds of Tan House Farm but the authority for this is uncertain and the story does not agree with the tithe map location.

The buildings of the tannery which give Tan House Farm its name, are now all lost. In the *Taxatio Ecclesiastica* of 1291, there is mention of a tannery grange.[25] The building of a tannery within the precinct would have been a later medieval development when tenants were increasingly involved within the precinct, and the monks administered the economic life of the abbey. At Rievaulx the southern end of the east range of the cloister, together with a large area to the south of the frater, was in use as the abbey tannery in the sixteenth century. According to the Rievaulx 'Survey' made in 1538/9 the area included a bark house with tanning vats, the bark house garth, a bark mill with associated lime kiln, a house for the storage of bark and also a

133

Fig. 87. Aerial photo of the precinct, with the depressions visible in the field to the east
© Crown Copyright/MOD (1949)

house for the barker, who was clearly a lay tenant.[26] A similar range of buildings would have been present at Dore Abbey, and would have covered a relatively large area. The substantial woodlands held by Dore Abbey would, despite the extensive assarting of the thirteenth century, have provided ample supplies of oak bark for use in the tanning process.[27] The hides also would have come from the abbey's lands, though records of the number of cows and oxen are scant and seem underestimated.

Just downstream of Tan House farm, marking the boundary of Mill Meadow, is a drain or leat which leads back to the river. It is uncertain whether this drain is of post-medieval date or whether it diverted some of the water from the tannery and mill from the leat which continued through the claustral ranges serving as a drain for

the reredorter, infirmary and abbot's lodgings. As it passed to the north of the cloister, the course of the leat is now no longer visible, but in 1893 there were masonry remains arching over the leat 'all along its length, where opposite the Abbey' (i.e. the claustral buildings) and the leat was visible as a stream about 4 feet (1.2 metres) wide.[28]

This water system was for industrial and agricultural use and for drainage, but would not have been for drinking water for which there was always a separate source.[29] No wells or springs are known within the precinct, but there is a spring on the hill beyond the precinct, to the south of the church. This spring was brought into use to serve Tan House Farm early this century and prior to this the area was marshy.[30] It is possible that this was the source for the community's drinking water and that it was piped from here to the monastery, where it would have fed ultimately into the main drain running past the north range of the cloister.

Further east there is very little evidence of the layout of the Outer Court, apart from a series of depressions in the field east of the church (Fig. 87), at a distance of some 100 metres from it, which Roland Paul considered to include fish-ponds.[31] For most of the year this area is well drained, but after heavy rain two separate pools can be seen, joined by narrow water courses. In this area the subsoil is river gravel at a depth of 1.5m or less[32] and if these were fishponds they would have needed a clay seal to retain the water.

The Outer Court was doubtless largely meadow and pasture, but some crops were culti-vated, such as flax. The monastery's dovecotes were probably in the two large fields bordering the river, which were known as Upper and Lower Pigeon Close when the tithe map was compiled. These provided a staple food, particu-larly in the earlier medieval period with its restrictions on meat-eating at a time when poultry was not considered to be meat as it walked on two legs rather than four.

During the course of the medieval period the Cistercians gradually moved from a system in which work was generally done by the monks and the lay brothers to one in which the monks were administrators and their servants and the local laity did most of the manual work. This gradual relaxation came to include women as labourers or servants. However, the account of the visitation of 1318 shows that this was unac-ceptable, at this period at least, and women were forbidden admittance to the abbey for picking, washing and preparing flax.[33] The scale of this crop is unknown, but the reference gives a hint of the wide diversity of land use that might be found within the precinct.

A further indication of this changing nature of priorities in the monastic life is the presence of a tailor, one Harry ap Glyn, in the sixteenth century. Earlier, in the middle of the thirteenth century there is a reference to Walter, one of the monks, fulfilling this role under the title of keeper of the wardrobe.[34] There would have been a workshop for him within the precinct, but as he does not seem to have had a lodging, this may not have been a dedicated building, and if it was it may have been an insubstantial structure. Such buildings are likely to have been scattered throughout various parts of the Outer Court, serving the many needs of the community.

The economy of Dore Abbey was reliant in part upon woodland exploitation and this resource would have provided the building mate-rial for most of the structures needed. Sheep farming was also of great importance, as for many Cistercian houses, with the estates of Dore Abbey supporting some 3,000 sheep in the late thirteenth century, compared with the 4,000 of Hailes.[35] The Dore wool, however, was of better quality. The best of the sixteen sacks exported annually through the Italian factor Pergalotti was worth 28 marks, compared with a maximum of 18 marks for the best of Hailes' twenty sacks.[36] One of the prominent buildings is therefore likely to have been a woolhouse, enabling a centralised control of the wool production of the many granges to be maintained. There may also have been areas for specialised functions asso-ciated with sheep farming, as at Fountains Abbey where there was a clipping garth and a shearing garth.[37]

At Fountains the woolhouse with its dye vats was next to a semi-detached building which housed a malthouse, brewhouse, and later a smithy.[38] Similar combinations of different func-tions can be expected at Dore Abbey, and all these buildings would have to be somewhere in the precinct. In the later years the size and range of buildings is likely to have grown, and increas-ingly the workmen would have been given accommodation within the precinct, as the earlier restrictions on laity within the precinct were relaxed. At Rievaulx Abbey at the dissolution a smith, plumber and baker were all housed.[39] All communities would have had buildings for housing workers and the 'house by the wayside next to the bridge', mentioned in the 1537 sale of goods of Abbey Dore, may have been one of these.[40] Certainly it is likely to have been rela-tively substantial as few buildings outside the

Fig. 88. The earthwork platform of the Inner Court buildings, from the east

claustral core are mentioned and at its sale would have been of value only for stone, timber or slate. At Dore Abbey there is now little visible evidence in the landscape for masonry structures and any timber structures would be even more ephemeral in the archaeological record. Without considerable survey work or archaeological excavation it would be hard to locate and identify the remains of such structures.

The Inner Court and the House

Earthworks, documents and maps allow for a broad indication of the layout of a substantial part of the Inner Court and the peripheral buildings of the House. In general it would encompass an additional area roughly the same size as the church and claustral complex. The major buildings besides the claustral ranges were the abbot's lodging and the infirmary which were considered part of the 'House'. Although there was no prescribed location for these buildings the Cistercians generally followed one of two forms.

The more formal of these had a complex of abbot's lodging and infirmary grouped around one or two cloisters or yards close to the east and of the church and the chapter house, as at Jervaulx and Tintern. The other form was of two separate complexes, generally not forming quadrangles and often further from the church and chapter house as at Furness and Fountains. Abbey Dore belonged to this second category.

A note on Roland Paul's plan of 1931 states that he found 'considerable remains of walling' 150 feet (46 metres) east of his plan.[41] An unpublished sketch plan indicates the extent of these remains, which are of two separate buildings.[42] The western-most, which he records as 130 feet (40 metres) from the east end of the church, comprised a 15 foot (4.6 metres) long stretch of walling with traces of a cross wall spanning the great drain. It can therefore be identified as a reredorter or latrine block, and Paul considered it to be part of the infirmary. To the north of the drain in this area an earthwork platform survives which must represent the continuation of this complex (Fig. 88). The shape of the platform, together with the remains that Paul found, suggests that the building was half H-shaped. The arm perpendicular to the leat would have included the reredorter, perhaps with the infirmary hall at right angles and another building, perhaps the chapel, in the northern arm. In 1330 there was a mention of the 'great infirmary' within the precinct, which suggests that there may have been another, perhaps including provision for sick guests and the laity.[43]

About 35 feet (11 metres) east of this wall there were more substantial remains. The irregularities of the plan suggests that the building was of more than one phase. It was 41 feet (12.5 metres) long internally and 10 foot 8 inches (3.2 metres) wide at the west. The eastern wall continued further north, at least 18 feet (5.5 metres) and had a narrow cross wall, probably a partition wall. In the south wall, alongside the drain (which was here some eight feet (2.4 metres) wide) an uninterpreted feature is shown. It it not clear whether this was of timber or stone. It appears to have included an opening 2 foot 6 inches (0.8 metres) wide internally. This could have taken a mill wheel and the complex may have been for some industrial process. If this were the case this structure would undoubtedly have been in the Outer Court. Although it has been suggested that this was part of the abbot's lodging, it is quite a distance from the church and this interpretation does not explain the feature alongside the drain. From the available evidence it seems more likely that this was part of a second mill in the precinct and that the abbot's lodging was elsewhere, as yet undetermined. Masonry can still be seen in this area on both sides of the leat, and further investigation may confirm the nature of the structure.

Another major feature of the Inner Court was the cemetery, which is presumed to have lain to the south and east of the church.[44] In 1286 it was noted that the Abbey garden was adjacent to the cemetery. Besides there being a cemetery for the monks several benefactors of the abbey were buried within the church, and according to Gerald of Wales, in his antipathetic depiction of

the practices at Abbey Dore, the monks brought the dying to the monastery from Ewyas Harold and Bacton, hastening their death.[45] The intention was to benefit from the income from the funeral and doubtless to encourage the dying to leave money and possessions to the abbey in return for burial within the monastery, thus increasing the likelihood of reaching heaven. Although this may have been an isolated occurrence it is evident that there was a lay cemetery as well as one for the members of the community, though perhaps there was no formal separation between them.

Also within the Inner Court were buildings associated with the best attested of Dore's corrodies, that granted to Thomas Cleubery, a former abbot of Dore. Three years after his retirement in 1523 he received, in addition to a substantial pension, a corrody consisting of three chambers, a parlour, and an adjacent chapel, 'situated on the north side of the monastery' together with a servant, fuel and land and fodder for two horses as well as food and drink.[46] In the sale of 1537 after the dissolution this was called the New Chamber, and two other chambers were separately itemised—St. Thomas of Lancaster's chamber and the Little Chamber—the former being more richly furnished than the New Chamber, and the latter less so.[47] These other chambers could have been for corrodians but may equally have been Inner Court accommodation for visiting monks.

The guest house, perhaps with its own kitchen and stabling, is most likely to have been between the gatehouse and the church. Such a position is found at Fountains and at the excavated guest house at Tintern.[48] The bakehouse, brewhouse, buttery and kitchen are all mentioned in the 1537 sale.[49] They are likely to have been situated to the north or north-west of the cloister, but as with so many of the precinct's buildings no evidence of them can any longer be seen in the landscape.

An outline of the probable extent of the Inner Court and the House is given in Fig. 84. There are no medieval walls to indicate the boundary and only crude approximation, based on later walls, the landscape and divisions marked on the tithe map, can be used. The Inner Court was roughly rectangular, at the north being close to the north end of the frater, turning southwards between the infirmary and mill, then returning close to the east end of the church. The inclusion of the present cemetery to the south of the church is uncertain, the boundary would not have been far from the west front of the church.

Conclusion

The information presented above is based on several site visits at different times of the year and in different weather conditions, augmented by documentary study. More information can be given about the disposition of the precinct than is at first apparent. The entrance was at the west, leading to the industrial centre of the Outer Court, with its corn mill, tannery and barns. Beyond were the Inner Court and House, separated by a further gate. The eastern part of the precinct was devoted largely to agricultural production rather than processing, though there may have been another mill here. The level of detail provided by visual examination and documentary study remains variable, however, and although some flesh has been put on the bones of the precinct much more could be understood by further selective study. Geophysical and earthwork survey would give greater insights into the disposition of the precinct, the area to the east of the frater being particularly susceptible to such future investigation. Excavation, nowadays frowned upon if there is no threat to a site, should not be undertaken lightly but should not it be excluded as an option to answer specific research-driven questions. Monastic precincts remain under-studied and every possible method should be brought to bear in an attempt to get a more detailed picture of the changing land use of these critical social and economic units.

CHAPTER XIII

The Engineer Monks

by Francis Evans

Dore Abbey is part of a much greater whole, just one out of nearly 800 Cistercian abbeys. From Portugal to the Holy Land, from Italy to Norway and Latvia, these astonishing foundations spread across Christendom. Despite the pillaging by Henry VIII, by wars, or by rampant atheism, their remains still shelter in remote valleys. Because of their remoteness, they have rarely survived as living churches, unlike the great Benedictine and Augustinian abbeys of Gloucester, Selby and Tewkesbury where a town had grown up, large enough to take over the abbey church for the parishioners. For all their beauty, the Cistercian abbeys are as alien to the modern eye as the vestiges of Rome must have been to the barbarian tribes who replaced the empire. It is best to admit at once that they belong to a remote past which will not be easily explained in modern terms.[1]

It is well to remember that four hundred years separate St. Bernard of Clairvaux from the Reformation, nearly as long as the time between that upheaval and us. We have to clear our minds of layers of false impressions, not just the odd misapprehension, before we can even begin to approach the mystery; and it is not certain that we will solve it even then. Henry VIII's Commissioners and protestant Tudor public relations made sure that the monks got a bad press. Hollywood has fostered the same picture of fat, lazy, bibulous charlatans living off the work of others. Yet the first Cistercians were lean and

energetic. A new spiritual élite, they criticised the older Benedictine foundations, especially Cluny, for similar faults.

Another illusion grew up fed by the gaunt beauty of the ruins. As early as the seventeenth century, and increasingly in the eighteenth, the abbeys became symbols of Gothic mystery in the romantic mind. We recollect the delicious thrills of apprehension as Catherine Morland approaches Northanger Abbey and imagines the Gothic horrors that await her there. Wordsworth's lines on Tintern Abbey are exquisite but they show all the romantic preoccupation with the self and its consciousness. In the poem, there is not a word about monks. The reality was different from these later romantic imaginings. In their heyday, the abbeys were alive, functional and as unromantic as Arwright's mill at Cromford was in the eighteenth century. A great Cistercian abbey was a kolkhoz—a well-organised collective farm. J. Meade Faulkner's poem 'Cistercians' comes closer to the true past:

> All things in the beginning
> Before their Maker came,
> The wheatfield for the winning
> The furze-brush for the flame;
>
> The cattle in the cow-land
> The meadow-sweet and sedge,
> The plover on the plough-land
> The bullfinch in the hedge;

The sward the blackface browses,
The stapler and the bale,
The grey Cistercian houses
That pack the wool for sale;

The downland and the dewpond,
The drainland and the dyke,
The Friday-fishing stew-pond,
The netting of the pike;

The grass on hillside ranges,
The milk-froth in the pail,
The granaries and the granges,
The echo of the flail;

The applegarth and vineyard,
The Southern Cloister figs,
The dovecote and the kineyard,
The fat December pigs.

All things in the beginning
Before their maker came:
Labour to keep from sinning,
Fasting and prayer to tame.

Compline with *Qui cisternas*,
Exsurge with the lark;
The novice *Ad lucernas*,
The old monk in the dark.

The old monk dreams and drowses,
The young monk sings the scale;
The grey Cistercian houses
Pack all the wool for sale.

Remote in time and mood, not romantic, what else stands between us and a clear vision of the Cistercians? Perhaps we are not prepared to recognise how competent they were. Probably the modern mind is chiefly misled by pictures in old manuscripts. Though funny and appealing, the pictures are lacking in perspective and childishly distorted, so that the important people are drawn bigger, and large masons work on tiny castles. We take the ability to draw for granted and so we assume that people who draw crudely do everything else in the same fashion. We do not have to look far to see how wrong that idea

is. Compare a quaint medieval drawing of a castle with the reality that remains—Caernarfon, Harlech Castle or the mighty Krak des Chevaliers in Syria. Could anything be more businesslike? The competent military planning, the strength and quality of the work, the huge scale of construction at once strikes the eye. Compared with Leonardo da Vinci's drawings of machines, medieval illustrations are childlike. Yet it should be remembered that Leonardo's convincing drawings of ornithopters—men flying in a harness of wings that they flap—would not work; nor would his helicopter nor many other inventions of his ranging imagination. Medieval masons were different; they could build a cathedral vault but they could not draw it. Drawing and doing are two different things.

The Little Exord—the word means an introduction or beginning—tells how the first Cistercians, a small group of monks, in their determination to return to a purer observance of St. Benedict's Rule, decided that they should not take tithes nor be beholden to rich patrons, but should earn their own living. They would take and cultivate lands remote from human dwellings, vineyards and woods; and streams to power mills or provide fish. The work would be more than the monks could achieve alongside their main duty of prayer and contemplation, and so they took up one of the essential keys to their eventual success—the bearded lay-brothers 'whom they would treat as themselves in life and in death—the status of monk apart.'[2] Logically, this led on to the building of granges to exploit lands too far from the abbey for daily travel; but only lay-brothers could live on these granges for monks were not allowed to sleep away from the abbey.

The English often like to think of their medieval history as a rather fortunate, haphazard, unguided evolution—A.F. Pollard called his book on the origins of parliament *The Evolution of Parliament*, for instance, as if like Topsy it just growed. The thinking which led to the rules of the Cistercian order was not haphazard, but strongly purposeful and for a century and more it worked out as the planners intended. Historians are in general agreement that this clear planning was largely due to the third abbot of Citeaux, Stephen Harding the Englishman. His quality of mind comes across clearly in the way he tackled the problem of establishing a more accurate text of some Old Testament books. Harding was concerned that certain texts translated by St. Jerome did not tally with each other. He approached learned Jews and explained the problem. They then unrolled their own scrolls and explained in French what their Hebrew and Aramaic sources contained. Harding then amended his texts. This way of settling a problem reveals a clear and at that time unconventional mind. The example is important because the deep spirituality of the Cistercians often comes to us in the form of a thought which is mystical, and works by analogy and metaphor rather than analytical reason. Though this was true of their theology, their practical doings show them to have been pragmatic and very effective people.

The abbey and its granges under an abbot was the basic Cistercian unit and was self-contained, but the multitude of these units also formed the unity of the whole order. Modern management theorists think in terms of models, and have the skill of designing management structures for this or that purpose. The early Church had had to wrestle with these problems too, as we can see from the Creeds which set out a core of belief which all should agree. The Church's management structure was based on the Roman Empire, with the church in each province under the leadership of a bishop. It is less apparent in England, but the Roman provincial pattern is still visible in France, with ancient dioceses centred on Roman provincial capitals. The Cistercians, however, set up a management structure *de novo*.

When there were enough monks, they would 'swarm', often twelve like the apostles, and set off to found a new monastery. Thus Citeaux gave off her four daughter monasteries, and they in turn spread their daughters and granddaughters across Christendom. Discipline, adherence to the Cistercian code of conduct, was assured by each abbot being the inspector of his abbey's daughter houses so there was a chain of responsibility from the most remote place to the centre. Furthermore, the General Chapter of all the

abbots at Citeaux was the only regular international convention of the twelfth century, and was used by the Popes as a most sure and rapid means of disseminating information. One can scarcely refrain from pointing out how like all this was to the working of a modern multinational corporation. From the point of view of 'engineer monks' these excellent communications offered a further advantage—the rapid spread of know-how.

Secrecy, indeed mystery, has nearly always surrounded any new technical progress and for good reason. It would be a foolish government that told its military competitors how to make better gunpowder. Steelmakers in Sheffield were noted for their willingness to conceal their own technical secrets and to winkle out the secrets of others. Medieval guilds and crafts were equally unwilling to share their knowledge with others. Consequently, in earlier times, the dissemination of new techniques was usually slow. Within the Cistercian order, it was clearly otherwise. Not only did the party of monks leaving an abbey carry with them the knowledge they had gained there, but there are such strong resemblances in the early Cistercian style of different abbeys that clearly information was readily exchanged. Nor was building the only technique transferred. A successful new variety of apple from Burgundy soon found its way to the German abbeys, and— a transfer of genetic information—Burgundian monks would bring good breeding cattle from Italy.

Burgundy's position at the cross-roads of important east-west and north-south European routes undoubtedly helped. Milos Kreps, a Czech historian, expressed doubts about the accuracy of a document implying that water power was being used in ironmaking at the Cistercian monastery of Velehrad so early as 1269. 'He demonstrates very little probability of existence of water wheels in Moravian industry at the end of the second half of the thirteenth century, because the time of their application in neighbouring countries is not supporting the possibility'. But given the Cistercians' communications it was not necessary for the technology to diffuse gradually.[3] The Czech Cistercians might well have set up their *'molendina que vulgo hutte dicuntur ad ferrifodinas pertinentia'* with consultants bringing the 'know how' directly from Burgundy.

Jean Gimpel has shown how strong the Cistercian iron industry was in Burgundy.[4] The area had important iron-making even before Roman times, and by 1330 the Cistercians already owned between eight and thirteen forges making iron in the region. Imagine monks forging red hot iron with heavy hammers. The forge at Fontenay Abbey is still well preserved, a long handsome building with vaulted workshops. It has been suggested that the forge was using water-powered tilt hammers as early as the twelfth century. Another laborious task was working the bellows and this too could be undertaken by water power. Stephen Harding's bible includes a clear drawing of an organ driven by multiple bellows which could just as well have served a hearth.[5] In Champagne too, the Cistercians were the leading iron producers from 1250 until nearly the industrial revolution.

Their success in the quest for iron bearing lands was just as successful in Britain. Furness Abbey had rich supplies of excellent hematite and was using them by 1235; and Tintern exploited ores in the Forest of Dean. Was it a coincidence that Buildwas Abbey lay only a few miles from one of the great homes of the British iron industry? This was Coalbrookdale, where in the eighteenth century Abraham Darby first used coke to smelt iron successfully. Yet perhaps it was Yorkshire that witnessed the greatest monkish activity in ironmaking. Kirkstall Abbey in Leeds had a forge on whose site metal is still being worked today. Kirkstead Abbey in Lincolnshire had four forges round Sheffield, and dug ore at Kimberworth and Ecclesfield. Nearby Roche Abbey had its forge too and Fountains Abbey diversified its woollen industry with iron and lead mining at Niddersdale. The Cistercians were not the only ironmaking monks in Yorkshire. Monk Bretton Priory in Barnsley had forges and the Premonstratensian Abbey at Beauchief had at least five mills on the River Sheaf, including water-driven bellows and hammers.[6] These White Canons had a lot in common with the White Monks and Sheffield owes them a great deal.

Strangely enough no evidence is known for the making of iron in South Yorkshire between Roman times, when a forge existed at Templeborough, and the much later rapid development of monastic output in the twelfth century. Dr. R.A. Mott has put forward the interesting hypothesis that iron had been worked before the Conquest, but that the industry was ended by William the Conqueror's ravaging of Yorkshire as punishment for the massacre of the Norman garrison in York. Mott's suggestion was that production had continued on into Viking times, as suggested by place names like Scissett, Cinder Hill and Bole Hill. When, however, William struck at the North, his columns (Mott believed), chose routes which followed the outcrops of iron. In other words, a specific aim of the devastation was a pre-emptive strike against the weapon-making resources of this predominantly Norse area. The Mott hypothesis is appealing, but, unless archaeological work reveals evidence of ironmaking before the twelfth century, it remains not proven.[7] All the same, Kipling's Norman baron would have agreed with Mott:

Gold is for the mistress - silver for the maid -
Copper for the craftsman, cunning at his trade.
'Good!' said the baron, sitting in his hall,
'But iron, cold iron, is master of them all.'

Whatever the reasons, the British Cistercians grew fastest in the stormy times of Stephen (1135-1154) and Matilda, and in trouble spots like the ravaged Yorkshire or the Welsh Marches. Perhaps it was not just their ability to reclaim wastelands, but also their political trustworthiness. Iron was then a scarce material. Instead of using nails, carpenters and millwrights made elaborate joints and held things together with dowels; only their tools were of iron and steel. Even axles were wooden; and cogwheels in mills were built up from wood and had wooden teeth. Wood was the universal material, except where cutting edges were needed—scythes and swords; or a material to withstand them—mail made from rings of iron wire or plate. The abbey was a place of labour as well as of prayer and contemplation, and the ferrous fruit of that labour was well received in a warlike society. It was St. Bernard, after all, who composed the Rule which guided the Knights Templar, echoing in many ways what C.H. Lawrence calls 'the aggressive and élitist spirituality of the early Cistercian movement'[8]; it was St. Bernard, too, who preached the Second Crusade at Vézelay. There was a harsh side to Bernard.

Whatever the Cistercians set out to do, so far as I have been able to discover, they did well. It would not be remarkable that they made good wine in Burgundy—it would have been hard to do otherwise; but the Cistercians appear to have made the best. There is Stendhal's story of the

Fig. 89. Wine press at Clos de Vougeot

regiment, marching back north from Napoleon's campaign in Italy. At Clos de Vougeot, an old Cistercian vineyard, the general halted his troops and ordered them to give the general salute to the *terroir* of that quite exceptional wine. The list of famous Burgundian vintages produced by Cistercians is long; so is the German one. But they were adaptable too. They played to the strength of their hand, and if wine would not serve, then in Belgium and Dore they made excellent beer. Perhaps there is some lost knowledge that might have linked Herefordshire's Cistercians with the Normandy houses and good strains of cider apples—but I must not speculate.

Nevertheless, if the reader wishes to judge for himself the sheer competence of Cistercian wine makers, let him visit the grange which still survives at Clos de Vougeot. There one finds the original medieval wine presses, with beams that weigh seven tons to press out the juice (Fig. 89). The seven ton load on the grapes was applied over a large area so the actual pressure was relatively low. My wife made a rough calculation suggesting that the pressure was close to that of the human foot. Interesting, too, is the form of the huge wooden screw that lifted the beam. Villard de Honnecourt was close to the Cistercians[9], and left one of the few collections of drawings of medieval buildings and machines. One drawing shows a powerful lifting screw.[10] It bears a clear resemblance to the device to lift the beam at Clos de Vougeot.

There was a widespread saying, 'Bernard in the valley, Benedict on the hill', which highlights the Cistercian choice to be near water, and their abbeys were famous for the elaborate hydraulic systems which can still be seen today. Byland Abbey was a marshy site but the monks set about draining it, and built fish ponds. A few hundred metres up the valley are the remains of a long earth dam. At Roche, too, there is a magnificent dam, though artistic landscaping in the eighteenth century has made it harder to visualise the full extent of the medieval water system. Villiers la Grange, 35 kilometres south-east of Pontigny Abbey (Fig. 90) had no source of water, so a great underground cistern was built, five metres deep, to catch any surface water. The

Fig. 90. Pontigny Abbey

cistern is composed of two side-by-side barrel vaults which are supported in the centre by an arcade of ten round arches. It measures 8 metres by 16.1 metres.[11]

At abbey after abbey, such traces are to be found, and many of the names reinforce the importance of valleys and water to the monks: Clairvaux, Rievaulx, Jervaulx; Fountains, Fontenay, Troisfontaines. It entered into their language too. Gilbert of Hoyland says that when Aelred of Rievaulx was interrupted, 'He would break off while the other opened the sluicegates of his spirit. And when the tumultuous flood of speech had ebbed away would take up the thread of his argument.'[12]

The scale of the works undertaken to channel, store and control water was sometimes immense, much more costly in labour than the building of the wheels and machinery which they powered. There is a pleasing word picture of the completeness of the hydraulic system of a big abbey written by a twelfth century monk[13]. The writer follows the river Aube as it flows through Clairvaux's land, irrigating fields and vineyards, and filling ponds for fish. Then it splits, and a part comes into the abbey to work. The scale and variety of work it performed must surprise the modern reader. Water power grinds and then sieves corn. It fills a vat for beer-making (in case there is a poor vintage). More wheels drive the heavy fulling stocks that beat woollen cloth to condition it. On it goes where it is needed in 'cooking, sifting, turning, whetting, watering, washing, grinding and softening.' If this is to be believed—and it does ring true—then power technology was being used on a broad front in a wholesale manner.

The industrial revolution of the eighteenth century took off even though there were almost no sources of power exceeding ten horsepower. Most waterwheels were small, being made of wood, and it was only towards the end of that century that steam engines became capable of running machinery. From the modern perspective this is a surprisingly paltry supply of energy—even a little 2CV car has a 25 horsepower engine. Instead, think of it from an earlier viewpoint, when water power was what we would call 'high tech'. The ten horsepower wheel is giving fifty man power, without fatigue and free from cost. 'From how much backbreaking travail for horses and arm-aching labour for men does this obliging torrent free us, to the extent that without it we should be neither clothed nor fed.'[14]

This document also makes one wonder how the machines worked, what were the details of their construction, how big they were—for so little has survived. With machines made of wood in a wet environment, water-powered works need constant renewal as we find today with places like Wortley Top Forge and Abbeydale. Even when they are run lightly, the decay is rapid and large timbers have to be renewed in as little as twenty years. Consequently it is worth looking very carefully at the machines in Villard de Honnecourt's sketchbook. Their meaningfulness has been questioned, but it seems to the present writer that these were drawings of devices that existed. Admittedly, there is a perpetual motion machine—a wheel with hingeing weights; but even this could have been built, though it would not have worked.

Make allowances for the difficulty of drawing a three-dimensional machine for a thirteenth century man. We can check this difficulty by comparing Villard's sketch of a tower in Laon with the actual tower of the cathedral. He could draw the facing view pretty well, but he was in difficulty with any oblique surfaces, and he was also tempted to show what he knew was there rather than what could be seen from one viewpoint.[15] Nevertheless, wherever they can be checked, the drawings are truthful. Villard, for example, draws a windlass with twelve arms or levers. Twelve men would be able to put a very large force onto the axle. If the arms passed through holes chiselled into the wood it would be weakened and then break under the strain. Villard's sketch shows the axle square, with the levers firmly fixed to a box clamped round the axle. The surviving medieval treadmill used to lift building material up to Salisbury's spire has an axle and arms fitted like Villard's picture.

Another of Villard's drawings shows a water powered saw—*Par chu fait om une soore soir par li sole*—'by this means one makes a saw saw by itself' (Fig. 91). The axes of the sketch flow in a manner worthy of Esscher, with the verticals and horizontals laid out flat for the viewer to disentangle; but the mechanical elements are all there. A schematic water-wheel, probably undershot, turns an axle. This drives a spiked wheel to advance the log, and also four arms stick out of the axle representing a mechanism to pull the saw blade down. This makes a lot of sense, as the saw is powered downwards by the water on the cutting stroke, and pulled back up by a springy piece of wood pegged down at one end and resting in a forked wooden rest. The linkage between the saw and the four arms on the axle is particularly interesting because it may be a

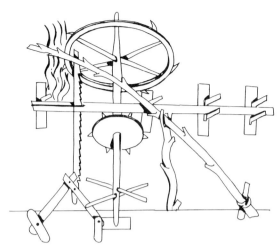

Fig. 91. Villard's water-powered saw (B.Byron)

jointed mechanism to restrict the saw's motion to a straight line. If this interpretation of Villard's drawing is correct—that it represented a working machine—then power was being applied to complex actions far in advance of the simple corn grinding mill.

Lastly, we come to the Cistercians' building, the side of their engineering which we know best because it has lasted so well. Unfortunately most of the British abbey churches represent the later medieval period when the Cistercians had abandoned their individual style and adopted the common forms of Gothic. Britain has no Fontenay or Pontigny to exemplify the simple purity which Stephen Harding and St. Bernard made a hallmark of the order. The towers at Dore Abbey and Fountains would not have met with their approval. Bernard was scathing about the elaborateness and rich decoration, even fantasy in sculpture, which he found elsewhere. The simplicity and beautiful proportions of Fontenay and Pontigny are breathtaking.

However, the churches and even the adjacent monastic buildings were only a part of the Cistercians' building campaign. A wonderful heritage of granges has survived too, and it is a pity that there is not a greater awareness that fifteen or twenty granges were very much an integral part of a big abbey. The statement that everything the Cistercians did was done well

Fig. 92. Barn at Ter Doest Abbey

applies especially to their building. The walls and vaulting of the forge of Fontenay are of the highest quality. The grange at Ter Doest near Zeebrugge is about 180 feet long by 72 wide, with low side walls and high gables to support the soaring tiled roof (Figs. 92 & 93).

It would be fair to say that the Cistercians did not invent Gothic but that they did a great deal to spread it. The aesthetic beauty of Gothic must not be forgotten of course, but for the moment consider its functional advantages. As a structural form its thinking owes as much to the carpenter as it does to round-arched romanesque. This implies the true meaning of the word carpenter, as the French use it—not just a general worker in wood but the creator of *charpente*, the great frameworks like the roofs of barns or the skeletons of spires.

The world is divided into two kinds of structure—the shell and the skeleton. Crabs and beetles have shells; fish and mammals have skeletons. The dichotomy still flourishes: the early aeroplanes were skeleton structures made of wood and covered with fabric; the Spitfire and Dakota were metal monocoques, meaning shells.

Romanesque vaulting in its essence was shell thinking, the building of curved shapes out of surfaces. It is very difficult to work out the shape of the stones to build a curved surface for the part of a vault where another vault crosses it.

But at first there were only barrel vaults (like a drum cut in half longways). It was easy enough to build a barrel vault, just a matter of moving the wooden centering along, and making the arch broader and broader. But then the whole length of the side walls had to withstand the thrust and weight of the vault—this meant big thick walls, with no scope for good windows or large doors. When the mason tried to move on from that and construct cross vaults to take the strain off the walls and allow openings, he was in a minefield. A passable cross vault can be built with round arches if the span of both is the same. But if different spans are attempted then irreconcilable problems arise, because if the arches are semicircular, then increasing the span increases the height. There are little side arches in the arcade needing to spring from high up and big arches across the nave needing to spring from the same pillars, but from lower down. It was going to be

Fig. 93. Barn at Ter Doest Abbey

spaces are doing virtually nothing structurally. So long as the skeleton is there, the intervening surface can be a non-load bearing wall, glowing stained glass, or even empty space. This raises a new problem—but Gothic masons solved it. Even the skeletons (the ribs) push; how could there be thin walls with the vaults pushing them outwards? The glorious answer, which meant that the European mind had really started to think again, was the flying buttress to take the thrusts outwards and downwards as simply and cleanly as a prop holding a wall up—which is more or less what it was. Now that the violent sideways pushing forces of the vault were dealt with, the fat Romanesque pillars could be replaced by light and elegant Gothic ones. Stone carries downward forces easily—it was the sideways thrusts that had been causing the main problems.

If the reader looks at a Gothic vault and sees how the forces are carried by the ribs, he will see why that structure is more like the wonderful carpenters' wooden roofs than the heavy shells of Romanesque.

We do not know how much of this technology, except for the building, existed at Dore Abbey, but we can be sure that the monks knew of its existence, and that they could have introduced any of the techniques had they needed to. Dore was a part of that Cistercian world which transcended its age and foreshadowed better ways of doing things. Little was written to tell us how they achieved their aims. Even today, craftsmen and other practical people rarely have the skill with words to match what their hands can do. Bakers, blacksmiths, carpenters and

very difficult to develop better stone roofs if the Romanesque style was kept to.

Here is the first beauty of Gothic. Once again the French have the best words, *arc brisé*—broken arch—you can move the centres from which the curves are drawn, so that although the arches are different spans, they can be the same height. If we see technology as liberation—books liberating our memories and telephones how far we need to shout—then the pointed arch counts among the greatest.

Gothic brought another, equally great, liberation. Shells are hard to design - as anybody will see who sits down and tries to work out the shapes of stone blocks to build a cross vault. Four arches form the sides of the rectangle, and then two longer diagonals cross it. It is infinitely easier to built this well cut skeleton of stone and then fill in the intervening spaces with whatever rubble is needed to fit them. Even better, the skeleton carries the thrusts and the intervening farmers teach better by example. Foolishly, we equate knowledge with books. Thus it was, perhaps, that the Cistercians came to be seen as something of backwoodsmen.

The subsequent development of analytical thought leads historians of science to favour the schoolmen at Paris and Oxford who argued, theorised and dissected all knowledge; and reason is favoured over the apparently simple faith which Bernard preached. Yet, in all honesty, who would trust a schoolman to build a vault, make good iron from the ore, or produce a heavenly vintage? He would undoubtedly win an argument against the man who could do these things. Even in the twelfth century, those who could, did, and those who couldn't, taught. Wherever the philosophical truth lies, we have to recognise the practical triumphs of those simpletons for whom *laborare erat orare*.

CHAPTER XIV

The Dissolution

by David H. Williams

The abbey of Dore was suppressed on 1 March (St. David's Day) in 1537, when up to 9 monks and 16 or more servants may have been resident[1], though only four monks are recorded as receiving payments between the unknown day of 'dissolution [or survey] and the suppression.'[2]

The last abbot, John Redborne, received a state pension of £13 per year, of which he was still in receipt in 1556.[3] That year he appears to have joined the reconstituted Benedictine community at Westminster, having with him there a Welsh servant named Ap Thomas. Redborne died at Westminster in September 1557, aged about 77.[4] Former Abbot Cleubery moved into his own house in Hereford, and was still alive in 1557 when aged about 71 years old (See also chapter III). After the Suppression Cleubery was still paid his pension (agreed in 1526) of £16 13s. 4d.; it was received in half-yearly instalments via intermediaries. Cleubery's and Redborne's receipts exist for their pension payments in 1549.[5] In 1540 both had been required to pay a 'first subsidy' of 2 shillings in the pound on their pensions.[6]

Little has so far been traced of the fate of the remaining monks after their eviction from the monastery. Apart from Redborne and Cleubery, the known community at Dore in 1536 included Richard Burford (sub-prior and about 35 years old), Richard Alberton (a monk of Dore for at least 54 years, and by then nearly eighty years old), John Dydebroke (39 years), Ralph

Westbury, Thomas Bristol, and Rhys Williams (27 years old). Five or so of the monks had scarcely been ordained ten years. There was also Richard Dean, who moved to Hailes Abbey until its later suppression in 1539, and William Marbye (alias Merbury) who remained for a year or two at Dore, as one of the two chaplains appointed to serve the parishioners.[7] The monastic lay officials at the suppression of the house included its steward, Thomas Baskerville, John Watkin, bailiff, and Richard Warncombe, auditor.[8]

A sale of goods was made at Dore that St. David's Day[9] 'at the dissolution of the house there', and brought in some £53. Nearly all the goods were bought by John Scudamore, the Particular Receiver appointed by the Crown for Dore and some other Herefordshire houses. Clearly he was well placed to do so. Scudamore bought (for only £2) the roof, slates and timber, of the refectory, 'the old house by the wayside next to the bridge', and also the 'organs in the quire'. Together with Thomas Baskerville and Miles ap Harry, (and for 64s.) he also purchased 'the old infirmary' and 'all the glass and iron of the windows of the dorter (dormitory), the frater (refectory), and the chapter-house'. Several buyers accounted for the vestments of the church, which all told consisted at the time of the sale five chasubles (the priest's vestment at Mass; one being blue, another green), four pairs of tunicles (for the deacon and sub-deacon at Mass), and three copes (used at Lauds and Vespers). Of these the last abbot bought the cope of 'blue silk with angels', a chasuble and two tunicles. William Parry bought two tunicles 'of blue satin bruges' and William Sayce a cope of the same material and colour—blue clearly played some part in medieval liturgical colours. Other ecclesiastical goods sold included eight altar cloths, thirteen palls and four 'stained' frontals (these to abbot Redborne), a holy water stock, a copper pyx, a cross of beryl, and a censer.

Scudamore bought practically all the household goods. These included, from the kitchen: eight platters, six pottingers (soup-basins), three saucers, a broach (spit for roasting meat), a chafern (for heating water), two grid-irons, two brass pans, an iron dripping pan, a frying pan, and a hogshead; from the parlour: a table-board, two trestles, a chair and a cupboard; from the buttery: four table-cloths (two were of linen, two of hurdyn—a coarser flax), three linen towels, six napkins, five candlesticks, four salt-cellars, a basin and a ewer of pewter, and an ambry (cupboard). Sold from the brew-house were, amongst other goods, two brass furnaces, a kneading trough, two bran tubs, a 'great trough to keep corn', a moulding board, a mash vat, and a hogshead. Abbot Redborne bought a carpet and a brass mortar with the ponners (crushing instruments).

Three of the chambers were itemised separately. The grandest, whose contents included two beds (one a feather-bed), a green coverlet, three trestles and two table-boards, a cupboard and two chests, was called St. Thomas of Lancaster's Chamber after the never officially canonised earl who received much popular acclaim as a saint following his execution in 1322. The Little Chamber's contents only brought 14d., but those of the New Chamber (abbot Cleubery's old lodging) fetched 6s. 7d., and included a feather-bed and a tapestry coverlet. Scudamore bought four corn wains, 24 oxen, 20 cows, two sows, four horses, eleven iron taws, four plough-shares, four cultirons, 12 yokes and 2 pairs of horse harrows, and also, 3 qts. of wheat in the barn and $10^1/2$ qts. sown in the ground, as well as 2 qts. of barley and $12^1/2$ qts. of oats in the barn.

As the Crown Receiver Scudamore took the abbey's gold plate to London, but shortly after the Dissolution there still remained at Dore (perhaps in his hands) $35^1/2$ ozs. of other plate, and a six-ounce gilt chalice. A parcel-gilt chalice was also retained at Dore 'because of the clamour made about it by the parishioners.'[10] There was £1 worth of lead on 'the spire—le Steple', and £7 6s. 8d. worth on the roofs, with a further 20d. worth in the webs and gutters. The roof lead was melted down soon after the Dissolution and weighed $2^1/2$ fothers (almost 50cwt). It remained on site in ten pieces (sows) in Scudamore's custody. There were six bells (seven in one record); they weighed together $27^1/2$cwts. and 28lbs.[11] Four were retained by the Crown, but two were bought by the churchwardens and continued in parochial use. They were later the subject of a lengthy enquiry.[12] By 1545 the Crown had demised or sold much of the former monastery lands. John Scudamore had received the site of the abbey with certain demesne lands and Gilbert Hill's Wood, Llanfair Cilgoed passed to Antony Foster, Morlais Grange to James Gunter, Morehampton to Stephen ap Parry, Whitewall to Richard Andrews and Nicholas Temple, and Llyncoed to John Cokkes, to mention but a few.[13] By about 1540 (if not before) the Mill Close (a 3 acre pasture) had been sown with barley, and the Home Sheep House field (a 20 acre pasture) had also been converted to arable.[14]

In the years following the Suppression there was widespread litigation regarding former monastic properties. Dore was no exception, and former abbot Redborne was required to give evidence before at least two boards of inquiry. The first was held at Peterchurch on 11 June, 1539[15], into a dispute between David ap Thomas ap Rhys (defendant) and Watkin Seysil (plaintiff) as to whom was the rightful tenant of Hollings Grange. The commissioners were Miles ap Harry (see also chapter III), George Delabere, and Thomas Vaughan. Both defendant and plaintiff claimed that abbot Redborne and the community had leased the property to them by indenture. It does appear that two indentures were in fact prepared, but the abbot claimed that the first did not hold good. The depositions made bring to light several points of interest, but as is so often the case the findings of the commissioners are not extant.

Fig. 94. An extract from the first post-Suppression Ministers' accounts (PRO SC6/Henry VIII 7319)

The defendant claimed that the monastery had granted Hollings Grange to him on 27 April 1530, that the indenture had been 'sealed with their conventual seal', and that the abbot had written on the back that it was 'the very true deed' of the community. The plaintiff countered

that on 1 May, 1532, he had been granted the reversion of the grange once the then tenant's lease expired (on 10 November, 1536). Further, at the time of the Suppression, the abbot told him that no valid lease had been made to the defendant, and that on the back of his deed had noted that it had never been made. In his evidence, John Redborne agreed that he did write certain words upon the back of the defendant's lease, but that he could not remember what they were— 'they be not new in his memory'. Other former monks called to give evidence included the sub-prior, Richard Burford—who claimed to have been staying at the daughter-house of Vale Royal in Cheshire from 1531 to 1533; John Diddebroke (Dydebroke)—who said there had been 'dissension in the community' over the matter, and that 'if the abbot had been an honest man' the defendant's lease would have held good. Both Diddebroke and young Rhys Williams agreed that they had received part of the money the plaintiff paid for the making and sealing of his lease. A lay witness pointed out that the matter had been previously ventilated before the king's Commissioners for the Marches of Wales, sitting at Bewdley in about 1532.

The inquiry was re-opened on 20 September[16], when John Redborne was re-examined. He agreed that an earlier lease was made to the defendant, but that after its making, and during its inscribing on parchment, he had to go on 'great business' to Vale Royal, by the king's command. So he delivered the box containing the common seal to the sub-prior for him to seal this and other leases. Six months later, when the plaintiff asked for a lease of the grange, he had said that he could not honestly do this, but 'people of influence brought pressure upon him' and so he granted a lease to the plaintiff 'against the mind of the whole convent'. He also said and wrote that it was of no effect, telling the plaintiff that if the lease did not stand, he, the abbot, was 'therewith contented'. The case is another example of how external forces in Tudor times (and before) might limit the free action of a monastic community. (The sitting tenant was David W(e)ythe; and his lease, as described in the first post-Suppression Ministers

151

Accounts (Fig. 94)[17], was not for a term of years but for life).

Then, in 1541, Richard ap Thomas ap Richard of Dore alleged to the Court of Augmentations[18], 'as it becometh his duty to do':

(1). that John Redborne, the former abbot, and Thomas Baskerville, the former Steward, still had in their possession £160, coming from the time before the Suppression when the abbot had been collector of a king's subsidy in the diocese of Hereford.

(2). that the abbot a little while before the Suppression 'gave away to the parish church there a suit of vestments which was surveyed by the king's Visitors, and he craftily after the surveying thereof gave away a cross of gold called "a little relic cross", and one gospel book plated with silver'.

(3). that the abbot, a little before the Suppression and within the period disallowed by statute, had granted a lease to Thomas Baskerville and Philip Tewe (his servant) for only 33s. 4d. per year, whereas the lease had previously been worth £3 6s. 8d.; he said that as a result 'the king is defrauded and deceived of 33s. 4d. yearly.'

(4). that the lessees were bound by the abbot that 'if the monastery should stand still [i.e: not be suppressed] that the lease should be surrendered and yielded up to the community.'

An inquiry was held concerning these allegations at Hereford on 25 June, 1541, before a commission consisting of John Scudamore (the former Receiver), Simon Hyett, and Richard Warncombe (Mayor of Hereford in 1526). Former abbot Redborne said that the subsidy had been payable over two years, that he had acquittance ('which he would not shewe us') for the charge of the first year. As for the second year he had made William Jones, one of the informers, his under-collector who had given him £200; of this he paid £80 to Thomas Baskerville for the redeeming of a pension of 20 marks yearly granted by abbot Glynn (possibly that awarded Thomas Cleubery, see chapter II) and that he had paid to the late bishop of London (Dr. John Stockesley, 1530-39) by the hands of the monastery bailiff (John ap Watkin—now deceased) 'whether £40 or £50 he perfectly knoweth not, and of the said sum he hath no acquittance'. He agreed that he possessed the vestments, the cross and the gospel book referred to. He described the cross as 'being a little cross of wood containing in length eight inches and in breadth three-quarters of an inch covered with a thin plate of silver, and in that cross was a little bone of a saint which was reputed a relic and it was named "a little relic cross"'. As for the lease (it was of the tithe and hay of Dore) he insisted (as did Philip Tewe) that it had been granted well before the period nullified by the Act of Dissolution, but Redborne admitted that 'whether it was sealed before the statute was made or after, he perfectly knoweth not'. He also contradicted the suggestion of any financial irregularity.

The closing years of the monastery's life were perhaps ones of ominous predictions of the wholesale Suppression of 1536; there was jockeying in some monasteries for the position of abbot (to be sure of a decent pension when the end came), and clearly there were those local laity who wanted to capitalise out of the monastery with favourable leases whilst there was still time. Hence, superiors like Redborne came under great pressure—with few friends left in high places it is not surprising that they sometimes succumbed. The consequence was, not just at Dore but throughout the kingdom, that a considerable number of such formal inquiries took place in the years immediately following the Suppression. Redborne's clinging to the 'little relic cross' and the gospel book, his buying up of vestments—as if hoping to continue some form of religious community, and his dying at Westminster, suggests a monk of a spiritual nature who only wished to protect that which was holy. It is a pity that the last abbot and monks have left no written word of their feelings, not only on being cast out, but on seeing their monastery plundered and the monastic life of four hundred years discontinued.[19]

CHAPTER XV

After the Dissolution
by Jim Tonkin

As one of the less wealthy religious houses Abbey Dore was dissolved in 1536 with all those whose annual income was under £200. Its yearly value was assessed at £101 5s. 2d. and its other possessions at 60s.[1]

The estate of the abbey was granted by the king to John Scudamore of Holme Lacy on 30 March, 1540. At the same time the rectory and tithes were granted to Henry Courtney, Earl of Devon, and passed through several hands before being bought by John Scudamore, who was in receipt of a pension of 50s. per annum, awarded by the Crown, which he used to pay a priest-in-charge.

From the time of the Dissolution services were held here for a century, and one incumbent, John Gyles, was reported as reading the services from under an arch to keep his book from getting wet. The nave, conventual buildings and vaulting were destroyed and used as a 'quarry' during this time. It seems that the church and transepts had a wooden roof at this period which was in a poor state of repair. There appears to be no evidence as to who the other incumbents were during the period 1536-1633.[2]

Evidence for this period is hard to come by, but by c.1890 two watercourses north of the abbey were cleared out close to where the domestic buildings and dormitories of the monastery were situated and nine old keys ranging from 2 to 6 inches in length were found, some of them cut into very unusual wards. One

resembled an intricate modern key; perhaps it opened a form of padlock. A silver groat of the reign of Elizabeth was also found.[3]

Leland in his *Itinerary* lists important people buried in the abbey including 'Caducanus [Cadwgan] sumtyme Byshope of Bangor, after monke of Dour', but does not mention an effigy, whereas Gibson in his account of the abbey in 1727 quotes from Leland and then writes 'Of whom I suppose there remains in the South-Isle an almost entire effigy, made of the Heart of Oak: Nothing being either decay'd or broken, but the Top of his Pastoral Staff'. A rough sketch in the Hill Mss was made about 1716 (Fig. 12) and under it is written 'This effigies is of wood and lies under the southern Isle'. The figure is dressed in a long gown with large sleeves, a hood open at the neck and a cap on his head. From the left arm hangs a maniple, derived from the napkin used by a Roman consul to start the games, and in this hand is a cross staff (not a crozier or pastoral staff), with its lower end in the mouth of a lion at his feet. In his right hand is a book or possibly a mirror. The son of an Irish priest, Cadwgan was successively the Cistercian abbot of Strata Florida and Whitland. He was removed from this post as a result of a fraud investigation into wool sales conducted by a party from Clairvaux. However, he was made bishop of Bangor in 1215 before the archbishop of Canterbury became aware of the details. He retained the post until 1236, when Pope Gregory

IX gave him permission to retire and become a monk of Dore, where he died on 11 August, 1241.[4]

The effigy seems to have been sent by a Dr. Miles to his friend, Lord Bateman, in London some time after 1731 and before 1769. It is possible that this figure still exists, probably undocumented, in some private collection or in a museum.[5]

Of the non-ecclesiastical property the Abbot's Lodging was valued at £10. This was presumably in or very near the cloisters. The 'Chapel of Dore' listed under 'Spiritual' property was valued at £2. In the list of farms and other possessions of the Abbey was an entry which reads in translation 'Dore - Rendered for the site of the monastery with lands, meadows, pastures and rights of pasture ... £13 11s. 4d.' In this there is no real clue as to how much of the abbey's temporal buildings was destroyed or otherwise.[6]

CHAPTER XVI

The Altar and the Vestments
by Ruth Richardson

Altar

Perhaps the most evocative survival in Dore Abbey is the great stone mensa, the very altar used at the consecration ceremony.[1] If the evidence is correct then the celebrant was Thomas Cantilupe, Bishop of Hereford, 1275-1282, who carried out the service in a terrifying atmosphere with armed men outside. The frightened congregation of monks little knew that they were listening to a future saint, canonised in 1320, but they would have been bitterly aware of the potential for conflict.[2] Thomas Cantilupe had to be heavily protected as Bishop Thomas Bek of St. David's claimed that the abbey was a part of the Ewyas district and therefore in his diocese, a claim local lords tried to support with military force. Despite this, the day apparently passed peacefully.

The altar slab is large, 12 feet long, 4 feet wide and 3 inches thick. It bears the five consecration crosses carved after the sacred oil had been poured onto it and would have contained a relic. It now stands on the remains of three pillars and the low wall behind, 4 feet high and 1 foot wide, was thought by Roland Paul to have been part of the reredos.[3]

In 1260 Bishop Peter de Aquablanca had granted an indulgence to raise money to finish building 'the sumptuous church of Dore.'[4] Completion had been difficult but by *c*.1282 the church was colourful, beautifully decorated, and already quite full. The church did not have the open vista seen now and was a more complicated structure than the first austere building of 1147, as there would have been stalls, monuments, and partitions (parclose screens) around numerous altars. Little of this has survived, apart from the sculpture, though the lenten rings can be seen.

A free-standing altar often had a processional cross slotted in a socket behind it.[5] The word 'altar' comes from the Latin *altare* meaning a structure where sacrifice takes place. Christ's celebration of the Last Supper, as described in the New Testament, probably took place at a wooden table. However, the custom of using stone altars seems to have arisen in the early church due to the celebration of the eucharist on a saint's tomb in the Roman catacombs. Later a saint's body was often buried beneath a cathedral altar, but elsewhere the custom of having a saint's relic embedded in a cavity of the altar slab or mensa was considered sufficient,[6] the altar having to be formally consecrated by a bishop.

By the tenth century the service consisted of the sprinkling of the whole church and altar with holy water, a rite repeated in monasteries each Sunday. This was followed by twice tracing the alphabet in sand or ashes, in the shape of a St. Andrew's cross, on the pavement in front of the altar to claim it for Christ, through the initial of Christus in Greek. The relics were carried in procession, the service including several processions, incense being used and candles carried. The mortar was prepared and the altar was washed and then anointed by the bishop with consecrated oil (the chrism), the five consecration crosses showing the exact spots. The relics were deposited in the altar cavity and sealed in. Henceforth, the place would be kissed by the priest in the mass. The consecration service ended with mass, which by the thirteenth century included a lighted torch or candle held by one of the assistant ministers at the elevation of the host,[7] the celebrant being the bishop.

The abbey is recorded as acquiring two crosses,[8] but no mention was made of the altar relic. The altar has an oak insert in its centre front, made at the restoration. Its exact position has the centre front of the altar at a point about three quarters along the insert from the north and a quarter from the south. The usual explanation, derived from the small curve on its lower lip, was that the cut was for allowing drainage when it was used for salting meat at the nearby farm.[9] However, it is rectangular and the cut marks can be clearly seen in the stone. It measures $1^1/2$ inches deep, 12 inches long, $3^1/8$ inches wide on its lower lip, which has the rounded cut in the centre that gave the later drainage idea, but 4 inches on the upper lip, with an additional $1^1/2$ inches removed along the edge of the north side. The oak is cut to fit exactly, with slightly acute internal corners, being symmetrically shaped (except for the northern scar) and the outer edge bevelled to fit to the lower lip. The position and shape show that the cut housed the relic which was kissed by the priest during the mass, the first probably being Saint Thomas Cantilupe at the consecration. The box was deliberately, though with difficulty, cut from the slab, in the process taking a fragment of the main stone, presumably at the Dissolution. If the box was of value—silver perhaps—then it could simply have been stolen. However, if rediscovered still in the original shape, it could be matched to the slab. The empty place, the small crosses and above all the huge slab itself are direct links to that fraught ceremony of c.1282.

Vestments and Altar Furniture

At the 1541 enquiry John Redborne, abbot 1529-1536, agreed he had a reliquary in the form of a small cross, 'a gospel book written in parchment with borders the one side covered with a thin plate of silver, estimated to value of five ounces or there about of silver' and a 'pair of vestments.'[10] The whereabouts of this book is unknown, but it is possible the vestments, or parts of them still survive!

The 1537 sale at Dore included the church vestments, some of which may have been made or repaired by Harry ap Glyn (or Harry Taylor) appointed in 1527 at 13s. 4d. a year. Of the several buyers, John Redborne's purchases included one of the three copes, described as of 'blue silk with angels', one of the five vestments or chasubles, and the four stained frontals. The colour worn by the celebrant at mass depended on the feast day. It seems reasonable that John Redborne would have bought a chasuble, worn for the eucharist, that matched his cope, worn for other services, that is a blue one. The other purchasers of the blue chasubles were Harry Hodnet, William Parry and John ap Watkin Vaughan.

In the nineteenth century a complete set of vestments and necessaria missae—a complete priest's kit, apart from amice, chalice and paten which would have been personal to each priest—was found in an oak chest in a farmhouse in Abbey Dore parish belonging to H.M. Gwillim Esq.[11] He was probably Henry Marsh Gwillim, son of John Gwillim and Elizabeth Lewis, who married at Clodock in 1825. Of their nine children, the first two were baptised at Much Dewchurch when they lived at Pool Farm, the next five being baptised at Kenderchurch when they farmed Howton Court. The 1844 Ewyas Harold tithe apportionment shows that the family had moved again, to the 380 acre Elm Farm which John Gwillim owned, and so the last two children, Henry Marsh being the youngest, were baptised at Ewyas Harold in 1847. However, by the 1851 census they were at Blackmoor Farm, in Abbey Dore and, though still there in 1861, they had moved yet again by 1871.[12] The only one of these farms in Abbey Dore was Blackmoor, which is probably the farm mentioned in the record.

According to the information given to the former South Kensington museum—now the Victoria and Albert museum—where the collec-

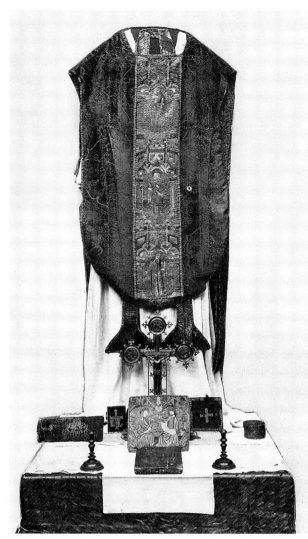

Fig. 95. The vestments and altar furniture (By courtesy of the Board of Trustees of the Victoria & Albert Museum)

Newport Pagnell, loaned the collection to the museum to whom it was sold in 1901.[13] There are no further details. Indeed, on 1 March 1913, the *Hereford Times* published a letter from Rev. Philip Cave-Moyle, Rector of Abbey Dore, appealing for information regarding the find and the current whereabouts of the items. The impression is that, despite local secrecy, H.M. Gwillim ensured that the collection remained intact and that it was placed with an organisation that would best preserve it. Fortunately, the items have remained together.

The collection consists of 21 items of vestments and altar furniture, 6 of which, because of their dates, could have been used in the abbey:

Burse
This is of English manufacture and was made between 1370 and 1430. It is a beautifully embroidered linen case made to carry the corporal, or cloth, on which the consecrated bread and wine are placed during mass. It was made from parts of orphreys which are narrow strips of braid, often woven with gold thread, used to cover the front and back seams of a chasuble.[14] The embroidery, in silver-gilt thread and coloured silks, is worked in split stitch and laid and couched work. It shows, on both sides, the Coronation of the Virgin with Christ blessing her. The figures on one side are on a diapered gold ground under part of a foliated canopy, but the other side has been repaired from fragments. It is 8¾ inches square and the lining is linen. The embroidered cross, as this was the earlier piece, would seem to have inspired the gilt bronze crucifix as the medallions appear to have the same design.

Crucifix
This crucifix, probably of fifteenth century date, is of gilt bronze with coarse open-work emblems of St. Mark, St. Luke and St. John on dark-blue enamel medallions. Each has an heraldic rose on the back. The edge is decorated with leaf-shaped crockets and the cross has an engraved diapered band down the centre of each part. Christ is

tion was deposited, they were supposed to have come into the family through H.M. Gwillim's great-grandmother who was a Vaughan. Although Welsh surnames were still not necessarily fixed, it is possible that there is a connection with John ap Watkin Vaughan—though it was John Redborne who bought the stained frontals. Certainly, in the seventeenth century, Vaughans and Gwillims were recorded as Roman Catholic and 'recusant' priests were frequent visitors to south Herefordshire and Monmouthshire. In 1884 H.M. Gwillim, then living at Churchfield, Mousloe, attached by three nails. As the lower end has been roughly shaped to fit a socket, and as St. Matthew is missing, this may have been re-fashioned as a processional cross as well as an altar cross, possibly for a chantry or side chapel, where it would have been slotted into a socket behind the altar. There is a small square stone with a shallow hole in its top in the centre of the wall opposite the southern effigy in Dore Abbey. Its position is such that it could be a surviving socket base. The height of the crucifix is $13^{3}/_{8}$ inches, width 12 inches. Until the late medieval period crosses were usually used in processions and placed, with candlesticks, on the pavement round the altar. Later they were sometimes placed on the altar.

Chasuble

Dating from between 1450 and 1500 this sleeve-less garment, worn by the celebrant at mass, is 4 feet 1 inch long and 2 feet $5^{1}/_{2}$ inches wide. This is Italian, dark-blue figured velvet, woven on an orange background with horizontal rows of lobed compartments, separated by leafy and flowering stems and containing radiating devices of pome-granate pattern—a symbol of the Virgin Mary also seen on the later screen. All Cistercian monasteries were dedicated to the Virgin so her motifs must have been common. The central linen orphreys are English and are so beautifully embroidered in gold and coloured silk threads, on linen in split and brick stitch and laid and couched work, that a monastic origin is a possibility.

They show figures on a diapered gold ground under architectural canopies. The back orphrey is cross-shaped: in the middle is Christ on the Cross, with two angels holding chalices, the Holy Ghost above shown as a dove. Below is St. John the Evangelist with a cup, and a Prophet. The front orphrey is straight and has a Prophet with a scroll, St. Thomas the Apostle with a carpenter's square, and Moses with a rod and the Tables of the Law. The lining is of printed linen with a black pattern of straight and wavy flow-ering stems printed on a mauve ground.

The set is completed by a stole and matching maniple.

Stole

A strip of material, 8 feet $5^{1}/_{2}$ inches by $8^{1}/_{2}$ inches at the widest ends, which derived from the scarf worn by Roman officials to denote rank. It hung round the neck and down to the knees.

Maniple

This is 3 feet $9^{3}/_{4}$ inches long by $8^{3}/_{4}$ inches wide at its ends and is derived from the napkin used by a Roman consul to start the games. It was hung over the left arm. Both the stole and the maniple are Italian, dating between 1470 and 1530, and are of brocade woven in blue silk and gilt thread. The wide ends have pointed corners and are made of fragments of English embroi-dered velvet, perhaps from older vestments. The linings of both match the chasuble.

Altar frontal

This dates from possibly the early 1500s. It is English, 3 feet 10 inches by 3 feet 8 inches, of olive-green, now greenish-brown, satin with a close pattern of slashes between diagonal stripes. Fitted frontals were introduced in the late medieval period, replacing the throwovers which hung in folds to the floor. Thomas Baskerville bought the abbey's set of green vestments, so green was used. However, it was John Redborne who purchased the frontals, though the colour is not given. He either took these to Westminster or perhaps gave them to the local Roman Catholic community. The pieces continued to be used over the years by succeeding itinerant priests when secretly administering mass.

Later additions

More than a hundred years later—in the 1600s to 1700s—further items were added or replaced. These were an alb, wafer box with lid, an embroidered panel, chalice veil, super-altar, chalice cover, two napkins, corporal, altar-cloths, a cushion for a missal and a pair of candlesticks.

Their dates show that none of these items could have been used in the abbey. However, the collection demonstrates the survival in the area of Roman Catholicism while the abbey was restored for use as the Anglican church of St. Mary.

CHAPTER XVII

Calvinists and anti-Calvinists

by Joe Hillaby

Calvinists and anti-Calvinists

When Dore was rebuilt and refurnished as a parish church by John, Viscount Scudamore in 1634, two factions were locked in conflict within the Church of England. The profound differences between Calvinists and Arminians was a major factor leading to the outbreak of civil war eight years later.

By 1600 doctrine was pre-eminently Calvinist with firm emphasis on divine predestination. The first three Lambeth Articles of 1595 declared:

'1. God from eternity has predestined some men to life, and reprobated some to death.

2. The moving or efficient cause of predestination to life is not the foreseeing of faith, or of perseverance, or of good works, or of anything innate in the person of the predestined, but only the will of the good pleasure of God.

3. There is a determined and certain number of predestined, which cannot be increased or diminished.'

For the Calvinists, preaching was 'that inestimable treasure which exceedeth all the riches of the earth.' There was thus a profound belief in an active, preaching ministry, and that appropriate behaviour was the sign of the elect.

In the following 20 years predestinarianism came under strong attack from opponents within the church, often described as Arminian, who insisted that Divine sovereignty *was* compatible with real free will in man; that Jesus died for *all*, not only for the elect. This theology of grace was closely linked to a belief in ritualised worship and an emphasis on order, obedience and uniformity through ceremony, for the church building was 'the presence chamber on earth of the king of heaven and earth.' Above all the divine presence manifested itself at the altar.[1]

The refurbishment of Dore as a parish church can only be fully understood in the context of the theology of grace but more particularly the way in which it was interpreted and put into practice by one man, William Laud. Laud's first major appointment came in 1617, as dean of Gloucester. One of his first acts was to persuade the chapter to remove the communion table from the middle of the choir and to set it altarwise, north-south on the uppermost steps, by the east wall. There it was railed off. Such rails served a double purpose. Superficially they were justified as defending the altar 'from the approach of dogs and all servile uses.' Far more important, however, communicants were now obliged to come up to the rails to receive the sacrament, kneeling, rather than, as previously, waiting seated in their various pews for the celebrant to come to them. The Gloucester rails are still in use, in the Lady Chapel. So angered was Bishop Miles Smith of Gloucester by Laud's actions that he swore never to enter the cathedral whilst he remained dean. He did not have long to wait. Laud was appointed bishop of St. David's in 1621.

With the accession of Charles I in 1625 and the election of Laud to the see of London in 1628, the chancellorship of the University of Oxford in 1629 and finally, on the death of Abbot, the archbishopric of Canterbury in 1633 Arminian views came into the ascendant. 'In all the ages of the church the touchstone of religion was not to hear the word preached but to communicate.' On the basis of this dictum the altar became the heart of the Laudian church.

Laud stated his position with great clarity. 'The altar is the greatest place of God's residence upon earth. I say the greatest, yea greater than the pulpit, for there 'tis *Hoc est corpus meum*, "This is My body", but in the pulpit 'tis at most but *Hoc est verbum meum*, "This is My word" and a greater reverence, no doubt, is due to the body than to the word of our Lord.' The archbishop's fundamental belief is revealed in his prayer before receiving the sacrament at communion. 'O Lord, I am thy son, thy most unkind, prodigal, run-away son, yet thy son ... O Lord, in thy grace I return to thee; and though I have eaten draff with all the unclean swine in the world, yet now Lord, upon my humble return to thee, give me I beseech thee the bread of life, the body and blood of my Saviour ... enrich me with all those graces which come from that precious body and blood, even till I be possessed of eternal life in Christ.' Thus did Laud reject Calvinist theology for making God 'the most unreasonable tyrant in the world.'[2]

By 1642 the grace of predestination and the grace of the sacraments had thus 'become rivals for the allegiance of English men and women' and to not a few of his opponents Laud's 'innovations' presaged a return to Rome, a charge which was, in fact, quite unjustified. Nevertheless, in January 1643 the Commons majority committed him, by a bill of attainder, to the scaffold on this very charge.

Scudamore's friendship with Laud apparently developed from his marriage in 1615 to Elizabeth, daughter and sole heiress of Sir Arthur and Lady Anne Porter of Lanthony by Gloucester. Certainly by 1618, that is before Laud's appointment to St. David's, it was flourishing. Scudamore's house at Holme Lacy was a

convenient resting place for the new bishop 'who generally visited him in his going to and returning from his diocese'. There he found 'Entertainment as kind and full of Respect as ever he did from any Friend.' This 'Strain of Love and Affection', so Scudamore's biographer, Matthew Gibson, tells us in his *View of the Church of Door*, (1727) 'runs through the constant Correspondence they kept. Certainly, true Friends they were, and heartily disposed to serve each other, in all the Vicissitudes of their Lives.'[3]

The refurbishment of Dore Abbey thus provides a remarkable insight into Laud's views on church worship, most particularly the position and setting of the altar and the design and imagery of the stained glass above it. The chancel was set wholly apart for the administration of the sacrament. Pews, music gallery and, significantly, pulpit were placed west of the screen. Only the minister's seat and reading desk were in the chancel. At the east end, beyond the rails, Scudamore replaced the great Cistercian stone altar with its five consecration crosses and chamfered under-edges.[4]

The story of this remarkable event is told by Gibson. The altar, he explains, had been 'prophan'd ... pulled down, and buried in the Ruins of the Church; till, carrying a great deal of Stone away for Common-Uses, it was dug up, among the rest; and appropriated (if by way of Abuse I may be allowed to call it so, tho' I tremble at it) to the salting of meat and making of Cheese. Thus it continued till it was very strangely (tho' without a Miracle) discovered what it was. Whereupon the Lord Scudamore, when he rebuilt this Church, with great Awfulness ordered it to be restored, and set upon three Pilasters of Stone: Where now it stands, the most remarkable Communion-Table of any in these Parts, being one entire Stone, 12 Foot long, 4 Foot broad, and 3 Inches thick.'[5] From Paul's notes we know that Scudamore replaced some of the green glazed tiles, identified by Rushforth as contemporary with Abbot Adam's presbytery, under the stone altar.

The altar rapidly became an object of awe with its own mythology of abuse. William

*Fig. 96. Archbishop William Laud by an unknown artist
(by permission of St John's College, Oxford [SGR5])*

Blundell, author of *A Cavalier's Note-Book*, describes how one servant who tried to make off with it was killed and another broke his leg. When used for pressing cheeses it ran with blood and when used in the laundry the sound of washing being pounded against it was heard throughout the night.[6]

In Elizabeth's reign most chalices had been replaced by communion cups. However, if the eucharist was 'the fount of eternal life' then the vessels for use at the altar assumed a much greater significance. Laud's tutor, John Buckeridge, later bishop of Rochester, reintroduced the chalice for use in his private chapel.[7] After his elevation to Canterbury Laud presented a cup, cover-paten and flagon for use at Lambeth Palace Chapel.[8] However the earliest known surviving 'gothic revival chalice' is at St. John's College, Oxford. It has been dated 'about 1615', that is to the period of Laud's presidency. It is therefore significant that as early as March 1618 Scudamore sought Laud's help in obtaining suitable vessels for use at the altar at Holme Lacy. As the workman contracted did not 'keep his promise', it was not until 1627 that Scudamore was able to give 'to the Use of the Parishioners in receiving the Sacrament, two Silver Flagons guilt, one Silver Chalice guilt, two Silver Patens guilt, with fayre Cases of Leather to put them in, and one Iron Chest, with three Locks to keep them in. Also he gave one large Damaske Cloth to cover the High-Altar, one Damaske napkin, and six framed Forms'—evidently to support the houseling or rail cloth spread over the altar rails to intercept any crumbs dropped during the administration of the sacrament. It is not surprising, given such concern with the propriety of the celebration of the eucharist at Holme Lacy, that at the consecration of Dore seven years later Scudamore gave 'at the Offertory ... a Purse of Gold' with which the silver flagon, chalice and paten, still in use, were bought for the service of the altar.[9]

Not merely space but decoration and light had to be concentrated on the altar if the congregation were to be in no doubt as to its significance and thus treat it with due respect. At Lambeth Palace Chapel Laud had a tapestry depicting the Last Supper placed behind the altar to serve as a reredos. Elsewhere the roof space above the altar was decorated to form a tester or canopy. Not surprisingly, at Dore Scudamore took the unusual step of placing a 'carved altar piece ... every way suitable to the honour of God' behind the altar.[10]

CHAPTER XVIII

The Scudamore Restoration
by Jim Tonkin

John Scudamore

Although he was about twenty-eight years younger John Scudamore was a friend of William Laud, who used to visit him. A remarkable series of letters written by Laud between 1622 and 1628 vividly show this friendship:[1]

'... All my fear is, that the great charges which these times have put me to in my beginnings will keep me so low that I shall have no liberty from good husbandry to attend myself and my friends; but such as I have is yours.' [1622] ... 'I had yesterday weeping weather, - it was fit I should not always brag of the fair. I got well to Gloucester before six, and might have been there sooner but that I had a greater mischance by the way than in all my journey beside. In the dirty bottom between Mr. Bridges his house and Ross, the careless man that led my sumpter went upon the side of a slippery bank, and overthrew my horse into a great slough. My horse had spoiled himself, if I had not caused one to lie upon his neck and to keep him down until his girths were undone. One end of my sumpter was full of dirt, and I rid after in jealousy for my papers, lest they had drunk such water; but I found them dry, and care not for the rest. I am now going to see my Lady Porter [Lady Scudamore's mother] and remember all respects to her from you and your lady ...' [1622]

Letters refer to John Scudamore's brother and sister and to John's letters being 'so full of kindness that I think you intended them for a new year's gift ...' [1627]

Perhaps these replies will be found one day. Laud himself is unfailingly kind in his references to the deaths in infancy of Scudamore's sons and makes solicitous enquiries after the health of poor Elizabeth Scudamore: 'For your lady, it does much trouble me to read the passion she has been in: and the best comfort that can be given her, under God, must come from yourself.' [1624] Elizabeth was obviously beside herself with grief as she had now lost three babies; she later lost two more and only one survived to manhood. John Scudamore tried to find a reason for his family tragedy and discussed it with Laud. His estates included Dore and Lanthony, Gloucester, both of which had been monasteries, and the tithes that had belonged to them. Laud sent him a very long letter in 1626 discussing the whole situation and giving as his opinion that 'you cannot hold impropriations to your own use without sin ... nor can the sale free you from sin, because you sell that which by divine law is God's, not yours.' Eventually, according to Gibson who used the Scudamore papers, John Scudamore spent about £50,000, not all at Dore, to expiate what he saw as his sin of having an estate founded on church property. The church was reconsecrated on his birthday.

Phase 1. 1630-40

The documentary evidence for the Scudamore restoration is contained in a series of documents at the Public Record Office and in Hereford

Cathedral Library. Copies of those at the Public Record Office are in Hereford Record Office and they tell the story of the work which was carried out in the 1630s on the instructions of John, Viscount Scudamore.

On 3 March 1632, a letter from Thomas Prichard to John, Viscount Scudamore, at Caradocke (Caradoc Court) states that 'Abel a carpenter' had made a survey for repairing the church and the mill and that he was willing to do the remaining work.[2] Abel had already written to Prichard on 23 February, 1632 about the water-mill and saying he would do the work in the Church for £230.[3]

This was followed on 21 March by a statement of what would be required:[4]

'The bodie of ye Church

Beames	16 Inches one waye, & 12 Inches ye other, in length 36 foote
Wall plates	double wall plats. 9 Inches broade, & 7 Inches thicke ev'ie wall plate
side rayles	4 courses. everie siderayle - tenne Inches broade, & 6 Inches & halfe thicke
Rafters	4 Inches square - the length 28 foote. the distance fro rafter to rafter, 13 Inches. the couples must bee 70.
Blads	as many payre as their are beames. 14 Inches broade & 7 Inches thicke
ffillinge timber to ye blads.	2 - coller beames, & 6 punchings to everie payer of blads.

Chancell — the chancell. the olde Rooffe to bee taken downe, & a newe ruffe to bee built according to ye reste of ye church. & the olde timber to be imployed about the Iles.

Iles — Beames. 20. tenne Inches one waye, & 8 Inches ye other waye, the length accordinge to the best order for ye good of ye buildinge.

Wall plates	sufficient everie wall plate 9 Inches broade, & 6 Inches thicke
side Rayles	3 - courses. everie side rayle to bee, 10 Inches broade, & 6 - Inches & halfe thicke, or accordinge to that sise
Rafters	4 Inches square, the length accordinge to ye places of ye Iles, the distance 13 Inches
Blades	20 - 14 Inches one waye & 6 Inches ye other waye.
ffillinge timber	necessarie & ffit. to make it substanstiall & stronge.

The ffirst to bee sised stronglye according to ye rest of ye worke

The steeple.	the ffirst floore, must consist of beames of a ffoote square, & other sufficient timber, with a hoele in ye middest of ye loft for drawinge up bels & other necessaries, wth plancks of 2 Inches thicke.
	the upper ffloor must consist of beames, of 14 Inches square & other sufficient timber, wth a houle in one pt of ye loft for drawinge up ye bels & other necessaries, wth plancks to cov' it of 2 Inches & halfe thicke.

The fframe for 4 bels; & to have space to hang two bels more. The frame to be made substantiall and stronge, to stocke the bels, & to make wheeles, & to hange the 4 bels sufficientlye & stronge the Iron worke beinge to bee done at the charge of the Viscount, the wheeles to be half wheeles. The Roofe of the steeple. One beame & two halfe beames, the beames to bee 15 Inches one waye & a ffoote the other waye, the beames of such a length as may be ffit for such a work. the roofe to come downe within the battlements 4 square, wth a spire up for holdinge a crosse and a weather cocke on the toppe; the sd roofe to be made wth such stronge & sufficient blads siderayles & other timber, as shallbee fitt for such a worke. ffor the Archinge wthin side the body of the Church & Chancell The pendents to bee belowe the beames tenne ffoote in length, wth compasse laces belonging to the pendents, & other fillinge timber betweene the beames, as shalbee sufficient & stronge to holde up such worke as shalbee sett up theron either by boardinge or playsteringe.'

Just over three weeks later on 15 April, 1633 a detailed estimate was received under the headings 'The Steeple'[5] and 'The bodie of the Church'[6] the total cost to be £326 1s. 10d.

The following three sections are not literal transcripts of the originals, but are based very closely on them.

The Steeple

   80 ft. high plus battlements 5 ft. at highest point

   16 ft. within the walls

   28 ft. without to the utmost part

   First loft 30 ft. - wall 6 ft, broad to be drawn in a foote

   Second loft 38 ft. from first

   The battlements to be 5 ft. high for the highest battlement

   The two walls of the steeple to bee made up to the Church walls come to - 100 - perche

   The 4 walls of the steeple to bee veryfied 30 - foote, will come to - 200 - perche

   The whole perches will bee - 300 - besides the battlements wch wilbe 5 foote high, the highest part

   The pyne ends mended:

     to mende the flre

     to pull downe the flr where the steeple must be founded

   The height of the wall - 50 ft.

   The compass of the steeple

550 perh at 2s -	£ 55	
Battlements 4 foot high	15	
The pyne ends	10	16s.
Mending the Iles	1	
Pulling down & digging stones for the steeple	5	
Tot.	86	16s.

The bodie of the church

   Beames 9 tonne of timber & 1/2

at 6s. 8d the tonne comes to	3	3s.	4d.
Wall plates 4 tonne at 6s. 8d.	1	6s.	8d.
Side rayles 6 tonne at 6s. 8d.	2		
Blades 8 tonne at 6s. 8d.	2	13s.	4d.
ffilinge timber 5 tonne at 6s. 8d.	1	13s.	4d.
Rafters 9 tonne at 14s.	6	6s.	
Tot.	17	2s.	8d.

The ffotte of the T.

6 tonne of newe timber at 10s.	3		
Rafters 5 tonne att 5s. 8d. ton, the falinge, squaringe & sawinge being deducted	1	8s.	4d.
for this pt of the church make up this some	13	6s.	8d.

Abell would have the wall plate - 1 tonne more

He would have 2 course of side rayles more, that is, 1 ton & 1/2 more of timber

The bodie of the Church 100 ffoote in length, that is the heade of the cross

Beames 10	16 ins. by 12 ins. - length 36 ft. - every beame contayninge 48 ft. [i.e. cub. ft.] The 10 beams contayne in total 9 ton of timber and a half and 5 ft.
Wall plates	double 9 ins. by 7 ins. Total length 400 ft. 4 tons of timber
Side rayles	3 courses Every side rail - 10 ft. by 6 1/2 ins. Total length 600 ft. 6 tons of timber
Rafters	4 ins. square 28 ft. long 13 ins. between rafters 70 couples. Every couple 6 ft. (cub. ft.) 9 tons of timber
Blades	10 payer 14 ins. by 8 ins. 40 ft. in every pair 8 tons of timber

ffillinge timber to the blade	2 collar beams and 6 punchings to every pair of blades. $\frac{1}{2}$ ton timber each pair. 10 payer - total timber for 10 payre will be 5 tons

Total timber 41$\frac{1}{2}$ tons & 5 ft.

Chancel

60 ft. long. Roof to be taken down and framed a new. Old timber to be used & 6 tons of new timber

Iles	240 ft. rounde. (not reckoning the tower)
Wall plates	double 480 ft. every wall plate 9 Ins. by 7 ins. 4 tons of timber & 40 ft.
Side rayles	2 courses at side of church and 3 at end of chancell 10 ins. by 6$\frac{1}{2}$ ins. 480 ft. in all & 66 ft. in chancel 5$\frac{1}{2}$ tons
Rafters	4 ins. square 24 ft. long 13 ins. between 140 single rafters Every three rafters will contain 8 ft. of timber Total for rafters 7 tons & 8 ft. allow 8 tons
Blades	20 - 14 ins. by 16 ins. 40 ft. of timber to every pair. Total 8 tons
ffillinge timber to the blades	10 ft. of punchinge to every blade 4 tons
Beams	20 - 10 ins. by 8 ins. 14 ft. long Every beam will contain 8 ft. of timber Total 3 tons & 20 ft. Allow 3$\frac{1}{2}$ tons
The ffirst	100 foot of timber which is 2 tonne

Total of timber for Iles - 35 ton & 40 ft.
Total of timber 83 tons and 20 ft.

The Steeple

First floor	4 beams each 22 ft. in length by 1 ft. square Total 1 ton & 38 ft. to make planks 1 ton & 12 ft. Total timber 3 tons
Upper floor	8 beams 25 ins, square 22 ft. long 33 ft. of timber to each beam Total timber 5 tons & 14 ft.
Planks	2$\frac{1}{2}$ ins. thick Timber 2$\frac{1}{2}$ tons

Frame for 4 bells & leave space for 2 more. 5 tons of timber to make frame, stocks & halfewheels

Roof of steeple	3 beams 1 ft. square by 22 ft. long. 2 tons & 16 ft. 3 pair of blades 15 ft. to a pair. Total 45 ft. 4 side rails 6 ins. by 10 ins. 40 ft. Two wall plates. 22 ft. of timber Rafters. 12 pair. Every rafter 13 ft. long. 3 ft. of timber in every pair. Total 36 ft.

Total of timber for roof 4 ton & 9 ft.
Total of timber for steeple 18 ton & 48 ft.
Total of timber for whole 102 ton & 18 ft.

Cost £326 1s. 10d.

Some of the terms used may need a little explanation. 'The pyne ends' under the heading 'Steeple' are what are normally called gables, the term still being in use in Carmarthenshire. 'Blades' are the principals, a term normally reserved for crucks, but used here for the main timbers in a truss.

It is interesting to note that Abel 'would have the wall plate - 1 tonne more' and '2 courses of side rayles - more'. This seems to be typical of timber-framing in the southern Marches; the timbers used are often much heavier than necessary. Presumably with so much good timber available a little 'over insurance' was acceptable. The measurement of timber in tons and cubic feet e.g. beams 36 ft. by 16 ins. by 12 ins. - 'every beame contayninge 48 ft', seems to the layman to be an odd way of working out the totals, but it would appear that 100 ft. of timber was estimated to be a ton. The difference in the weight of the principals (Blades) and the rafters is quite significant, the former being really heavy at 14 ins. by 8 ins. whereas the rafters are 4 ins. square. The term 'rayle' is used for what is normally called a purlin.

'Punchings' (puncheons) are the short, vertical timbers used in framing, more often known as studs.

The use of double wall-plates was common in wealthier buildings in this area, as for example in Bosbury Court, one of the palaces of the Bishop of Hereford. Ten of the beams were to be 36 ft. long and 16 ins. by 12 ins. This means the use of some fine trees; to find a tree which will give straight timbers of that length is comparatively unusual. Planks $2^{1}/_{2}$ ins. thick again shows the extravagant use of timber in this heavily forested county.

The term 'steeple' to an architect normally means tower and spire together as in the local rhyme at Weobley:

> *Poor Priest, proud People,*
> *Low Church, high Steeple.*

Presumably this is what was intended at Abbey Dore, but in the 'Articles of Agreement' made between Viscount Scudamore and David Adams of Rosse', mason, on 15th April, 1633[7] there is reference to a 'tower' not a 'steeple', though in the next document 'The manner of building' the term 'steeple' is used.

'Articles of Agreement made Indented and agreed uppon betweene'
Viscount Scudamore and David Addams of Rosse, mason, 15 April 1633.

Tower to be 80 ft. to roof, battlements to
  go 4 ft. higher 16 ft. square internally,
  24 ft. square externally
Walls 5 ft. thick to first level
To be built in angle on south side
Has to quarry stone for it.
To be paid £90. £5 weekly and balance to
  be paid within one week of finishing
Scudamore to supply scaffolding

In this agreement the position of the present tower is specified with some slight differences between it and the specifications in the section 'The Steeple'. Unfortunately it does not specify where the stone was to be quarried. There is no reference to the bell-frame in this contract, but this had already been agreed on 21 March, 1632.

Part of 'The Manner of building Agreed for Door church'[8] specifies:

'The Chancell roof to be taken down and
  new built up
The Body of the church to bee covered,
  wth the Iles
The steeple to bee built on the South-side
  upon the Ile, wth Battlements, &
  covered wth tile, for six bells, wth two
  lofts & a frame for the bells

Carpenter
The body of the Church 100 foot
Every rafter 13 inches in distance
The rafters wth 4 courses of side-rails on
  either side 4 inches square; the rafters
  in length 28 feet: 10 foote a sunder the
  bands, & at every band a beame 15
  inches one way and 12 another.
Double sills, 8 inches square apeece
the Iles

Mason
The steeple in height
The pine ends
The yarnding of the Isles

There is 38 foot difference betweene
Abell & Simmonds measure of the Isles.'

The 13 inches distance between rafters is quite common in Herefordshire and the sills at 8 inches square are more or less standard in the county. They are double sills, a sign once again of substantial and wealthy building. A rough plan of the tower is given showing angle buttresses at the two corners away from the church with a doorway into it and a stair turret.[9]

The final document in the series is 'An accompt of money delivered by my Lord Scudamore & paid by Ric Hands of Richard Marks towares the reedifying of the Church at Doore beginning the sixt day of Aprill 1633.'[10]

It is quite a long account and as some of it is repetitive not all is reproduced here. The first four sections are of considerable interest to the social and economic historian as they show the wages of workmen & the costs of materials.

Quarry for tile

		£	s	d
	5 men for 6 days in the quary at 8d	1	0	0
	1 man for 5 days in the quary at 8d		3	4
Apr. 13	5 men for 6 days in the quary at 8d	1	0	0
	1 man for 4 days in the quary at 8d		2	8
June 1	6 men for making 34,000 tile at 5s the 1000	8	10	0
June 7	5 men for making 7,000 tile at 5s the 1000	1	15	0
	Christopher Bowles for rearing of tiles	1	3	0
	Pd Parry for a daies work at the quary			8
	Fr Riddwis the watercourse	1	0	0
Dec. 6	Jo. Rollings & his fellowes for rearing 3000 of tiles at 5s		15	0
Jan. 27	Jo. Rollings etc. for rearing of 7000 tiles at 5s	1	15	0
May 26	For rearing 3000 tiles at 5s		15	0
Aug 2	For rearing 6000 of tiles at 5s	1	10	0
		19	9	8

Mason

		£	s	d
	David Adams for making the Tower	90	0	0
	To him for making two buttresses	13	6	8
		103	6	8

Tiler | | 53 | 9 | 8 |

Apr. 13   Making the lyme kill   5   0

Clearly men working in the quarry were being paid 8 pence a day and tiles were 5 shillings per 1,000. These are the sandstone tiles with which so many buildings in south and west Herefordshire were originally roofed. Unfortunately there is no clue as to the actual quarry from which they were cut. The making of the tiles is presumably the splitting with a bettle and chisel, a highly skilled craft, still carried out today at the great slate quarries in Wales and Cornwall. The actual tiling, 'reareing' the tiles, was paid for on a piece-work basis at 5 shillings per thousand tiles.

David Adams the mason was paid for making the tower and the two buttresses. The tiler and whoever made the lime kiln are not named, but it is interesting to see the local pronunciation being written almost phonetically, 'kill' and not 'kiln'.

In his original correspondence Abel made it clear that he was prepared to contract 'in gross for masons worke carpenters worke and tillers worke, you finding timber, tille ston & carriage & I to finde naiols and alle iron & irone worke.' However, to put all the work into the hands of one 'undertaker' was not felt to be the best way of working being 'a way of building not so allowable in works intended for posterity.' Thus Lord Scudamore was probably wise to contract separately with Adams for the masonry and the accounts show that he found the nails and Ironwork as well as the stone, tiles and timber.

In the next section the 'new lyme maker' is paid at 12 pence a day, so presumably this was a really skilled occupation, for the two men mentioned immediately below are not even paid at 8 pence a day whereas the man below is paid at 8 pence and gets an extra 6 pence for making a contract. These payments go on weekly from 6 July to 28 September, this presumably being the period when most of the actual building was done whereas the tiling itself seems to have been started in December and not finished until the following August.

'Digging stone for the Lyme burners' shows weekly payments from mid-July to mid-September totalling £1 10s. 2d. and on 'Drawing stone to the Kill', one payment in May, three in June and then weekly from 6 July to 20 October. This was totalled to £3 10s. 3d. and then a note added 'overspent 4d.' and the total reduced to £3 9s. 11d. Then follows 'Lyme bought' on various dates from 6 July to 27 November, totalling £21 5s. 0d.

The next two sections are about the costs of 'Cleeving,' The first is a quite straightforward series of payments almost weekly from 13 April to 14 September for 'Cleeving wood for the Lyme burners' totalling £5 3s. 10d. This was presumably simply firewood for the lime kilns, and almost anything that would burn well would do. The other is 'Cleeving Lath for the tiler,' a much more skilful task for these were to be the laths on which the tiles were hung. There are four payments altogether in August, September, October and the following May all to Henry Davis. The laths were 'cleeved' at a rate of 3s. 4d. (the old half mark) per 1000. Altogether he 'cleeved' 13,900 laths at a total cost of £2 6s. 4d. This was purely for the cleaving, the actual timber is a separate charge later in the account. It is interesting to note that this works out exactly; no question of charging for 14,000 when only 13,900 were supplied. Just like splitting the tiles, cleaving the lath was a skilled job. These would be split oak laths over which the tiles would be hung each with a nail through the top of the tile. The 'nails' were usually of copper, sometimes of sheep bone, sometimes of iron. Each tile hung in this way would have two more overlapping it so that only the bottom third of the tile would be exposed to the weather. The actual weight of such a roof can be very heavy—something like one and a half tons to a hundred square feet; so both the laths and the nails have to be strong and of good quality.

The next section is the cost of the 'Nailes', but what they are made of is not specified. There were nine payments between August and October in the following year totalling £13 11s. 4d.

After this follows a section headed 'Guifts given by my Lords appoyntment.' Quite what these were for is not made clear but over a period of almost two years they total £2 0s. 6d.

The actual 'Felling of trees for lath, gathering of woods etc' is listed for various dates covering four years and only totals 14s. 2d. The actual cost of timber is very much higher and these were presumably small trees felled simply for the cutting of laths.

The next section is 'Iron'

Oct. 20   Pd for 2 wire hookes for
           the church Doore   6
Dec. 6   Pd Th Ades for making one
           ton 18ct. 2qrs. 17l. of iron
           into barres for the windows

of the Church at three
farthings the pound
alowed for wast 15s
so paid   12   15   7
                  12   16   1

This is interesting in that it shows the use of iron for the windows here, but unfortunately does not say where it came from. The forges at Downton were working as early as the sixteenth century, but presumably the work here was done locally by blacksmiths at Dore.

There are two payments for 'Crests', almost certainly ridge tiles. These are probably of local sandstone and this seems more likely as they come immediately before the item 'Digging Paving' at various dates from December to the following October. 174 'crests' cost £2 3s. 6d.

The 'paving' will be the local sandstone flooring slabs dug at various dates from December to the following October at a cost of £7 14s. 0d. In addition to this eight loads of paving were bought in August costing 18s. 8d. Why this was bought and not dug with the other is not explained. Again the quarry from which they were cut is not named, but it is probably not very far away.

William Aleridge and David Adams seem to have had the task of paving the church, laying the floor tiles already quarried and bought and were paid for this in August and December. This also appears to have been paid for as piece-work at 7d. a square yard, totalling £25 4s. 0d.

Various accounts follow. Four of them in August are for lead work, plastering, mending broken walls and floor at £11 10s. 0d., £2 15s. 10d., £2 1s. 10d. and 8s. 0d. respectively. There are two payments for the 'Carriage of Iron', one in August and the other in October, totalling 17s. 0d. This is presumably the iron for the window bars which are mentioned again on four occasions between September and December 'Makeing holes in the windowes for the barrs' at a total of £3 5s. 6d. Before this in the list on 6 December is 'Making of Churchyard wall £12 11s. 0d.'

'Casting the bell' cost £4 15s. 0d. and is entered under 26 September.

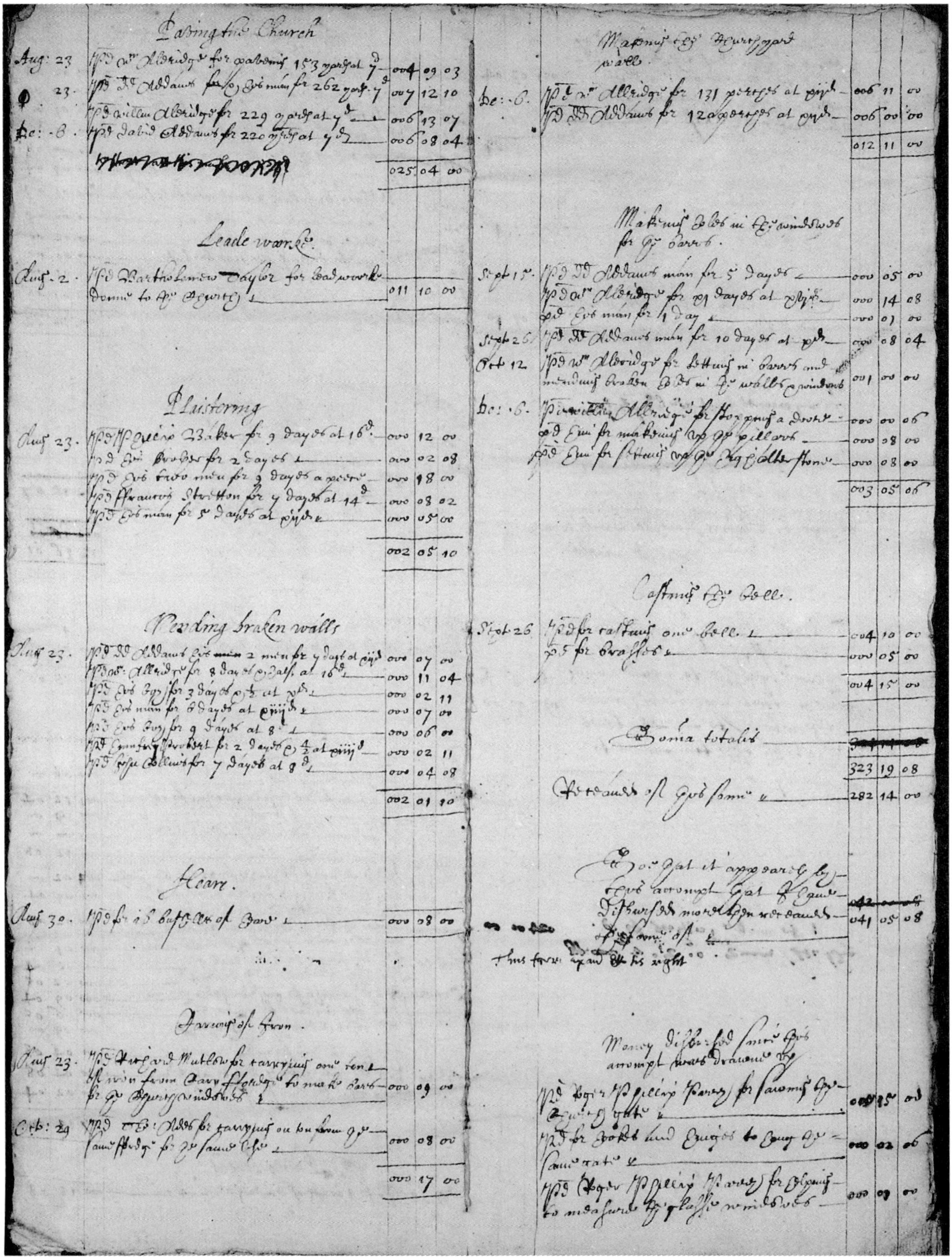

Paddington Church

Aug: 23	...	004 09 03
23	...	007 12 10
	...	006 13 07
De: 8	...	006 08 04
		025 04 00

Leade work:

Aug: 2	...	011 10 00

Plaistering

Aug 23	...	000 12 00
	...	000 02 08
	...	000 18 00
	...	000 03 02
	...	000 05 00
		002 05 10

Mending broken walls

Aug 23	...	000 07 00
	...	000 11 04
	...	000 02 11
	...	000 07 00
	...	000 02 11
	...	000 04 08
		002 01 10

Hearr.

Aug 30	...	000 08 00

Carriage from .

Aug 23	...	000 09 00
Oct: 29	...	000 08 00
		000 17 00

Making ... House yard wall.

De: 6	...	006 11 00
	...	006 00 00
		012 11 00

Making ... in ... windowes for ... barrs.

Sept 15	...	000 05 00
	...	000 14 08
	...	000 01 00
Sept 26	...	000 08 04
Oct 12	...	001 00 00
De: 6	...	000 00 06
	...	000 08 00
	...	000 08 00
		003 05 06

Casting the Bell.

Sept 26	...	004 10 00
	...	000 05 00
		004 15 00

Soma totalis

		323 19 08
		282 14 00

		041 05 08

Money disbursed ... accompt ...

	...	000 25 00
	...	000 02 06
	...	000 09 00

Fig. 97. The page from the account book detailing the expenditure on smaller items, including paving, leadwork, plastering and mending broken walls (PRO C115/D19 1915-1916)

This is then totalled:
'Suma totalis £323 19s 8d
Receaved of this some 282 14s 0d
Soe that it appeareth by this
accompt that I have desbursed
more than receaved 41 5s 8d

However, this is not the end of the story for the next item reads:

'Money disbursed since this accompt
was drawne up
Pd Roger Phillip Parry for sawing
the Church gate 15 0
Pd for hooks and hinges to hang
the same gate 2 6
Pd Roger Phillip Parry for helping
to measure the glasse windowes 1 0
Pd Humfrey Probert for makeing
up a doore in the end of the church
and a stile at the churchgate and
the broken walles of the Church
yard answearable to the rest 1 3 4
2 1 10
Some totalis 326 1 10
Soe laid out in the whole more
than received 43 7 10
For my paynes which yor. Ld{p}. please'

These accounts are for the finishing touches to the church, sawing and hanging the gate, a stile at the gateway and repairing a door, minor but essential items.

The next section reads:
'31 March Annor dni 1637
this Account wth ye paper for ye mill annexed on the other side of the leafe was then discharged & f d by Thomas Manfelde Clerke to mee
Richard Meeke'

Then follow two very significant items:
'Tymber felled for the same worke fifty and one trees wch were guesse to yeald about ffouer tons a piece wch comes in the whole to 204 tons wch at 5s the tone comes to in money 51 0 0
Lead of my Lords oven that went to make gutters for the Church
2 tons 0 cwts 2qr 4 lbs worth 24 0 0'

The fifty-one trees yielding four tons of timber each is a very interesting item for it gives some idea of the amount of timber needed for roof timbers and furnishings in a building the size of Abbey Dore Church. These were fine trees and show how valuable the Herefordshire oak forests were and the weight of timber a tree would produce.

The lead for the gutters is specified by weight. Lead was mined in Shropshire, and also in Devon and Cornwall. It could have been carted down from the Stiperstones area or brought by sea and river from one of the ports on the north coast of Devon and Cornwall which had a good trade with South Wales.

These accounts are followed by one of £6 0s. 10d. for repairing the mill at Doore and another which is an agreement with two miners to 'looke for coal'.

The final document is a summary item by item of the twenty-seven items in the account totalling £326 1s. 10d. Originally the Mill costs and the agreement to search for coal were included, but were crossed out before the total was finally arrived at.

Quarry of tile	019	09	08
Mason	103	06	08
Tiler	053	09	08
Makeing the lyme kill	000	05	00
Lyme making	010	16	08
Digging stone for the lyme burners	001	10	02
Drawinge stone to the kill	003	10	03
Lyme bought	021	05	00
Cleeving wood for the lyme kill	005	03	10
Cleeving lath for the tiler	002	06	04
Nailes	013	11	04
Guifts	002	00	06
ffalling trees for lath, rodds etc	000	14	02
Iron	012	16	01
Crests	002	03	06
Digging paveing	007	14	00
Paveing bought	000	18	08
Paveing the church	025	04	00
Leade worke	011	10	00

	li	s	d
Plaistering	002	05	10
Mending broken walls	002	01	10
Heare	000	08	00
Cariage of Irone	000	17	00
Makeing the Church yard wall	012	11	00
Makeing holes in the windoes for barrs	003	05	06
Castinge the bells	004	15	00
Disb: since this accot draweinge	002	01	10
	326	01	10

A further document concerning the rebuilding of the Church is among the Scudamore accounts in Hereford Cathedral Library and has been printed in the *Woolhope Club Transactions* on two occasions.[11]

	li	s	d
Roger Simons 9 daies at doore	0	9	0
Steeven Powell 8 daies there	0	8	0
Wm. Simons 6 daies there	0	6	0
a clapp (er) workmanship and baldring of a bell there	0	6	0
the bell wheele	0	6	0
the pines to fitt the wheele	0	1	0
the bellrope and nayles	0	4	0
a mason for placeing the font and stopping a window	0	7	4
a seame of lyme	0	1	2
sawyers for saweing timber for the Comunion table	0	2	0
labourers to helpe the sawyers	0	2	0
the Carpenter	0	2	0
Tot	2	14	6

This bears no date, but is among a lot of household and personal accounts headed 'Accounts of the Steward of the Rt. Hon, John Scudamore, First Viscount Scudamore, at Holme Lacy, 1632.' Simons and Powell occur in the documents quoted earlier, but here is evidence of the font being put in place, the sawing of timber for the communion table and the hanging of a bell with its wheel and clapper.

Phase 2. 1700-1710

During the reign of James II, 1685-8, the Church almost went back to Catholic discipline and this was followed by William III and Mary when the Church of England was finally established in 1689 more or less as we know it today. The Church entered a period when there was little regard for the sacraments in the way that there had been, communion sometimes only being celebrated twice a year. In most churches there were no week-day services and the emphasis was on the sermon and quite frequently on the singing. This was led in many cases by a small 'orchestra' and quite probably the gallery in Abbey Dore Church was used for this purpose.

Thus the 'broad' church outlook became common and it was not until the Evangelical and Oxford Movements of the nineteenth century that the Church really assumed spiritual leadership again. This lack of purpose led to the break away of the Methodists led by Wesley.

Two coins of this time were found when two watercourses were dug: a copper sixpence of James II, dated 1689, and a copper halfpenny of the reign of William and Mary with the inscription NUMMORUM FAMULUS and a double rose.[12]

CHAPTER XIX

The John Hoskyns' Tomb

by Ruth Richardson

On entering the main door of the Abbey turn right and you will be facing one of the original monastic chapels. Only two survive in this position as the thirteenth century extension changed the inner two chapels into part of the ambulatory. The north chapel is now the vestry while the south chapel is the Hoskyns Chapel, which contains monastic glass reset by Roland Paul. The 1899 screen, designed by Paul for Anna Wren-Hoskyns in memory of her sister Clare, is one of several Hoskyns family memorials. However, the central feature of this chapel is the tomb of John Hoskyns.

John Hoskyns was the Member of Parliament for Hereford during the reign of James I, from 1603/4 to 1611 and again in 1614. He helped draft the Petition of Right of 1628 and also chaired the whole House of Commons in committee when it was passed. He insisted that the doors were locked, with no-one allowed to leave, until the proceedings (which took all day) were completed.[1]

John Hoskyns was born at Monkton, a farm in the parish of Llanwarne, in 1566. Although there were several children, the family was sufficiently wealthy to allow them to be well educated. John briefly attended Westminster School and then Winchester College, and New College, Oxford. Winchester has a caricature entitled a 'Trusty Servant' which he painted, composing the Latin verse and English translation. His studies included Latin, Greek, Hebrew, Spanish, law, theology,

science, as well as grammar, logic, rhetoric, arithmetic, geometry, astronomy and music—a comprehensive gentleman's education and one that fitted him for public life. In his own time he was known as a famous poet, with a gift for satire, and a compelling speaker. According to his son's great friend John Aubrey, Hoskyns' bitingly satirical speech on the former Chancellor, Sir Christopher Hatton, who had served Elizabeth I completely unquestioningly, caused him to be sent to teach in Somerset for a year. Here he met his future wife.

Hoskyns was admitted to the Middle Temple in 1593 and called to the bar in 1600. About this time he published *The Directions of Speeche and Stile,* a book dedicated to Robert Harley of Brampton Bryan, that was widely read in literary circles. In August 1601 he married Benedicta Bourne (formerly Moyle), the rich widow of a colleague, who already had two children. Soon after, he rented, and later bought in 1609, a large house in Widemarsh Street in Hereford (the electricity showrooms now occupy part of the site).[2] By 1602 he had become a Justice of the Peace and, until 1609, because he was 'a man learned in the law', Deputy Steward, where he assisted the Mayor of Hereford at the Mayor's Court. He was the city's legal advisor and in 1612 was again listed as a J.P.

Records in 1624 show that John Hoskyns became the wealthiest man in Hereford but he never became Mayor. Evidence shows that this was di-

Fig. 98. The tomb of John Hoskyns

rectly due to the king. Hoskyns had contributed poetry to a memorial collection for Elizabeth I in 1603 but a distinctly less adulatory poem to an accession collection for James I. This second book also included a poem from Sir Walter Raleigh. In 1611 Hoskyns was a founder member of the Mermaid group, named after the tavern where they met, which convened once a month for conversation and to read their own poetry. It comprised many M.P.s as well as John Donne and Ben Johnson.

James I's new Parliament was dominated by the king's attempts to obtain finance to pay for his extravagances, while Parliament would only vote what it considered necessary for the government of the country. Hoskyns was apparently very concerned about James' promotion of favourites at court. His final speech in 1614, full of wit and satire, compared the situation with the oppressive rule of Charles of Anjou and his French favourites in Sicily and southern Italy

which was only ended by a massacre in 1282. Later he was to claim that he had not understood the allusion but James was so angry that, after Parliament was prorogued, Hoskyns was arrested, with four other M.P.s, and imprisoned in the Tower of London.

After some weeks of close confinement, Hoskyns was allowed to mix with other prisoners, which included Raleigh and many of the country's important mathematicians, astronomers and scientists. Indeed, Hoskyns is said by John Aubrey to have revised Raleigh's *History of the World*. The Tower became one of the main intellectual centres of England—in itself quite a comment on James I's rule!

John Hoskyns petitioned the King for his release and he was supported by Benedicta who cited her pregnancy with their second child, her fourth. During this time he wrote to his small son:

Fig 99. The Coat of Arms on the side of the Hoskyns tomb

'*Sweet Benedict, whilst thou art young*
And know'st not yet the use of tongue
Keep it in thral whilst thou art free
Imprison it or it will thee.'

Indeed, the family motto translates as: 'Bind the tongue or the tongue will bind thee.'

After a year Hoskyns was placed on probation and ordered to live in London, where his family joined him. But James I had still not forgiven Hoskyns. On 21 August 1616 he wrote to the Corporation of Hereford concerning the city's choice of Hoskyns as Mayor for the coming year. John Hoskyns is described as having 'fallen into our heavy displeasure, for wch cause he was removed from being yor. Recorder.' The king threatened that if this had happened by general consent he would have charged the Corporation with 'want of duty and discretion.' However, he provided a way out for the city by saying that he had been 'credibly informed' that Hoskyns had been chosen because of 'faction and underhand practises'

implying vote rigging. He directs the city to have a new election. There is no mention of the king's informant, but this letter was found in the Scudamore papers.

Nevertheless, in 1617 and 1618 John acted as a commissioner for land transactions between Hereford and Lord Abergavenny. In 1620 he was the second most important member, after Sir John Scudamore (1542-1623, see family tree), in the new Common Council of the City. By 1621 he was able to return to a more prominent role in public life when he was appointed Circuit Judge in Wales. In 1623 he was appointed Serjeant-at-Law and a member of the Council of the Marches.

In 1622 he bought an estate at Morehampton, between Vowchurch and Abbey Dore. He placed a Latin inscription on the outside of the house which translated read 'I admit, O Copernicus, the heaven stands still; the earth is moved.'[3] Copernicus' theory that the earth revolves around the sun would have been a part of his discussions in the Tower. Hoskyns is traditionally supposed to have entertained James I at Morehampton with ten Morris dancers whose combined ages totalled one thousand years. Hereford has been suggested as an alternative venue—there the combined ages were more than 1,200! However, considering James' known animosity to Hoskyns this all seems very unlikely.[4]

King James died in 1625 and in 1628 John Hoskyns was again elected as an M.P. for Hereford. This was Charles I's third Parliament, with a number of new members including Oliver Cromwell. In June Charles reluctantly gave his assent to the Petition of Right, which Hoskyns had

Fig. 100. Two portraits of John Hoskyns (by kind permission of the Duke of Buccleuch)

helped to draft. Parliament met again in 1629. The fiery debates were brought to a crisis when the king tried to adjourn the session only for the Speaker to be held forcibly in his chair—'God's wounds!' cried Denzil Holles, 'you shall sit till we please to rise.'[5] After much acrimony the House voted its own adjournment. Parliament did not meet again for eleven years, as the king attempted to rule alone, but by then John Hoskyns had died of gangrene of the leg, at Morehampton in 1638.

He was buried in Dore Abbey, where his tomb, in the chancel, was adorned with verses by among others John Donne. Hoskyns bequeathed books to Hereford cathedral library.[6] Although a supporter of the rights of law and Parliament, his friendship with men like Donne indicates that he was no Puritan, believing in the tenets of the Church of England. In his later life he had spent a great deal of time and effort settling his family into his large Herefordshire estates and, years later, in 1654, the family also acquired an estate at Harewood. His son Benedict, who had served as High Sheriff un-

der Cromwell's government,[7] purchased a baronetcy from Charles II. John Hoskyns' house at Morehampton was demolished after his, John's, death, but his tomb, now in the Hoshyns chapel, remains as an important feature of the abbey (Fig. 98).

The coat of arms on the side of the tomb (Fig. 99) includes the arms of John Hoshyns on the left which are described as:

'Per pale azure and gules, a chevron between three lions rampant or, on a canton the bloody hand.'

The crest above was described by John Aubrey:

'I have heard that when he came out of the Tower, his crest was graunted him (I believe) for his bold Spirit, and (I suppose) contrived by himselfe, viz. a Lyon's head couped or, breathing fire. The Serjeant would say jocosely that it was the only Lyon's head in England that tooke Tobacco.'[8] Hoskyns (Fig. 100) was a friend of Raleigh who did much to popularise smoking!

CHAPTER XX

The Woodwork

by Jim Tonkin

The Roof

The roof as reconstructed by Abel is a piece of first class seventeenth century carpentry typical of the Marches.[1] The actual roof construction, as opposed to the ceiling, could have been done by any good carpenter of the region at any time in the previous hundred and fifty years. It is of double queen-post construction with three purlins on each side. There are eight common rafters to each bay and unusually for this area Abel has used the butt-purlin type of construction rather than the more common Marches technique of trenched through-purlins. Each pair of queen-posts has diagonal braces to the collar above it, all well jointed with a mortice and tenon joint using two pegs at each joint. There is what is virtually a stub-collar beam lower again from the principal to the lower queen-posts. It reminds me of Carew writing in Cornwall in 1602 about their roofs 'packed thick with timber, seeking therethrough only strength and warmness.'[2] The latter quality is perhaps not very important here, but the former is.

The Ceilings

Below this roof is the flat ceiling of oak over the presbytery in three bays (Fig. 20). This also is the work of John Abel and his versatility and ability show well in the change from the heavy, traditional timbering of the roof to this right up-to-date ceiling showing the influence of the Renaissance. The tie-beams are carried on moulded wall posts which rise off the original stone vaulting shafts. Moulded braces, both longitudinal and transverse spring from these, the former being carved with the typical Herefordshire running foliage ornament and the latter with sunk quatrefoils with pendants under the beams carved with a bunch of grapes or hops, set within a pattern of four leaves. Below these braces are half-round shafts with square bases and capitals on which stand four carved consoles, one with more scroll work and foliage, a second with a typical Renaissance female bust and more scroll work, a third with monsters which have eagles' heads and horses' legs, and the fourth with more foliage and scroll work.[3]

The ceilings of the crossing and transepts are similar to those over the presbytery, but not as ornate. The wall posts have no shafts on their faces, but have carved consoles on the posts which are smaller than those in the presbytery. They include human faces and busts in the carving and on the west console of the south transept is a rather grotesque female figure carrying a shield. The small pierced pendants on the beams are typical pieces of Renaissance ornament.

Porch

The south porch is a typical early-seventeenth century timber-framed example built on low walls with plaster side panels, the east wall having been more recently filled with stone slates (Fig. 21).

The gabled front has arched braces below the tie-beam with two raking struts above to the principals. The posts are notched for the arched braces, but the mortices were cut too big for them or the whole truss has been dismantled and new braces put in. On the top of the west face of the south-west post is a cusped sinking which seems rather unusual.

The gable has barge-boards protecting the ends of the purlins and these have moulded edges and at the apex a pendant with a shaped end.

The inner doorway against the south wall of the south transept has a tie-beam on posts which are morticed for arched braces to the tie-beam but which are now gone.

Fig. 101. The thirteenth-century north door

Doors

One door survives from the monastic period. The doorway is in the north wall of the ambulatory and would have provided access to the church from the infirmary and the monastic burial ground. The door is close-battened with a two-centred head framed internally in the shape of a trefoiled arch. It has two wrought-iron ornamental hinges, the upper one with a beast's head; the lower one partly lost. The style is of the thirteenth century (Fig. 101).

In the south doorway the main door to the church is closely-battened and nail-studded, two-centred head, with moulded cover strips externally. It is hung on strap hinges with foliated ends and is contemporary with most of the seventeenth century work.

In the south-east angle of the south transept is the doorway of the staircase to the turret. It has a door of battens and is hung on strap hinges. In the upper storey of the tower leading to the roof space of the south-east chapel is a plain battened oak door with a small round-headed peep-hole in it. It is probably seventeenth century and is now boarded up.

The Screen

The screen is what catches the eye as soon as one turns to face the east end of the church (Fig. 102). It is under the eastern arch of the crossing and, along with the old market hall at Leominster (the Grange), shows that Abel was very much influenced by the Renaissance. It is of oak, of five bays divided by Ionic columns which stand on pedestals with no formal base and support an entablature with shaped consoles above each column. The columns have on either side of the central doorway grotesque carved heads, while above it are shaped brackets which meet in a carved pendant below the middle of the cornice. They are enriched with a standardised form of leaf ornament. The lower part of the screen is divided into four panels in each bay by heavy, moulded styles. In the upper part of the screen three of the bays are divided by turned balusters with trefoiled cusping between the heads. The fourth bay, that on the north side of the central opening, has pendants in place of the two

Fig. 102. The Renaissance screen

northern balusters. On the west face of the frieze are raised panels bearing the inscription *Vive deo gratus, toti mundo tumulatus crimine mundatus, semper transire paratus.* This is identical to the first part of the inscription on the old market hall at Leominster, now the Grange, which was the work of Abel in 1633, and used to stand at the top of Broad Street. Above the main cornice are four pierced finials and between them three large cartouches carrying coats of arms: the central is the Royal Arms (Stuart), that on the north of Scudamore with a coronet above, and on the south the See of Canterbury impaling Scuda-more's friend Laud, who was Archbishop 1633-40.

Seating
This all dates from the restoration of the 1630s. The pews have panelled ends and backs with carved panels at the top forming almost a type of frieze. One pew carries the initials T.M. There are pews at the rear for the churchwardens, with higher enclosures with arabesque panels at the end. At the east end are two desks.

Table
On the first floor of the tower is a five feet long table with chamfered and stopped legs, grooved or panelled top rails, all seventeenth-century work. It has a modern deal top and the top rail is missing at one end.

Poor Box
This is dated 1639 with an inscription following the date 'H(e) that from ye poo(r) h(is) eyes will turn aw(ay) t(he) Lord wil turn His ... V ... N yn later day yfro.' The oak box is square with a moulded rim to the lid and moulding mitred

179

round the base, carried on a small column with moulded capital and base. There are two old locks to the box, both no longer used.

Pulpit

The principal pulpit standing in the presbytery is a good example of the many early to mid-seventeenth-century pulpits in this county (Fig. 103). It is of oak, hexagonal with each side panelled and having a double arcaded head typical of the Renaissance ornament found so often about that time. Each of these heads is supported by enriched pilasters and has a pendant in the centre. At each angle of the pulpit flanking the arches is a Doric column and these support an entablature with an arabesque frieze, a moulded and dentilled cornice with shaped brackets above each column. The pulpit base below the panels is moulded and supported at each angle by a square leg. The hexagonal sounding board above the pulpit has an enriched frieze and a moulded cornice with pendants

Fig. 103. The pulpit

below and turned finials and cresting above. The board is supported on a standard panelled in the same way as the sides of the pulpit with a plain panel below. The pulpit stairs are modern. It used to stand west of the screen, as photographs demonstrate and where holes were made for it in the pillar.

Chest

The chest on the first floor of the tower is small and plain, probably dating from the seventeenth century.

Gallery

This is set against the rebuilt west wall of the church and is of four bays supported on circular oak columns with moulded octagonal capitals and bases standing on square pedestals. These support a beam above which is moulded panelling forming the front of the gallery which is divided into three bays by square posts with spherical finials. The floor of the gallery is carried on stop chamfered beams and at the south end is a door approached by a stairway with moulded strings and handrails and turned, mirrored balusters. The whole of this probably dates from the late-seventeenth century, probably the 1680s.

Other woodwork

The Communion Rails are quite advanced for their time with turned balusters seated in a square base-rail with a well-moulded rail at the top. The gate in the centre is flanked by baluster posts each with a square head and a ball finial.

The oak chair, usually in the sanctuary, has turned front legs which are carried up to support the curved arms. The back of the chair has diamond ornamentation inside a typical Renaissance semi-circular arch. It is an excellent example of the type of chair which is found in churches and houses of the early seventeenth century.

CHAPTER XXI

The Wall Paintings & Texts

by Jim Tonkin and Dennis Monger

Dore Abbey is fortunate in having an extraordinary series of illustrations and texts. They were painted on dampened plaster, probably using charcoal with a little red and yellow ochre — called the *secco* technique.[1] A detailed survey might reveal if other colours were used. Both paintings and texts were renewed from time to time, the underlying one being covered with limewash. At least two such sets of texts are apparent at Dore.

The Wall Paintings

The nature and extent of the pre-Reformation painting has been described in chapter V. The later series of paintings dates mainly from the early years of the eighteenth century, 1700-1710. On the south wall of the south transept, under the eastern lancet window, is the upper part of a skeleton, in an ornamental border, with the inscription *Memento Mori* (Remembrance of Death). To reinforce this message the figure leans on the spade that would be used to dig a grave (Fig. 104). This may date from the Scudamore restoration of 1630-40. On the west wall of the same transept, in the upper part of the north bay, is a large figure of 'Time' with his scythe and an hour-glass, which has been damaged over the years (Fig 105). Although images were not encouraged, Time and Death were survivals from medieval ideas of mortality. High up on the west wall, in the centre, in a laurel-leaf frame with a pointed head, is a painting of David with his harp, dated to *c.*1701.

In the centre of the north wall of the north transept is a quite detailed painting in a pair of

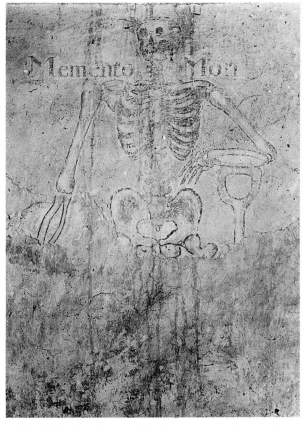

Fig. 104. The figure of death, leaning on his spade

181

Fig. 105. 'Time' with his scythe and hour glass adjoining the blocked arch of the south nave aisle

large, joined panels, each with an elliptical pedimented head containing the Ten Commandments in Roman lettering. The borders of these panels are enriched with laurel-leaf ornament. Above it is a painting of Jehovah with rays, not a common picture for this period.

Below this are the Royal Arms of Queen Anne (post-1702) 12 ft. by 12 ft. 6 ins. in red and yellow, with the motto *Semper Eadem* (Always the Same) and the initials A (R) for Anna Regina (Plate 3). After the Act of Supremacy in 1531, Henry VIII ordered that the Lord's Prayer, the Apostle's Creed, the Ten Commandments, and the Royal Arms should be prominently displayed in churches. Dore shows that these texts were re-written at least twice. As the Royal Arms of Charles I are on the Screen, it is likely that further Royal Arms could be discovered by photographic means.

The texts

Dore Abbey stands as a witness to the faith of many generations. Centuries of English church history have left their distinctive mark on its architecture and decoration. The Dissolution of 1536 was the end of a chapter but not of the story, which continues to this day. The seeds of a new era were being sewn even as ancient walls were being demolished. In 1535 Miles Coverdale produced the first complete Bible in English, basing his translation on the earlier works of William Tyndale, Martin Luther and the Latin scholars. Coverdale's translation formed the basis of the Psalter in the Book of Common Prayer. Other translations and revisions followed until in 1611 the Authorised Version was published, twenty-three years before the restoration of Dore Abbey.

One of the legacies of the Reformation was emphasis on Holy Scripture. With the restoration of the Abbey, scripture texts were written on the plastered walls. The work appears to have been done in two phases, 1630-1640 and 1701-1710 and it seems likely that the ones that can still be read belong to the second phase. The passing years have taken toll of their legibility. We can only imagine how they appeared in their pristine condition. They may be read beginning on the west side of the south door and continuing around the transepts in a clockwise direction.

1630-1640 inscriptions

The earlier texts are in the 'black-letter' style frequently used in churches in the years after the Reformation. It is possible that some of the later texts may also belong to this phase having simply been repainted in the 1700s. However, there is evidence of texts being beneath later texts. On the south wall, to the right of the skeleton, and partly covered by the later 'death' inscription, is an undeciphered text (Fig. 106). Two others are on the west wall, where black letters show beneath the 'fools' text and the 'children' text by the font.

Also on the west wall behind the gallery are three panels with decorative borders. The southern one contains the opening sentence of the Apostles Creed preceded by a text from St

182

Fig. 106. Slight traces of an earlier surround and text between the skeletal death and the linked text.

Paul's second letter to the Corinthians: *'I believed and therefore have I spoken, we also believe and therefore speak,'*(chapter 4, verse 13) followed by the opening sentence of the Apostle's Creed. The centre panel has about two decipherable letters and remains a mystery. The third, to the north, has the introduction to the Lord's Prayer in St. Matthew's Gospel: *'After this manner therefore pray ye'* (chapter 6, verse 9) and it may be assumed that this was followed by the Our Father. When the gallery was built, the Creed and Lord's Prayer could not be seen and so were re-written above it.

Continuing along the west wall, the 'young men and maidens' text is superimposed upon the earlier one which was probably two verses taken from the Book of Deuteronomy: *'You shall diligently keep the commandments of the Lord your God, and His testimonies, and His statutes, which He hath commanded thee. And thou shalt do that which is right and good in the sight of the Lord, that it may be well with thee.'* (chapter 6, verses 17 & part 18). The last seven words, with scroll work, are still visible. When the new text was written, probably during the second phase (1700-1710), only verse 17 was re-written and placed to the right of the original.

On the north wall, the Royal Arms of Queen Anne covers what is almost certain to be the Ten

Commandments from Exodus (chapter 20). They were re-written above.

1700-1710 Inscriptions

These texts are in Roman lettering and, unusually, the name of the painter is included in one frame. Under the western window in the south wall, and set in a laurel surround with ornamental cresting is: 'William ...er of H.....rd, painter, 1701.' Only two letters can be read of William's surname, but the space is sufficient for 'Hereford' to be his place of origin. The text beneath is one of the two quotations, with ornamental surround, placed appropriately near the entrance. *'I had rather be a door keeper in the house of my God than to dwell in the tents of wickedness.'* (Psalm 84, Verse 10 and *'Keep thy foot when thou comest to the house of God and be more ready to hear than to give the sacrifice of fools for they consider not that they do evil.'* (Ecclesiastes, chapter 5, verse 1.) (Fig. 107)

The third text with ornamental surround is near the font. *'And they brought young children that He should touch them, but His disciples rebuked them. But when Jesus saw it He was much displeased and said unto them "Suffer the children to come unto Me for of such is the kingdom of God."'* (St. Mark, chapter 10, verses 13 & 14.)

Fig. 107. The work of 'William ...er of H(erefo)rd, Painter, 1701'

God that we keep His commandments.' (I John, chapter 5, verse 3.). This small panel is in a foliated frame with cresting and swag ornament in red line.

On the upper part of the north wall, in the centre area, is a quite detailed painting in a pair of large, joined panels, each with an elliptical pedimented head containing the Ten Commandments in Roman lettering. The borders of these panels are enriched with laurel-leaf ornament.

To the right of this and matching the level and frame of the lower panel over the night-stairs doorway, is a timely word: *'For not hearers of the law are just before God, but doers of the law shall be justified.'* (Romans, chapter 2, verse 13)

The final text, which has greeted many who have left the building for the last time, is on the east of the south door, to the right of the skeleton figure of 'death.' *'O Death, where is thy sting? O Grave, where is thy victory? The sting of death is sin and the strength of sin is the law. But thanks be to God which giveth us the victory through our Lord Jesus Christ'* (1 Corinthians, chapter 15, verses 55-57.) (Fig. 106)

It is interesting to find all the wall texts in the transepts and crossing of the Abbey, reflecting that the pews were placed there at the church's restoration (see frontpiece), and now where people enter, congregate and leave the building. The Abbey was restored before the Commonwealth (1649-60) and continued to be a place of worship. This could well have been that part of the building where instruction was given. It is today the place where congregation and visitors meet, social occasions and refreshments enjoyed. Dore Abbey is a compendium of English church history and a symbol of the living church.

When the gallery was built two texts were re-written on the upper part of the west wall—the Creed to the south and the Lord's Prayer to the north. They are both in black lettering in frames of yellow foliage with ornamental surrounds.

Continuing on the west wall into the north transept, the first text is taken from Psalm 148: *'Young men and maidens, old men and children, praise the Name of the Lord, for His Name only is excellent and His praise above heaven and earth'* (verses 12 & 13). To the right of this is verse 17 from Deuteronomy which is in a foliated frame similar to those on the north wall.

On the lower part of the north wall, and running across the blocking of the monastic night-stairs doorway, is: *'For this is the love of*

CHAPTER XXII

'Beauty of Holiness': The East Window

by Joe Hillaby

The revival of church stained glass, c.1610-42

Far more significant than the use of such devices as testers or canopies, tapestries or reredos, was the re-introduction of stained glass into the eastern window. This was the principal means of magnifying the altar, an innovation all the more remarkable given the reformers' forthright rejection of such glass-painting as 'superstitious' imagery. The stained glass in the windows above the altar at Dore is of great interest not only for the light it throws on the then dominant theology within the church of England, but also for its stylistic distinctiveness.

At Lambeth Palace Laud himself 'caused to be repaired and beautified according to the former Figure' the medieval imagery of his chapel windows. Richard Butler was employed to mend the old glass and paint new (1635-6). In 1644 the principal charge brought against Laud by William Prynne in the House of Lords was that 'no chappel in Rome could be more Idolatrous, Popish and superstitious in regard to such offensive Pictures' than Laud's owne Kennel at Lanbeth.' This was one of the charges on which he was found guilty and beheaded on Tower Hill on 10 January 1645.[1]

Production of stained glass for ecclesiastical purposes had come to an abrupt end in the mid-sixteenth century. Edward VI's Injunctions of 1547 and Elixabeth's of 1559 had ordered the destruction of 'pictures, paintings and all other monuments of superstition so that there remains no memory of the same in walls, glass, windows or elsewhere within churches etc.' However, in 1577 William Harrison explained that when all monuments of idolatory had been 'removed, taken down and defaced; only stories in glass windows were excepted for want of sufficient store of new stuff, and by reason of extreme charge ... by alteration into white panes ... but little by little suffered to decay.'[2] The art of church window glazing thus fell into abeyance although a flourishing market developed in the production of flamboyant coats of arms.[3]

Even in the late fifteenth century the strict conventions of the medieval glazier's craft had given way to new and quite different forms derived from the Netherlandish Renaissance. The architectural framework of the window, its mullions, transoms, tracery and cuspings, was ignored. Scenes were painted which occupied the whole window. The larger the window the greater the opportunity. Notable local examples are the Crucifixion and Last Judgment in the east and west windows of Fairford Church, Gloucestershire (1495-1505) and the Magnificat window in the north transept of Great Malvern Priory (1501). Increasingly glaziers sought to emulate the styles of the great painters of the period, with large landscape scenes and elaborate interiors, rendered in full perspective. The great windows of King's College, Cambridge (1526-31) exemplify this well.[4]

There were other developments. In the middle ages pot metal, glass coloured throughout in the crucible or pot, had been used and was cut into shapes from small sheets. From the mid-sixteenth century the glazier's art was revolutionised by the use of sheets of white glass on which colours could be applied like ordinary paint, with a brush, using metallic oxide pigments. These were then fired with a flux of molten glass. The windows of the period are thus made up of rectangular panels, with much greater economy in the use of lead. The old pot metal colours, however, never completely disappeared. They were now employed to heighten effect, as in the garments of the principal figure.

When the revival of ecclesiastical glazing came, in the years c.1610-42, it depended largely on continental inspiration. In this revival the van Linge brothers played a leading role. Bernard, the elder, had come to England in 1621 after two years in France but had returned to his native Emden by 1628. His place was taken by his younger brother, Abraham.[5] For their inspiration they often turned to engraved book illustrations for religious as well as secular subjects. Thus for the east window of Wadham College Bernard van Linge turned in part to illustrations by Martin de Vos.[6]

The Oxford Colleges

Laud had been President of St. John's College from 1611-21. Eight years later he became Chancellor of the University and there advanced the custom of bowing towards the altar. By 1636 an observer wrote that the college chapels 'are much beautified, extraordinary cost bestowed on them; scarce any cathedral churches, nor Windsor nor Canterbury ... exceeds them, most of them newly glazed; richer glass for figures and painting I have not seen, which they have most from beyond the seas.'[7] This for Laud was all part of 'the beauty of holiness'.

The glass of the Oxford colleges shows that the glaziers looked in two directions. On the one hand they developed the late-fifteenth century convention of ignoring the architectural framework of the window. Thus Abraham van Linge's biblical scenes such as 'Jonah before Nineveh' at Christ Church College, and 'The Fall', 'Elijah taken up to Heaven' and 'Jonah and the Whale' at University College spread boldly across the mullions with landscape and townscape depicted in minute detail. Vegetation is luxuriant and painstakingly portrayed, such as the giant apple tree under which Adam and Eve stand and the great gourd tree beneath which Jonah sits. This intense concern for nature and landscape is one of the marked characteristics of the period. It can be seen already in the earliest apostle windows, at Wadham of 1614-16.

On the other hand, in terms of subject matter they followed medieval tradition in two respects. Firstly for the east window they favoured New Testament types and Old Testament antitypes that were held to prefigure them, as at Wadham, Lincoln and Queen's. Secondly they maintained the medieval convention of prophets and apostles facing each other to the north and south, as at Wadham and Lincoln.[8] Their use originated in the belief that each apostle had composed a section of the creed at the Council of Jerusalem before following his individual path to spread the Gospel, armed with this common standard of faith. A late medieval example can be seen at St. Laurence's, Ludlow and locally there was another in the now dispersed glass of Hampton Court Chapel.[9]

In 1631 at Magdalen, Scudamore's own college, the president, Accepted Frewen, replaced the communion table with an altar, 'the first set up in the university after the Reformation.' Upon this a crucifix was placed and above was suspended a corona. Behind he hung scenes from the life of Christ painted by Richard Greenbury who was commissioned to produce stained glass windows for the fifteenth-century ante-chapel in chiaroscuro glass of sepia tint, quite unlike any other work of the period at Oxford.

Lay patronage

The use of stained glass was not restricted to the chapels of colleges and ecclesiastics. The movement also found support amongst the laity. Indeed the chapel at Hatfield House marks the 'major change in the relationship of art and religion in early-seventeenth century England.' It was built by Robert Cecil, first earl of Salisbury, who had become Elizabeth's chief minister on the death of his father, William Cecil, first lord Burghley, in 1598 and had then served James I in the same capacity. With 'both his doctrinal and aesthetic sensibilities moving in the direction later identified with Laudianism' we should not wonder that Cecil had stained glass windows placed above the chapel altar: twelve panels of types and antitypes, mostly the work of Dolphin and Butler, 1610-20.[10] William Langton, Robert Cecil's personal chaplain at Hatfield at this time, was President of Magdalen during Scudamore's studentship at the college in 1616-17. It may well be, therefore, that he should be included with Laud as a formative influence on Scudamore, in particular on his views on the position and setting of the altar.

Lord Maynard, son of one of Burghley's secretaries and a property developer, built a private chapel at Easton Lodge, his Essex home in 1621. The glass, painted by Battista Sutton, depicting five Passion scenes including the Crucifixion, was 'amongst the first of its kind in an English Protestant context.'[11] In the same year Sir Henry Slingsby of Moor Monkton near York, one time High Sheriff and 'as opposed to Catholicism as to Puritanism', commissioned a crucifixion by Butler for his private chapel.[12]

In Herefordshire Scudamore was not the first to seek to breathe new life into the ruins of a medieval ecclesiastical institution or to heighten the status of the altar by the use of stained glass. Sir Thomas Coningsby of Hampton Court founded a hospital for The Company of Old Servitors in Widemarsh Street, Hereford, in 1617. This he built on the site of the hospital of the Knights of St. John of Jerusalem to perpetuate the memory of that order. Parts of the hall and chapel range appear to have been incorporated. The owner in fee of Hampton Court was to be considered and styled Commander of the Hospital 'in memory of those worthy governors who once presided over the military society in this place.' In the revival of a medieval monastic institution in a modern form he thus anticipated Scudamore by seventeen years.[13]

In other respects Sir Thomas was parsimo-nious. Even after his son Fitzwilliam's marriage to Cecilia Nevill, eldest daughter of Henry, lord Abergavenny, he had looked so 'sharply' after his son's expenses that he was 'hardly his own master'. Once Fitzwilliam succeeded to the estate in 1625 and became high steward of the county the next year, he sought to restore Hampton Court to some of its former glory. The chapel windows then contained 'a very important and stylistically homogeneous collec-tion' of what was 'among the finest painted glass in England of the first half of the fifteenth century.' Auctioned in 1924 the collection was broken up. Much is now in the United States although two figures were acquired by the Victoria and Albert Museum and four panels are in Hereford Cathedral.[14]

Coningsby graduated from Lincoln College, Oxford, in 1619 and would therefore have known the recently installed Wadham Chapel windows well. Indeed his own college chapel was reglazed in the new style in 1629. In that year, as part of his refurbishment scheme, Coningsby inserted a small panel of stained glass into the window immediately above the chapel altar at Hampton Court. He made no attempt to match the remarkable display of late medieval glass. Instead he commissioned a panel from Abraham van Linge depicting The Deposition bearing the inscription 'the truth hereof is historicall, devine and not superstis-sious.' Now in the Victoria and Albert Museum, it is described by Rackham as, in artistic terms, 'a somewhat lifeless derivative from an early Flemish altar piece by Roger van der Wyden (of which a replica is at Buckingham Palace)', continuing 'the technique with its sparing use of ruby glass and its muddy enamels is characteristic of its period.' In terms of its subject matter and text, on the other hand, it has been called 'one of the most remarkable pieces of religious glass to survive from the period.' This is not surprising for Coningsby knew Laud, whose help he had sought in successfully persuading a friend not to quit the Anglican for the Roman church.[15]

The Seventeenth Century glass of the Dore East Window (Plate. 2)

This was the milieu in which Scudamore commissioned glass for the three early thirteenth century lancet windows above the high altar at Dore. The liturgical importance of the glazing is reflected in the price Scudamore was prepared to pay. For 'one tower, ... covered with tile ... two lofts and a frame for six bells, of 80 Foote into the roofe' together with 'tiles, stone, timber, nails and iron', Scudamore paid David Addams of Ross a total of £90. For the structural woodwork of the roofs and tower, but not the screen, gallery etc., John Abel received £120. According to Gibson the Dore glass was provided at the expence of one hundred pounds.'[16] This is quite remarkable given that Bernard van Linge the leading glazier of his age received merely £120 for the east window of Wadham College.

Scudamore, who like Coningsby graduated at Oxford, matriculated from Magdalen in 1619. Therefore he too must have known the glass at Wadham and in all probability that at Lincoln. Yet Scudamore rejected the Renaissance forms developed over the last century and a half. Stylistically he looked back more than three centuries for his inspiration. The window is not a child of its time; it is overwhelmingly retrospective. The Ascension panel alone is in the style of the great revival.

The only glass similar to that of Dore is in the small east window at Sellack which is made up of fifteenth, sixteenth and seventeenth-century glass and bears the initials RS and date 1630. Rowland Scudamore, a younger brother of the viscount's grandfather, had bought Caer Caradoc manor house in Sellack from the Mynors of Treago in 1594. Rowland never married. When he died in January 1630/1 he bequeathed his estate to John, his great-nephew. The initials RS have led people to assume that the seventeenth century reglazing was Rowland's work. The evidence indicates otherwise, that it was the viscount's memorial to his great-uncle. The date 1630 is the year of Rowland's death Old Style. The use of 25 March as the opening of the new year was only formally abandoned in 1752. Scudamore used the house as his second home

until 1648 when he passed it to James, his fourth and only surviving son, who was to die there in 1668. Significantly his fifth son, who died within the year, was christened Rowland at Sellack Church on 22 May 1631, a further commemoration of his issueless great-uncle.[17]

Given its history, some locals, possibly even the viscount himself, had reason to believe the family was blighted, for the inheritance in the senior line had skipped a generation ever since the time of his great-great-grandfather, John Scudamore. This man, Henry VIII's Receiver 'of divers abbeys within county Hereford ... to be suppressed', acquired the Dore estates and later bought up the tithes, thus creating the dilemma so to exercise the viscount. His eldest son, William, predeceased him and the estate passed to John, his grandson, in 1571. Again the son died before the father and the grandson, John, who became first viscount, succeeded in 1623. The process now seemed to be repeating itself. He and his wife had poor health. In November 1632 Richard Prichard, vicar of Sellack, granted the viscount 'his Lady and their son, in respect of manifest sickness and infirmity to eate flesh upon dayes prohibited.' When the viscount had twins, John and John, in 1621 both died within a year. A third son, also John, born in 1623, died the next year. James, the fourth son, born in 1624, was to attain manhood and to live at Caer Caradoc. The fifth son, William, born in 1629, was dead within the year, as was Rowland, the sixth and last, born in 1631. This, it has been suggested, was a factor in the viscount's decision to refurbish Dore.[18] In the event, however, James also predeceased his father and was buried in the church at Holme Lacy in 1668. There his spectacular monument can still be seen (Appendix 5).

For seven years after his succession in 1623 Scudamore had experienced serious financial problems. In addition to an annuity to his mother, as well as his responsibility for her debts and those of his uncle, he had to find dowries for four sisters. From 1625 he had to sell family lands in Worcestershire and his salt works in Droitwich to meet these obligations. The death of Rowland in 1630/1 brought the first relief. The death of his father-in-law, Sir Arthur Porter, in March 1630/1, followed by that of Lady Anne Porter brought him their Lanthony by Gloucester estates. This double inheritance secured his financial position, enabling him to fund not only the work at Sellack but also the restoration of Dore in 1634.[19]

It was not only the east window which was replaced at Sellack. As at Holme Lacy, the church underwent a thorough Laudian remodelling at this time, with altar table, panelling in the chancel around the east end, communion rails, a three-decker pulpit and a gallery at the east end. Further, it had corporal, pall and damask rail cloth, suggesting celebration of communion with 'a degree of ceremonial uncommon even in cathedrals.'[20] It thus appears a prelude to Dore but a comparison of the two east windows can come only after the Dore window has been fully described.

In reglazing the Sellack east window and glazing that of Dore afresh Scudamore was merely following a trail blazed by others, laymen and ecclesiastics. What is unique is his rejection of the current style of reglazing in favour of the gothic. Whether this was survival or revival will be discussed later.

The iconography was Scudamore's personal choice. Gibson refers to 'The fine East-window ... made by the Lord Scudamore ...; and the Glass so painted by him.'[21] This is corroborated by a preliminary sketch of the proposed glass for 'the greate windowe in Doore church', unsigned and undated, but in an early-seventeenth century hand, now amongst the Scudamore papers at Hereford City Library (Fig. 108).[22] The Dore east window is a characteristic early-thirteenth century Cistercian triplet with smaller lancets on either side of a large central lancet. The sketch shows lower panels of the outer lancets with Peter, identified by his key; Andrew by a saltire; an unidentified figure, in all probability James; and John, shown beardless. In the central light two groups of three apostles look upwards to the image of the Ascension, a figure enshrouded in cloud from the waist upwards. On either side are the four evangelists (without symbols), John alone holding book and pen. To the left of the Ascension are a pair of angels with further pairs at the head of each of the three lights. Finally in the central window, above the Ascension, are two figures. One holds what appears to be a rod, or possibly a martyr's palm. If the former this would signify Moses, who now occupies this space with John the Baptist to his right in the actual window at Dore. In terms of figures portrayed the sketch bears a close relationship to the existing window but important changes were made. In the sketch there is no hint of canopy work nor is room provided. The figures occupy all the lateral and, in the middle band, all the vertical space. Thus in the final composition the angels were sacrificed to enable the figures to be placed within tabernacle work. Furthermore, the Ascension is depicted according to quite a different tradition.

As we see the window today, the glass of the lancets to the north and south form a pair. Each is decorated by figures under canopies in two bands. The upper depicts the four evangelists, from left to right, Matthew, Mark, Luke and John. Matthew and Mark lack only parts of their cloaks but John has lost his head. Of Luke only the body from waist down now remains. Each was identified by his proper symbol, one of the four beasts of the Apocalypse:

'Before the throne there was a sea of glass like unto crystal: and in the midst of the throne and round about the throne, were four beasts full of eyes before and behind. The first beast was like a lion and the second beast like a calf, the third beast had a face as a man, the fourth beast was like a flying eagle.'[23]

Of these Matthew's angel, in blue and gold, and Mark's lion, in gold, can still be seen above their right shoulders. Luke has lost his calf but John's silver eagle is visible, also above his right shoulder. By the early-seventeenth century, with the spread of literacy, imagery, however, was not all: each figure was named at the base. 'Luke' can still be made out.

Originally each evangelist carried his gospel book. These were open and bore inscriptions. Only three remain. They were copied down by the glaziers when the windows were removed in 1912 for restoration and releading. They read:

Fig. 108. The preliminary sketch of the proposed glass for 'the greate windowe in Doore church'

Liber genration
This Mathew - that Angell
doth imply Chriestes Royall ligne
in his humanitie Man like him-selfe
deriving downe the same
To Josephs Tribe faithful Abraham

Markes Lion as his Gospel
Doth beginne a criers voice
The Wilderness within make straight
His paths the same is only Hee
of Judah's Tribe - who was
fortould to bee

Looke, How the quick sight Eagle
Mounts on High Beholds the Sunne
with her all piercing eie
So unto Christes Divinity I soar
Beyond the Straine of those that
are before[24]

The lower band across the smaller lancets carries the canopied figures of the first four apostles as listed in Matthew Chapter 10, Verse 2— Peter, Andrew, James and John. Each bears his attribute but again imagery was supplemented by a brief biographical description below. On the north Peter carries his key and Andrew his cross. 'Peter 44 years after the death [of] our Saviour went to Rome to confute Simon Magus and there lived 25 years. He was condemned by Nero to be crucified, which Peter desired to be done with his head downwarde.' The next reads 'Andrew, brother to Peter, he lived at Patris in Achaia where he at last was crucified, joyfully embracing the cross [with] his arms.' James carries his pilgrim staff and scrip but has been deprived of the broad brimmed hat with its scallop shell badge as seen on most late medieval portrayals. 'James, brother of John', the inscription tells us, 'was beheaded by Herod his [accuser] likewise confessing Christ suffered martyrdom with him.'

St. John is as usual depicted as a young man, the only apostle without a beard. In his right hand he holds a chalice which he blesses with his left. This is a reference to the poisoned cup offered him, according to one tradition, by Aristodemus, priest of the temple of Diana at Ephesus which he had cast down. Another version is that John himself requested the cup to prove the validity of his teaching to the emperor Domitian. Significantly, what is missing at Dore is the small dragon fleeing the chalice after John had blessed it with the cross 'through which virtue it lost its malice and did him no harm.' Also missing is John's palm. This is often believed to be a martyr's palm, quite wrongly — according to tradition John lived to be a centenarian. It is in fact the Virgin's palm. After Christ had committed Mary to John's care at the foot of the cross, saying 'Woman, behold thy son' and to John 'Behold thy Mother', John took the Virgin with him to Ephesus, where what is claimed to be the Virgin's house can still be seen. It was there that an angel brought the palm to Mary to signify her imminent death. This, as a sign of regard, she gave to John to carry before her coffin. John himself was buried at Ephesus and about his tomb Justinian built, by 565, a great ecclesiastical complex, some 400 feet in length. These events are alluded to in the inscription. 'John the beloved desipel was banished by Domicion to the Isle of Pathmas where he write the Revellation. He died 60 years after Christ and was buried neer to Ephesus.'

Although John's chalice was acknowledged, dragon and palm were not. Similarly the exclusion of the pilgrim's hat and cockle shell from the image of St. James was not accidental. Retrospection could be taken only so far.

The taller central lancet is divided into three, not two, horizontal bands. The upper is, for the most part, now a jumble of fragments including two pairs of feet on a black and white background, probably belonging to the apostles in the Ascension scene, and three crowns, probably interlopers. However the remnants of canopy work indicate that this band originally contained two further figures, possibly a pair of angels, as in the preliminary sketch.

The left hand panel of the middle band carries the named figure of Moses holding his rod. Since the time that Paul in his first epistle to the Corinthians wrote that all did 'drink the same spiritual drink: for they drank of that spiritual Rock that followed them: and that Rock was Christ' the church has regarded the rod struck by Moses as a type of Christ. Later commentaries suggested that the spring which gushed from the rock was the water and blood that gushed from Christ's side when it was pierced by the lance of the centurion. The right hand panel shows St. John the Baptist, also named, with book and Paschal Lamb. He is not quite the ascetic figure described by Matthew as coming out of the Judean wilderness with 'his raiment of camel's hair and a leathern girdle about his loins; and his meat was locusts and wild honey.' John is clothed similar to his fellows but the head of the camel does rest between his feet. The mane, an eye and an ear can be seen above a prominent glazing bar. Beneath Moses and the Baptist is the portrayal of the Ascension but this is in quite a different style and will be examined later.

The Dore glazier followed, with surprisingly clear understanding, the essential characteristics of the style of the early decorated period. Each figure is placed in an elaborate gold architectural framework. Figures in canopied niches had graced the west fronts of the cathedrals of Wells, Lincoln and Salisbury in the Early English period. Such decoration was extended to other architectural features, small—such as tabernacles, the cupboard in which the reserved sacrament for the eucharist was kept, and large—such as shrines, screens and tombs, like those of bishops Cantilupe and Aquablanca and of Peter de Grandison at Hereford Cathedral. The convention was also followed by woodworkers in their screens, choir stalls, bishops thrones etc. and by the braziers and glaziers. Indeed some of the earliest English medieval glass, in the Canterbury choir clerestory, has figures under simple semi-circular arcades. These are antecedents of the niche and canopy work developed by the glazier at the end of the thirteenth century and adopted by Scudamore for the Dore east window.

'Tabernacle work', as the elaborate decorative niches in which the figures were placed came to be described, was the dominant characteristic of church glazing c.1300-50. It consisted of pillars with bases and capitals carrying a gabled canopy decorated along the upper edge with leafwork, with cusping below and finial on top. On either side crocketted pinnacles rose above the supporting shafts, as with the buttresses of choir, nave and transepts of major churches.

Other marked early-fourteenth century features included the use of yellow stain, chloride of silver fired at a low temperature. Employed particularly for tabernacle work, it gave the appearance of a gilded shrine. Diapering, the application of a flat often foliage pattern, usually to the background of the figures in their tabernacles, provided further enrichment. Finally the whole composition was usually enclosed in a narrow ornamental border of running stalk and leaf design or individual alternating patterns. The only discordant note at Dore is the checky ground on which the four apostles stand. This is a fifteenth century feature.

Tabernacle work, with yellow stain representing gilding, diapering and patterned borders are all found in the Dore window although admittedly in a debased form. The tabernacle work above the apostles, Moses and John the Baptist is elaborate but that of the evangelists and the two missing figures at the top of the central light is rudimentary. In that respect it is very similar to that above the upper band of figures at Sellack. At both Dore and Sellack diapering is applied to the white and blue background glass, but it lacks the vitality of the foliage patterns of the original red, blue and green glass reset in the Hoskyns, the southernmost transeptal chapel which it appears to be emulating. The borders are composed of alternate panels of blue with a four-lobed leaf and gold, black and silver decorated with a lozenge enclosing a quatrefoil. At Dore the border runs only between the figures in the three lancets. It is very similar to, but less sophisticated than, the Sellack border which frames both sides of the figures.

At Dore and Sellack the figures and their tabernacle frames are a world apart from the apostles and prophets in their large classicised gothic canopies at the Oxford colleges. With the Dore Ascension panel, however, we do enter that world. It occupies more than a third of the central light. It belongs firmly to the first half of the seventeenth century although incongruously surmounted by a pair of 'gothic' canopies. As the glass was reset in 1912 it is possible that this relationship is not original. In the panel Christ is shown clothed in blue gown and red cloak with hands outstretched to left and right. The glazier sought to give Christ a lifelike appearance by the use of flesh-coloured glass for the face and a redder tint for the lips. This is thoroughly contemporary and can be paralleled at Oxford. In marked contrast the faces of the apostles immediately below, like those of all other figures in the window, are sketched in black on white. Christ's head is in a gold glory, radiating against the blue background. He is surrounded by a whirl of puffy white clouds, amongst which fly six bodiless putti, three on either side, each with cherubic face, a lock of gold hair and wings. It is not only the putti but also the clouds of the Dore Ascension which are highly characteristic of their period. Described by some as 'plate-like', they first appear in Bernard van Linge's Passion sequence at Merton and then in Abraham's Passion cycles at Lincoln and Queen's. Below, looking up in the traditional manner are eleven apostles in gowns and cloaks of gold, blue, red and green. A medieval touch comes with the division of the group by two vertical bands of bordering in the centre. This peters out in the clouds.

The forms of the Ascension as originally proposed and as eventually executed at Dore are of considerable interest.[25] In the late medieval form the twelve apostles form a group, with the Virgin, on a small conical hill on top of which are Christ's footprints, a reference to the church of the Ascension where, Bede tells us, the footprints were always renewed even though the pilgrims removed the earth. Only Christ's feet and the lowest part of his dress are visible as He ascends in a cloud at the very top of the picture. This is portrayed at Fairford and at Great Malvern Priory. At Oxford it is found at Balliol (1529), Wadham (1622), Lincoln (1631), and Queen's (1635). But, significantly, in seventeenth century Oxford glass the Virgin was excluded. The Laudian church was not prepared to go that far. In the preliminary sketch of the Dore window the Ascension follows this tradition in an abbreviated form, possibly due to lack of space; all that is seen is the lower part of Christ's tunic and His feet disappearing into the clouds. However this late medieval form was ultimately abandoned by Scudamore.

The earlier form represented the apostles, with the Virgin, gazing up at Christ in Glory surrounded by angels. It can be seen at Poitiers Cathedral and at York Minster. At Dore it reappears but the Virgin was omitted. As this early form is not found in contemporary English glass Scudamore was on this occasion ahead of his time. In all probability the inspiration came, possibly through the intermediary of the Roman Missal[26], from Perugino (1446-1523) who revived it in his great altarpiece of the Ascension for San Pietro at Perugia.

In the now scattered Scudamore papers there is evidence as to other craftsmen working at Dore but not a hint as to the glazier. Those amongst the Additional Manuscripts in the British Library, examined by Blashill at the turn of the century, provide details of the work of John Abel.[27] The so-called Duchess of Norfolk's collection in the PRO was searched by H.M. Colvin who found the contract of Addams of Ross, builder of the tower.[28] An important set of accounts for this period, acquired by Hereford City library at one of the sales of Sir Thomas Phillipps' collection, include the steward's accounts from October 1635 to March 1636 but no earlier.[29] Those for 1632 are in the cathedral library.[30] Although sketches of the 'Great Window' are amongst the City's Scudamore manuscripts, there are no glazing accounts. For most extant glass c.1610-42 we know the author from discreetly placed initials.[31] A close examination of the Dore glass may fill this gap in the documentary evidence.

Does the Dore window represent gothic survival or gothic revival? Continuity certainly characterised the ecclesiastical architecture of the period. Prior to Charles II's restoration in 1660 the only genuinely classical church built in England was St Paul's, Covent Garden by Inigo Jones. In church architecture the gothic lived on. Two major examples are St. John's, Leeds (1632-3) and Staunton Harold, founded 1653, 'when all things sacred were throughout the nation either demollisht or profaned', by Sir Robert Shirley 'whose singular praise it is to have done the best things in the worst times, and hoped them in the most calamitous.' In Herefordshire, at Monnington-on-Wye, under the patronage of Uvedale Tomkyns, the perpendicular style retained its attractions well beyond the restoration, until 1679. Whilst these buildings are late gothic the internal fittings, as at Dore, are quite ambiguously of their own era. Only at Sedgefield, county Durham, was a wooden gothic screen attempted—a clear case of revival.[32]

For the glazing of the Dore east window, apart from the Ascension panel, there is no question of continuity. No stained glass of this type had been produced for some 300 years. This is gothic revival.

What was the source of its inspiration? At Sellack Scudamore re-used some medieval material and his own glass may in part have been influenced by earlier designs. In 1640 John Abrahall was so impressed by what he saw at Sellack that he left instructions in his will for the provision of an east window at Foy 'in the same manner as such ... is placed in the church at Sellack'. In 1675 Foy got its copy of the Sellack window and glass. There is a creditable amount of glass of the period still to be seen in Herefordshire, at Brinsop, Credenhill, Eaton Bishop, Madley and the cathedral but we do not know what was lost during the interregnum, and later. Was the Dore glass so inspired or was it an attempt to reconstruct an earlier window? All that can be said is that the majority of the glass found and preserved by Paul during his work in the presbytery was of the decorated period, in all probability from the abbacy of Straddell.

CHAPTER XXIII

The Bells & Bellframe

by Dr. John Eisel

It is most likely that bells were in use at the abbey in connection with the liturgy from soon after its foundation, but no evidence survives until the Suppression. At that time there were apparently six bells in the central tower (although another record indicates there might have been seven)[1], and the accounts of John Scudamore, the Crown Receiver, for 1536/7 show that they weighed 27½cwt. and 28lbs. Two of these, valued at £7 10s., were bought by the churchwardens to continue in the use of the parishioners while the other four, valued at £15 6s. 8d. remained in Scudamore's possession at the site and it is inferred that they were sold or otherwise disposed of.[2] In 1538/9 the two bells still served the parish, and they were later the subject of a lengthy inquiry. Thomas Baskerville, last steward of Dore, was ordered by the Court of Augmentations to pay £8 for the two bells, but it was clearly stated that while it was acknowledged that the bells were part of the profits of the Crown, the parishioners had paid for the use of them.[3] In modern times it has been stated, quoting an old tradition, that the bells were removed to Madley church after the Suppression.[4]

But the fate of the bells is not so clear. On 30 September 1552 the Commissioners of King Edward VI compiled inventories of the goods of the parishes of Webtree Hundred, which lies mainly to the south-west of Hereford. Not all of the membranes have survived and of those that

do some are damaged. But among the survivors is one for the parish of 'Dowre' which records, among other things:

'Item iiii[or] belles whereof the least of xxvii[ti] ynches the second of xxx[ti] ynches the third of xxx[ti] ynches the iiii[th] of xxxvi[ti] ynches brode over in the mouthes.[5]

The parish referred to is clearly Abbey Dore and the inventory shows that there were four bells then in the tower, the largest being about 9cwt. in weight. However, it is possible that the diameters were underestimated.

Scudamore's Restoration

After the Edwardian Inventory of 1552, there is no further information available for the next eighty years. The next reference comes with Scudamore's restoration in the 1630s, for in the surviving papers relating to the restoration there are several references to the bells and frame, each of which adds a little more to our knowledge.

On 23 February 1632 John Abel, who had already done some repairs to the watermill and to the church, wrote to Thomas Partridge, agent for Viscount Scudamore, offering to do further repairs to the church:

'I will likewise builde you a substantiall strong steeple with a frame for fower bells with too loftes & there to new hang your three bells the too that their canons are broke I will hange with iron boultes.[6]

195

It seems that a meeting took place on 21 March 1632. One surviving specification is endorsed:

'The particulars of ye timber worke cast up by Slade and Simmons for ye Church of Doore, March 21th (*sic*) 1632.'

and states:

'The fframe for 4 bels & to leave space to hange two bels more. five tonne of timber to make the frame the stocks & wheels, the wheels to be halfe wheels.'[7]

Abel's notes of the same date state:

'The fframe for 4 bels, & to leave space to hange two more bels more. the fframe to bee made substantiall and stronge, to stock yᵉ bels, & make wheels, & to hange the 4 bels suficientlye & stronge the iron worke beinge to be done att ye charge of yᵉ Viscount, the wheeles to bee halfe wheeles.'[8]

As can be seen, only three bells seem to have survived from the four recorded in 1552, two of these in a damaged condition. Because of the damage to the canons it was necessary to hang these bells with bolts through the crown, not the usual practice at the time.[9] The reference to half wheels is also unusual and is consciously backward looking as at the time the three-quarter wheel, with consequent greater control and the ability to be rung full-circle, had come into vogue.[10]

However, this was not the end of the work on the bells. An account dated 26 September states that 'Casting the bell' cost £4 10s. and that the brasses cost 5s. 0d.[11] An undated account for 1632[12] has payments relating to hanging a bell, and this may relate to the casting of this bell. No founder is mentioned for this bell, but it was most likely to have been John Finch of Hereford; it is possible that a damaged bell was being recast rather than a new bell being supplied.

In the early part of the eighteenth century, six bells were cast for Dore Abbey by Abraham Rudhall I of Gloucester, and it was no doubt in this period that the frame was rebuilt. The 1751 *Catalogue of Bells cast by the Rudhalls of Gloucester* states that six bells were cast for 'Abby-Door'.[13] However, the former second bell of the ring of six bells was cast in 1712,[14] and if a complete ring of six bells was supplied—as is most likely—then one of them at least had to be recast within two years.

Over the years it was found necessary to recast various bells of the ring. Thomas Rudhall recast the treble in 1770, while Charles and John Rudhall recast the tenor in 1782. At the same time much work was done on the bells, with five new wheels being made and the bells restocked. 'Mr. Rudhall' was paid £21 9s. 6d. on 25 January 1783 for his work.[15] John Rudhall, half-brother to Charles and John, recast the fourth bell in 1810 but was not paid £25 until 20 May 1811. The amount of £10 outstanding was apparently loaned by the rector, the Rev. Mr. Duncumb,[16] and he was reimbursed by the churchwardens on 21 March 1812.[17] Finally, the second bell was recast by Llewellins and James of Bristol in 1892. Thus only the third and fifth bells of the ring cast in 1710 survive, and of these the fifth bell is badly cracked in the crown due to the rusting of the cast-in crown staple.

At the time that the second bell was recast the new bell and the fifth bell were refitted, and the other four bells were rehung in new fittings by Llewellins and James of Bristol in 1912. This was at the expense of Mary F.E. Partridge as is recorded on a plaque in the ringing chamber. This is the last time that they have received any major attention, although subsequently—probably in the 1930s—two north-south RSJs were installed below the supporting beams of the frame.

Details of bells

Only the second bell has canons, the other bells having had them removed and hung by bolts through the crown. The fittings, consisting of elm stocks, plate gudgeons and plain bearings, together with traditional-type wheels, stays and sliders, are of two periods, but all by Llewellins and James of Bristol, that of the second and fifth bells dating from 1892, while that of the remainder was installed in 1912. The detail of the wheels varies, the earlier wheels having spokes of heavier section and more elaborate fillet holes, while the plate gudgeons also have two different patterns.

Details of the the bells

Bell	Inscription	Diameter (inches)
Treble	RECAST BY T : RUDHALL GLOCESTER 1770 (Border)	$26^{5}/_{8}$
2	RECAST 1892/LLEWELLINS & JAMES/BRISTOL (Reverse)ALFRED PHILLIPS RECTOR	$27^{5}/_{8}$
	CHARLES WALL } CHURCHWARDENS GEORGE EVANS	
3	PHILLIP WILLIAMS & THOMAS LEWIS CH. WARDENS (Bell) A R (Bell) 1710 (Border)	$30^{1}/_{4}$
4	(Five-dot cross)IOHN RUDHALL GLOCESTER FECT. J8J0 (Border)	$31^{1}/_{8}$
5	PEACE & GOOD NEIGHBOVRHOOD (Border) A : R (Bell) 1710 (Border)	$33^{7}/_{8}$
Tenor	P : LEWIS & I : DAVIS C : W : (Border) 1782 (Border)	$37^{1}/_{2}$

The frame

The whole frame is of considerable interest, for a substantial part of the frame installed by John Abel still survives, although in a much altered form (Figs. 109—111).

At present the frame consists of four parallel pits, more or less central in the tower, with the bells swinging east-west and the widest pit on the north side. The two smallest bells hang in a transverse pit on the west side of the frame, the bells swinging mouth-to-mouth. As a consequence the rope circle is anti-clockwise (Fig. 109).

There are redundant mortices and other marks in the frame that enable the sequence of development to be deduced. The first phase was a frame of four parallel pits, with trusses of the form shown in Fig. 110, each truss having end posts and main braces, but no king post. The brace between the end post and the cill is the most likely interpretation of the redundant mortices but this form is rather unusual. Between the cills and bearers there was a lapped dovetail joint, while the transverse head tying the trusses together at the upper level was just halved over the heads and pegged through. The bearers are made from reused timber having ovolo mouldings.

How Abel made his provision for space for two more bells is indicated by the subsequent extension. It is likely that the frame was originally placed centrally, but since it did not span the tower completely east-west, it could be moved over so that a pair of pits, with the bells swinging mouth-to-mouth, could be built on one side or the other. This in itself is most unusual, as the design with bells swinging mouth-to-mouth is in general a later development, and at this period was only used in special circumstances. There is no evidence to suggest that Abel's frame contained more than four pits.

A major remodelling of the frame took place, almost certainly at the time when the ring of six bells was provided in 1710. In this the pits were reduced in length and one of the braces was moved west so that the main braces cross

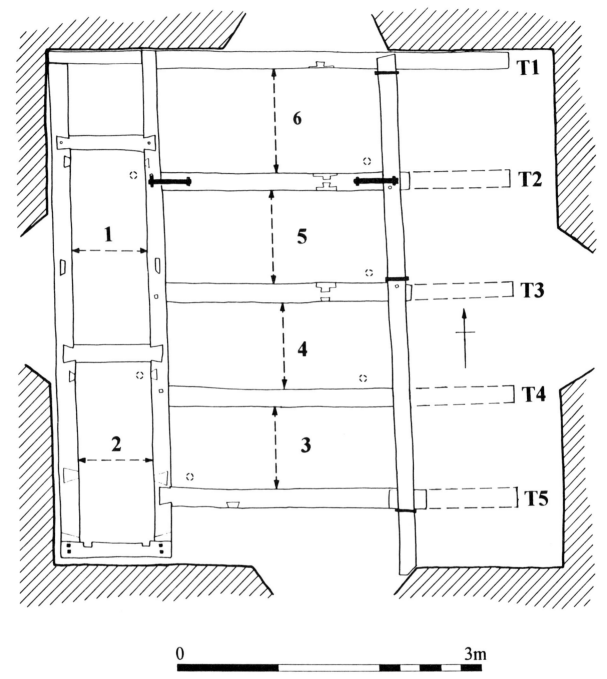

Fig. 109. Plan of frame at frame head level

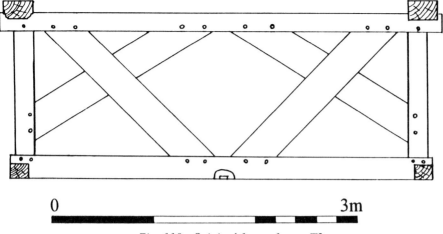

0   3m

Fig. 110. Original form of truss T2

(Fig. 111). This is best seen in trusses 1, 2 and 3 as the other two trusses were rebuilt rather more, and the head of truss 4 was reused as the cill of the truss. As part of the work the trusses were moved closer together, the evidence being seen in the redundant joints in the bearers. As there are no redundant joints in the transverse heads these must have been replaced. The spacing of the trusses between centres is now 47, 42, $40\frac{1}{2}$ and $38\frac{1}{2}$ inches, whereas formerly the spacing was 52, 46, $45\frac{1}{2}$ and 45 inches. This implies that there was a reduction in size

in the bells, perhaps the metal of the former bells being used without much addition to cast the ring of six bells. The diameter of the present tenor is about the same as the mediaeval tenor recorded in the 1552 inventory. Curiously, the head of the north truss of the frame was not cut down in length when the frame was rebuilt, and projects to the east for its full length, confirming the length of the pits of Abel's frame.

In order to accommodate the increased number of bells, an outer elevation was built on the west side of the frame to form a transverse pit to hold two bells swinging mouth-to-mouth. It is possible that the frame was moved a few inches to the east to make enough space for the transverse pits. The elements of the transverse elevation are rather slighter in section than the remainder of the frame, and its lower elements have been replaced. The position of the redundant bearing indents in relation to the braces in the elevation shows that this took place before the work carried out in 1892.

The importance of the frame

Any dated frame is important as it provides evidence of how frames develop in a particular area. As part of his general work on timber structures John Abel did other work on frames,

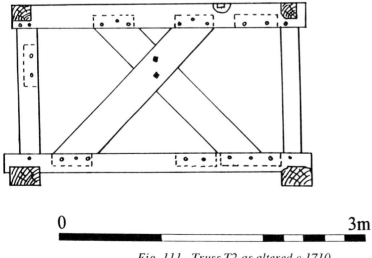

0   3m

Fig. 111. Truss T2 as altered c.1710

and his name occurs in Madley churchwardens' accounts as having done work in the belfry in 1623 and 1627. What was done is not known and over the years all evidence of seventeenth century work there has been destroyed.

There are a number of seventeenth century frames in Herefordshire with which to compare that at Abbey Dore. That at the Cathedral can be dated, from the mouldings on the clearance grooves, to the first half of the seventeenth century, probably *c*.1630-40, and is of a hollow square form, the trusses having braced kingposts and corner-posts. While the cills are covered over, they are tenoned together on the level. At Hentland the frame almost certainly dates from *c*.1630 and is very tall, with wide, upright, braces, but no kingposts. Of four parallel pits and one transverse, the four bell unit has posts at the outer corners only. The cills of the parallel pits are tenoned to the bearers and since they are not as deep as the bearers, the weight is carried by the bearers and not distributed evenly over the cills. A slightly later frame is that of five parallel pits at Holmer, where the trusses are tall and also lack kingposts, and the braces are very wide but not so upright as those at Hentland. Here the trusses are lap-jointed to the bearers, with a peg through the joint, and there are corner posts only. Probably only just post-Civil War is the tall frame at Woolhope, where the bells may have been augmented to a ring of five in 1649. It answers the same general description as that at Hentland, except that the braces are at a lower angle. Slightly later still is the frame at Hampton Bishop, again of the same general description as the frame at Hentland and possibly dated by two bells cast for the tower by John Finch in 1654. If this is so, then Finch was probably the maker of the frame, as he seems to have begun his career as a carpenter before diversifying into bell-founding.[18] The frame at Hampton Bishop, however, is rather lower than the frames described above and there are no posts at all in the frame, except for two inserted when the frame was extended in 1904 to accommodate an extra bell.

In the context of the frame discussed above, lap joints were going out of fashion at the time that the Dore Abbey frame was constructed, and although they were still used for the internal trusses of a frame built for Clun, Shropshire, in 1668, it was much more usual for mortice and tenon joints to be used instead. Frame makers were gradually realizing that any sort of vertical post was detrimental to the stability of the frame, and it is noticeable that Abel did not use king posts but still used end-posts in each truss. Abel also used the extra braces from end-post to cill of truss, a form not so far recorded anywhere else in the Welsh Borders, and braces to the end-posts in the transverse elevations. The method of tying the trusses together at head level was also rather backward looking, and the overall impression is of someone who was trying his own ideas but was not really in the forefront of frame development.

Thus while the frame at Dore Abbey is not an important example in the story of frame development, it has its own interest as showing how a carpenter, more used to standard timber constructions such as houses and roofs, albeit of a high standard, would turn his hand on occasion to other structures using the same techniques.

CHAPTER XXIV

The Paul Restoration

by Joe Hillaby

In July 1901 Thomas Blashill, by then 'father' of the Woolhope Club and president in its jubilee year, took members once again to Dore. There he described the condition of the church, 'suffering from the decay of three centuries' and drew their attention to the recently launched appeal for work on drainage and floors, roofs and ceiling, the general fabric including glazing, and the tower.[1] Given the resources of a sparsely populated parish little had been done since the Scudamore reconstruction. The drive behind the restoration came, of course, from Roland Paul. In 1898 he published an appeal for the abbey's repair, outlining the church's architectural and historic importance before describing its current state and proposed repairs. He emphasised that a sound roof and dry floor were necessities for any building and estimated the cost of repairs and proper heating at £2,500. Contributions would be gladly received by the rector or the Capital and Counties Bank, Hereford.[2] The records of the parochial church council betray no interest in the state of the church at this time. Their concern was with the adminis- tration of parochial social services: appointment of wardens, overseers of the poor, way warden (surveyor of highways), and occasional appren- tices.[3] The appeal fell on deaf ears.

November 1900 was apparently the turning point, for the parochial church council then went so far as to minute their anxiety about the 'unsafe condition of the belfry'. In the following May a meeting was called at the Bishop's Palace under the presidency of the bishop who explained that, whilst he recognised that there were a great many demands on people's generosity 'owing to the death of Queen Victoria and other causes', he had called the meeting because of the 'extreme urgency' of the matter. A subscription list, published in *The Hereford Times*, had obtained a total of £1,058. It was headed by Capt. Thomas Freke-Lewis of Abbey Dore Court (£200), Sir Joseph Verdin of Garnstone, Weobley, Mr. G. Winsor Clive, and the Rev. A. and Mrs. Phillipps (£100 each). Roland Paul presented his report in which necessary repairs were estimated at £5,600.

In 1634 rubble from within the church had been dumped immediately outside. The problem of damp was now critical for the accumulated soil, nearly 6 feet deep on the west and 3 feet on the north, covered the plinth and lower parts of the walls. Burials inside the church, as evidenced by the remarkable series of late-seventeenth and early-eighteenth century floor slabs, aggravated matters, 'vitiated air arising from these numerous interments.'[4]

To ensure a degree of warmth, chairs and rough forms had been brought into the presbytery, around which a series of 'hideous screens of canvas and baize' had been placed to keep draughts at bay. It was possibly this which a visitor, about 1816, referred to when he wrote 'I fear the present incumbent does not much appre- ciate the beauties of his church. It is unfortunate something is not done to control incumbents from mutilating these monuments of antiquity.' Two stoves provided some heat but also drew draughts of cold and humid air from the body of the church. Sections of the plaster ceilings of Scudamore's day were breaking off and falling whilst other parts were merely secured by boards screwed to the joists. The stone roof tiles required relaying with felt and boarding beneath, and the window glazing required attention. Finally, after inspecting the tower, Paul decided that the parapet and string course needed to be replaced and the roof timbers renewed.[5]

By September 1901 a tender by Collins and Godfrey of Tewkesbury for £4,395 had been accepted. Work began in October. Inside the church it was found that the debris which had accumulated since the dissolution had been roughly levelled at the time paving was laid in 1634. Into this layer, for almost 200 years, burials had been made. To lower the paving to its original, medieval level a 'considerable thickness of debris, tiles, glass, worked stone, rubble, earth, skulls and bones' had to be removed. All was carefully examined and human remains were reinterred. A concrete raft was then laid and the old paving reinstated except where oak blocks were set under the Laudian pews, brought in from their original position in the crossing west of the screen to replace the chairs and rough forms. A special service at the end of June 1903 marked the completion of the work in the presbytery.[6]

The second stage involved the repairs to the crossing and transepts: the renovation of the roof and the replacement of the lathe and plaster ceilings by oak boarding on the seventeenth century joists. In addition the whitewash was to be stripped from the walls to reveal the wall paintings on the south, west and north walls and the sandstone on the east. Here again old paving and grave slabs were relaid in their original positions on a bed of concrete.[7] Within the church these now form a valuable series, with sixteen dating from the seventeenth century.[8] This stage was completed by August 1909, but this was not the end. A heating system was installed in 1911 and the Laudian east window was releaded the following year. A timber lectern 'In Memory of James Hopton of Dulas Court d.1855' and an elaborate timber reredos with the 5 wounds of Christ on it to match the screen, the gift of the architect, were presented to the church. Both were designed by Roland Paul.

As previously described these works gave Paul an opportunity to establish important details of the original ground plan: the position of the high altar, the screen walls of the eastern chapels and foundations of three of their altars. Removal of earth and rubble on the exterior and the reduction of internal levels led to the discovery of large numbers of medieval tiles. Paul was fully aware of the importance of this find; amongst his papers are 170 drawings of the best preserved, most in water colour, the rest in pencil; 80 sketches of larger fragments, and the plan for 'Tiles to be laid in Sacrarium, 1902.' Although his finds included more early lozenge-shaped green-glazed tiles, most were of the later slip variety. Amongst the latter were many heraldic tiles with, in all, twenty-one different shields. Paul also uncovered inscribed tiles where the letters appear backwards, several examples of the winged bull of St. Luke, 'apparently belonging to a set of evangelistic symbols', and a very beautiful tile with squirrels in trees. Most interesting of all, however, was a tile 6.5 inches square with the circular inscription *Martin me fecit* within which were the head and shoulders of a monk blowing a trumpet from which hung a banner. The character of the tiles so carefully preserved by Paul has been analysed in chapter VII, but it must be recorded that the affinity of many of these Dore tiles to those at Bredon was recognised by Paul. The best preserved he reset north of the altar, in other parts of the presbytery, in the east chapels and around the font; those considered unsuitable were carefully stored in boxes, scarce touched to our own day.[9]

It was fortunate for Dore that Paul had a similar enthusiasm for and knowledge of stained glass. In 1901 he had published a monograph on the medieval heraldic glass of Great Malvern Priory. Few architects of his day could have identified and rescued so many fragments of Cistercian glass amongst the loose earth, stones, bones and skulls removed from beneath the paving in the north aisle and north transept.[10] There Paul found more medieval glass than has been recovered from any other Cistercian site in Britain. This was carefully sorted into three categories: early grisaille and later grisaille, the so-called grey-glass, and coloured and figured glass of c.1350. The best preserved pieces were reset. Paul is quite explicit that prior to restoration there was no glass at Dore earlier than the east window of 1634. He thus provided Dore not only with the sole English examples of early Cistercian grisaille but with the best collection of mid-fourteenth century Cistercian glass in Britain. From 1134 the Cistercian General Chapter ordained that windows should be 'white, without cross, without colours' and the order was re-enforced in 1182. Even so, windows were built with simple geometric patterns and natural motifs, especially foliage, sketched in black, even with occasional small coloured panes as in the Five Sisters window at York Minster.[11] In the glass, as in the architecture, we can trace the move from the early austerity of the order to the mainstream, the artistic norms, of the medieval church in the first half of the fourteenth century.

Fig. 112. *The only record of the early Cistercian grisaille glass from the westernmost window of the south aisle* (Photo: R. Marks)

Fig. 113. *The design of overlapping concentric circles*

Most important were the fragments of early grisaille glass which he reset in the westernmost window of the south aisle. Its significance was undetected even by the acute and well-trained eye of the Royal Commission's investigator who here merely noted 'fragments of painted glass - too much work for the patterns represented to be recognised.' The first person to appreciate Paul's achievement was Richard Marks who drew attention to the unique character of this glass ten years ago. The 'two rows of white glass with a scale-like pattern formed by overlapping concentric circles' were 'a unique design in early Cistercian glass.'[12] However, similar 'scale' designs are found in other early Cistercian art forms—in painting on the jambs of the cloister door of the outer parlour at Fountains and, formerly, on the north doorway of the Rievaulx refectory. In France it appears on tile patterns at La Benisson-Dieu. Early geometric designs can be seen in the grisaille at Obazine in the Limousin and at Santes Creus in Catalonia[13]

This remarkable and solitary example of early Cistercian grisaille, possibly contemporary with the building of the presbytery, has since been removed. The vestry minutes of 20 March, 1973 record that John Hall and Sons (Bristol) Ltd had agreed to repair windows for £1,276. E.A. Roiser's specification for reglazing, including derusting and painting of iron work, refers to windows 1, 2 and 4 from the east of the south ambulatory. Thus did Dore, and most probably the country, lose a remarkable treasure. A record remains, for Marks had photographed it on an earlier visit (Figs. 112 & 113). The somewhat later grisaille glass was not removed. Three roundels made up from Paul's finds are now in the westernmost window of the south aisle. This glass differs from the earlier grisaille in that, whilst the latter was made up of abstract design, this is decorated with foliage, with a few pieces of red and blue glass for contrast,.

The glass of the third period was brought together by Paul and set in the south and east windows of the Hoskyns Chapel, that is the south-east transeptal chapel. This is in marked contrast to the grisaille. The Cistercian glazing at Dore had now abandoned its early austerity and was now in the mainstream of English medieval stained glass. It is characterised by the use of intense colour—gold, blues, reds and greens—and figures, human and angelic, in addition to foliage. Just as the colour is intense, so are the figures boldly drawn. From the fragments Paul recovered it is clear that the latter were large in size and striking in appearance.

The east window has at the top pieces of heavily feathered angels in deep gold/bronze; close by, Paul placed a luxuriant (prophet's?) beard sketched in black on gold and beneath a head with golden locks and eyes with the striking black pupils. This is surmounted by a (separate?) mitre. The deep blue and red pieces with foliage diaper, made up with brownish fabric to suggest the form of a body, are companions of the green fragments in the south window. Other pieces of this diapered blue glass were used by Paul to make up lost material in the east window. They can be seen by the head and waist of Luke and the left foot of John. The south window is a satisfying melange of foliage diapering in deep green, quarries with a sprig of pear and another of pomegranate, a kneeling monk(?) with hands clasped in prayer, the winged lion of St. Mark and winged bull of St. Luke, three elaborate gold crowns and part of another inverted, a gilt cup and black letter work, surrounded on three sides with a border of varying designs and a band of lozenges at the base, all in black and gold.

Once again we are deeply in Paul's debt. Not only has he provided us with some sense of the quality and character of Dore's glazing of the first half of the mid-fourteenth century but he has also enabled us to speculate as to its relationship with the figures found in the important Jesse windows at St. Mary's, Madley, and St. Laurence, Ludlow. These depict the descent of Jesus in the form of a tree springing from the body of Jesse, father of David, with intermediary descendants on the branches. At Madley there is similar deep red, green and blue glass with foliage diaper in the three Jesse panels and amongst the fragments in the adjacent southeast window of the apse. At Ludlow the heads in the tracery of the Jesse window are on blue, ruby and green grounds, the blues and rubies with a pronounced diaper pattern. More critical, the affinity between the heads in the three churches is striking. Each is characterised by the application of silver stain by which process the white of the face and gold for hair, beard, crown etc could be produced on a single piece of glass. Here the faces are white, not as in the similar Merevale, Warwickshire, Jesse, flesh-coloured; smear shading is used to emphasise eyes and nose. All are boldly painted with piercing eyes in a side-long glance and luxuriant hair and beards. One of the ecclesiastics in the Madley southeast window has hair swept back over the ear, as at Dore. The Dore crowns resemble that of a king, originally part of a Jesse tree in the east window of Bristol cathedral, now in the cloister.[14]

Are these Dore fragments the remains of a Jesse tree? To be effective the tree's branches need to spread from the central light across adjoining lights, for which large east windows give most scope. Local examples were found in the five-light east windows of the Chilstone Chapel at Madley and the lady chapel at Ludlow. In the three narrow, widely spaced eastern lancets at Dore this effect could not be achieved. Without Paul's *Diary* we do not know where the various pieces were found. Thus we can only be grateful that he preserved these vestiges of the former glories of Dore's glass for our pleasure, and curiosity.

On the re-opening of the presbytery in 1903 Sir George Cornwall quoted the warning made by Sir George Gilbert Scott years previously: 'I would say as emphatically as I can find words to express, that in any future restorations and repairs it is the duty of all concerned to pay as pious and reverential a regard to the works of this admirable man Scudamore as to those of the original builders.' Scott feared that any restoration of Dore would destroy the building's unique character, derived from the extraordinarily happy combination of medieval and early seventeenth century features. His fears were unfounded. Paul not only maintained this balance but went further: the restoration of the original levels and incorporation of medieval tiles, glass etc. made the interplay of the two elements of the character of Dore even more satisfying.

CHAPTER XXV

Dore Abbey today

by Rt. Revd. John Oliver, Bishop of Hereford

'A serious house on serious earth it is,
In whose blent air all our compulsions meet,
Are recognised, and robed as destinies.
And that much never can be obsolete,
Since someone will for ever be surprising
A hunger in himself to be more serious,
And gravitating with it to this ground,
Which, he once heard, was proper to grow
  wise in,
If only that so many dead lie round.'
          (from 'Church Going' by Philip Larkin)

I first saw Dore Abbey by accident, like so many visitors to the Welsh Marches. I vividly remember my sense of amazement and wonder at the vast building set so gloriously in the shadow of the Black Mountains, and guarding the southern approach to the beautiful Golden Valley. We were on holiday in one of our favourite parts of England, the first of many visits which were to last over thirty summers. Armed in due course with architectural handbooks, we discovered with great excitement the origin of the building, and on occasions were able to attend the ordinary parish services on Sundays. I also remember our sense of surprise and delight at how successfully Dore Abbey can accommodate a small village congregation, without any sense that the handful of faithful people are overwhelmed by their huge and inspiring surroundings.

It is one of the particular blessings of Dore Abbey that, for all its formidable splendour, it can still function effectively as a village church. It was part of the wisdom of Lord Scudamore's restoration of the remains of the great abbey that it provided an enclosed space where the worship of a parish church could continue, set at the heart of the choir of the ancient church, but far less intimidated by the sheer scale of the building than is the case in many much more modest churches.

Over many years we have returned to Dore Abbey as visitors and holidaymakers; for five years I have now had responsibility for the church as bishop of the diocese of Hereford and I still marvel every time I visit it, as I do from time to time, to join in an act of worship or attend one of the concerts which are now a regular part of the Dore Abbey Festival. When I arrived in the diocese I found the Ewyas Harold Team Ministry well-established, with three clergy caring for thirteen parishes, among them Abbeydore. The Team Ministry had been set up in 1984 to bring together the pastoral care of no less than thirteen small parishes, Ewyas Harold being the only place of any size at all. The official staffing was two clergy—a team rector and a team vicar—but the opportunity was subsequently taken to make use of the benefice as an ideal place in which to train somebody in rural ministry, so there was a third team member, a curate in training.

Fig. 114. 'The church of Door' in 1727, a century after it had been restored for use as a parish church

it to continue to serve its local congregation as a place of regular worship Sunday by Sunday. The outcome of that meeting was the formation of the Friends of Dore Abbey, and the happy result of their hard and devoted work has been the safeguarding of the great church for the foreseeable future.

I am personally delighted by the outcome of the negotiations, because I believe that every church we have inherited from the past, particularly a building of such outstanding beauty, holiness and splendour as Dore Abbey, should continue in use as a place of prayer and sacrament, of preaching and teaching, of building up the people of God.

As I look to the future, my hope is that the Ewyas Harold Team Ministry will be able to take advantage of new schemes of lay training and team building, so that the life of the parishes may be sustained in a fuller and more vigorous way by a local ministry team. This will ensure the continued existence of the great abbey as a parish church, a focal point for pilgrimage, and a place where people from all over the world may rejoice at the devotion which built it up as a Cistercian abbey, and which has sustained it across the centuries through times of great difficulty and trouble, and enabled this generation to inherit as a priceless treasure.

An important new initiative, which is still in its very early stages, involves a plan to try to re-establish some kind of regular round of prayer in the abbey church. Founded by the Cistercian monks in 1147, Dore Abbey was for 400 years a place where monastic worship was offered, and pilgrims and those in need came from far and wide to find both the love of God and the practical care and help which the monastery could offer. It seems entirely right that we should once again think in terms of using Dore Abbey as a place for retreats and quiet days, for reflection

In view of the very small number of parishioners it was a generous allocation of clergy, despite the extensive area which the team covers. When the team rector moved to a new post in 1993, the staffing was reduced to two, one full-time stipendiary priest and a trainee curate, and the curacy is not one which we can guarantee to maintain in view of the diminishing number of stipendiary clergy. New forms of ministry are beginning to emerge, and there are encouraging signs of lay people being willing to take on increasing responsibility. But it was not surprising that the 1993 quinquennial inspection report, which underlined the necessity for major repair work, was the signal for a careful appraisal of whether Dore Abbey should continue in use as a parish church.

The temptation to seek redundancy, in the hope that the Churches' Conservation Trust would take over responsibility for the building and enable it to be preserved and still occasionally used, was a very strong one. But it was wisely decided to hold a major public meeting, and to see whether any way could be found of raising the large sums that were necessary to put the abbey into a sound state of repair and enable and recollection and building people up in holiness. These plans would involve some modest addition to the existing buildings, to enable people to spend a day in the abbey, meeting, praying, talking, listening and sharing in meals together. I warmly welcome the idea that the religious life should be re-established in Abbeydore, in a way which, although so very different from that for which the abbey was established, will be meeting the needs of today's church, and drawing people from far and near to make creative use of what is one of the great churches of Britain, even of Christendom; truly a place where we may be 'lost in wonder, love and praise'.

Fig. 115. Abbey Dore church as it is today, viewed from the east.

Dore Abbey has survived many crises, and it came perilously near to complete abandonment at the time of the Dissolution of the Monasteries. That it was preserved as a parish church is a ground for great gratitude, but it seems right that its future should be one which serves far more people than the small community of the parish of Abbeydore. I hope and pray that they will continue to use and support their own parish church, but I believe it to be important also that the worldwide interest in Dore Abbey should be harnessed and focussed in a number of important ways. There will of course be a significant and I hope increasing number of people who come to visit it as tourists, students of architecture, or those who simply love the Welsh Marches. But I hope too that the development of Dore Abbey as a centre of devotion and of the religious life in a

form which is accessible to busy people at the end of the twentieth century, will give it back its raison d'être and help it to become a resource for mission in the years that lie ahead. I welcome too the reintroduction of the Dore Abbey Festival, and the use of the great abbey church for so many concerts and other events which exploit its wonderful acoustics, and enable people of all Christian persuasions and of none to spend time in its incomparable surroundings.

'You are not here to verify,
Instruct yourself, or inform curiosity
Or carry report. You are here to kneel
Where prayer has been valid.'
(from 'Little Gidding' by T.S. Eliot)

APPENDIX 1

References in the Annals of Dore to the Monastery

(Translated from the transcription of BL. Egerton MS 3088, in Waitz, G. (ed) *Monumenta Germaniae Historica, Scriptorum* XXVII (Hanover, 1885), pp.514-31. For a description of the whole MS, see: *Isis* XVII (Nov. 1937).

1147   This year was begun the abbey of Dore.

1226   The sending of a convent [i.e: a community of monks] from Dore to Grace Dieu on the 24th April, to wit, on the vigil of St. Mark the Evangelist.

1257   On April 1st died Reginald, 6th abbot of Dore.

1273   On November 20th died Henry, the 7th abbot.

1274   On January 1st William of Hereford was elected abbot.

"   On January 25th a convent was sent to Dernehale.

1281   Abbot William (9th) Wroth died, of gracious nature, prelate of Dore, he was buried at L'Arrivour [a Cistercian monastery near Troyes in France, at which abbey William was probably staying on a journey to or from the General Chapter at Cîteaux further south].

1296   On March 12th died William of Hereford, sometime 10th abbot of Valley Dore.

1310   John of Grosmont died, sometime 11th abbot of this house.

1312   Hugh Cromus died, sometime 12th abbot of this house.

"   In this year, on the 12th of April, master Richard de Straddel, lord and abbot of the house of Dore, of the Cistercian Order, in the diocese of Hereford, began theology at Oxford, not only with honour, but right worthily, with the help of God and the support of the clergy.

1318   In this year shewed God his hand, namely in the manifestation of a miracle in this place by the virtue of a holy virgin, which grace indeed He gave to the venerable matron, Matilda Burnel, who lies before the high altar.

1321   On October 6th, and then a Tuesday, came to Dore the lord W[illiam] de Grandison and bringing with him a portion of the wood of the holy cross, very beautifully adorned with gold and precious stones; on the morrow, in honour of the Holy Trinity, and on account of a grace and favour of the lord Richard de Straddel, abbot of the said house, (namely a debt that was owed to him), he handed it over to the monastery, cancelling his obligation, being completely pardoned by the said lord abbot Richard.

1347   On the 29th July died master Richard de Straddel, a distinguished doctor of theology and 12th abbot of this house. [An editorial error here, as Hugh Cromus is previously noted as being the 12th abbot].

1362   On 22nd June died Robert Wroth, 13th abbot of this house.

APPENDIX 2

Extract from Cadwgan of Bangor's
Tract on the Blessed Virgin Mary

'She went up into the hill country of Juda with haste,
     entered into the house of Zacharias,
          and saluted Elizabeth.
She went up out of Nazareth,
     together with Joseph,
          unto Bethlehem.
She went up into the Temple of the Lord,
     together with Joseph,
          that she might place her Child,
               in the presence of the Lord.
She went up out of Egypt,
     together with Joseph,
          into the land of Israel.
She went up to Jerusalem, that she might pray
     together with Joseph,
          after the custom of the feast.
She went up again to Jerusalem,
     together with Joseph,
          that she might seek the Child Jesus.
She went up at length into heaven,
     to take her place by her blessed Son.
          'upon thy right hand did stand the queen (Ps. 45/10)

The first ascension, was to visit and to minister,
The second, to beget and to obey.
The third, to present her Son, and to offer a pair of turtledoves, and two young pigeons.
The fourth, to keep vigil, and to make her dwelling.
The fifth, to pray.
The sixth, to seek her Child, and to find Him.
The seventh, to have joy, and to reign.'

APPENDIX 3

Extract from Richard Straddell's
Sermon 'Of St. Benedict'

(based upon the text, 'Blessed art thou in the firmament of heaven', Song of the Three Holy Children, verse 34.)

These are the words of the children walking in the midst of the furnace. Indeed, we read that king Nebuchadnezzar sent them to burn in the fire of the furnace, but the angel of the Lord descended and saved them unscathed. Through the furnace we can appreciate three things: present unhappiness, into which the devil, as the proud king, sends the human race by his deception, and inflames the seven senses, procuring our sevenfold vices. But God sends his angel into the furnace, that is the man Benedict, who extinguishes the flame by the doctrine of his word, and by the example of his life turns its midst into a gushing fount of dew, so that, walking in it unhurt, and prizing highly our glorified father, now with God, we say: 'Blessed art thou in the firmament of heaven'.

[These form the opening sentences. The sermon concludes with rhyming phrases difficult to preserve when rendered into English]:

Blessed art thou -	The war with vices most strongly undertaking, The profit out of virtues most fully gaining, The furthest from unlawful things most devoutly withdrawing.
In the firmament -	Most sure in the protection of God, Most secure in the abundance of grace, Most splendid in the excellence of glory.
Of Heaven -	For which thou scornest earthly things, For which thou lovest virtuous things, In which thou hopest for eternal things.

APPENDIX 4

The Seals of Dore Abbey

Various statutes of the General Chapter regularised the seals which a Cistercian abbey might employ. Throughout the thirteenth century no common seal was used, only the seal of the abbot, and this was not to bear his personal name. As for design, the seal might bear an emergent hand holding a staff, or else the simple effigy of the abbot alone bearing his staff (and usually a book, presumably for the *Rule of St. Benedict*).[225] Generally speaking, the hand-and-staff type gave way to the effigy by the mid-thirteenth century, but Dore, after using the effigy type in 1252 (and again about 1275-90; Fig. a) re-used its hand-and-staff seal in 1263. The seal used by Dore in 1329 seems still to have been the effigy-type, and was noted that year by a notary as being impressed 'in red wax, with the image of an abbot standing clothed in abbatial vestments with a crozier in his right and a book in his left hands, on the right side of a shield.'[226]

The Statute of Carlisle (1307) required that each English monastic house had a common seal; this injunction was reinforced by the papal Constitution for the Cistercian Order of Benedict XII (1335) and a related statute of the General Chapter. From 1335 onwards each Cistercian abbey was to have a common seal 'rounded, of copper, and engraved with the image of the Blessed Virgin, in whose honour are founded all the monasteries of the Order'. The abbot's seal henceforth was to bear his personal name. In this way it would be easier to tell 'by whom and in whose time' a deed had been executed.[227] As the deed of acknowledgement of Henrician supremacy for Dore Abbey is missing, the only common seal of Dore (known from a later drawing, and attributed in usage to the reign of Edward IV [1461-83], like the common seal of its daughter-house at Grace Dieu, bears not Our Lady but the abbot standing in an alcove, a shield either side (Fig. b). The more traditional seal was perhaps that stolen about 1397 and possibly never regained. Another abbatial seal extant is that of Jordan Bykeleswade (1398-1403); the matrix, found prior to 1806 among the effects of Mr. Somerville, a Stafford surgeon, is now held in the Society of Antiquaries of London, an impression is in Hereford Cathedral Library.[228] This does depict the Virgin and Child, the tonsured abbot being shown three-quarters length in a niche below (Fig. c).

Fig. a. Abbot's Seal (Later form) (PRO DL 25/326)
Brown Wax, pointed oval, 41x 26mm c.1275-90
....IGILLVM : ABBATIS : DE : DOR.

Fig. b. Common Seal (BL, ADD. MS 24, 101, f.5)
? engraved about 1330-34, this drawing by B.
Howlett in 1823
Sinister: shield: two bars, in chief a lion sejant
guardant, TREGOZ[229]
Dexter: shield: plain
Legend: S.C.........De Dora

Fig. c. Seal of Abbot Jordan Bykeleswade
Modern impression, Hereford Cathedral Library
S : fratris : iordani : ab/atis : de: monstri : de
dora

213

APPENDIX 5

The Scudamore Family Tree

by Ruth Richardson & Joe Hillaby

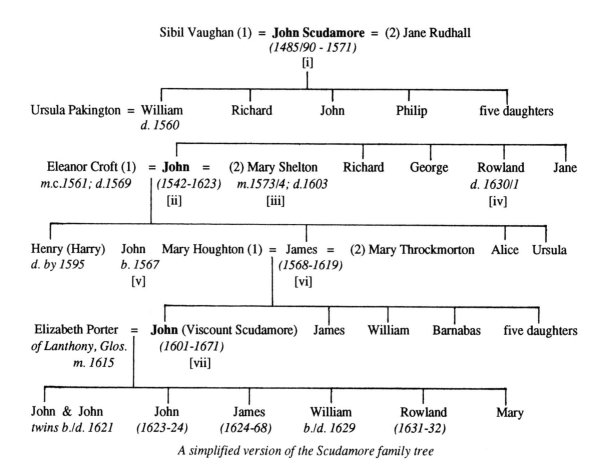

A simplified version of the Scudamore family tree

APPENDIX 6

Floor Tiles

Petrology

Twelve thin-sections were prepared by A G Petrology. They are numbered L2091 to L2102. Samples L2091 to L2096 were relief tiles and L2097 to L2102 the two-colour tiles. The thin-sections are in the author's possession.

Tile drawings

The drawings of the tiles were prepared by Lyn Harper with advice and help from Steve Clarke.

IPCS (Inductively Coupled Plasma Spectroscopy) The same twelve samples were submitted for ICPS analysis. Oxides and elements were determined as percentages (for major and minor oxides/elements), or ppm (for trace elements) Summary statistics for this data (below) show that for almost every oxide/element measured there is a clear difference between the two groups. In several instances the element ranges do not even overlap. This is a remarkable result, given that the two fabrics are shown by thin-section analysis to both have used the Devonian marl.

(a)   Minor Elements (%)

Group		Al2O3	Fe2O3	MgO	CaO	Na2O	K2O	TiO2	P2O5	MnO
Relief	Mean	13.42	5.39	2.45	3.69	0.91	1.74	0.68	0.20	0.16
	Standard Deviation	0.49	0.15	0.11	0.99	0.02	0.10	0.04	0.02	0.02
	Range	1.45	0.42	0.29	2.90	0.05	0.27	0.12	0.06	0.06
	Minimum	12.78	5.16	2.35	1.83	0.89	1.61	0.64	0.17	0.13
	Maximum	14.23	5.58	2.64	4.73	0.94	1.88	0.76	0.23	0.19
Two-colour	Mean	14.52	5.95	1.82	0.91	1.35	2.57	0.73	0.12	0.07
	Standard Deviation	0.65	0.33	0.10	0.10	0.06	0.15	0.02	0.02	0.01
	Range	1.87	0.91	0.29	0.22	0.15	0.43	0.05	0.04	0.03
	Minimum	13.35	5.48	1.66	0.83	1.27	2.30	0.70	0.09	0.05
	Maximum	15.22	6.39	1.95	1.05	1.42	2.73	0.75	0.13	0.08

(b)   Trace Elements (ppm)

Group		Ba	Co	Cr	Cu	Li	Nb	Ni	Sc	Sr
Relief	Mean	874.83	15.83	118.17	41.17	44.00	12.33	55.00	15.00	77.83
	Standard Deviation	56.92	0.75	5.56	11.16	1.41	0.82	1.41	0.63	12.34
	Range	133.00	2.00	14.00	26.00	4.00	2.00	4.00	2.00	34.00
	Minimum	800.00	15.00	111.00	30.00	42.00	12.00	53.00	14.00	68.00
	Maximum	933.00	17.00	125.00	56.00	46.00	14.00	57.00	16.00	102.00
Two-colour	Mean	584.00	13.17	102.00	23.50	51.33	13.50	49.17	13.67	92.50
	Standard Deviation	27.52	2.93	3.63	3.39	2.94	0.55	2.23	0.52	4.51
	Range	72.00	7.00	10.00	9.00	8.00	1.00	6.00	1.00	13.00
	Minimum	541.00	10.00	96.00	19.00	46.00	13.00	46.00	13.00	85.00
	Maximum	613.00	17.00	106.00	28.00	54.00	14.00	52.00	14.00	98.00

Group		V	Y	Zn	Zr*	La	Ce	Nd	Sm	Eu	Dy	Yb
Relief	Mean	156.50	56.33	73.67	68.33	55.00	91.33	52.83	11.38	2.12	7.63	3.33
	Standard Deviation	12.57	1.86	5.82	7.69	2.10	4.27	1.83	0.56	0.08	0.23	0.08
	Range	36.00	5.00	15.00	20.00	6.00	10.00	4.00	1.50	0.20	0.60	0.20
	Minimum	142.00	53.00	69.00	57.00	52.00	86.00	51.00	10.40	2.00	7.30	3.20
	Maximum	178.00	58.00	84.00	77.00	58.00	96.00	55.00	11.90	2.20	7.90	3.40
Two-colour	Mean	87.00	22.17	76.50	46.50	43.33	81.00	33.83	7.05	1.23	3.18	1.45
	Standard Deviation	4.52	1.17	6.57	4.04	1.75	3.29	1.47	0.42	0.08	0.26	0.08
	Range	12.00	3.00	20.00	12.00	5.00	9.00	4.00	1.10	0.20	0.70	0.20
	Minimum	81.00	21.00	67.00	40.00	40.00	76.00	32.00	6.80	1.10	3.00	1.40
	Maximum	93.00	24.00	87.00	52.00	45.00	85.00	36.00	7.90	1.30	3.70	1.60

The ICPS summary statistics

REFERENCES

STANDARD ABBREVIATIONS
BL: British Library.
CS: *Hereford Cathedral Registers*, Cantilupe Soc., Canterbury and York Society.
HCL: Hereford City Library
HRO: Hereford Record Office
PRO: Public Record Office
RCHM, I, II & III: An *Inventory of the Historical Monuments in Herefordshire,* 3 vols. (1931-4)
TWNFC : Transactions of the Woolhope Naturalists' Field Club

COMMON REFERENCES
Monasticon (1846): Dugdale, W., *Monasticon Anglicanum* , 5, (1846)
Statuta: Canivez, J., *Statuta Capitulorum Ordinis Cisterciensis* , Louvain (1933)
Blashill (1985): Blashill, T., 'The architectural History of Dore Abbey,' *J. Brit Arch Ass,* 41 (1885) 363-81
Cowley (1977): Cowley, F.G., *Monastic Order in South Wales, 1066-1349* (1977)
Gibson (1727): Gibson, M., *View of the Ancient and Present State of the Churches of Door ...* (1727)
Hillaby (1984 & 1985): Hillaby, J., 'Hereford Gold ... ' *TWNFC,* Pt. 1 (1984) 358-419; Pt. 2 (1985)193-270
Hillaby (1987);Hillaby, J., 'Early Christian & pre-Conquest Leominster,' *TWNFC* 45 (1987) 557-685
Hillaby (1989): Hillaby, J., 'The House of Houses, The Cistercians of Dore and the origins of the polygonal chapter house,' *TWNFC,* 46 (1989) 209-45
Malone (1984): Malone, C.M. 'Abbey Dore: English versus French Design' in *Studies in Cistercian Art and Architecture* 2 (1984) 50-75
Morgan (1955): Morgan, F.C., *Guide to Abbey Dore* (1955)
Norton & Park (1986): Norton, C, & Park, D., (eds) *Cistercian Art and Architecture in the British Isles* (1986) 305
O'Callaghan(1995): O'Callaghan, B.,'An Analysis of the Architecture of the Cistercian Church at Abbey Dore' *Medieval Art, Architecture and Archaeology at Hereford: Brit Archaeol Ass Conf Trans,* 15 (1995), 97, pl.XIB
Paul (1893): Paul, R.W., 'Abbey Dore,' *The Builder* (8 April 1893) 265-9
Paul (1896):Paul, R.W., 'Abbey Dore' *The Builder* (4 April 1896) 298-300
Paul (1898): Paul R.W., *Dore Abbey, Herefordshire: A Short Account of its History and an Appeal for its Repair* (1898)
Paul (1899): Paul, R.W., 'Bosses, Abbey Dore Church,' *The Builder,* (8 July 1899) 34
Paul (1902a): Psaul R.W., 'Abbey Dore,' *The Builder,* (19 April 1902) 307
Paul (1902b): Paul, R.W., 'Abbey Dore Church, Hereford,' *The Builder* (15 Nov. 1902) 448
Paul (1903): Paul, R.A., 'Abbey Dore, Hereford,'*The Builder,* (3 Jan. 1903) 15

Paul (1904a): Paul, R.W., 'The Church and Monastery of Abbey Dore, Herefordshire' *TBGAS,* 27 (1904) 117-26
Paul (1904b): Paul, R.W., 'New Lectern and Reredos, Abbey Dore Church, Hereford,' *The Builder,* (28 May 1904) 583
Paul (1927): Paul, R.W., 'Abbey Dore Church, Herefordshire' *Archaeol Camb* 82 (ii) (Dec. 1927) 269-75
Paul (1931): Paul, R.W., 'Abbey Dore Church, Herefordshire,' *The Builder* (25 Sept. 1931) 500
Sledmere (1914): Sledmere, E., *Abbey Dore, Herefordshire, Its Building and Restoration,* (1914)
Smith (1964): Smith, L.T., *Leland's Itinerary in England and Wales,* 5 vols. (1964)
Williams (1966): Williams, D.H., 'Abbey Dore', *Monmouthshire Antiquary* II:2 (1966).
Williams (1976): Williams, D. H., *White Monks in Gwent and the Border* (1976)
Williams (1984): Williams, D.H., *The Welsh Cistercians, (*1984)
Williams (1990): Williams, D.H., *Atlas of Cistercian Lands in Wales* (1990)

CHAPTER I (Dore before the Abbey)
1 Camden, W., *Brittania* (1568)
2. Children, G. & Nash, G., *A guide to prehistoric sites in Herefordshire,* (1994) 15
3. Stanford, S.C., *The archaeology of the Welsh Marches,* 2nd edition, (1991) 58
4. Notes on 3rd Field Meeting, *TWNFC* (1900-April 1902) 180-199
5. Notes on 3rd Field Meeting, *TWNFC* (1900-April 1902) 180-199
6. Jack, G.H., 'Some notes on Roman Herefordshire,' *TWNFC* (1908-11) 68-74 and plates between pps. 70 & 71
7. Shoesmith, R., *Castles and moated sites of Herefordshire* (1996) 168
8. Margery, I.D., *Roman Roads in Britain* (1967)
9. P.R.H., 'Possible Roman Roads,' *Herefordshire Archaeogical News,* No. 58 (Sept. 1992) 34
10. *Loc. cit.* note 3, 76
11. Thomas, M., 'Investigation of a possible Roman Road in the Golden Valley,' *TWNFC* (1985-7) 186-92
12. Andere, M., *Arthurian links with Herefordshire* (1996)
13. Davies, W., *The Llandaff charters* (1979) 74f
14. Gelling, M., *The West Midlands in the early Middle Ages*, (1992) 69-70 & fig 34. Indeed Gelling comments 'In the greater part of Herefordshire, Welsh speech cannot have been exceptional.' The language tradition was to continue even in Hereford city into the seventeenth century (Shoesmith, R., *The Civil War in Hereford,* 1995, 39)
15. Davies, W., *The Llandaff charters* (1979) 104 (Charter 162b)

16. *Loc. cit.*, note 15, 105 (charter 165). *Podum* means district or estate. *Cynmarchi* is considered to be Chepstow; *podon Mafern*, Dore, *Lann Cerniu*, Dorstone and *Mochros*, Moccas. The position of *Lann Calcuchis* is unknown.
17. Coplestone-Crow, B., *Herefordshire Place-Names* (1989) 20
18. *op. cit.*, 17, 162
19. *op. cit.*, 3-5
20. Fox, C., *Offa's Dyke* (1955)
21. Gelling, M., *Offa's Dyke Reviewed by Frank Noble* (1983) 14
22. Morris, J., (gen. ed.) Thorn & Thorn (eds.) *Domesday Book—Herefordshire* (1983). *Wadetune* was one of the many settlements in the Golden Valley area that suffered a name change after the Norman Conquest [Coplestone-Crow, *Herefordshire Place-Names* (1989) 196]
23. Sledmere (1914) 81
24. My thanks to Ruth Richardson for bringing this to my notice. The tithe map and apportionment are in HRO
25. *Loc. cit.*, note 22. *Almundestune* with a church and a priest could well be Peterchurch. It is suggested that *Alcamestune* was at Urishay
26. *Loc. cit.*, note 17, 20
27. Information from Ruth Richardson
28. Smith (1964)
29. *Loc. cit.*, note 17, 20

CHAPTER II (The Cistercians)
1. Brooke, C., *Monasteries of the World, The Rise and Development of the Monastic Tradition* (1982) 136
2. Matarasso, P., (ed.) *The Cistercian World, Monastic Writings of the Twelfth Century*, (1993) 3, 5-6
3. *Op. cit.*, note 2, 3
4. *Op. cit.*, note 2
5. Pennington, M.B., *The Last of the Fathers, The Cistercian Fathers of the Twelfth Century*, (St. Bede's Publications, Still River, Mass., 1983)
6. Quoted by Southern, R.W., *Western Society and the Church in the Middle Ages* (1970) 251, from Walbram J.R. (ed.) *Memorials of Fountains Abbey*, Surtees Soc. 42 (1863) i, 15
7. McGuire, B.P., 'The Meaning of Cistercian Spirituality,' *Cistercian Studies Quarterly*, Vol. 30.1, 1995, 104
8. Williams (1990) 16
9. I have taken these figures from Southern *op. cit.* note 6, 254
10. Knowles, D., & Hadcock, R.N., *Medieval Religious Houses* (1953) 29
11. *Loc. cit.*, note 6, Southern, 255
12. Prologue to the Charter of Charity quoted by Pennington, M.B., *The Last of the Fathers, The Cistercian Fathers of the Twelfth Century*, (St Bede's Publications, Mass., 1983) 8
13. Sermon 18.6 From Pennington *op. cit.*, note 12, 9 note 47
14. Morson, J., *Via Veritas et Vita: Christ in the Sermons of Guerric of Igny*, quoted in Matarasso *op. cit.*, note 2, xv
15. Pennington, B., *op. cit.*, note 10

16. I owe this to Matarasso *op. cit.*, note 2, xv
17. This is largely due to *The Cistercian Fathers* series, Cistercian Publications, Kalamazoo, Michigan, and *Cistercian Studies* subsequently *Cistercian Studies Quarterly*

CHAPTER III (The Abbey of Dore)
1. King, A.A., *Citeaux and her Elder Daughters* (1954) 330
2. O'Callaghan, J.F., 'The Affiliation of the Order of Calatrava', *Analecta S.O. Cist.* 16 (1960) 48-52
3. Gwynn, A. and Hadcock, R.N., *Medieval Religious Houses, Ireland* (1988) 122, 5. I am grateful to Brian Galway for drawing my attention to Macosquin; it is however not listed by Anselme Dimier in his 'Liste Alphabétique des Monastères de la Filiation de Morimond,' *Analecta S.O. Cist.*, 14 (1958) 112-16
4. *op. cit.*, note 1, 341
5. Eydoux, H.P., 'L'Eglise abbatiale de Morimond', *Analecta S.O. Cist.*, 14 (1958) 13, 32, and plan
6. Williams (1976) 1
7. Conway Davies, J., *Episcopal Acts relating to Welsh Dioceses* I (1946) 276; *Monasticon* (1846), 555b; *cf.* PRO, E 315/50, f.74
8. *Statuta* I, 111 (1189/3), 295 (1204/2)
9. Brewer, J.S. (ed.), *Giraldus Cambrensis, Opera*, 4 (Rolls Ser., 1873) 206
10. Williams, D.H., 'Grace Dieu Abbey: An Exploratory Excavation', *Monmouths Antiq* 3:1 (1970-71) 55-58
11. Williams (1976) 13-4
12. *op. cit.*, note 1, 330
13. Williams (1976) 1
14. *Cal. Papal Registers* (Letters) III, 1
15. *Cal. Patent Rolls*, 1405/65
16. Smith (1964) III, 49
17. Baring-Gould, S., *The Lives of the Saints* 11: [October 1] (1944) 44
18. CS, *Reg. Richard de Swinfield* (1909) 58-61; *Camden Soc.* (Old Ser., 1853) 232-36; Dew, E.N., *Hereford Cathedral Registers* (1932) 24-5; Williams (1976) 1-2
19. Williams (1966) 84-6
20. Williams, D.H., 'Fasti Cistercienses Cambrenses', *Bull. Board Celtic Studies* 24:2 (May, 1971) 181-229; 25:2 (May, 1973) 156-57
21. Harper-Bill, C., 'Cistercian Visitation', *Bull. Inst. Hist Research*, 53 (1980) 105-06
22. PRO, E 326/B. 12582
23. *op. cit.*, note 21, 105-06
24. Jack, R. Ian., *Medieval Wales* (1972) 122
25. Ker, N.R., *Medieval Libraries of Great Britain* (1964) 58; Williams (1966) 99
26. Mynors, R.A.B. and Thomson, R.M., *Catalogue of the Manuscripts of Hereford Cathedral Library* (1993) P.v.5
27. Trinity Coll. Cambridge, MS 1272
28. BL, Egerton MS 3088
29. BL, Harleian MS 218; Watson, A.G., 'A book belonging to Thomas Cleubery', *TWNFC* XL (1970) 133-36; Williams (1976) 26.
30. Appendix 1 *(infra)*

31. Hereford Cathedral Library MS P.i.13; Bannister, A.T., 'Miraculous Happenings at Dore', *TWNFC* (1927-29) 209-11
32. *op. cit.,* note 21, 105-06
33. Appendix 2
34. PRO, E 321/32, f. 84; Williams (1976) 29-30
35. Williams (1976) 8-9
36. Williams (1984) I, 30
37. Brewer, J.S. (ed.), *Giraldus Cambrensis, Opera* 4, R.S. (1873) 220-23; cf. *Statuta* I, 111 (1189/3), 295 (1204/2)
38. *op. cit.,* note 37, IV, 192-3
39. Hardy, D.T. (ed), *Descriptive Catalogue of MSS relating to the History of Great Britain and Ireland* III (1871) 31; Talbot, C.H., 'Cadogan of Bangor', *Citeaux* 9 (1959) 19; *cf.* Gibson, Matthew., *Churches of Door, Home Lacy and Hampstead* (1727) 16
40. *Statuta* I, 472 (1217/30)
41. *Monasticon,* (1846) 555
42. Williams (1976) 10-11, *cf.* Sumption, J., *Pilgrimage* (1975) 139, 156-57
43. Peterhouse, Cambridge, MS 119 (pencilled footnote at base of page 111); Harper, C.G., *Abbeys of Old Romance* (1930) 268-69
44. PRO, E 326/B. 12582; Cowley (1977) 122-23; Williams (1984) I, 28; BL, Add. MS 4533, f. 120b
45. Talbot, C.H. *op. cit.,* note 39, 19
46. *Statuta* II, 206 (1239/20)
47. *The Reliquary* (Jan. 1903); Hereford City Libr., Hill MSS III, 228; Marshall, A., 'Wooden Monumental Effigies', *TWNFC* (1918-20) 189-97
48. PRO, C. 115/D. 19/1895
49. *Cal. Patent Rolls* 1265/429, 1266/660
50. PRO, E 135/6, m.9
51. PRO, SC 1/11
52. *Statuta* III, 118, (1273/12)
53. Williams (1976) 11
54. PRO, E 315/40, m, 146
55. *Cal. Patent Rolls* 1265/431
56. *Cal. Close Rolls I*1272/2
57. Appendix 1
58. CS, 65 (1968) *Register of John Peckham,* II. 182-84
59. Talbot, C.H., 'Richard Straddell', *Downside Review* (Jan. 1943) 18-20
60. Appendix 3
61. Brownbill, J. (edit), *The Ledger Book of Vale Royal,* Lancashire and Cheshire Rec. Soc. 68 (1914) 6
62. *Cal. Close Rolls* 1321/367
63. *Cal. Close Rolls* 1321/404
64. *Cal. Patent Rolls* 1327/95
65. Haines, R.M., (ed), *Reg. Adam de Orleton,* Worcs Hist. Soc. N.S. 10 : Hist MSS Comm, 27 (1979) 112 (No. 449)
66. *Cal. Close Rolls* 1335/518; *cf.* Williams (1976) 17-8
67. PRO, E 101/311, mm. 11, 17; transcribed in Williams (1966) 92
68. *Cal. Patent Rolls* 1330/513, *Cal. Close Rolls* 1335/370
69. Leland, J., *Commentarii de Scriptoribus Britannicis* (1709) 329
70. Sledmere (1914) 18; (Sledmere quotes the Welsh work, *Llyfr Baglan,* as saying that one Sir Robert Wroth, knight, built a great part of the abbey)
71. *Cal. Patent Rolls* 1396/30, 106; Williams (1976) 19
72. *Papal Registers (Letters)* V, 167, 302
73. *Cal. Patent Rolls* 1403/438
74. *Cal. Patent Rolls* 1398/362
75. PRO, SC 8/213/10624
76. Williams (1984) I, 75-6
77. *Cal. Patent Rolls* 1405/65
78. *Cal. Close Rolls* 1410, 44, 449; cf. 1411/160, 450
79. *Statuta* IV, 157 (1411/85)
80. Bannister, A. T. (ed.), *Register of Thomas Spofford* (CY, 1917) 186-88
81. Williams, D. H., 'Gwent Seals, VI', *Monmouths Antiq, 10* (1994) 21-3
82. Williams (1976) 21-2
83. Jones, G. H, 'Celtic Britain and the Pilgrim Movement,' *Y Cymmrodor,* 23 (1912) 376-77
84. *Statuta* V, 185 (1466/33)
85. *Cal. Patent Rolls* 1453
86. Williams (1976) 21
87. *Statuta* V, 280 (1471/10)
88. PRO, C 1/304, m. 38)
89. PRO, C 1/304, m. 34, 36
90. PRO, E 315/35, f. 29
91. PRO, E 315/238, ff. 72, 75d; Blashill, T., 'Abbeydore', *TWNFC* (1886-89) 9
92. PRO, E 315/35, f. 29 of 1490); *Cal. Papal Registers (Letters)* XVIII, 493 (No. 714, of 1506)
93. PRO, E 111/28; SP 1/231, f.24; 1/240, f. 223; Williams (1966) 91
94. PRO, E 315/405, f. 22
95. PRO, E 315/405, f. 20
96. PRO, E 315/405, f. 21; E 315/51, f. 229; Williams (1976) 23
97. PRO, E 111/28
98. PRO, E 315/39, f. 43
99. PRO, E 315/19, f. 17; cf. E 111/24
100. PRO, E 315/405, ff. 22-25.
101. Williams (1976) 24-5
102. PRO, C 1/899, ff. 14-15
103. PRO, Stac. 2/26, m. 163
104. PRO, SC 6 (Henry VIII)/ 7319, m. 17d; Williams (1966) 98
105. Bodleian Libr. Oxford, Tanner MS 334, f. 1; Hereford Cathedral Archive 5602; Williams (1976) 54 (n.135)
106. Williams (1976) 27
107. PRO, E 315/51, f. 53; Williams (1984) I, 101
108. Williams (1976) 35
109. PRO, E 318/875, f9
110. Williams (1976) 35
111. Williams (1990) 118 (Fig. 36b)
112. PRO, SC 6 (Henry VIII)/ 7319, m. 10r
113. Williams (1976) 324 (map of grange boundaries), 36; Llyncoed was granted by Henry III and Hubert de Burgh in return for obit Masses sung in the abbey church by 'four priest-monks'.
114. Williams (1976) 36

115. *Ibid.* 36; *Council for Brit Archaeol* (Group12, Wales) Report (1973) 49
116. Williams (1976) 33, 36
117. *Ibid.* 33; *cf.* PRO, E 326B. 12453 (Licence in mortmain)
118. *Monasticon,* V, 557; *cf.* PRO, E 315/287, f6
119. At HRO, pub. by Herefordshire Field-Name Survey
120. Williams (1976) 33-35
121. Bannister, A. T., *History of Ewyas Harold* (1902) 47
122. Williams (1976) 71-2
123. *Ibid.* 39; (the abbey's grange here was formed by enclosing part of the 'pasture of Benfield'
124. *Ibid.* 39
125. *Monasticon* (1846) 555b
126. *Catal. Ancient Deeds* I, 277 (B. 673)
127. PRO, E 315/43, f. 62
128. *Catal. Ancient Deeds* II, 396 (B. 3372)
129. Williams (1976) 39
130. *Catal. Ancient Deeds* I, 250 (B. 379)
131. *Catal. Ancient Deeds* I, 337 (B. 1275)
132. Williams (1976) 37; *Cal. Charter Rolls* I, 1241/ 261; it was a holding referred to as 'Gwern Devog' in the 16th century
133. Edwards, J. Goronwy, *Littere Wallie* (1940) 101
134. Williams (1976) 37-8
135. *Catal. Ancient Deeds* I, 282 (B. 727)
136. PRO, E 326/ B. 11586., *cf.* B. 8398
137. Williams (1976) 38
138. Owen, E., *op. cit.* IV (1922) 902 (No. 1766: BL, Addit. MS 4505), cf. (No. 1766b) Addit. MS 4527
139. *Monasticon* (1846) 555-56
140. *Cal. Charter Rolls* 1327/14-5
141. *Cal. Ancient Deeds* III, 294 (B. 4106); *cf.* PRO, E 315/53. f. 160
142. PRO, E 326/5541
143. Williams (1976) 40; *cf. Cal. Close Rolls* 1265/ 126
144. PRO, E 329/B.S. 469; *cf.* E 326/B. 4100
145. PRO, E 315/52. f. 98
146. PRO, E 111/28
147. PRO, SC 6 (Henry VIII)/ 7319, m. 13r
148. PRO, E 315/238, mm. 58-87; *cf.* E 303/5, ff. 88-130
149. Williams ('976) 40
150. Williams (1976) 40-1
151. PRO, SC 6 (Henry VIII) m. 8r; Williams (1966) 95-6
152. *Ibid.* m. 9r; Williams (1966) 96
153. Williams (1976) 42-5
154. *Cal. Patent Rolls* 1351/188, 1352/308; PRO, DL/ LS 326; *Reg Bishop Norbury* (Staffs Rec Soc. O. S.) I, 281
155. *Cal Chancery Warrants* 320, PRO, C 143/81/3; *Monasticon* (1846) V, 554
156. Williams (1976) 44
157. *Cal. Close Rolls* 1446/443-44
158. Bannister, A. T.(ed), *Register of Adam de Orleton* (CY, 1907) 144
159. *Op. cit.,* note 65,143 (No. 611)
160. *Op. cit.,* note 65, 197
161. *Op. cit.,* note 65, 148-49 (No. 634)
162. *Op. cit.,* note 65, 202-04; *cf.* Parry, J. H. (ed), *Reg. John de Trillek* (1911-12); 122; Bannister, A. T. (ed), *Reg. Charles Bothe* (1921) 297-300
163. PRO, SC 6 (Henry VIII) 7319, m. 17r; *Cal. Papal Registers (Letters)* II, 321
164. *Op. cit.,* note 65, 103-04 (No. 396), *cf.* 168 (No. 767), 178 (No. 839)
165. *Cal. Patent Rolls* 1327/20; Staffs Rec. Soc. O.S. I, 256;Williams (1976) 43-4
166. *Cal. Papal Registers* (Letters) 167; *Monasticon* (1846) 554b
167. Williams (1976) 44
168. PRO, SC 6 (Henry VIII)/7319, m. 18r; *Monasticon* (1846) 556
169. PRO, E 315, 238, f. 64
170. PRO, E 303/50, m. 96
171. PRO, SP 1/240, f. 224; Williams (1966) 91
172. Williams (1976) 45
173. PRO, E 326/ B. 5539
174. *Statuta* III, 118 (1273/13)
175. *Statuta* III, 210 (1281/21)
176. *Cal. Close Rolls* 1295/447
177. *Cal. Close Rolls* 1340/641
178. Williams (1976) 45
179. *Ibid.* 45; in 1477 three tenants alone owed over £160 to the abbey
180. *Valor Ecclesiasticus* (Record Commission) III (1817) 33
181. *Monasticon* (1846) 556; *Cal. Charter Rolls* 1, 261
182. *Monasticon* (1846) 556
183. *Cal. Charter Rolls* 1, 2-3; also 1265/55, 1327/14; cf. Brewer, J.S. (ed), *Giraldus Cambrensis, Opera* 4, RS (1873) 186-92
184. *Cal. Close Rolls* 1254/58
185. *Monasticon,* (1846) 553-54, 557
186. PRO, E 318/2, f. 30
187. NGR: 407353
188. Williams (1976) 47
189. *Monasticon* (1846) V, 553a
190. *Cal. Charter Rolls* 1327/14
191. Owen, E. (ed) *Catalogue of MSS relating to Wales in the British Museum,* 4 vols (1900-22) 3 (1908) 538 (No.803), 192
192. *Monasticon,* (1846) 557.
193. Harper-Bill, *op. cit.* 105.
194. E 303/5/101, C 115/D 19/1898, C 115/D 21/ 1936
195. Williams (1966) 93
196. *Catal. Ancient Deeds* I, B. 36
197. Williams (1976) 48
198. *Ibid.* 48
199. *Monasticon* (1846) 556
200. University of Kansas - Spencer Research Library, Dept. of Special Collections, MS Flat (Abbey Dore Collection) 1/10
201. *Cal. Charter Rolls* 1, 121
202. *Monasticon* (1846) 554, 556
203. *Monasticon (1846)* 556; Owen, *op.cit.* note 191 533 (No 792)
204. PRO, E 315/41, f. 148
205. PRO, E 326/ B. 871
206. Evans, A. (ed.) Pegolotti, F.B., *La Pratica della Mercatura* (1936) 261

207. Williams (1976) 49
208. *Cal. Close Rolls* 1216/3
209. PRO, E 326/ B. 9234
210. *Cal. Close Rolls* 1275/254
211. PRO, E 326/ B. 5539
212. PRO, E 326/ B. 5527
213. PRO, E 315/40, f. 231
214. PRO, E 315/54, f. 30
215. *Cal. Patent Rolls* 1233/32
216. Paul (1904a) 125
217. *Cal. Charter Rolls* 1265/55, 1327/14
218. Williams (1976) 50
219. *Monasticon* (1846) 556
220. *Monasticon* (1846) 555b
221. *Cal. Charter Rolls* 1, 347
222. PRO, E 315/54, f. 209
223. PRO, E 315/48, f. 293
224. *Cal. Ancient Deeds* I, 339 (B. 1294)
225. *Statuta* I, 251-52 (1200/15, 17)
226. PRO, E 326/B.8850
227. Williams, D.H., *Catalogue of Seals in the National Museum of Wales*, I (1993) 16.
228. *Archaeologia* 21, 542; *Gentleman's Magazine* 81I (1806): 2) 212, 793; *Soc Antiq Cat* (1847) 28; *Loc. cit.,* note 227, M 68; Douët D'Arcq, M., *Collection Des Sceaux De L'Empire* III (1868) 8699, draws attention to a Jordan, abbot of Dorat in France
229. *Monasticon* (1846) 553

CHAPTER IV (The Opus Dei)

1. *RIBA Kalendar*, 1890 176-8
2. Paul's plans are in: Paul (1893), (1898), (1904a), (1927) & (1931)
3. *The Builder* (8 Nov. 1935) 812 & (15 Nov. 1935) 859; another brief obituary was published in *Bristol Evening Post* (29 Oct. 1935). On Bristol Cathedral see Paul, R.W., 'Description & Plan of the Church & Monastery of St. Augustine, Bristol, *Archaeologia*, 63 (1911-12)
4. Paul's further reports and comments are in the standard abbreviations
5. *Loc.cit.* notes 2 & 4
6. Dimier, M.A., *Recueil de Plans d'Églises Cisterciennes*, 2 vols (Commission d'Histoire de l'ordre de Citeaux, Paris 1949) & *Supplément,* 2 parts (Paris 1967). The same comment applies to Dimier's *l'Art Cistercien: France* (3rd ed. la Pierre qui Vire, 1982)
7. St John Hope, W.A., 'The Abbey of St Mary in Furness, Lancashire' *Trans Cumb and West Antiq & Archaeol Soc,* 16 (1900) plan facing 302; Russell, J.C., *Dictionary of Writers of Thirteenth Century England,* Bull Inst Hist Research Suppl, 3 (1936) 4; Chad, D.F.L., 'Liturgy and Liturgical Music: the limits of uniformity' in Norton & Park, (1986) 305; *Statuta* (1933) 472; Williams (1976) 31 quoting PRO, C115/D21/1937
8. At the German house of Maulbronn the great rood, carved by Conrad von Sinsheim in 1473, still exists, a rare survival
9. Vallance, A., *Greater English Church Screens* (1947) 89-91, 99-100, 121-2
10. Hillaby (1987) 642-4

11. Walbran, J.R., *A Guide to Ripon, Fountains Abbey ... & of several places of interest in their vicinity* (1875), 107-8; St. John Hope, W.H., 'Fountains Abbey,' *Yorks Archaeol J.*. 15 (1900) 307-8 on rather similar arrangements excavated at the secular cathedrals of York, Lincoln and Wells
12. Paul (1931) 500; Paul (1927) 270-1; Paul (1896) 299
13. For discussion of French *porches* see Aubert, M., *L'Architecture Cistercienne en France,* I (1947) 364-5
14. For Dore's polygonal chapter house see Hillaby (1989) 209-45; For the 'certain chamber,' see Haines, R.M., (ed) *Cal. Reg Adam de Orleton, 1327-33,* Worcs Hist Soc/Hist MSS Comm (1979) 148 no. 634.

CHAPTER V (Architectural History)

1. Fergusson, P. *Architecture of Solitude: Cistercian Abbeys in Twelfth-Century England* (1984) 128
2. Wilson, C. 'The Cistercians as "missionaries of Gothic" in Northern England' in Norton. & Park (1986) 86-116
3. Malone, (1984) 50-75
4. Brakspear, H. 'A West Country School of Masons' *Archaeologia*, 81 (1931) 1-18
5. Esser, K.H. 'Uber den Kirchenbau des Hl. Bernhard von Clairvaux' *Archiv fur Mittelrheinische Kirchengeschichte*, 5 (1953) 195-222
6. *Loc. cit.,* note 1.
7. *Loc. cit.,* note 1, 84, 129
8. *Loc. cit.,* note 1, 139-40, 152
9. Gilyard-Beer, R. and Coppack, G. 'Excavations at Fountains Abbey, North Yorkshire, 1979-80: the Early Development of the Monastery' *Archaeologia*, 108 (1986) 147-88
10. Wilson, C. 'The Sources of the Late Twelfth-Century Work at Worcester Cathedral' *Medieval Art and Architecture at Worcester Cathedral, Brit Archaeol Ass Conf Tran,* 1975 (1978) pl. XIVc
11. *Loc. cit.,* note 1, pl.12
12. O'Callaghan, (1995), 97, pl.XIB
13. *Loc. cit.,* note 12, 97
14. Halsey, R. 'The earliest architecture of the Cistercians in England' in Norton & Park, 1986, 72-3; Thurlby, M. 'The Romanesque Priory Church of St. Michael at Ewenny' *Jnl Soc of Archit Historians*, 47 (1988) 281-94
15. Evans, D.H. 'Further Excavation and Fieldwork at Llanthony Priory, Gwent' *Monmouths Antiq* 5 (1982-4) 7
16. Paul (1904) 120-1
17. Thurlby, M. 'St. Andrews Cathedral-Priory and the Beginings of Gothic Architecture in Northern Britain' *Medieval Art and Architecture in the Diocese of St. Andrews: Brit Archaeol Ass Conf Trans* 1986 (1994) 47-60
18. Eydoux, H-P. 'L'église abbatiale de Morimond' *Bulletin Monumental,* 115 (1956) 25
19. Colchester, L.S. and Harvey, J.H. 'Wells cathe-

20. *Loc. cit.,* note 10
21. *Loc. cit.,* note 3, 52
22. *Loc. cit.,* note 12, 22
23. *Loc. cit.,* note 1, pls 7 & 32
24. Jalabert, D. 'La flore gothique: ses origines, son evolution' *Bulletin Monumental,* 91 (1932), 181-246 esp. 190-9; Jalabert, D. *La flore sculptée des monuments du moyen age en France* (1965) 96-8
25. Halsey, R. The 12th-Century Church of St. Frideswide's Priory' *Oxoniensia,* 43 (1988) 131-2
26. *Loc. cit.,* note 10, 80-90
27. Thurlby, M. 'The Lady Chapel of Glastonbury Abbey' *Antiq J,* 75 (1995) 107-70
28. Willis, R. 'The crypt and chapter house of Worcester Cathedral' *Trans RIBA,* 1st Ser., 13 (1862-3) 222, reprinted in *Architectural History of some English Cathedrals* II (Chicheley, 1973)
29. Willis, R. *The Architectural History of Canterbury Cathedral* (London, 1845) 60, reprinted in *Architectural History of some English Cathedrals* I (1972)
30. Paul (1931)
31. Paul (1893) 266 & 267
32. Paul (1896) 299
33. *Loc. cit.,* note 30
34. *Loc. cit.,* note 32, 298
35. Thurlby, M. & Kusaba, Y. 'The Nave of St. Andrew at Steyning and Design Variety in Romanesque Architecture in Britain,' *Gesta,* XXX/2 (1991) 163-175
36. Harrison, S., Lewis, J., Park, D., Robinson, D. and Turner, R. 'Strata Florida Abbey' (forthcoming)
37. Bony, J. 'The Resistance to Chartres in Early Thirteenth-Century Architecture,' *J Brit Archaeol Ass,* 20-21 (1957-8) 48, pl. XXV 1 & 2)
38. Gem, R. 'The Bishop's Chapel at Hereford: the Roles of Patron and Craftsman' in Macready S. & Thompson, F.H. (eds.) *Art and Patronage in the English Romanesque* (London, 1986) 87-96; Halsey, R. 'Tewkesbury Abbey: some recent observations' *Medieval Art and Architecture at Gloucester and Tewkesbury: Brit Archaeol Ass Conf Trans* 1981 (1985) 16-35
39. Norton & Park (1986)
40. *Loc. cit.,* note 1
41. *Loc. cit.,* note 32
42. Shoesmith, R., 'Survey work at Abbey Dore' *TWNFC,* 43 (1981) 255-66
43. Tudor-Craig, P., in Alexander, J. and Binski, P. (eds) *Age of Chivalry: Art in Plantagenet England 1200-1400* (1987) 320, cat. 289
44. Dawton, N., in Alexander and Binski (*Loc. cit.,* note 43) 233, cat. 101
45. Heslop, T.A., in Alexander and Binski (*Loc. cit.,* note 43) 316-9
46. Griffiths, R.G. and Capes, W.W. (eds) *Registrum Thome de Cantilupo, Episcopi Herefordensis* (1907)
47. Hillaby (1989) 209-45
48. *Loc. cit.,* note 4
49. *Loc. cit.,* note 1, 75
50. Harrison, S. *Byland Abbey* (1990)

51. Fergusson, P. and Harrison, S. 'The Rievaulx Abbey Chapter House' *Antiquaries* J, 74 (1994) 211-55
52. Stalley, R. and Thurlby, M. 'The Early Gothic Choir of Pershore Abbey' *J of the Soc of Architectural Historians,* 48 (1989) 351-70, fig. 15
53. *Loc. cit.,* note 4
54. *Loc. cit.,* note 52, fig. 26
55. Hoey, L. 'Pier Alternation in Early English Gothic Architecture *J of the British Archaeol Assn,* 139 (1986) 45-67; Hoey, L. 'Piers versus vault shafts in Early English Gothic Architecture' *J of the Soc of Architectural Historians,* 46 (1987) 241-64;
56. *Loc. cit.,* note 12, 102-3
57. *Loc. cit.,* note 52, 368-9
58. Thurlby, M. 'The Early Gothic Transepts of Lichfield Cathedral' *Medieval Archaeology and Architecture at Lichfield, Brit Archaeol Ass Conf Trans* 1987 (1993) 50-64
59. Park, D. 'Cistercian wall painting and panel painting' in Norton and Park (1986) 181-210
60. Tristram, E.W. *English Medieval Wall Painting*: The Thirteenth Century, 2 vols (1950)
61. *Loc. cit.,* note 50
62. *Loc. cit.,* note 32
63. Paul (1893) 267; Geddes, J. 'Cistercian metalwork in England' in Norton & Park (1986) 256-65

CHAPTER VI (The Loose Architectural Detail)

1. Blashill (1885) 368
2. Paul's papers and drawings in the Library of the Society of Antiquaries
3. Blashill(1885) 368-369
4. *Op. cit,* note 2
5. *Op. cit,* note 2
6. Paul(1904a) 122-3
7. *Op. cit,* note 2 annotated sketch plan
8. Paul (1931)
9. Robinson, D., *Tintern Abbey Guide* (1995) 48
10. *Op. cit,* note 2 annotated sketch plan
11. Paul (1896) 299
12. Paul (1904a) 120
13. *Op. cit,* note 2
14. *Op. cit,* note 2 annotated sketch plan
15. Paul (1896) 299
16. Paul (1902b)
17. Williams (1966) 66
18. Paul (1902b)
19. Biddle, M., 'Restoring the Shrine,' *The Alban Link,* 1992, 7-13
20. Adair J. *The Pilgrim Way : Shrines and Saints in Britain and Ireland* (1978) 15
21. Paul(1927) 271
22. Paul(1931) 500
23. *Op. cit,* note 2
24. Paul (1931) 500

Chapter VII (The Medieval Floor Tiles)

1. Ward-Perkins, J.B., English Medieval Embossed Tiles, *Archaeol. J.,* 104, 128-53; Vince, A.G., 'The Medieval Ceramic Industry of the Severn Valley,' (Unpublished PhD thesis, University of Southampton, 1984) Ch. 3.

2. Vince, A.G. & Wilmott, T., A Lost Tile Pavement at Tewkesbury Abbey and an Early Fourteenth-Century Tile Factory, *Antiq. J.*, 71 (1991) 138-173

3. Vince, A.G., 'The ceramic finds', in Shoesmith, R. (ed.)., *Hereford City Excavations: The Finds,* Vol. 3. (1985) 34-82

4. Chatwin, P.B., The Medieval Patterned Tiles of Warwickshire, *Trans. Birmingham Warwickshire Arch. Soc.*, LX, (1936) 1-41, Fig. 3

5. *Op. cit.* Fig 5.1

6. *Op. cit.* Plate 1

7. *Op. cit.* p. 8, Figs. 7.3 & 7.4

CHAPTER VIII (People in the Abbey)

1. Rouse, C. E., *Medieval Wall Paintings*, (1991)

2. Account of the appeal given in *The Hereford Times*, 1 June 1901. This view was mistaken as the stone of the walls was not intended to be seen by the original builders.

3. The figure of Time in particular has been heavily restored in Dore

4. The existence of a 'shrine' is debatable

5. Paul (1896)

6. Sledmere (1914) 55

7. Williams (1976) 13

8. *Loc. cit.* note 5. The stone is also mentioned in *Arch. Camb.* XV.; Sledmere (1914) 81

9. Williams (1976) 1

10. Williams (1976); Coplestone-Crow, B., The Fief of Alfred of Marlborough in Herefordshire, *TWNFC*, (1986) 387

11. Williams (1976) 13

12. *Loc. cit.* note 5; Pevsner (1963) 312

13. Williams (1976) 18

14. Sledmere (1914) 18

15. Sledmere (1914) 40; Walford,W.S., On a Diminutive Effigy of a Bishop at Abbey Dore, Herefordshire, *Arch. J.*, (1862) 24-31

16. Compare the drawings in Sledmere (1914) 5 & 40

17. Davies, J.G. (ed.) *A New Dictionary of Liturgy & Worship,* (1986) 248 says: "The elevation itself was first formally recognised in 1210 when the Bishop of Paris ordered that before the 'consecration' the bread should not be held more than breast-high, and only after the words 'This is my body' should the host be raised high enough for everyone to see."

18. *Op. cit.* 536; Skilbeck, C.O., *The Vestments,* (1948). I am most grateful to Rev. Kay Garlick for her help

19. Sledmere (1914) 60, quotes an account of 1602 when the inscription was legible

20. Fryer, A. C., Monumental Effigies made by Bristol Craftsmen (1240-1550), *Archaeologia* 74,(1925) 17

21. Moir, A.L., *Bishops of Hereford*, (1964) 24

22. Sledmere (1914) dates them to late thirteenth century, Pevsner, N., *Buildings of Herefordshire* (1963) 61, to early fourteenth century.

23. Halliday, F.E., *Cultural History of England* (1967) 67, shows an example of Christ with hand on an orb from the early fourteenth century East Anglian Book of Hours in the Fitzwilliam Museum, Cambridge. It is a fairly common motif of the time

24. *Op. cit.* 71 concerning Psalters of the East Anglian School of *c*.1280-1340

25. Sledmere (1914) 55

26. Addleshaw, G.W.O., & Etchells, F., *The Architectural Setting of Anglian Worship,* (1948)

27. Laver, J.A., *A Consise History of Costume,* (1982); Houston, M.G., *Medieval Costume in England and France,* (1950)

28. Sledmere (1914) 55

29. John Leland was told about him—Williams (1976) 14-18, 42-43; see also the list of abbots. Richard of Madeley (Madley?) was abbot 1305-1312 followed by Richard Straddell 1312-1346. It is not known for certain if this was the same man—if it was, it is interesting to know Straddell's home area

30. It was featured in the 'Age of Chivalry' Exhibition in London in 1987/88 and later in Paris.

31. Sledmere (1914) 56

32. Attwater, D., *The Penguin Dictionary of Saints* (1965) 209, 350

33. Sledmere (1914) 59

34. Harvey, J., *Medieval Craftsmen,* (1975) 134

35. *Loc. cit.*, note 20, 27

36. *Loc. cit.*, note 20, 26

37. *Loc. cit.*, note 20, 27, 63

38. Research by the Church Monuments Society. See also Tummers, H.A., *Early Secular Effigies in England. The Thirteenth Century* (Leiden, 1980); Stone, L., *Sculpture in Britain: The Middle Ages* (1955)

39. *Loc. cit.*, note 20, 30, 64

40. Stolen between July and August 1985. The replica was kindly made and donated in 1995 by Simon Armstrong, stone-mason of Wells Cathedral

41. Hillaby (1985) 245. John of Monmouth died 1248 so this tomb would have been the earlier.

42. *Loc. cit.*, note 20, 21

43. Personal comments by B Coplestone-Crow & Rev. D.H. Williams

44. Williams (1976) 1

45. Skidmore, W., *The Scudamores of Upton Scudamore, a Knightly Family in Medieval Wiltshire, 1086-1382,* 2nd edn. (1989) 29, 70

46. Williams (1976) 1; *Loc. cit.*, note 10, Coplestone-Crow, 387

47. *Liber Feodorum: Book of Fees, Part 1, 1198-1242* (PRO)

48. Hillaby (1985) 247; Blount, T., 'MSS collections for Herefordshire,' (no. 358 in HRO, B56/12) says 'She *(Sybil)* was first married to Robert de Tregoz, whom she survived, and in 2 Hen. 3 *(1218)* gave nyne Hundred Marks fine to the King, that she might enjoy her Dower, and not be compelled to marry, but where Herself pleased whereupon she took Roger de Clifford for her second Husband.'

49. Hillaby (1989) 229

50. Hillaby (1985) 250; Three marks equal £1. The approximate equivalent to £1 in 1290 is £550 today; Jancey, M. (ed.) *St. Thomas Cantilupe, Bishop of Hereford,* (1982) 147

51. Hillaby (1985) 250
52. Taken from Hillaby (1984); Hillaby (1985); Cople-stone-Crow (1986); Williams (1976); *Loc. cit.* note 50; Walker, D., The Register of the Churches of the Monastery of St Peter's, Gloucester ... , *BGAS* Records Section (1976); pers. res. by Remfry, P., & Taylor, E., (with grateful thanks)
53. Hillaby (1984) 404: *Loc. cit.*, note 48, Blount says Sybil 'dyed about 20 Hen. 3 *(1236)* leaving Robert de Tregoz her son and Heyr by her first Husband.'
54. *Loc. cit.*, note 50, 15
55. *Loc. cit.*, note 50, 15
56. *Loc. cit.*, note 50, 80
57. *Loc. cit.*, note 50, 77
58. Grant made by Sir John de Tregoz, 19 Oct. 1268 *Descriptive Catalogue of Ancient Deeds in PRO*, 6 vols, (1890-1915) 3, C3025) (info. E Taylor)
59. *Loc. cit.*, note 50, 14
60. *Loc. cit.*, note 58
61. Williams (1976) 7
62. *Loc. cit.*, note 21, 23
63. *Loc. cit.*, note 21, 25
64. Williams (1976) 14
65. Williams (1976) 14
66. Hillaby (1985) 251
67. Hillaby (1984) 404
68. Hillaby (1985) 251
69. Williams (1976) 14

CHAPTER IX (Cults, Patrons and Sepulture)
1. Baddeley, St Clair., 'The Holy Blood of Hayles,' *TBGAS*, 23 (1900) 276-84; Brakspear, H., 'The Architecture of Hayles Abbey', *TBGAS*, 24 (1901) 126-35; Denholm-Young, N., *Richard of Cornwall* (1947), 174, quoting Hailes Annals from *MGH*, 16, 483 (see note 6)
2. Stalley, R., *The Cistercian Monasteries of Ireland*, (1987) 115-9: Leask, H.G., 'Holy Cross Abbey,' *Archaeol J.*, 117 (1960) 168-70; Leask, H.G., *Irish Churches and Monastic Buildings*, 3 (1960) 64-7; Gwynn, A. & Hadcock, R.N., *Medieval Religious Houses: Ireland* (1988) 135; Champneys, H., *Irish Ecclesiastical Architecture* (1919 reprinted 1970) 175. A fragment in a silver case of medieval date with the arms of Butler and de Burgo at the base is described in Crawford, H.S., 'A descriptive list of Irish Shrines and Reliquaries,' *J Ryl Soc Antiq Irld*, 103 (1923) 89-90; Comerford, M., 'Relic of the Holy Cross ... in the Ursuline Convent, Blackrock, Cork,' *Ossory Archaeol Soc*, 1 (1874-9) 130-35
3. Dore Annals *sa* 1321 in Pertz, G. (ed.) *Monumenta Germanicae Historica Scriptores*, 27 (1805) 514-31
4. On the Grandison brothers generally: G.E.C. (okayne) *CompletePeerage*, 6 (1926) 60-5, 69-73; Kingsford, C.L., 'Sir Otho de Grandison, 1238?-1328?,' *Trans Ryl Hist Soc*, 3 (1909) 125-95; Colvin, H.M., (ed.) *The History of the King's Works*, 1 (1963) 244, 371, 377; Prestwich, M., *Edward I* (1988) 22
5. *Complete Peerage*, 6 (60-65); *Loc. cit.* note 4, Kingsford, 140-71; Smith, 1 (1964) 236. For

Bishop John de Grandison as a major patron of the arts see Smith, 1 (1964) 236; Pevsner, N., *S. Devon* (1952) 135, 218-23
6. *Complete Peerage*, 6 (1926) 69-73; *Loc. cit.* note 4, Kingsford, 140-71; Holder-Egger, O., (ed.), *Chronica S Bertini, Monumenta Germaniae Historica: Scriptores*, 25 (1880) 856
7. Runciman, S., *A History of the Crusades III: The Kingdom of Acre* (1954) 413-9; 'Acre: A Crusader City' in Riley-Smith, J., (ed.) *Atlas of the Crusades* (1991) 102-3
8. Capes, W.W., (ed.) *Charters and Records of Hereford Cathedral* (1908) 186, 195; Haynes, R.M., *The Church & Politics in Fourteenth Century England* (1978) 8, 20-5, 48-9
9. O' Sullivan, J.F., *Cistercian Settlements in Wales and Monmouthshire* (1947); Donnelly, J.S., *The decline of the Medieval Cistercian Laybrotherhood* (1949) & 'Changes in the Grange Economy of English and Welsh Cistercian Abbeys, 1300-1500,' *Traditio*, 10 (1954) 399-458; Donkin, R.A., 'Cattle on the Estates of Medieval Cistercian Monasteries in England and Wales,' *Ecc Hist Rev*, 15 (1962) 31-53; Cowley (1977) 83-89, 117-21. On drunkeness and general indiscipline see Hillaby, (1989), 227 & 233; *Statuta* (1933), 123, 138, 149, 191, 193, 181.
10. Fergusson, P., *Roche Abbey* (1990) 11
11. Aubert, M., *L'Architecture Cistercienne en France*, 2 (1947) 330-36; Smith, 5 (1964) 178; Marshall, G., 'Wormsley Church,' *TWNFC* (1926) 161
12. *Loc. cit.*, note 1, Denholm-Young, 112, 151; Roche, T.W.E., *The King of Almayne* (1966), 166-168; Bazeley, W., 'The Abbey of St. Mary, Hailes,' *TBGAS*, 22 (1899) 257-8;. Baddesley, St Clair, 'Richard, Earl of Cornwall and Henry of Almaine,' *TBGAS*, 22 (1899) 111-14
13. Coppack, G., *Fountains Abbey* (1993) 64-7
14. Barrow, J. (ed.) *English Episcopal Acta VII : Hereford 1079-1234*, (1993) 254-5; Williams (1976) 35
15. *Monasticon* (1846) 557; Haines, R.M. (ed.) *Cal Reg Adam de Orleton, Bishop of Worcester 1327-1333*, (Hist. MSS Comm JP 27, 1979) 143, no.611
16. Smith (1964) 178;
17. *Monasticon* (1846) 554; Smith, 5 (1964) 168; Bannister, A.T., (ed.) *Orleton Reg*, CS (1908) 386; Sanders, I.J., *English Baronies: A Study of their Origin and Descent 1086-1327*, (1960), 73-4; *Complete Peerage*, 10 (1945) 555. Leland wrongly describes her as the daughter of the Earl of Hereford and has her married to John de Kilpeck. See also Melland Hale, J., 'Haresfield: Manors and Church,' *TBGAS*, 19 (1894-5) 288-90. In 1319 Alan II was negotiating with the dean and chapter of Hereford cathedral for exchange of his church of Lugwardine for Holme Lacy, a manor with a lengthily troubled history; *Orleton Reg* 95-6. *Loc. cit.*, note 8, Capes, 208-9, 210-15; Capes, W.W. (ed.) *Thomas de Charlton Reg* CS (1918) vii on significance of the grant.

18. *Cal Patent Rolls, 1319,* 347; *Cal Charter Rolls, 1327,* 15; *Op. cit.,* note 17, *Orleton Reg* 144, 174, 197, 202-4, 387; *Loc. cit., note 15,* Haines, 143, 148.

19. *Cal Close Rolls, (1296-1302)* 477; *Cal Fine Rolls (1272-1307)* 432, 435; *Cal Inq Post Mortem (1291-1300)* no.603; *(1316-27)* no.249; *(1327-36)* no,676; *(1336-47)* no.51; *Complete Peerage,* 12 (1959) 22 note e

20.*Loc. cit.,* note 8, Capes, 208-215, 229-230; *Loc. cit.,* note 17, Capes, *Charlton Reg.* 16-17, 34-40. For the quality of Joanna de Bohun's tomb in the Hereford cathedral Lady Chapel see Gee, L., '14th century Tombs for Women in Herefordshire,' *Medieval Art, Architechture and Archaeology at Hereford, Brit Archaeol Ass Conf Trans* (1995) 132-137; Pevsner, N., *Herefordshire,* 261, 161. Peter de Grandison's wife, Blanche, chose to be buried in the chancel at Much Marcle her 'astoundingly beautiful and interesting' tomb and effigy (1347) can still be seen. The splendid tombs of Joanna, Peter & Blanche are clear witness to the resources which local families were prepared to devote to appropriate places and forms of sepulture. This was the market Straddell wished to tap.

21. Parry, J.H., (ed) *Trillek Reg,* CS (1910) 147-148; Smith, 5 (1964) 176-177. Williams (1976) 31, quoting PRO C115/D21/1937, see note 1.

CHAPTER X (Superfluity and Singularity)

1. Nopen,J.G., rev. Rigold, S.E., *The Chapter House, Westminster Abbey: Official Guide* (HMSO, 1952) 3-8, 17-19; Rigold, S.E., *Chapter House And Pyx Chamber, Westminster Abbey* (HMSO, 1976) 3-6, 10-17; Coldstream, N., 'York Chapter House,' *J. Brit. Archaeol. Ass.,* 35 (1972) 15-23; Pevsner, N., *Yorkshire: York and the East Riding* (1972) 85-6

2. For comparative plans, illustrations and detailed consideration of the chapter houses of Dore and Margam see Hillaby (1989) 209-45

3. RIBA, *Directory of British Architects 1834-1900* (1993) 90; *RIBA Nomination Papers,* A, IV, 14; *Herefordshire Portraits,* (1908) 63; obituaries in *The Builder* (28 Jan, 1905) 98-9; (4 Feb. 1905) 127; *RIBA J.* (1905) 211-12, 309-11

4.*Archaeol J.,* 34 (1877) 492.In 1870 at a meeting of the Association, he exhibited Roman tiles and pottery which he had found at Putley church.

5. 'Report of Golden Valley Field Meeting, May 25th 1882,' *TWNFC* (1882) 164-9; Mowat, C.L., *The Golden Valley Railway* (1964)

6. Blashill, T., 'Abbey Dore,' *TWNFC* (1882) 168 & 'Abbeydore,' *TWNFC* (1883) 5-10; Blashill (1885) 363-71

7. Paul (1893), 265-9

8. Birch, W. de G., *A History of Margam Abbey* (1897) 36-81, 122-32; David, H.E., Margam Abbey, Glamorgan, *Arch Camb,* 84 (ii) (1929) 318; Hillaby (1989) 222-7 & Figs 3, 7, 8 & 10.

9. Stratford, N., 'Notes on the Norman Chapter House at Worcester', in *Medieval Art and Archi-tecture at Worcester Cathedral, Brit. Archaeol Conf Trans,* 1975 (1978) 64, n.8

10. Webb, G., *Architecture in Britain: The Middle Ages,* (1956) 87-8; RCHM I (1931) 100-3; Haslam, R., *Powys* (1979) 287; Champneys, H., *Irish Ecclesiastical Architecture,* (1919, reprint 1970) 139-42

11. Lloyd, J., *A History of Wales,* 2 (3rd ed, 1939) 547-8; Dimock, J.F., (ed) *Giraldus Cambrensis: Opera 6,* RS 21 (1861-91) 49-53; Luard, H.R., (ed) Annals of Margam, in *Annales Monastici,* 1, RS 36 (1864) *sa* 1213-1214

12. *Statuta,* 151-2

13. Pevsner, N., *Herefordshire,* (1963) 60

14. Translated in Lekai, L.J., *The Cistercians: Ideals and Reality,* (1977) 442-66 from Bouton, J. de la C., & van Damme, J-B., (eds) *Les plus anciens textes de Citeaux,* (1974) 51-86, 107-25, 132-42

15. Melczer, E., & Soldwedel, E., Monastic Goals in the Aesthetics of St. Bernard in Lillich, M.P., (ed) *Studies in Cistercian Art and Architecture,* 1, Cistercian Studies 66 (1982) 31-44 quoting St. Bernard, *Sermon on the Song of Songs,* i-iv trans. Walsh, K., Cistercian Fathers Series 7 (1976) xiii; *St. Bernard: Sermon for the Seasons & Principal Festivals of the Year,* trans. Priest of Mount Melleray (1925) vol 2, 282 & vol 3, 303. See also Stiegman, E., The Aesthetics of Authenticity in Lillich, M.P., (ed.) *Studies in Cistercian Art & Architecture,* 2, Cistercian Studies 69 (1984) 8, & n.32. 'Divine capacity, however, comes to naught when the soul is lured by curiosities and moves towards outward things.' Here he refers to St. Bernard's, *Liber de gradibus humilitatis et superbia*

16. *Carta Caritatis,* XXV, XXVI; *Exordium Parvum,* XVII; *Statuta,* I, (1933) 1157, 13

17. *Apologia,* XXVIII. The most recent translation is by Casey, M., in *Bernard of Clairvaux: Treatises,* I, Cistercian Fathers Series 1 (1970)

18. *Carta Caritatis,* III; Cowley (1977) 127, ns.102 & 103

19. Butler, L.A.S., 'The Cistercians in England and Wales: A Survey of Recent Archaeological Work', 1960-1980 in note 15, Lillich (1982) 96;Hillaby (1989) 209-45; Gilyard-Beer, R., 'The Graves of the Abbots of Fountains', *Yorks Archaeol J.,* 59 (1987) 45-50; Butler, L.A.S., 'Cistercian Abbots Tombs and Abbey Seals' in Lillich, M.P., (ed) *Studies in Cistercian Art and Architecture,* 4; Cistercian Studies, 134 (1993) 78-88; Gardner.,W.S., The Role of Central Planning in English Romanesque Chapter House Design, unpublished Princeton PhD thesis (1976); Fergusson, P., & Harrison, S., The Rievaulx Abbey Chapter House, *Antiq J.,* 74 (1994) 211-55

20. Fergusson, P. & Harrison, S., *Loc. cit.,* note 19, 240; Dutton, M.L., 'The Conversion and Vocation of Aelred of Rievaulx: A Historical Hypothesis' in Williams, D. (ed.) *England in the twelfth century: Proceedings 1988 Harlaxton Symposium* (1990) 31-49. See also Grosjean, P., 'La preten

due canonisation d'Aelred de Rievaux par Celestin II' *Analecta Bollandiana*, 78 (1960) 124-9

21. The first reference to Adam I as abbot comes in a grant to Haughmond Abbey, in which he appears as first witness, between 10 August 1186 and August 1187. The dating is derived from Cheney, C.R., *et. al.*, (eds.) *English Episcopal Acta, 2: Canterbury 1162-90*, (1986) 238. The charter is printed in Rees, U., *The Cartulary of Haughmond Abbey* (1985) 213:Fergusson, P., *Architecture of Solitude: Cistercian Abbeys in twelfth-century England* (1984) 102. 99: Brakspear, H., 'A West-country School of Masons', *Archaeologia*, 81 (1931) 1-18; Prior, F.S., *History of Gothic Art in England* (1900) 86

22. James, M.R. (ed. & trans.), revised Brooke, C.N.L., & Mynors, R.A.S., *Walter Map: De Nugis Curialium* (1983) 85

23. Brewer, J.S., (ed.) *Giraldus Cambrensis: Opera 4*, RS 21 (1873) 200-7. Some of Gerald's stories are related in Bannister, A.T., *History of Ewyas Harold* (1902) 23, 45-7 & Williams (1976) 88-9; *Charter Rolls 1327*, 15 for the grant by Sybil's grandaughter. Brooke & Mynors, *Loc. cit.*, 84-5; Hart, W. (ed.) *Historia et Cartularium Monasterii Sancti Petri Gloucestriae*, 1, RS 33 (1863) iii, lxxv-lxxviii

24. Holesworth, C.J., John of Ford & English Cistercian Writing, 1167-1214, *Trans Ryl Hist Soc*, 5S, 11 (1961) 136

25. Russell, J.C., 'Hereford and Arabic Science in England, 1175-1200', *Isis* 18 (1932) 14-25; Burnett, C., 'Mathematics and Astronomy in Hereford and its Region in the Twelfth Century', *Medieval Art, Architecture and Archaeology at Hereford*, BAA Conf Trans for 1990 (1995) 50-9; Hunt, R.W., 'English Learning in the late Twelfth Century', *Trans Ryl Hist Soc*, 4S (1936) 19-42

26. BL Reg MS 8Av ff110-32; Bodley Rawlinson MS C67, ff22-85; Russell (1936) 4; *Statuta* I (1933), 232

27. James, M.R., Pictor in Carmine, *Archaeologia*, 94 (1951) 141-6; Brown, T.J., Pictor in Carmine, *Brit Mus Quart*, 19 (1954) 73-5. Recent doubts about this attribution, Norton & Park (1986) 199-200 are not strong enough to overthrow the deeply informed judgment of James

28. Norton & Park (1986) 305

29. 'Annals of Waverley' in Luard, H.R., (ed) *Annales Monastici*, 2, RS 36 (1865) sa 1187, 1188, 1199

30. *Statuta* I (1933) 123, 138, 149, 191, 193, 281; Donnelly, J.S., *The Decline of the Medieval Cistercian Brotherhood*, (1949) 23-4; Cowley (1977) 117-21

31. O'Callaghan (1995) 102

32. Brakspear, H., *Waverley Abbey*, (Surrey Archaeol Soc, 1905)

33. Painter, S., *The Reign of King John*, (1949) 156; Hewlett, H.G., (ed) *Roger of Wendover: Flores Historiarum*, 3, RS 84 (1889) 235; Stevenson, J., (ed.) *Ralph de Coggeshall: Chronicon Anglicanum*, RS 66 (1875) 164; Poole, A.L., *From Domesday Book to Magna Carta, 1087-1216* (1954) 449; *Annales Monastici*, 1 (1864) 29-30

34. Pertz, G.H., (ed.) 'Dore Annals' in *Monuments Germaniae Historica: Scriptores*, 27 (1885) 514-31 sa 1214

35. *Cal Close Rolls, 1213*, 148, 154; *1214*, 165; *1217*, 227; *1219*, 398; *Cal Patent Rolls, 1216*, 192, 193

36. *Cal Close Rolls, 1223*, 564; *1226*,

37. *Giraldus Cambrensis: Opera 4* (1873) 194; Griffiths, R.G., (ed.) *Cantilupe Reg*, Cantilupe Soc (1906) xxxiv

38. Hope, W.H.StJ., 'Foutains Abbey', *Yorks Archaeol J.*, 15 (1900) 343;Walbran, J.R., *Guide to Ripon, Fountains Abbey, etc* (12th ed, 1875) 120-2; Gilyard-Beer, R., *Loc. cit.*, note 19, 45-50

39. Malone, C.L.M., 'West English Gothic Architecture' unpub Un. of California, Berkeley, PhD thesis (1973) xxvi, 38; *ibid*, 'Abbey Dore: English versus French Design' in Lillich, M.P., (ed.) *Studies in Cistercian Art and Architecture, 2* (1984) 50-75

40. Bilson J., The Architecture of the Cistercians with special reference to some of their Earlier Churches in England, *Archaeol J.*, 66 (1909) 208-20; Aubert, 1 (1947) 2, 51-70, 109; Peers, C., *Byland Abbey, Yorkshire* (1952); Fergusson (1984) 73-82, 98

41. Malone (1973) 190-3

42. For English examples see Godfrey, W.H., English Cloister Lavatories as Independent Structures, *Archaeol J.* 106 (1952) Supplement, 91-7; Dimier, M.A., *L'Art Cistercian hors de France* (1971) 132, 136, 251, 253, 297-8. Aubert, 2 (1947) 26 incorrectly describes Poblet as octagonal. Grüger, H., 'Cistercian Fountain Houses in Central Europe' in Lillich (1984) 201-22

43. Paul (1893) 268; Bilson, J., 'On the Discovery of some Remains of the Chapter-House of Beverley Minster', *Archaeologia*, 54 (1895) 430; Willis, R., *Architectural History of some English Cathedrals*, 2 (1973) 213-24; *op. cit.*, note 9, Stratford (1978) 52-63

44. Stalley, D.R., *The Cistercian Monasteries of Ireland*, (1987) 171-72

45. Fergusson & Harrison (1994) *loc.cit.*, note **19**, 250, n. 44; Gardner, 173-221, 288-9

CHAPTER XI (The Cloistral Range and a fresh look at the Chapter House)

1. Harrison, S.A., *Byland Abbey Official Guide*, (1990)

2. Hope, W.StJ., 'Kirkstall Abbey,' *Thoresby Soc.*, (1907); Fergusson, P., 'The twelfth-century refectories at Rievaulx and Byland Abbeys,' in Norton & Park (1986) 160-80

3. Hope, W.StJ., 'Fountains Abbey,' *Yorks Arch J.* I15, 269-402

4. Robinson, D., *Tintern Abbey Guide,* (1995)

5. *Loc. cit.*, note 3

6. *Loc. cit.*, note 3

7. Stalley, R,, *The Cistercian Monasteries of Ireland* (1987)

8. Coppack, G., *Abbeys and Priories* (1990)

9. *Loc. cit.,* note 2, Fergusson
10. Gilyard-Beer, R., 'Boxley Abbey and the Pulpitum Collationis,' in Detsicas, A., *Collectana Historica : Essays in Memory of Stuart Rigold,* (1981)
11. Hope, W.StJ. & Brakspear, H., 'Jervaulx Abbey,'*Yorks Arch J.* 21, 303-44
12. Coppack, G., *Fountains Abbey* (1993)
13. *Loc. cit.,* note 4
14. *Loc. cit.,* note 1
15. Robinson, D., *Neath Abbey, card guide,* (1989)
16. *Loc. cit.,* note 2, Hope
17. *Loc. cit.,* note 2. Hope
18. Paul, R.A. notes and drawings in the Library of the Society of Antiquaries
19. Paul (1931)
20. Paul (1931)
21. *Op. cit.,* note 18
22. Paul (1904a)
23. Paul (1893)
24. Blashill (1895)
25. *Op. cit.,* note 18
26. *Op. cit.,* note 18
27. Paul (1931)

CHAPTER XII (The Monastic Precinct)
1. Horn, W., & Born, H., *The Plan of St Gal* (1971)
2. Fergusson, P., 'Porta Patens Esto': Notes on Early Cistercian Gatehouses in the North of England, in Fernie, E., & Crossley, P. (eds) *Medieval Architecture and its Intellectual Context* (1990), 47-59
3. Coppack, G., *Abbeys and Priories, (*1990) 81
4. *Monasticon,* 5, 556-7; PRO, 1540, 189
5. Smith (1964) 75
6. Hope, W.H.StJ., 'The Abbey of St Mary in Furness, Lancashire,' *Trans Cumb & West Ant & Arch Soc.,* 16 (1900) 221-302; *Loc. cit.,* note 3, 100
7. Coppack, G., *Fountains Abbey,* (1993)
8. Courtney, P., 'Excavations in the outher precinct of Tintern Abbey,' *Med Arch,* 33, (1989) 99-143
9. Williams (1976) 30
10. Coppack, G., 'Some descriptions of Rievaulx Abbey in 1538-9 : The disposition of a major Cistercian precinct in the early sixteenth century,'*J. Brit Arch Assn,* 139 (1986) 100-33
11. *Loc. cit.,* note 6, Hope, 232; Coppack G. & Fergusson, P., *Rievaulx Abbey* (1995) 13
12. Brears, P.C.D., *Kirkstall Abbey Leeds' Cistercian monastery,* (Leeds, nd.) 6; Robinson, D.M., *Tintern Abbey Guide (*1990) 10 and 53
13. *Loc. cit.,* note 6, Hope, 236
14. Williams, D.H., 'Sale of Goods at Abbey Dore,' *Monmouths. Antiq.,* 3, (1978) 193
15. Paul (1904a) 119
16. Williams, D.H., 'Layfolk within Cistercian precincts,' *Monastic Studies,* 2 (1991) 111
17. Williams (1976) 17
18. *Loc. cit.,* note 16, 89; Williams (1976) 23
19. Brown, W., 'Description of the buildings of twelve small Yorkshire priories at the Reformation,' *Yorks Arch J.,* 9 (1886) 197-215
20. Williams (1976) 13
21. Paul (1893) 266; Paul (1896) 300
22. Mr. Powell, pers. comm.

23. Williams (1976) 31
24. *Loc. cit.,* note 19, 203-7
25. Williams(1966) 93
26. *Loc. cit.,* note 10, 113
27. Williams (1976) 47
28. Paul (1893) 267
29. *Loc. cit.,* note 3, 81
30. Mr. Powell, pers. comm.
31. Paul (1927) 274
32. Mr. Howes, pers. comm.
33. *Loc. cit.,* note 16, 111
34. Williams (1976) 27
35. Williams (1976) 49; Winkless, D., *Hailes Abbey, Gloucestershire : The story of a medieval abbey* (1990) 32
36. Williams (1966) 81; *Op. cit.,* Winkless, 33
37. *Loc. cit.,* note 10, 114-5
38. *Loc. cit.,* note 7, 95
39. *Loc. cit.,* note 10, 113-4
40. *Loc. cit.,* note 14, 193
41. Paul (1931) 500
42. Paul, R.A., Notes and drawings in the Library of the society of Antiquaries
43. Williams (1976) 5
44. Williams (1976) 5
45. Williams (1976) 8
46. Williams (1966) 98
47. Williams(1976) 31
48. *Loc. cit.,* note 8,, 101
49. *Loc. cit.,* note 14, 192

CHAPTER XIII (The Engineer Monks)
1. Lawrence, C.H., *Mediaeval Monasticism,* 2nd edn (1989) is a good introduction to monasticism generally. Lekai, L.J., *The Cistercians : Ideals and Reality,* (1977) is an excellent broad study. Tobin, S., *The Cistercians,* (1995) tells the story well and has excellent illustrations, but lacks references. A useful guide in France is Peugniez, B., *Routier des Abbayes Cisterciennes de France,* (Editions du Signe, 1994)
2. Matarasso, P., *The Cistercian World: Monastic Writings of the Twelfth Century.* (1993) 7.
3. Kreps, M., *The First Ironworks in the Territory of Bohemian lands.* (Rozpravy narodniho technickeho muzea v praze, 1969, no. 39, Prague) 41.
4. Gimpel, J., *The Mediaeval Machine (*1976) 67-69.
5. Duby, G., *L'Art Cistercienne,* (Flammarion, 1993) 19.
6. Mott, R.A., 'The Water Mills of Beauchief Abbey'. *Trans. Hunter Arch. Soc.,* IX (1964) .203-220.
7. The Ironbridge Gorge Museum holds an unpublished manuscript of Mott's work on this.
8. *Loc. cit.,* note 1, 206-213
9. Bowie, T. (ed.) *The Sketchbook of Villard de Honnecourt,* (Indiana University, 1959) 3-4
10. Erlande-Brandenburg, Pernoud, Gimpel and Bechmann(eds.) *Carnet de Villard de Honnecourt;* (Editions Stock, Paris, 1986) Plate 44, d
11. Kinder, T.N., 'De Profundis: Une descente archéologique dans la citerne de Villiers-la-Grange,' *Bulletin des Amis de Pontigny,* 3 (1992) 25-32
12. *Loc. cit.,* note 2, 222

13. *Loc cit.*, note 2, 287-291
14. *idem.* 289
15. *Loc. cit.*, note 4, 125.

CHAPTER XIV (The Dissolution)
1. PRO, E 315/289, f.4; LR 6/152/1
2. PRO, E 315/278, f.145
3. PRO, E 315/289, f.4
4. Aveling, H., in Mc Cann, J. and Cary-Elwes, C., *Ampleforth and its Origins* (1927) 60, 62, 273; Nash, C., 'Fate of English Cistercian Abbots', *Cîteaux* 16 (1965) 113; Bodleian Libr. Oxford, Jones MS 9
5. PRO, E 314/31 (7)
6. *Cal. Letters and Papers, Foreign and Domestic (Henry VIII)* 1540/731
7. Williams (1976) 32; PRO, E 315/289, f. 12d
8. Williams (1966) 94. Life at Dore after the Suppression still reflected local feuding, as witnessed by an affray 'on the bridge of Dore' about 1541: PRO, Stac. 2/31, f. 32
9. PRO, C 115, Bundle D.21, No. 1937. (For a full transcription, see: Williams, D. H., 'Sale of Goods at Abbey Dore', *Mon Ant*, III:3-4, (1979)
10. PRO, E 315/278, f. 136, 315/289, f. 7
11. PRO, E 315/278, f. 137; E 315/289, f. 7
12. PRO, E 321/16, f. 27, E 321/10, f. 32
13. Williams (1976) 46.
14. Williams (1966) 95 (after *Monasticon* (1846) 557).
15. PRO, E 315/109, ff. 127-134.
16. PRO, E 315/109, f. 134.
17. PRO, SC 6 (Henry VIII)/ 7319, m. 10d; Williams (1966) 96.
18. PRO, E 321/32, m. 84.
19. Something of those days may be seen in a letter written to (perhaps the last) abbot of Dore by Thomas Havard, when he advises the abbot that: 'John Hyere, your bedeman is gone to London, and for them that cometh I beseech your lordship to haste them forth, as for why, they be well attest they cannot get owt': PRO, SP 1/240, f. 224. Noteworthy too, is the annuity of 13s. 4d. granted by Dore on 1 August, 1535, to Thomas Berington (Byrynton) for 'good advice.'
20. See note 7 *supra*.

CHAPTER XV (After the Dissolution)
1. *Monasticon (1846)*, 522-7
2. Bannister, A.T., *Institutions etc (A.D. 1539-1900)*, (1923)
3. Watkins, M.G., 'Antiquarian Discoveries at Abbey Dore,' *TWNFC*, 1890-2, 146-7
4. *ibid*.
5. *ibid*.
6. *Loc.cit.* note 1

CHAPTER XVI (The Altar and the Vestments)
1. Williams (1976), 3
2. Moir, A.L., *Bishops of Hereford* (1964) 22-25, Williams (1976), 25
3. Sledmere (1914), 40
4. Williams (1976), 3

5. Davies, J.G., (ed) *A New Dictionary of Liturgy and Worship,* (1986) 201
6. *Loc. cit.,* 7
7. *Loc. cit.,* 138
8. Williams (1976), 16, 30
9. Morgan (1955) 5
10. Williams (1976) 30
11. Sledmere (1914) appendix
12 I am very grateful to Mrs. Muriel Tonkin for this research from the census returns, parish records and tithe apportionment in HRO.
13. Information from the Victoria and Albert Museum where the collection can be seen by appointment. I am most grateful for the help of the Assistant Curator, Miss L. Woolley.
13. *Op. cit.*, note 5, 526. My thanks to Rev. Kay Garlick.

CHAPTER XVII (Calvinists & anti-Calvinists)
1. For the background refer to Tyacke, N., *Anti-Calvinists: The Rise of English Arminianism, c1590-1640* (1987) & Scott, W., and Bliss, J. (eds.) *The Works of William Laud,* 7 vols (1847-60)
2. *Op. cit. Laud: Works* VI, 57; III, 74-5; Tyacke, N.,. 'Archbishop Laud' in Fincham, K., (ed.) *The Early Stuart Church, 1603-1642* (1993) 66, n33
3. Gibson (1727) 127, quoting a letter from Scudamore to Laud of 18 March 1618, 64-5; Trevor-Roper, H.R., *Archbishop Laud* (3rd ed, 1988) 437-56 publishes 16 of Laud's letters to Scudamore 1621-28. For the Scudamore family see Collins, A., *Early History of the Scudamore Family,* (1931) and Skidmore, W., *Thirty Generations of the Scudamore/Skidmore Family in England and America* (2nd ed., 1989)
4. Atherton, I., 'Viscount Scudamore's "Laudinanism": The Religious Practices of the First Viscount Scudamore' *Hist J.*, 34 (3) (1991) 586, but also see Addleshaw, G.W.O., & Etchells, F., *The Architectural Setting of Anglican Worship* (1948) 131
. 5. Gibson (1727) 40-1
6. Gibson, T.E., (ed.) *W. Blundell: A Cavalier's Note-Book* (1880) 170-1
7. *Loc. cit.*, note 2,Tyacke, 61, n22
8. RCHM, *West London* (1925) 82
9. *Loc. cit.*, note 2,Tyacke, 71; Gibson (1727) 126-8, 41; RCHM I (1931) 8; Stanhope, B.S., & Moffat, H.C., *The Church Plate of the County of Hereford* (1903) 1
10. *Loc. cit.*, note 4, Addleshaw & Etchells, 139, n3; Gibson (1727) 38

CHAPTER XVIII (The Scudamore Restoration)
1. Given in the appendix of Trevor-Roper, H.R., *Archbishop Laud,* (2nd. edn.1962)
2. PRO, C115 D19X/LO1519; HRO, X55/7
3. PRO, *op. cit.*; HRO, X55/8
4. PRO, *op. cit.*; HRO, X55/9
5. PRO, *op. cit.*; HRO, X55/1
6. PRO, *op. cit.*; HRO, X55/2
7. PRO, *op. cit.*; HRO, X55/4
8. PRO, *op. cit.*; HRO, X55/5

9. PRO, *op. cit.*; HRO, X55/6

10. PRO, *op. cit.*; HRO, X55/10

11. Morgan, F.C., 'The Steward's Accounts of John, First Viscount Scudamore of Sligo (1601-1671) for 1632,' *TWNFC* (1975) 312-7

12. Watkins, M.G., 'Antiquarian Discoveries at Abbey Dore,' *TWNFC* (1891) 146-7

CHAPTER XIX (The John Hoskyns Tomb)

1. Whitlock, B. W., *John Hoskyns, Serjeant-at-Law*, (Washington, USA, 1982) provides the basis for this brief account. I am also greatly indebted to Sir Benedict Hoskyns, Bt. for information.See also *TWNFC* (1957) 249 & (1960) 306-9

2. Whitlock, B.W., 'Hereford City Properties of John Hoskyns,' *TWNFC* (1961) 62-66

3. Wood, A.S., 'Vowchurch and the Hoskyns family,' *TWNFC* (1961) 92-93

4. Morgan (1955) 7; Templar, P.J.T., *Some further notes on Arms Bearing Families of Herefordshire ...*, (1946) VI-XVII, esp. VIII

5. Gregg, P., *King Charles I* (1981) 186

6. Hurley, H., *Historic Harewood, Herefordshire* (Ross Civic Soc., 1996)

7. Morgan (1955) 7

8. *Loc. cit.*, note 2 13; Strong, G., *The Heraldry of Herefordshire* (1848) 64 & pl.LV

CHAPTER XX (The Woodwork)

1. PRO, C115D19 X/L01519; HRO, X55/2,/3,/5,/9

2. Halliday, F.E. (ed) *Richard Carew of Antony 1555-1620, The Survey of Cornwall etc* (1953) 124

3. PRO Loc. cit. note 1; HRO, X55/9

CHAPTER XXI (Wall paintings and texts)

1. Rouse, E.C., *Medieval Wall Paintings* (1991)

CHAPTER XXII ('Beauty of Holiness': The East Window)

1. Prynne, W., *Canterburies Doome or the First Part of the ... Tryall ... of William Laud* (1646) 59-62, 466; Wharton, H. (ed.) *W. Laud, History of the troubles and tryall of Laud, wrote by himself,* (1695) 312-18; Heylyn, P., *Cyprianus Anglicus or the History of the Life and Death of ... William ... Archbishop of Canterbury* (1671) 467-92; Rushforth, J., *Historical Collections* (1659-1701) IIIi, 196-9; Aston, M., *England's Iconoclasts* (1988) 340-1

2. Phillips, J., *The Reformation of Images: Destruction of an Art in England, 1535-1660* (1973); Edelen, G., (ed.) *William Harrison's Description of England* (1968) 35-6

3. Rackham, B., *Victoria and Albert Museum: A Guide to the Collections of Stained Glass* (1936) 119-20, pl 57c

4. For description & illustrations see: Wayment, H., *The Stained Glass of the Church of St. Mary, Fairford*, (1984); Rushforth, G.M., *Medieval Christian Imagery: Great Malvern Priory Church*, (1936); Wayment, H., *The Windows of King's College Chapel, Cambridge* (1972)

5. For our knowledge of this revival and the work of the van Linge brothers and others we are indebted principally to M. Archer. See for example his 'English Painted Glass in the Seventeenth Century: The early work of Abraham van Linge' *Apollo* 101 (1975) 26-31; *The Painted Glass of Lydiard Tregoze* (Swindon, nd); and 'Richard Butler, glass-painter' *Burlington Magazine,* 130, no. 1046 (May 1990) 308-15

6. *Op. cit.*, Archer (1975) 27-8; Archer, M., Brown, S. & Cormack, P., *English Heritage in Stained Glass: Oxford* (1988) 24-5; *Loc. cit.*, note 3, Rackham, 117, plate 57c; *Loc. cit., note 5,* Archer (1990) 311-12

7. *Calendar of State Papers*, 1637, 113

8. *Loc. cit.*, note 6, Archer *et al* for early seventeenth century glass at Oxford). RCHM, *City of Oxford* (1939) provides descriptions and black and white illustrations under the respective college entries

9. RCHM, *Oxford*, pls. 191, 124, 176; Anderton, E.W.., & Lafond, J., *Ludlow Stained and Painted Glass* (1961) 43-6; Caviness, M.H., 'Fifteenth-century Stained Glass from the Chapel of Hampton Court, Herefordshire : The Apostles' Creed and other subjects,' *Walpole Soc.*, 42 (1968-70) 35-70

10. Croft, P., 'The Religion of Robert Cecil' *Hist J.,* 34 (4) (1991) 773-96; Wilkinson, A.L., 'The Great East Window of Hatfield House' *J Br Soc Master Glass Painters* (1955-9) 245-50; *Loc. cit.,* note 5, Archer (1990) 309-10; Auerbach E., & Kingsley Adams, C., *Painting and Sculpture at Hatfield House* (1971) 20, 26-7, 106-8; Stone, I., 'The Building of Hatfield House' *Archaeol J.* 112 (1955) 122-3; Atherton, I., 'John. 1st Viscount Scudamore (1601-71): A career at Court and in the Country 1601-43' unpublished Cambridge University PhD (1993), 373

11. Archer, M., 'Seventeenth century painted glass at Little Easton' *Essex J.* (1977) 3-10; Tyacke N.,*Anti-Calvanists The Rise of English Arminianism c.1590-1640* (1987) 192-4

12. *Loc. cit.*, note 5, Archer (1990) 310-11. The furnishings are almost intact and four of Butler's heads remain in the glazing of the east window tracery

13. RCHM, I, 129-30; *Report of the Commissioners Concerning Charities: Herefordshire*, 53-6; Webb, T.W., *Memorials of the Civil War in Herefordshire,* 1 (1879) 209

14. RCHM, III, 68-9; *Loc. cit.*, note 9, Caviness 35-60

15. *Loc. cit.*, note 3, 120-1;*Loc. cit.*, note 11, Tyacke (1987) 219; Scott, W., & Bliss, J. (eds.) *The Works of William Laud,* 7 vold. (1847-60) III, 413

16. Addams' contract, printed in part by Colvin, H.M., 'Abbey Dore' *TWNFC* (1948) 235-7, is in PRO C115/D19. (Items 1907, 1908 front, 1909-12 front, 1913-16 & 1924 are available as photocopies in HCRO.) I am obliged to Mr Christopher Pickford for information on this and on Blashill's architectural work. Abel's contract in BL Add MS 11044 f267 is referrred to by Blashill, T., 'The Seventeenth Century Restoration of Dore

Abbey Church' *TWNFC* (1901) 184-8; *Loc cit.,* note 5, Archer (1990) 31-4; Gibson (1727) 41

17. Robinson, C.J., *A History of the Mansions and Manors of Herefordshire* (1873) 248 quoting 'Title Deeds'. RCHM, I, 236-7; Morriss, R. & Shoesmith, R., *Caer Caradoc: Interim Report* (1989); HRO BE7/1, Sellack Parish Register, 1566-1678, *sa* 1668 & 1630/1

18. *Complete Peerage* 11 (1949) 572-4; *Op. cit.,* Robinson, 142-3; Trevor-Roper, H.R., *Archbishop Laud,* (3rd Edn. 1988) 437-9; HRO BE7/1, Sellack Parish Register, 1566-1678, inner cover

19. *Loc. cit.,* note 10, Atherton, ch. 3 & 4

20. RCHM, I, 234-6; HRO AL 17/1; *Loc. cit.,* note 10, Atherton, 585

21. Gibson (1727) 41

22. HCL pLC 726.7

23. Revelations, 4: 6-10

24. HRO K38/Cd/5

25. *Loc. cit.* note 4, Rushforth 386-7; RCHM, *Oxford,* pls 74, 124, 176, 191. For the early iconography of the Ascension see Male, E., *Religious Art in France - the Twelfth Century: a study of the origins of medieval iconography* (1978) 92-8

26. Foquel, G., *Missale Romanum, ex decreto Sancrosancti Concilii Tridentini restitutum,* (Salamanca, 1587) 369

27. BL, Add MS, 11044 f267; *Loc. cit.,* note 16, Blashill 184-8

28. PRO, C115/D19. (Items 1907, 1908 front, 1909-12 front, 1913-16 & 1924 are available as photocopies at HRO (1948) 235-7)

29. HCL, MS LC647.1 & 3 boxes of Scudamore papers, 949.203 formerly Phillips MS 22287. Herbert Reade, 'Some Account Books of the First Lord Scudamore ...' *TWNFC* (1924) 119-29

30. Morgan, F.C., 'The Steward's Accounts of John, first Viscount Scudamore ... for the Year 1632' (transcription) *TWNFC* (1950) 155-84

31. *Loc. cit.,* note 5, Archer (1990) 311-12; (1975) 25-30

32. Summerson, J., *Architecture in Britain 1530-1830* (1953) 106-11; Clapham, A., 'The Survival of Gothic in Seventeenth Century England' *Archaeol J.* 106 (1949) 4-9; Stocks, J.E., 'The Church of St John the Evangelist, Leeds' *Thoresby Soc Pub* 24 (1919) 190, 224

CHAPTER XXIII (The Bells and Bellframe)

1. Williams (1976), 3. No evidence has so far been found to suggest that the abbey had a west tower, and it is inferred that there was a central one. If so, it was not a substantial structure despite its height, for the arches supporting it are only 39 inches wide; it may thus have been a lantern tower. It is at least possible that there was a separate campanile such as formerly existed at Grace Dieu (*ibid.* p. 66) and at Tewkesbury. That at Tewkesbury was converted to a House of Correction in 1582 and was eventually demolished in 1817. (Massé, H.J.L.le, *Tewkesbury and Deerhurst,* 1901, 16 & 17)

2. Williams (1976), 31

3. *ibid,* 5

4. Wade, G.W. & Methuen, J. H., *Herefordshire,* nd, 209

5. Stanhope, B.S.S., & Moffatt, H.C., *Church Plate of Herefordshire* (1903) 212

6. HRO X55/8

7. HRO X55/3

8. HRO X55/9

9. How unusual this was at that period can be judged from an episode at Exeter Cathedral. In 1676 a number of the bells there were recast by Thomas Purdue, but he ran short of metal while casting and one of the bells came out of the mould without canons so that it had to be hung by bolts through the crown. This worried the Dean and Chapter to such an extent that they made Purdue sign a bond to recast the bell without charge if it failed within 20 years, rather than the usual year and a day. However, their fears were groundless as the bell is still there today. Scott, J.G.M., 'Exeter Cathedral Bells,' *Friends of Exeter Cathedral Thirty Fourth Annual Report* (to 31st March 1964)

10. For a history of the development of bell wheels see Eisel, J.C., 'Developments in Bell Hanging' *Change Ringing -The History of an English Art,* Vol. 1 (1987)

11. HRO X55/10. Brasses were the bearings in which the gudgeons rested, usually made of bell-metal or similar.

12. Morgan, F.C., 'The Steward's Accounts of John, First Viscount Scudamore of Sligo (1601-1671) for 1632,' *TWNFC* (1949-51) 155-84

13. From a photostat taken from the original in the Bodleian Library

14. HRO AC 16/91

15. HRO AC 16/27

16. The Rev. John Duncumb is better known as the author of *Collections Towards the History and County of Hereford,* Vol. 1 (1804) and Vol. 2, Part 1 (1812)

17. HRO AC 16/26

18. For a discussion of Finch's career see Eisel, J.C., *The Bells of Hereford Cathedral,* (1977) 6-8

CHAPTER XXIV (The Paul Restoration)

1. *TWNFC* (1901) 181-3

2. Paul (1898)

3. The register from which this information comes has been rebound and given the title 'Abbey Dore Parochial Church Council.' However, the first entry is dated 1886 and (civil) parish councils were only established by Fowler's Local Government Act in 1894. From that year until 1920, when the 'first meeting of the parochial church council of qualified electors' met Abbey Dore was apparently governed in a hybrid manner. I am much obliged to G.H. Hollom for considerable assistance on this and other parochial matters

4. Sledmere (1914) 76 quoting Paul (1902a) 11

5. Paul (1902a) 10-12; *Gentleman's Magazine,* 99 (Dec 1829) 497

6. *Hereford Times:* 'Abbey Restoration: Urgent Appeal' (1 June 1901); Rev. A. Phillipps, 'Letter'

(15 March 1902); 'Re-opening of Presbytery' 4 July 1903)
7. Paul (1904b)
8. Marshall, G., 'Monumental and Other Inscriptions in the Church of Abbey Dore, Co. Hereford' *Genealogist,* NS 30 (1914)
9. Describing the heraldic tiles in an undated note amongst his papers at Burlington House, he says 'These tiles ... resemble the fine series of 40 shields still to be seen at Bredon church in Worcestershire.'
10. Paul, R.W., *Some Notes on the Heraldic Glass in Great Malvern Priory Church* (1901) (reprinted from *Archaeologia* 57, (1901) 353-8; Paul (1902a)
11. Aubert, M., L'Architecture Cistercienne en France 1 (1947) 144-5, 311-12
12. RCHM, MSS notes on Abbey Dore at NMR, Swindon; Marks, R., 'Cistercian window glass in England & Wales' in Norton & Park, 212-15 & ill. 89
13. Norton & Park, fig. 27 & ills 75 & 78; Brisac, C., 'Romanesque Grisailles from the former Abbey

Churches of Obazine & Bonlieu' in *Studies in Cistercian Art and Architecture,* 2 (1982) 130-39; Vita-Grau, J., 'Cistercian stained glass windows at Santes Creus' in *Studies in Cistercian Art and Architecture,* 4 (1993) 154-60
14. Marks in Norton & Park (1986) 219; Woodforde, C., 'A Group of Fourteenth Century Windows Showing the Tree of Jesse' *Br School of Master Glass Painters J.* 6 (1937) 184-90; Newton, P.A.,'Schools of Glass Painting in the Midlands 1275-1430' Unpub Un of London PhD (1961) 62-71; Marshall, G., 'Ancient Glass in Madley Church' *TWNFC,* (1924) 66-71; Brown, S., 'The Fourteenth Century Stained Glass of Madley,' *Medieval Art, Architecture and Archaeology at Hereford, Brit Archaeol Conf Trans* (1995) 122-31, illus Ai-iv; Rackham, B., 'The Coventry School of Glass Painting,' *Walpole Soc.,* 19, (1930-1) 92

CHAPTER XXV (Dore Abbey today)
  No references

INDEX

Other books from Logaston Press

OWAIN GLYN DWR :
THE WAR OF INDEPENDENCE IN THE WELSH BORDERS
by Geoffrey Hodges. 256pp with photographs £9.95
ISBN 1 873827 24 5

This book concentrates on the background to and the actual fighting in the borders. The tensions leading up to the revolt are considered, as are the politics of early fifteenth century England and Wales. The battles of Pilleth and Hyddgen are examined in detail, as is the Franco-Welsh advance on Worcester. Finally the evidence is detailed for Owain spending his last days with his daughters in Herefordshire.

THE MAN IN THE MOONE
by Francis Godwin, Bishop of Hereford between 1617 and 1633.
80pp, hardback, with photographs, £8.95
ISBN 1 873827 64 4

A science fiction story that predates Jules Verne by some two centuries and, despite Godwin's appreciation of gravitational theory, the birth of Newton by at least ten years. A Spaniard, set ashore on St Helena to recuperate, starts to train the tame wildlife to lift loads with a series of pulleys. He uses a white signal to encourage the birds to rise and, after a few adventures en route, he is whisked off to the ultimate white signal—the Moon. A modern introduction by Andy Johnson and Ron Shoesmith sets Godwin's scientific views against the knowledge of the age, and also considers the wider implications of the book which appears to have been both a cover for scientific debate as well as a political call for greater seaborne exploration. It also attempts to unravel the Herefordshire sources of Godwin's geographical information with some surprising results.

ARTHURIAN LINKS WITH HEREFORDSHIRE
by Mary Andere. 160pp with maps and photographs. £9.95
ISBN 1 873827 44 X

The author of previous books on Herefordshire, Mary Andere makes a welcome return with an investigation into the Arthurian connections with Herefordshire. Enthused by reports of a friend who felt she had had an 'experience' near the site of St. Dubricius' seminary at Hentland, Mary sets the scene by analysing what we do know of the Arthurian period in general, what is myth and legend, and where such myths and legends could contain germs of the original truth. Spreading out from Hentland, she details the possible basis for Mordred's connection with Mordiford, for Gawain's connection with both Hereford and the old kingdom of Erging; with Uthyr Pendragon's possible siege of Vortigern at The Doward and for the same area to be the site for Arthur's eighth battle. Much history is given of the early British and Welsh kings and families, and connections made back to the days of the Roman Empire.

THE CIVIL WAR IN HEREFORD

by Ron Shoesmith. 176pp with maps and photographs. £8.95

ISBN 1 873827 34 2

This book uses documents from the Civil War to bring out the story of the four sieges of Hereford by the Parliamentary forces. Ironically the best prepared army, led by one of the most experienced generals of age, that of the Scots led by Alexander Leslie, Earl of Leven, was the one which failed with much loss of life. Two earlier attempts succeeded after brief skirmishes, with resultant court martials for some of the Royalist officers; the final attempt resulted in a well-read pamphlet entitled A new tricke to take Townes.

A VIEW FROM HEREFORD'S PAST

by Richard Stone and Nic Appleton-Fox

80pp with 44 photographs, maps and illustrations. (A4 format, bound) £9.95

ISBN 1 873827 34 2

This tells of the excavation and finds in the precincts of Hereford Cathedral in preparation for the building of the new exhibition centre for the Mappa Mundi and Chained Library. It relates several surprising finds, including over 1,100 complete skeletons and charnel with an additional 5,000 bodies. The excavation has also shed new light on the road layout and style of buildings of the Saxon city; of the diseases that prevailed amongst the medieval population and much besides. Whilst serving as the interim archaeological report, the text is written in a way that anyone interested in finding out in substantial detail what has so far emerged from the archaeological work can do so.

JAMES WATHEN'S HEREFORDSHIRE 1770-1820

His sketches and paintings

by David Whitehead and Ron Shoesmith, 228pp, over 90 colour illustrations. £65

ISBN 1 873827 04 0

A high quality production, of which only a few numbered copies remain, this work details the life of James Wathen, including his early years in Hereford's gloving industry before his turning to watercolour painting. The paintings show the city gates before demolition, street scenes now disappeared, country houses as they were being rebuilt with the profits from a buoyant agriculture, the Wye at the time of the Wye Tour and rural scenes and villages before mechanisation. Also included are his contributions, turned to engravings, for *The Gentleman's Magazine*, together with his descriptions of the antiquities and churches.